Pakistan Since
Independence

Pakistan Since Independence

A History, 1947 to Today

STANLEY B. SPRAGUE

McFarland & Company, Inc., Publishers
Jefferson, North Carolina

This book has undergone peer review.

LIBRARY OF CONGRESS CATALOGUING-IN-PUBLICATION DATA

Names: Sprague, Stanley B., 1940– author.
Title: Pakistan since independence : a history, 1947 to today / Stanley B. Sprague.
Description: Jefferson, North Carolina : McFarland & Company, Inc., Publishers, 2020 | Includes bibliographical references and index.
Identifiers: LCCN 2020042597 | ISBN 9781476681511 (paperback : acid free paper) ∞
ISBN 9781476641706 (ebook)
Subjects: LCSH: Pakistan—History. | Pakistan—Politics and government.
Classification: LCC DS384 .S63 2020 | DDC 954.9105—dc23
LC record available at https://lccn.loc.gov/2020042597

BRITISH LIBRARY CATALOGUING DATA ARE AVAILABLE

ISBN (print) 978-1-4766-8151-1
ISBN (ebook) 978-1-4766-4170-6

© 2020 Stanley B. Sprague. All rights reserved

No part of this book may be reproduced or transmitted in any form or by any means, electronic or mechanical, including photocopying or recording, or by any information storage and retrieval system, without permission in writing from the publisher.

Front cover image © Mehaniq/Shutterstock

Printed in the United States of America

McFarland & Company, Inc., Publishers
  Box 611, Jefferson, North Carolina 28640
    www.mcfarlandpub.com

Table of Contents

Preface and Acknowledgments   1
Abbreviations   3
Chronology   5
Glossary   8
Maps   10
Introduction to Pakistan   13

Part One—Pakistan's Early Years

1. Independence and Partition   19
2. Pakistan Under Jinnah   23
3. Pakistan Under Liaquat Khan   32
4. Transition to Military Rule   39
5. General Ayub Khan's Military Rule   53
6. General Yahya Khan and Civil War   74

Part Two—Pakistan After Dismemberment

7. Zulfikar Bhutto's Missed Opportunity   85
8. General Zia and the Death of Bhutto   106
9. The Soviets Invade Afghanistan   116
10. Zia's Last Years   125
11. Benazir Bhutto's First Term   132

Table of Contents

12. Sharif's First Term — 145
13. Benazir Bhutto's Second Term — 154
14. Sharif's Second Term — 163
15. General Musharraf Takes Control — 170

Part Three—Pakistan After Al-Qaeda's Attack on America

16. Musharraf Joins America's War on Terrorism — 179
17. The End of Musharraf's Reign — 194
18. Civilian Rule Under Gillani and Zardari — 218
19. Sharif's Third Term — 242

Epilogue — 251
Appendix: List of Pakistan Army Chiefs — 255
Chapter Notes — 257
Bibliography — 273
Index — 275

Preface and Acknowledgments

When I was 24 years old, I spent a month traveling solo around India, and then spent a few days in Pakistan waiting for a flight home. This experience sparked my curiosity of faraway countries, and I began a life-long study of foreign countries. My readings took me to the Afghan-Soviet War, and they revealed how important Pakistan had been in expelling Soviet troops from Afghanistan.

As I began reading books on Pakistan, I noticed how many books had been written on Pakistan, but how few recent books covered its key events in chronological order. It was then that I decided to write a book to fill this void.

Pakistan is an important country with a fascinating history. It is located in the center of a volatile region of the world and borders Russia, China, India and Afghanistan. It is inhabited by more than 200 million people. It is also a dangerous country, since a number of Islamist terrorist groups are based there, it possesses nuclear weapons, and it has fought four wars with its neighbor India. It was Osama bin Laden's home when his al-Qaeda terrorists hijacked airliners which destroyed New York City's World Trade Center. Bin Laden was living there when he was killed ten years later.

I had several objectives in writing this book. First, I wanted to offer a chronological history of Pakistan's political events, foreign affairs, military operations, and terrorist activities. I have made extensive use of endnotes to make the book valuable as a research tool for use in libraries.

My second objective has been to make this book as objective as possible. I have tried to simply describe the key events in Pakistan's history as accurately as possible using the most credible sources available. I have described both the strengths and weaknesses of each of Pakistan's key leaders. Any errors of fact or interpretation are mine alone.

My third objective has been to make this history relatively easy to understand, and this has been a challenging task since Pakistan's history is quite complicated. The country has had three constitutions, and has alternated between civilian and military rule. During civilian rule, it has operated under presidential and parliamentary systems of governments. Also, Pakistan has been home to more than 30 political parties and 20+ Islamist extremist groups.

To simplify things, I have included an "Introduction to Pakistan" which offers a quick overview of Pakistan's geography, government, armed forces and religions. To further simplify the book, political parties and Islamist extremist groups are usually referred to by abbreviations, such as PPP and PML (a list is provided). Following the list of abbreviations are a chronology and a glossary. To further simplify the book, I have referred to the head of Pakistan's army as simply the "Army Chief" instead of that official's changing official titles. A list of Pakistan's army chiefs is included as an appendix, along with their official titles.

I wish to acknowledge several persons who have helped me with this book. I want to thank my family for their help. My daughter Katherine offered to read some of my early chapters. She was an excellent editor. My daughter Allison offered to help with the maps, and I thank her for her talent and infinite patience in developing the two maps. I thank my wife Celine for putting up with me with minimum complaint for the last 15 years as I researched and wrote this book. In addition, I want to thank my friend Tom Gratzek for his helpful suggestions on improving the manuscript. I also thank Steve Pearsall for the many hours he spent modifying the end notes for the manuscript. I also want to thank Professor Jeff Jones at the University of North Carolina at Greensboro for his encouraging me to keep writing and for recommending that I contact McFarland. Finally, I want to thank Layla Milholen and the staff at McFarland for their support and for their suggestions on improving my manuscript.

Abbreviations

AJK—Azad (Free) Jammu and Kashmir (Pakistani-controlled territory in Jammu and Kashmir)
AL—Awami League (an East wing political party)
ANP—Awami National Party (secular party representing Pashtuns, especially in Karachi)
BDs—Basic Democrats (electors in Ayub Khan's "democracy" scheme)
CAP—Constitutional Assembly (body set up to write a constitution)
CMLA—Chief Martial Law Administrator (martial law leader)
ConML—Convention Muslim League (political party of Ayub Khan)
COP—Combined Opposition Party (anti–Ayub Khan coalition)
FATA—Federally Administered Tribal Areas (merged with KP in 2018)
FC—Frontier Corps (paramilitary force under Interior Ministry)
FSF—Federal Security Force (Zulfi Bhutto's private army)
GHQ—General Headquarters of Pakistan's army
HIH—Hekmatyar's Islamist extremist Afghan group
HuM—Harkatui-ul-Mujahideen (JI's militant wing in Kashmir)
IAEA—International Atomic Energy Agency (U.N. agency)
IB—Intelligence Bureau (Pakistan's civilian intelligence agency)
IED—Improvised explosive device (homemade roadside bomb)
IJI—Islami Jamhoori Ittihad (anti–Benazir Bhutto coalition)
IJK—India Jammu and Kashmir (Indian-controlled territory in Jammu and Kashmir)
IMU—Islamic Movement of Uzbekistan (an Uzbek Islamist group)
ISI—Inter Services Intelligence (Pakistan Army's intelligence agency)
JeM—Jaish-e-Mohammad (militant group seeking to liberate Kashmir)
JKLF—Jammu and Kashmir Liberation Front (Kashmiri anti–India militant group)

Abbreviations

JI—Jamiat-i-Islami (religious party desiring an Islamist state)
JuA—Jamaat-ul-Ahrar (Pakistani Islamist terrorist group)
JUI—Jamiat-ul-Ulema i-Islam (moderate Islamist Party)
JUP—Jamiat-e-Ulema Pakistan (West wing religious political party)
KHAD—Afghanistan's security service
KP—Khyber-Pakhtunkhwa (NWFP's new name after 2010; merged with FATA in 2018)
LeJ—Lashkar-e-Jhangvi (anti–Shia religious group)
LeT (also LT)—Lashkar-e-Taiba (jihadist group fighting in Kashmir)
LFO—Legal Framework Order (law offering constitutional framework)
LOC—Line of Control (cease-fire line separating AJK and IJK)
MI—Military Intelligence (the army's intelligence agency)
MMA—Mutahhida Majlis-i-Amal (anti–Musharraf Islamist coalition)
MRD—Movement for the Restoration of Democracy (anti–Zia group)
MQM—Mohajir Qaumi Mahaz (East wing political party representing the mohajirs)
NAP—National Awami Party (East wing political party)
NC—National Conference (political party in Kashmir)
NGO—Non-Governmental Agency (non-profit charitable organization)
NWFP—North-West Frontier Province (one of four provinces of Pakistan; renamed KPP in 2010)
PAEC—Pakistan Atomic Energy Commission
PML—Pakistan Muslim League (a major mainstream political party)
PML(N)—Pakistan Muslim League (Nawaz Sharif faction)
PML(Q)—Pakistan Muslim League Queen (Musharraf's party)
PNA—Pakistan National Alliance (Anti–Zulfikar-Bhutto Alliance)
PPP—Pakistan People's Party (a major mainstream political party dominated by Bhutto family)
PTI—Pakistan Movement for Justice (party of Imran Khan)
RSSS—Rashtriya Swayamseuak Sangh (Indian terrorist group)
SMP—Sipah-e-Mohammed Pakistan (Shia military group)
SSP—Sipah-i-Sahaba-i-Pakistan (rabidly anti–Shia sectarian group)
TNSM—Tehriki-e-Nifaz-e-Shariat-e-Muhammadi (Islamic extremist group with the goal to enforce Sharia law inside Pakistan)
TTP—Tehrik-e-Taliban ("Pakistan Taliban") a united front of Pakistan's Taliban groups

Chronology

1947 August—Pakistan gained independence with Karachi its capital. Jinnah took control as governor-general

   October—First Kashmir War (became First Indo-Pak War)

1948 September—Jinnah died. Prime Minister Liaquat Khan took control

1951 October—Liaquat Khan assassinated. Pro-army triumvirate led country, with Ghulam Muhammad as governor-general

1953 August—India set up puppet government in IJK Kashmir and began integrating IJK into India

1954 May–Pak-American Mutual Defense Treaty signed

1955 August—Iskander Mirza replaced Ghulam as governor-general

   October—Pakistan adopted "One Unit" voting system

1956 March—Pakistan's First Constitution came into effect, with Iskander Mirza as the first president. Governor-general position abolished; National Assembly created

1958 October—General Ayub Khan removed Mirza in military coup. Prime minister post abolished for the next 13 years

1962 March—President Ayub Khan imposed a second constitution on Pakistan, with a strong president; no prime minister

1963 October—first workers moved into new capital in Islamabad

1965 August—Second Kashmir War began (became Second Indo-Pak War)

1967 December—PPP Party founded

1969 March—General Yahya Khan replaced Ayub Khan as president; second period of martial law

1970 July—Yahya Khan ended "One Unit" voting system

   December—Mujib's East wing AL Party won National Assembly elections

1971 March—Pakistani troops attacked East wing. Civil War began.

Chronology

December—India defeated Pakistan in Third Indo-Pak War. East wing became Bangladesh. Yahya Khan resigned and named Zulfi Bhutto president

1973 April—Pakistan adopted Third Constitution. Strong prime minister; weak president. Senate created; Zulfikar Bhutto prime minister

1977 March—Zulfikar Bhutto won elections, but with massive rigging

July—Gen. Zia seized power. Prime minister position abolished

1979 March—Zulfikar Bhutto executed

December—Soviet troops occupied Afghanistan, starting 10-year Afghan-Soviet War. Zia and U.S. jointly support Afghan rebels

1983 March—Pakistan's first cold test of a nuclear device

1985 March—Zia restored prime minister post. Junejo prime minister

November—8th Constitutional Amendment gave president power to dismiss prime ministers

1988 August—Zia killed in mysterious plane crash

December—PPP head Benazir Bhutto started first term as prime minister. Start of "Lost Decade of Democracy"

1989 February—Soviets completed withdrawal from Afghanistan

1990 January—Kashmir's four-year mass uprising (intifada) began

August—Saddam Hussein's Iraq Army invaded Kuwait

November—PML leader Nawaz Sharif started first term as prime minister

1992 April—Afghan communist regime toppled. Four-year Afghan civil war began

1993 October—Benazir Bhutto started second term as prime minister

1994 September—Afghan Taliban formed by Mullah Omar

1996 May—Osama bin Laden arrived in Afghanistan

September—Taliban took over Afghan government, ending Afghan civil war

1997 February—Sharif started second term as prime minister

April—13th Amendment ended president's power to dismiss PMs

1998 May—Pakistan hot-tested its first atomic bomb

August—Benazir Bhutto indicted; left for nine-year exile

1999 March—Third Kashmir War began and soon became Fourth Indo-Pak War

October—Gen. Musharraf seized power. Abolished post of PM until 2002

2001 September—al-Qaeda destroyed New York's World Trade Center

December—U.S.-supported Northern Alliance drove al-Qaeda and Taliban out of Afghanistan; many survivors fled to Pakistan

2003 December—17th Amendment adopted; restored presidential power to dismiss prime ministers

2007 March—Musharraf fired Supreme Court Chief Justice Chaudhry

July—Musharraf attacked the Red Mosque

October—Benazir Bhutto returned to Pakistan from exile

Chronology

November—Musharraf gave up position as army chief

December—TTP ("Pakistan Taliban") formed; Benazir Bhutto murdered

2008 March—Gillani elected prime minster

September—Zardari elected president after Musharraf resigned

2010 April—18th Amendment adopted. President lost power to dismiss prime ministers. NWFP renamed Khyber Pakhtunkhwa (KP)

2011 May—U.S. Navy SEALs killed Osama bin Laden inside Pakistan

2012 June—Supreme Court dismissed Prime Minister Gillani for contempt of court

2013 June—Nawaz Sharif started third term as prime minister

2017 July—Supreme Court disqualified Prime Minister Sharif for dishonesty

2018 May—25th Amendment adopted; merged FATA with KP

July—Imran Khan elected prime minister

Glossary

Ahmadis—members of the persecuted minority Ahmadi Muslim sect
Army chief—unofficial title of head of Afghan Army
Barelvi—a tolerant school of Sunni Islamic thought
Bengali—native or resident of Bengal (region mainly in East wing)
burka—tent-like garment covering women from head to foot
daicot—bandit
Deobandi—a rigid, intolerant school of Islamic thought
East wing—informal title of East Pakistan
fatwa—religious decree handed down by Muslim religious leader
feudals—wealthy landowners who dominated Pakistan's politics
Frontier Constabulary—military force providing border security
Haqqani network—Taliban group based in North Waziristan
intifada—mass uprising
Islam—Muslim religion with belief in Allah and Prophet Muhammad
Islamist—a Muslim or Muslim group that advocates an Islamic state
Jammu—the region south and west of the Kashmir Valley
jihad—a good Muslim's struggle for spiritual perfection, or for war against nonbelievers
jihadist—one who fights for a religious cause
Koran—Islam's book of sacred writings based on Allah's revelations to Muhammad
loya jirga—a national assembly convened to make major decisions
madrassa—a religious school devoted to training boys in the way of Islam
mohajirs—migrants from India, especially those settling in Sindh Province
Muhammad—a prophet and the founder of the Islam religion
mujahideen—jihadist fighters against the Soviets in the Afghan-Soviet War

Glossary

mullah—religious leader

Muslim—a follower of Islam religion

National Assembly—Pakistan's national legislature

Northern Alliance—north Afghan group opposing the Afghan Taliban.

One Unit—system whereby East and West wings given voting equality

Pakistan Taliban—another name for the TTP (a united front of Taliban groups in Pakistan)

Pashtun (also Pushtun) ethnic group living in Af-Pak border region

Pashtunistan—name of hoped-for Pashtun independent country

pirs—rural religious leaders

political agent—official who administers a FATA agency

Punjabi Taliban—network of militants in Punjab Province providing support to the TTP

sectarian—an adherent to a sect which is intolerant of others

secular—not overtly religious

Sharia (also "Shariat")—interpretations of the Koran and lessons learned from Muhammad's life

Shia—also Shiite (a Muslim of the minority branch of Islam)

Shiite—see "Shia"

shura—council of elders responsible for village governance

sufi—a mystic sect that worships saints

Sunnah—Prophet Muhammad's code of personal conduct for Muslims

Sunni—A Muslim of the majority branch of Islam

Taliban—Afghan Islamist religious group founded by Mullah Omar

ulema—religious scholars and leaders in the cities

West wing—informal title of West Pakistan

zakat—tax that Muslims pay to support the poor

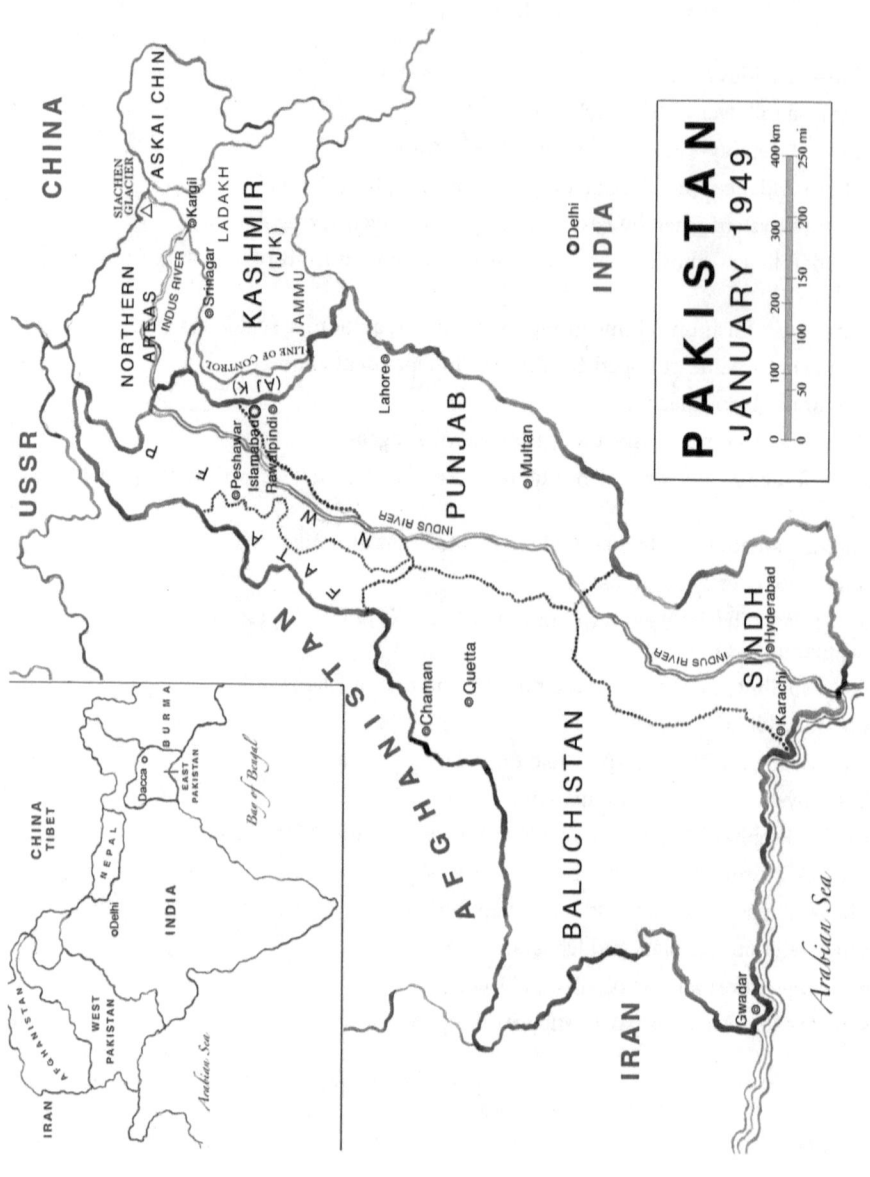

Map of Pakistan (courtesy Allison Cosmos).

Map of FATA and NWFP (courtesy Allison Cosmos).

Introduction to Pakistan

The Provinces

After Pakistan became an independent nation in 1947, it consisted of West Pakistan (the "West wing") and East Pakistan (the "East wing"). The West wing's western border abutted Afghanistan, while its eastern border abutted India. The East wing was larger in population than the West wing, but had a much smaller land area. In 1971, a civil war resulted in the East wing's breaking off from the West wing and becoming the independent country of Bangladesh.

After this dismemberment, and still today, Pakistan consists of four provinces and a tribal region called FATA. Punjab Province in the north is home to 53 percent of Pakistan's people (2017 census). It also is the country's richest province in agricultural output since the Indus River flows through it. Sindh Province in the south contains 23 percent of the country's population. The province includes Karachi, which is Pakistan's commercial capital and the country's most important port. Baluchistan is the largest province in land area but is largely uninhabited, with just 6 percent of the country's people. It is home to several deserts, including the Thar Desert—the seventh largest desert on the planet. It contains large natural gas fields. The Northwest Frontier Province (NWFP) is the smallest province in land area and contains 14 percent of the country's people.

In addition to Pakistan's four provinces, there is a tribal region called the Federally Administered Tribal Areas (FATA). FATA is a sparsely populated arid, mountainous region, with only 3 percent of the country's population. In 2008, it merged with the NWFP.

Religions

Most Pakistanis are Muslims. Three-fourths of the country's Muslims belong to the Sunni branch of Islam, while one-fourth belong to the Shia (Shiite) branch. Most Pakistani Muslims take their religion seriously. Most support Pakistan's blasphemy laws, which make it a crime punishable by death to desecrate the Koran or make derogatory remarks about the Prophet Muhammad.[1] For centuries, the Sunnis and Shiites have quarreled with each other throughout the world, largely because of a dispute over who succeeded the Prophet Muhammad as the spiritual leader (caliph) of Islam.

There are also millions of followers of non–Muslim religions living in Pakistan. These include 20 million Christians and 4 million Ahmadis. Muslim Sunni extremists have become more and more intolerant toward these minority religious groups—and even toward Muslim Shias.

Education

Pakistan's educational system is not impressive. Pakistan's literacy rate is just 57 percent, and 40 percent of people have never received any schooling. Only 15 percent of people have graduated from high school.[2] Of those enrolled in schools, some 60 percent attend state-operated public schools, 30 percent attend private schools, and 10 percent or less attend religious schools (madrassas).[3] Literacy rates and school enrollment rates are lower for women than men. However, despite Pakistan's low literacy rates, it has more than 190 private and public universities.

State public schools are underfunded, understaffed, and overcrowded. Teachers use thin standardized government textbooks with an emphasis on memorizing material so that their students can pass "matric exams" needed to graduate from high school.[4] Most religious madrassas teach students to memorize the Koran and other Muslim texts. The madrassas have their greatest impact on the country by graduating students who will influence others with radical Islamist ideas as they preach in mosques or teach in public schools.[5] Some madrassas teach religious intolerance and even violent jihad.

The Military

Pakistan's army has become the country's dominant "class," with its own budget, rules, and economic interests. Civilians have minimal control over Pakistan's army, although the head civilian leader (prime minister or president) does have the authority to appoint a general to be the army's leader (the "Army Chief"). The 550,000-man army dominates the country's navy and air force. To control the border regions, the army is supported by poorly trained and poorly equipped troops in the 90,000-man Frontier Corps and Frontier Constabulary. The leader of Pakistan's army—the "Army Chief"—is the most powerful person in Pakistan. Army generals have become quite wealthy, since military dictators have given them large plots of state-owned lands, and the generals have used their wealth to form large businesses in the farming and commercial sectors ("Milbus").[6]

The army operates an intelligence agency called Inter-Service Intelligence (ISI). The ISI has become Pakistan's most dreaded organization due to its constant spying on citizens and its punishing those it believes threaten the country.[7] The ISI also conducts its own aggressive foreign policy in Kashmir and Afghanistan. The army theoretically controls the ISI and appoints its officers. However, the ISI has its own headquarters, and often conducts missions without the army's knowledge. The ISI sometimes has intervened in national elections in support of pro-army candidates.[8]

The Government

General

Pakistan has operated under three different constitutions. The first two constitutions (1956 and 1962) provided for rule by a strong civilian president. However, the Third (current) Constitution of 1973 provides for a parliamentary system. Under this constitution, National Assembly elections are held and the political party which wins the most seats is called on to select a prime minister from that party—subject to National Assembly confirmation.

Pakistan has sometimes been governed by civilian politicians and sometimes by army generals. During the 50 years between 1958 and 2008, military dictatorships alternated with civilian governments—usually at ten-year intervals. Army leaders have always had the ability to remove civilian governments by force, and they often have used this power to take over the government, claiming that the army is Pakistan's "guardian." These bloodless military coups normally have been led by the army chief with full army support and with the blessing of Pakistan's Supreme Court. The army has justified these takeovers on grounds that the civilian politicians were corrupt and endangered the nation's security. Army leaders have been careful to seize power only when there was reasonable justification for doing so—such as when civilian leaders have been unable to control violence. Pakistan's politicians often played into the army's hands by giving it justification for taking over, since most politicians have been self-serving and unwilling to compromise among themselves to enact needed reforms.⁹

The government's power has always been limited by its inability to secure sufficient government revenue to meet the needs of the people. Tax revenues have been stunted because of widespread income tax evasion, smuggling by criminals, and corruption of government officials.¹⁰ Government sales tax revenues are low because smuggled consumer goods are sold on the black market.¹¹ Also, many wealthy persons and businesses refuse to repay money loaned to them by national banks, even though they can easily repay them. Moreover, for decades the government refused to impose a tax on agricultural income and it has abolished taxes on gifts, estates and capital gains.¹²

During Periods of Military Rule

During periods of military rule, military dictators generally have acted almost as selfishly as civilian politicians. However, army leaders know that they must gain the support of the masses if they are to retain control for long periods. The generals have noticed that after a few years of military rule, the people want the generals to return to their military duties and return the country back to civilian control.¹³ Military rulers often have tried to delay their departure by portraying their regimes as "democratic"—by adopting civilian titles and holding referendums on their rule.

During Periods of Civilian Rule

THE EXECUTIVE BRANCH: PRIME MINISTERS AND PRESIDENTS

Under Pakistan's Third (and current) 1973 Constitution, when a civilian government is in power, the prime minister leads the government. The president is just a figurehead head of state. The prime minister stays in office for five years or until he loses control of a majority of seats in the National Assembly—whichever comes first.

Pakistan has had many political parties, but only two or three parties have had a national following. The main national parties have been controlled by a wealthy feudal landowner family (the Bhuttos) and more recently by a wealthy urban industrialist family (the Sharifs). The power of the feudals is even stronger than that of the industrialists, since the fomer has been able to direct the votes of their farmhands and tenant farmers, whereas factory owners haven't been able to direct the votes of their workers. These ruling elites have had no incentive to promote legislative reforms that might improve the literacy or well-being of the lower classes, since prosperous, educated voters might challenge their control of the country. It has been easy for the elite to maintain control since the state controls the content of radio and television, and most voters are illiterate and cannot comprehend the little written information that does reach them.[14]

While the prime minister is the most powerful official in a civilian government, he usually has only a precarious hold of the government. He still must retain majority support in the National Assembly, but he can't even count on the support of all his own party members. Many were elected due to their own fundraising and vote-getting abilities, and so don't depend on their party to help them be reelected.[15] The prime minister's task of retaining his majority in the Assembly becomes even more difficult if his own party members didn't secure a majority of National Assembly seats, forcing him to form a coalition with other parties. These coalition parties sometimes withdraw from the coalition for trivial reasons—thereby depriving the prime minister of his majority and forcing him out of office.[16]

Even if a prime minister has absolute control of the National Assembly, he still can quickly be removed from office. First, a prime minister can be forcibly removed by army at any time. Also, the prime minister's powers have twice been diluted by constitutional amendments which have allowed prime ministers to be dismissed by the president if the president simply declares, even without proof, that the prime minister has lost majority control of the National Assembly. Moreover, during the past eight years, the Supreme Court has become more assertive and has dismissed two prime ministers for contempt of its decisions or for having been dishonest.

The Legislative Branch

During Pakistan's first decade, its legislature was called the Federal Assembly. It was a weak, docile institution which often quickly passed all bills submitted to it by the prime minister with little debate.[17] In 1956, the first Constitution was adopted and a National Assembly became the legislature. The National Assembly was a wild and uncivil body in which majorities steamrolled through legislation, while the Opposition responded with violent speeches, protests and walkouts.[18] In 1973, a less powerful Senate was added.

Throughout Pakistan's history, legislative candidates have needed to raise a lot of money to run a successful national election campaign and so most candidates have been wealthy.[19] Most candidates sought legislative seats primarily so they could receive substantial legislative salaries, allowances, and low interest loans from national banks.[20] Most legislators just wanted to stay in office and refused to compromise with their rivals. The legislators stopped serious discourse and debates. The majority pushed legislation through while the Opposition fought back with absenteeism, and abusive threatening behavior.[21]

Meaningless Elections

Pakistan's elections have always been relatively meaningless for the masses. There simply aren't enough literate voters capable of holding candidates and political parties accountable—especially since the parties seldom have definable objectives.[22] Candidates campaign on simple slogans, and stir up emotions by attacking minority religions or unpopular foreign countries.[23] As mentioned, since most voters are illiterate, they vote based on personalities instead of issues and can't even choose their favorite party unless they can recognize its symbol on the ballot. Many farm workers and tenant farmers vote for candidates recommended by the landowners who own the land on which they work.[24] Many Pakistanis attended rallies out of curiosity, boredom or the promise of a few rupees for a meal.[25] Most voters realize that the candidates who promise to improve their lives by building schools and roads in their villages have no intention of carrying out these empty promises.[26] They also know that whoever wins the election will waste government funds due to corruption, and that the extent of corruption will never be discovered until the next government comes to power.[27] Voter confidence in the election process is further diminished because of the ballot tampering and vote count rigging that accompanies most elections.[28]

The Judicial Branch

Pakistan's judicial system consists of a national Supreme Court, an appellate "High Court" in each province, and numerous lower district courts. Powerful military rulers, presidents and prime ministers have often appointed their own supporters to the appellate courts. Some military dictators have even made these judges take oaths of allegiance to them. For decades the Supreme Court legitimated military takeovers, even though they violated the Constitution. However, recently the Supreme Court has shown more independence, and has prevented the rulers from packing the courts with their supporters.[29] In Pakistan's lower courts, provincial lawyers are often corrupt, and judges often insure that poor litigants don't receive justice.[30] The courts are so slow resolving cases that law and order is administered by brutal local police who wield absolute power within their jurisdictions.[31]

PART ONE—PAKISTAN'S EARLY YEARS

1

Independence and Partition

During the six-month period covered in this chapter (March–August 1947), Britain would decide to cede independence to its prized colony India. At the same time it would decide to divide the Indian subcontinent into two countries: Hindu-dominated India and Muslim-dominated Pakistan. In August 1947, the British would formally give independence to the new countries, and a few days later would announce the boundaries of the countries—having been given that boundary-setting authority by the leaders of both Pakistan and India.

Jinnah Leads the Muslim Independence Movement

The story of how Pakistan became independent began with Mohammed Ali Jinnah. He would become the leader of India's Muslim League party, which claimed to represent India's 100 million Muslims. In February 1937, India's Congress Party prevailed in India's general elections, while Jinnah's Muslim League only managed to win 25 percent of the seats reserved for Muslims.[1]

Jinnah refused to give up, especially when Nehru's Congress Party ignored his request that Congress share power with the League in those provinces where Muslims lived in significant numbers.[2] Jinnah began by launching a drive to increase Muslim League membership.

He won over many Muslims to the League by claiming that Muslims could not trust India's government to protect the rights of the 100 million Muslim residents in a 400-million person India. He would claim that "Islam Is in Danger" as long as India's Muslims remained in the country.

When the Second World War broke out in Europe in September 1939, Britain demanded that India join the war against Germany. However, India's Congress Party refused, since Britain wouldn't first give India independence. In contrast, Jinnah's All-India Muslim League supported the British war effort. Jinnah was hoping that the British would repay this Muslim loyalty by supporting its call for a post-war independent Pakistan. During the next four years, Muslim League membership greatly increased. India's Muslims flocked to the League's rallying cry that "Islam was in danger" and that the Hindus would oppress them if they remained in India.

On July 26, 1945, British Labor Party leader Clement Attlee replaced Winston Churchill as Britain's Prime Minister. Attlee immediately declared his intention to quickly give India its freedom. Britain had accumulated a huge war debt and simply couldn't afford to continue occupying and administering India and its other colonies.

On August 16, 1946, to secure its goal of an independent Pakistan, a Jinnah-called "Direct Action Day" was observed to support the formation of an independent Pakistan. The demonstrations led to a massacre in Calcutta as groups of Muslims, Hindus and Sikhs attacked each other in the streets. The violence spread to the countryside and within a week, 15,000 people were dead. This communal violence forever ended the possibility that Muslims would give up their demand for a separate Muslim Pakistan. On February 20, 1947, Prime Minister Attlee declared that Britain would transfer power to the Indian people by June 1, 1948.

Britain Cedes Independence to India and Pakistan

On March 22, 1947, the 46-year-old British war hero Lord Louis Mountbatten arrived in India and became the Viceroy of the British colony of India. He had a mandate from Prime Minister Attlee to arrange for the transfer of British sovereignty of the Indian subcontinent to a single independent nation—India. Mountbatten began trying to win over India's key leaders to this idea, in the hope of leaving behind a united India. However, Mountbatten soon realized that Jinnah never would abandon his demand for a separate Muslim nation, and so he began promoting a plan for redrawing the boundaries of the Indian subcontinent into Hindu and Muslim regions. This plan called for granting the Hindu-dominated regions to India, while granting the Muslim-dominated regions to the separate new nation called Pakistan.

On June 3, 1947, Pakistan's leader Jinnah and India's leader Jawaharlal Nehru formally approved the general outline of the British partition plan. The details of dividing assets between the two new nations still had to be worked out. Mountbatten then shocked everyone by moving up the date for

British transfer of power to the new nations to August 15.[3] This left only 73 days to complete three major transfer tasks. First, the lands of the Indian subcontinent had to be divided between the new nations of India and Pakistan. Another task was to divide the Indian subcontinent's other tangible assets and debts between the two new nations. The last task was to get the subcontinent's provinces and princely states to declare whether they would join ("accede to") India or Pakistan. Mountbatten took it upon himself the job of persuading the hundreds of Indian princes to decide whether to accede to India or Pakistan.

The British ended up being responsible for drawing the boundary lines which would divide the two new nations. At British insistence, Jinnah and Nehru agreed to allow an Englishman to chair two Boundary Commissions to divide the subcontinent's lands—the Punjab Commission and the Bengal Commission. The British chose the distinguished British lawyer Sir Cyril Radcliffe to head the two commissions, and he arrived in India on July 8, 1947. The two five-person commissions had a five-week deadline to determine the boundary lines. Four judges on each commission were to present to Radcliffe their joint recommendation as to where the boundaries were to be. However, it quickly became apparent that the two Hindu judges never would agree with the Hindu and Sikh judges on the location of any boundary, and so it fell to Radcliffe to make most of the boundary decisions himself.[4] Mountbatten secured promises from the leaders of both governments-to-be that they would accept the British Radcliffe partition decision no matter what it would be, with no right of appeal.[5] The final Radcliffe awards favored India, and at the last minute, Mountbatten probably pressured Radcliffe to change a key boundary in India's favor.[6]

On July 18, 1947, Britain passed the "Indian Independence Act," which divided British India into the new separate nations of India and Pakistan, effective August 15. The Act called for the creation of the office of governor-general in each country to represent the British Crown. It also called for creating a Constituent Assembly in each nation with authority to act as a temporary legislature and to write a permanent constitution. Until a constitution was enacted, each country would be governed by the old Government of India Act of 1935.

On August 14, 1947, at 9:00 a.m., the official Pakistan Independence Day ceremonies began in Karachi, Pakistan. Mountbatten delivered the King's good wishes, while Pakistan's leader Jinnah declared that he hoped the two countries could remain friends. Soon after these Pakistani ceremonies, Mountbatten flew to New Delhi to participate in the Indian transfer of power ceremonies.

While Pakistan formally became independent when the new day began on August 15, 1947, it would celebrate August 14 as it Independence Day. On

August 15, 1947, when the new day began, Britain officially surrendered its authority in the Indian subcontinent to India and Pakistan. At 8:30 a.m., Lord Mountbatten was sworn in as governor-general of the new Indian nation. Jinnah had offended the vain Mountbatten by refusing his offer to also be Pakistan's governor-general. This refusal led Mountbatten to favor India over Pakistan while he remained India's governor-general.[7]

By now, Mountbatten had persuaded most of the Indian princes to give up their independence, and most had acceded to India. However, the princes ruling Kashmir, Hyderabad and Juinagadh still chose to keep their states independent. Mountbatten purposely delayed announcing Radcliffe's partition awards until after Independence Day in order to prevent boundary award discontent from marring the festivities.[8]

The Pakistani and Indian independence ceremonies were peaceful and friendly. Most Indians had a good feeling toward the British, and held the naive belief that the British departure would solve all their problems. However, the ceremonies soon would be followed by the world's greatest migration and by unprecedented suffering and death.

2

Pakistan Under Jinnah

During the 13-month period covered in this chapter (August 1947–September 1948), Pakistan and India would become independent, and Britain would announce their national boundaries. There followed the greatest migration in human history. Millions of Muslims would migrate westward to Pakistani-awarded territory, and millions of Hindus would migrate eastwards to Indian territory. When the great migration ended, Jinnah would try to unify Pakistan and insure its survival. In October 1947, the long fight over control over the princely state of Kashmir would begin when Pakistani-backed tribesmen crossed into Kashmir and sought to make it part of Pakistan. The chapter ends with Jinnah's death by cancer.

Pakistan Sets Up Its Government

On August 15, 1947, Pakistan became independent. The name "Pakistan" was chosen largely to describe the regions it presumed would be included. The "P" was for Punjab, "A" was for Afghans, "K" was for Kashmir, "S" was for Sind, and "tan" was for Baluchistan.

Pakistan's government declared Karachi to be its temporary capital. Karachi was chosen because it was Jinnah's birthplace, had some modest facilities for housing the government, and its harbor gave Pakistan access to the outside world. Pakistan's army set up its headquarters in the former headquarters of the Indian Army's Northern Command in the town of Rawalpindi—1,000 miles north of Karachi.

Pakistan's initial government would follow the framework of the

Government of India Act of 1935 until it adopted its own constitution. Pakistan's government would consist largely of a Constituent Assembly (CAP), a governor-general, and a prime minister. The CAP was Pakistan's temporary legislative body with responsibility for writing a constitution. It named Jinnah as Pakistan's governor-general, and Jinnah named Muslim League leader Liaquat Ali Khan as prime minister. Governor-General Jinnah immediately assumed very strong powers, while Prime Minister Liaquat Khan willingly assumed a subordinate role. Jinnah diminished Liaquat's authority by his tendency to assume great powers and make the final decision on most substantive matters. He handpicked Liaquat's cabinet (with Jinnah himself heading two ministries) and chaired Liaquat's cabinet meetings. While the Constituent Assembly was the federal legislature, it submissively rubber-stamped all legislation proposed by Jinnah, since the Assembly was packed with Muslim League members and there were no opposition parties.[1]

While the Assembly's main responsibility was to write a constitution, it would take the CAP seven years to agree on the wording of this important document. The long delay would be partly due to differences of opinion on how power should be shared between the two wings. Also, rigid Islamists opposed the constitution until it included provisions making the country an Islamic state.

Jinnah had many strengths. First, he was a brilliant lawyer who was able to critically analyze Pakistan's problems.[2] He was a charismatic leader who had become extremely popular as the "Father of the Nation." As "the Quaid" ("Great Leader"), he was able to keep the country together during its critical first year. His mere presence insured that the Federal Assembly members deliberated in a calm and respectful manner.[3] Also, Jinnah promoted solid, sensible goals for Pakistan which he urged his followers to accept. These goals included developing Pakistan into a secular, democratic state honoring the rule of law and protected by a strong army. In addition, Jinnah called for tolerance between Pakistan's many religious communities. He wanted Pakistan to be a state for Muslims, but not an Islamic state in which all its citizens had to adhere to Islam and its dictates.

Jinnah had some weaknesses. First, he perpetuated the British colonial tradition of viceregal rule, whereby the governor-general made all important decisions. While Jinnah was an unselfish, benevolent dictator, the concentration of power in his hands set an unfortunate precedent for autocratic rule. Also, Jinnah didn't delegate authority well. When he discovered that he had terminal lung cancer, he never groomed Prime Minister Liaquat Ali Khan or anyone else to be his successor. In addition, Jinnah was stubborn and uncompromising, which hampered his ability to work with others in administering the country.

2. Pakistan Under Jinnah

The World's Greatest Migration

On August 16, 1947, India's Governor-General Mountbatten announced the Radcliffe decision. This established the boundaries of India and Pakistan. There was no dispute over the boundaries, since Jinnah and Indian leader Nehru had agreed in advance to abide by the British Radcliffe boundary award.[4] However, an immense problem arose when the boundary decision was announced, since five million Muslims began migrating west to Pakistan, while four million Hindus began traveling east to India. The greatest migration in human history had begun. Religious minorities fled their homes due to intimidation and death threats by their neighbors. In both India and Pakistan, the strong attacked the weak just because they practiced a different religion. Many Muslim refugees were killed while traveling to their new homelands, mainly by groups of well-organized Sikhs.[5] Muslims retaliated by killing defenseless Sikhs and Hindus. When trains couldn't carry all the fleeing refugees, many set out on foot, bicycles and mules. Many in these slow, unguarded refugee columns didn't survive due to exhaustion and lack of food and water.[6] During the six weeks of the Great Migration, four million largely productive civilians from Pakistan left, while five million mostly destitute persons from India arrived.[7] During the migration, 400,000 or more people died.[8]

There were several repercussions to this great migration. First, the mass migrations led to huge refugee problems in both Pakistan and India, when the eight to nine million survivors reached their destinations. Pakistan suffered even more from the migrations than India, since it received a million more refugees than India, and the refugees they received tended to be poorer.[9] Also, the forced evictions and killings left a permanent impression on the survivors which greatly increased the distrust between Indians and Pakistanis.

During the early days after independence, Pakistan's leaders were forced to focus their attention on their country's survival. This narrow focus would have significant long-term consequences. Pakistan's leaders became preoccupied with the threat of being invaded by their large neighbor India.[10] These fears would lead Pakistan to spend over half of its budget on strengthening its military forces. The earmarking of these huge sums for the military reduced the funds available for building public schools, health clinics and roads. Also, the focus on survival led Pakistan's civilian leaders to rely heavily on the army and allow it to dominate the country. Moreover, the focus on survival led Pakistan's leaders to support Islamist religious parties and groups as a way to unify the country. This support would enable Islamist extremist groups to grow so powerful that they eventually would threaten the government itself.

Pakistan's leaders realized that the country was weak and isolated and would need outside military assistance should hostilities break out with

India. Pakistan secured some of that help when on September 30, 1947, Pakistan gained United Nations' membership. Pakistan would play an active role in the U.N., and would become a major promoter of independence for Afro-Asian countries still under colonial rule.

Pakistan's foreign policy would center around several principles. First, Jinnah sought to have good relations with all nations—especially Muslim countries. Also, Jinnah quickly turned against India. India's leaders openly predicted that Pakistan would collapse, and thereby allow India to reclaim it.[11] Jinnah's hostility toward India grew as India intentionally delayed distributing desperately needed assets located in India that it had agreed to turn over to Pakistan. In addition, Jinnah would try to secure military and economic support from the United States. He believed that Pakistan's close proximity to Russia would lead the United States to choose it as an ally to block Soviet territorial expansion in the region.

Pakistan's Huge Problems

During Jinnah's short rule, he immediately faced two sets of major problems. The first set involved Pakistan's shortage of tangible resources. Since Pakistan had broken off from India, it had to start from scratch, and it inherited a weak economy. Its agricultural production was small and lacked diversity. The country's main agricultural export products were jute and cotton—jute being used for sacks and carpet backing. However, all the jute processing mills were in India and jute was being challenged by new materials.[12] Also, Pakistan had a weak industrial base, since Pakistan had been awarded just 10 percent of the subcontinent's industrial base. In addition, Pakistan's government facilities were practically non-existent, since most government staff and equipment was still in India. The Treasury was almost empty, and India was slow to turn over to Pakistan its share of cash and sterling balances. The treasury had difficulty paying for the food and shelter of the five million largely destitute Muslim refugees from India. Also, Pakistan had a small weak army, since it had been awarded just 140,000 troops compared to 260,000 to India. Also, Pakistan's army was ill-equipped—partly because India failed to transfer to Pakistan its allotted share of military equipment.[13]

Pakistan also faced a second set of problems, which involved intangible factors which threatened its fragile national unity. First, West and East Pakistan (Pakistan's West and East "wings") were 1,000 miles apart. The west and east wingers didn't feel part of the same country. Also, the residents in Pakistan's diverse regions didn't share a common language or ethnicity, and most didn't consider their common Muslim religion as justification for joining together in one country. Pakistan's leaders contributed to the disunity by setting up a strong central government to control the provinces and then not listening to the provincial grievances. In addition, Pakistan's leaders lacked experience in representative government, and so there was no tradition of politicians compromising to take action for the good of the country. Instead, politicians in power suppressed their opponents, while the opposition was only interested in removing the incumbents from power.[14] Also, there was no strong political party to lead the country. While Jinnah's Pakistan Muslim League (PML) had gained popularity for its role in securing independence, the party was dominated by the refugees who had fled from India. These party leaders were reluctant to share their power with non–PML members. The PML would gradually transform itself into a decentralized group of provincial and local branches which ignored the vestiges of national PML ideals that still remained.[15]

The First Kashmir War and First Indo-Pak War

The suffering and deaths during the six-week Great Migration had largely ended by the end of September 1947. It soon would be followed by fighting between Pakistan and India over which country would possess the princely state of Kashmir and Jammu. This princely state still was ruled with an iron hand by the ruthless Maharaja Hari Singh. The maharaja was one of the few princes who had not made his choice whether to join India or Pakistan. Pakistan's leaders had assumed that he would choose to join Pakistan, since although he was a Hindu, most Kashmiris were Muslims, and Kashmir bordered Pakistan. The matter came to a head on October 23, 1947, when a force of 2,000 or more ill-disciplined Muslim tribesmen from Pakistan crossed into Kashmir on trucks to seize it on behalf of Pakistan. They justified their invasion as an effort to liberate their fellow Muslims from the Maharaja, who recently had conducted a three-month reign of terror against rebellious Muslims in the Poonch region of Western Kashmir.[16] That campaign had resulted in the deaths of some 200,000 Muslims. While Pakistani soldiers were not part of the invasion force, the army actively aided the tribal invaders, who were led by a collection of military veterans.[17] The invaders only had to drive their trucks down 135 miles on undefended paved roads to reach Kashmir's capital Srinigar. They should have reached the capital in just one or two days. However, many of the raiders began looting and raping in the villages on the invasion route, and when they reached the outskirts of Srinagar, they decided to relax for several days before entering the city.[18]

On October 24, the day after the tribal invasion began, Muslims proclaimed the formation of the "Provisional Government of Azad (Free) Kashmir"—AJK. The AJK would control a strip of land in the southwestern corner of Jammu and Kashmir. It set up its own government and raised its own army—mainly from demobilized Second World War veterans in the Poonch region. The AJK wanted Jammu and Kashmir to join Pakistan. While the AJK would form its own local government, Pakistan would control it.

India's Governor-General Mountbatten became concerned about the Pakistani tribal invasion of Kashmir. On October 25, 1947, in the morning, Mountbatten agreed with India's leaders that Indian military intervention would be justified—but only if Kashmir's Maharaja Hari Singh first officially agreed that Kashmir join ("accede to") India. That afternoon, Indian official V.P. Menon flew to Kashmir's capital Srinagar on an Indian military plane, presumably to obtain from the maharajah a signed letter of accession of Kashmir to India. Shortly before midnight, Maharaja Singh fled from Kashmir's capital to Jammu, leaving no administration behind in Kashmir. It is unclear whether the Maharajah had signed a valid accession agreement to India before he left the capital. If Kashmir's leader didn't officially accede Kashmir to India before he fled, Kashmir's accession to India and India's military intrusion could be considered invalid.[19]

On October 27, India airlifted troops to the deserted Srinagar airfield—days before the Pakistani tribesmen arrived. The Indians set up strong defensive positions, enabling them to prevent the poorly armed tribesmen from entering the city. Within two weeks there were 5,000 well-armed Indian troops in Srinagar. Protected by these troops, Indian authorities set up a rudimentary Indian Jammu Kashmir (IJK) administration in Srinagar. There were now two rival governments competing for territory in Kashmir and Jammu—India's IJK and Pakistan's AJK. Jinnah had tried to deploy Pakistani troops to counter the Indian troop deployment, but the British general commanding Pakistan's army refused to deploy the troops, claiming that Kashmir had already acceded to India.[20]

Indian leaders wanted to secure support among the Kashmiri people for their intervention. Therefore, on October 30, 1947, they arranged for the popular Kashmir Sheikh Abdullah to be installed as the emergency administrator of their newly formed IJK. Sheikh Abdullah (the "Lion of Kashmir") had gained political power in the Kashmir Valley by his impressive oratory and by his having acquired control over most of the Valley's mosques and their congregations.[21] He also controlled Kashmir's popular, well-organized National Conference Party. India's Prime Minister Nehru agreed to let Abdullah temporarily govern the IJK in return for Abdullah's pledge to help integrate IJK territory into India.[22] Then on March 5, 1948, India arranged for the Lion of Kashmir to become IJK's prime minister—a position that he would retain for five and a half years.

Until now, Pakistani troops had stayed out of Kashmir, and the Indian forces were overwhelming the tribal invasion force. As Indian troops were on the verge of seizing all of Kashmir, General Gracey, the newly appointed chief of Pakistan's army, agreed to send in troops. Pakistan Army troops entered Kashmir on May 24, 1948, and took up defensive positions to prevent any further Indian advances. With Pakistani and Indian soldiers now fighting each other for control of Kashmir, the nine-month First Indo-Pak War began (May 1948–January 1949). Pakistan's troop strength in Kashmir never would match Indian troop strength, but Pakistan's army would prevent India from seizing all of Kashmir and Jammu. A stalemate developed, with neither side able to win an overwhelming victory.

The First Indo-Pak War ended on January 1, 1949, when a cease-fire came into effect. Both sides were exhausted and convinced that they no longer could make significant territorial gains against the other. The prolonged failure to resolve the Kashmir issue would increase the hostility between the two countries, would prevent the two sides from reaching a fair settlement, and would lead both countries to strengthen their armies. Seven months later, India and Pakistan would agree to the location of a cease-fire line, which would become known as the "Line of Control." While not an official border, for decades it would serve as an unofficial line separating Pakistan's AJK from India's IJK.

The Twilight of Jinnah's Rule

While the First Indo-Pak War was being fought, Pakistan's "Great Leader" Jinnah was fighting a battle for his own life. He had been diagnosed with lung cancer. He had kept his condition secret, and as his health steadily deteriorated, he became less and less able to address the affairs of state. His sister Fatima took over many of his duties. He would die within a year.

While Jinnah exercised less and less control, Pakistan's infant government limped along trying to solve its many problems. Its problems centered on how the new government could unify the diverse groups of people living within its borders. Many of these problems became evident during Jinnah's rule, and he confronted them with varying success.

One of the early problems was that Pakistan lacked a strong, unified intelligence agency. This problem was resolved in January 1948 when Pakistan joined together most of its small intelligence agencies into one central organization within the army—forming the Inter-Services Intelligence Agency (ISI). The ISI would be staffed largely by career army officers, who would serve in the ISI for two- or three-year tours. The ISI also hired retired army officers on contract. Once the ISI was formed, Pakistan would have just three primary intelligence agencies—the ISI, Military Intelligence (MI), and the civilian Intelligence Bureau (IB). The ISI gradually would become Pakistan's most important intelligence agency. It would also become one of Pakistan's most powerful and feared institutions.

Jinnah did a poor job in meeting Pakistan's language problem. He was so focused on unifying the country that he initially insisted that there must be just one national language, even though many of its ethnic groups spoke their own language. Jinnah compounded this mistake by insisting that this national language be Urdu—the language of India's Muslim elite. Urdu was spoken by only 7 percent of Pakistanis, and was not the primarily language spoken in any of Pakistan's provinces. In contrast, half of Pakistanis spoke Bangla, which was spoken largely by the Bengali ethnic group living in the populous East wing. The seriousness of this language issue was highlighted on March 11, 1948, when 50 Bengali students in the East wing city of Dacca demonstrated to have Bangla made Pakistan's national language. The students were beaten by police. Despite this protest, Jinnah's government would fail to comprehend the depth of discontent in the East wing over the Urdu-Bangla language issue. This discontent would only be partly defused when the central government allowed Bangla to be the official language of the East wing, while keeping Urdu as Pakistan's national language. When Pakistan's first constitution was adopted years later, both Urdu and Bangla were made official national languages.

Jinnah's government had to solve the problem that the giant, sparsely populated princely state of Baluchistan was still not part of Pakistan. The Khan of Kalat ruled this state located in the south of West Pakistan. The Khan stubbornly insisted that Baluchistan remain independent. Pakistan put enormous pressure on the Khan of Kalat to join Pakistan, and on March 27, 1948, the Khan finally officially acceded Baluchistan to Pakistan. In retrospect, Pakistan's pressure may have been excessive and may have been responsible for the Baloch people insisting on securing independence (or more autonomy) from Pakistan for decades to come. The Baloch people were willing to fight the central government for these goals, and during the next decades Baloch nationalists would conduct a series of revolts against Pakistan's central government. But the Baloch never would have enough manpower to defeat Pakistan's army, although their fighters would tie down the army using guerrilla hit-and-run tactics.

Jinnah hoped that the problem of Pakistan having weak armed forces might be solved when on May 1, 1948, Pakistan and the United States agreed to establish diplomatic relations. However, it would be years before the United States would give or sell weapons to Pakistan. Also, the relations between these two countries always would be strained, since America favored Pakistan's enemy India—a country better able to impede Communist Chinese expansion.

Pakistan's problem of unifying a country with diverse religions became more difficult with the growth of Islamist political parties which sought to impose their beliefs on others. The fundamentalist JI (Jamiat-i-Islami) had always been Pakistan's most powerful religious party, and the newly formed JUP (Jamiat-e-Ulema-e-Pakistan) became Pakistan's next most important religious party. On May 7, 1948, the JUP observed a country wide "Shariat Day" to publicize its demand that the government introduce Islamic Shariat holy laws throughout Pakistan.

A new problem developed in Sindh Province. On July 27, 1948, Pakistan's government declared that its capital would be located in Karachi—the populous city in Sindh Province. During the next month, Jinnah pressured Sindh Province to allow hundreds of thousands of refugees from India ("mohajirs") to settle there. When these mohajirs flooded into Sindh, tensions developed between these outside "intruders" and the native Sindhis. The natives resented the intrusion of the well-educated, Urdu-speaking mohajir refugees who didn't bother learning the Sindhi language and made only limited efforts to assimilate into the population.[23] At the same time, the mohajirs treated the native Sindhis with disdain and considered them to be backward peasants. The mohajirs further antagonized the natives as they gradually came to dominate Sindh's economy. They took away jobs from the natives and took over businesses abandoned by Sindhis who had fled to India.[24]

On September 11, 1948, Pakistan's 71-year-old Governor-General Jinnah died of lung cancer—an enormous blow to the new country. Jinnah had created Pakistan by the sheer force of his indomitable will, and during his short rule his great prestige and leadership had allowed Pakistan to survive. His towering personality, intelligence and honesty would be greatly missed.

There were several repercussions to Jinnah's death. First, without Jinnah's leadership, it would become difficult to hold the government together. Provincial leaders would feel emboldened to challenge the central government's authority, and would take even less interest in unifying the country. Also, Jinnah's vision of a secular government would disappear, since his successors lacked his commitment to religious tolerance. They would allow Islamists to grow in strength and they would submit to Islamist demands for pro–Islamic measures.

3

Pakistan Under Liaquat Khan

During the three-year period covered in this chapter (September 1948–October 1951), Liaquat Khan would lead the country as prime minister. Pakistan would return to peace after its war with India, and Pakistan would turn to Communist China as an ally. Prime Minister Liaquat Khan would appoint General Ayub Khan as Pakistan's Army Chief. The chapter ends with Liaquat Khan's assassination.

Liaquat Khan Takes Over

When Governor-General Jinnah died on September 11, 1948, Prime Minister Liaquat Khan was the natural choice to take over the government. He was the only popular national leader in the country, and he had been Jinnah's prime minister and trusted lieutenant. Liaquat Khan would control the government as prime minister, while his appointee Khwaja Nazimuddin succeeded Jinnah as governor-general. The weak Nazimuddin wouldn't interfere with Liaquat's management of the government, and the governor-generalship became a ceremonial position.[1]

Liaquat Khan had several strengths. First, he had considerable stature—having been the deputy of Pakistan's beloved leader Jinnah. His nationwide popularity, his leadership of the PML Party, and his majority support in the National Assembly gave him real power. Also, he was honest, hard-working and unselfish, and he had a strong commitment to improve the country.

However, Liaquat Khan also had several weaknesses. First, he lacked Jinnah's charisma, political acumen, and ability to command obedience. He never had developed leadership experience and political savvy while serving as Jinnah's prime minister because Jinnah had made all the major decisions by himself. He hadn't tried to train Liaquat as his successor. Also, Liaquat had only recently emigrated from India to Pakistan. Therefore, he lacked a political base inside Pakistan and he wasn't very familiar with Pakistan's leaders and people.[2] In addition, Liaquat would refuse to listen to the grievances of provincial leaders, and would dismiss officials who challenged or criticized him. Also, Liaquat felt that to unify the country, he must develop Islam into the country's sole religious ideology. His government would promote the notion that non–Muslims in Pakistan were potentially dangerous since they might support a Hindu-Indian plan to reintegrate Pakistan into India.

Liaquat Khan faced several obstacles when he took office. First, He had to govern Pakistan without the support of a strong national party. His own Pakistan Muslim League (PML) had deteriorated in part because its leaders hadn't offered any bold new programs to strengthen the country. Instead they sought to perpetuate themselves in power by recruiting no new members and by appointing party officials instead of electing them. Another obstacle was that Pakistan's officials lacked interest in developing a truly representative government.

While Pakistani troops had blocked India from seizing all of nearby Kashmir, this did not prevent India from seizing the princely state of Hyderabad. Hyderabad was totally surrounded by Indian territory, and most of its inhabitants were Hindus. However, when Indian troops invaded Hyderabad on September 13, 1948, and permanently occupied it, Pakistanis were very disturbed. They watched in dismay as India totally absorbed Hyderabad into India, with no country willing or able to stop this naked aggression. Pakistan's leaders worried that India might next try to seize all of Kashmir.

Kashmir's Hot War Turns into a Cold War

On January 1, 1949, the U.N.-promoted Pak-Indian cease-fire went into effect, thereby ending the 15-month fighting in Kashmir. However, the location of the cease-fire line separating the two belligerents still had to be determined. The end of the Kashmir fighting would be followed by a 16-year period of relative peace in that region.

Each side held on to the territory that it had seized. India's territory in Indian-controlled Jammu and Kashmir (IJK) included two-thirds of this land. Its territory was home to ten million people and included most of the coveted central Kashmir Valley. In contrast, Pakistan controlled just one-third of Jammu and Kashmir—the "Azad" (Free) Jammu and Kashmir (AJK). AJK territory consisted of a long north-south strip west of the IJK, and was home to three million people. Pakistan would directly administer this AJK territory without even pretending to give its people representation.[3]

On July 27, 1949, India and Pakistan agreed to the location of a temporary cease-fire line, and the United Nations sent in unarmed observers to help prevent the armies from violating this line of separation. This cease-fire line (later renamed the "Line of Control") would separate Pakistan-controlled AJK from Indian-controlled IJK for the next 16 years. During these years the Pakistani and Indian armies would honor the cease-fire line—although neither country gave up its claims to all of Kashmir and Jammu. During these years of relative peace, Pakistan would try to pressure India to hold a plebiscite—as Nehru once had promised. When this effort failed, Pakistan's ISI intelligence agency would encourage Pakistani-based Islamist jihadist groups to cross the Line of Control into IJK and attack Indian occupation troops there. The ISI hoped that these jihadist attacks would weaken India's resolve to remain there.

Unlike Pakistan, India was content to make the Line of Control a permanent boundary, since that would solidify its control of the larger IJK. However, Kashmir would become a huge problem for India. India would set up harsh puppet governments to rule IJK residents, and would even maneuver to integrate IJK into India. India's mistreatment of the Kashmiris in IJK would generate growing discontent. Also, to suppress the Pakistani-based jihadist groups which attacked Indian forces, India would eventually have to deploy over 250,000 troops and security police in IJK. India never would consider giving up this territory, partly because Nehru was personally attracted to Kashmir—his ancestral home.

During the next decade, India would take measures to make its stake in Kashmir permanent by absorbing its IJK territory into India. Pakistan would be too weak to stop this Indian absorption of IJK territory. It also would be unable to persuade the United States and Britain to pressure India to hold a plebiscite among the Kashmiris to determine how they wished to be governed.

Liaquat Tries to Increase His Powers

Prime Minister Liaquat Khan tried to strengthen his powers, since he didn't have sufficient prestige to get rivals and provincial leaders to do his bidding. On January 6, 1949, Liaquat had Pakistan's Constituent Assembly enact PRODA (the Public Representative Offices Disqualification Act). PRODA allowed the governor-general, provincial governors and ordinary citizens to file a complaint against any elected official suspected of corruption, favoritism or mismanagement. The charges would be investigated by a two-judge tribunal, and violations would lead to exclusion from holding public office for ten years. Liaquat would abuse PRODA by using it to subdue his rivals and unruly provincial leaders, and this abuse would diminish the image of all the country's politicians.[4]

The prospect of better Pak-American relations improved when Harry Truman was inaugurated as America's president on January 20, 1949. Truman sought good relations with both Pakistan and India and he tried to position himself as a neutral mediator in the Kashmir dispute. While he personally tended to favor Pakistan, he held back from establishing a military relationship with Pakistan for fear of antagonizing India.

Liaquat Khan wanted Pakistan to gain the respect, friendship and support of other Muslim nations. Therefore, Liaquat organized a World Muslim Conference, which convened in Karachi in February 1949 to promote pan-Islamism. All Muslim countries sent representatives and the delegates ended up agreeing to form a World Muslim Congress. The Congress would promote the feeling that Muslims were being victimized by non–Muslim nations, and this would encourage the growth of a global Islamist jihadist movement against the West.[5]

Pak-Indian relations, already damaged by the Kashmir fighting, became further strained over currency devaluations. India, following Britain's devaluation of the British pound, greatly devaluated its currency on September 21, 1949. However, Pakistan didn't devalue its currency, since it had favorable balance of payments with the rest of the world. Indian leaders were angry at Pakistan's refusal to devalue, and they retaliated by blocking all trade with Pakistan. However, Pakistan was barely affected by the loss of India's trade, since Pakistan quickly compensated by increasing its trade with China and other countries.

President Truman's personal preference for Pakistan over India grew stronger during Indian Prime Minister Nehru's official visit to Washington which began on October 11, 1949. Nehru's cold neutralist attitude during this four-week visit generated more irritation than goodwill. After Nehru's visit, the United States began shifting its support from India to Pakistan, which seemed much more willing to serve as a bulwark against communist expansion.

Pakistan Loses Another Key Leader

Pakistan's leaders realized that Pakistan needed assistance from one or more major foreign powers to help it survive, since some Indian leaders threatened to invade it. Pakistan's leaders were willing to accept help from any powerful country willing to offer it protection or arms. Hoping that China might become its protector, Pakistan on January 4, 1950, recognized mainland China's communist government—the first Muslim country to do so. This early recognition was greatly appreciated by China's isolated leaders, and it marked the beginning of a long cordial relationship between the two countries. Pakistan also decided to retain its close ties with Britain, and on March 23, 1950, Pakistan announced that it would remain in the British Commonwealth.

Pakistan also hoped to secure American support, and on May 3, 1950, Prime Minister Liaquat Khan traveled to Washington for a three-week visit. Liaquat was hoping to secure American military aid. Liaquat was given an unusually warm welcome by President Truman, who even met him at the airport. Liaquat's straight-forward talk and his pro–American statements impressed many American officials, who began to look to Pakistan as a necessary and willing ally.

Two months later, Pakistan got a chance to demonstrate to the United States its usefulness as an ally. On June 25, 1950, North Korean troops invaded South Korea and soon afterwards Pakistan endorsed America's military intervention in Korea. Pakistan's backing of America's intervention contrasted favorably with India's neutralist position. The Korean War increased American interest in Pakistan, since the communist invasion stirred concern about growing Communist Chinese and Soviet expansion in Asia. The Korean War also helped Pakistan's economy by increasing America's wartime demands for Pakistan's raw materials.

While supporting the United States during the Korean War, Pakistan simultaneously continued to improve its relations with Communist China. On September 25, 1950, when Communist China argued in the U.N. that it should take the Chinese seat instead of Nationalist China, Pakistan supported Communist China's claim. Furthermore, when Chinese Communist troops crossed into North Korea and attacked UN forces, Pakistan abstained from voting on the American-backed resolution to brand China as an aggressor.

While Prime Minister Liaquat Khan was befriending the United States and China, he was having trouble managing discontent in East Pakistan (its "East wing"). The East wing had many legitimate grievances. First, Pakistan's central government was located in the West wing, and it had been dispensing far more funding to the West wing than to the East wing. Also, West wingers looked upon the poorer Bengali East wingers with disdain and treated them with disrespect. In addition, most of Pakistan's military forces were located in the West wing, leaving few troops in the East wing to defend it from invasion. Army leaders had even declared that if India attacked the faraway East wing, that the army would not rush to its defense. Instead, the army would respond by capturing Indian territory, and then barter these captured lands for territory lost in the East wing.

On November 4, 1950, East wing discontent was brought into the open

3. Pakistan Under Liaquat Khan

with the convening of a two-day East wing convention. The delegates called for giving the East wing more autonomy. Under the convention's plan, the central government would be reorganized so it would control only defense and foreign affairs, while each region would control all remaining matters. When the central government ignored this proposal, East wingers responded with anti-government protests.

On January 16, 1951, Pakistan's government secured more control over its military forces when British General Douglas Gracey retired as Pakistan Army Chief. Prime Minister Liaquat Ali replaced Gracey with Pakistani Muhammad Ayub Khan. Liaquat believed that a Pakistani Army Chief could be depended on to better look after Pakistan's interests than a foreigner. He chose Ayub Khan believing that Ayub had a balanced personality needed to strengthen the armed forces, while holding in check the army's more aggressive risk-takers.[6] Ayub Khan would remain army chief for over seven years—serving both Liaquat and his successors. During that time, Ayub would quietly monitor and pressure Pakistan's civilian leaders to be sure they looked after army interests.

While most of Pakistan's generals were pleased with Liaquat for his having appointed a Pakistani to lead the army, one general was not. General Arbar Khan was so dissatisfied with Liaquat that he organized a coup to overthrow Liaquat's government (the "Rawalpindi Conspiracy"). On March 9, 1951, Liaquat informed the country that the coup had been foiled. He announced that General Arbar Khan had conspired with Pakistan's communists to overthrow the government.[7] The conspirators were arrested and convicted, but given only light sentences. The conspiracy convinced Liaquat Ali to place Pakistan firmly on the side of the anti-communist West in the Cold War, and he used the plot to justify outlawing Pakistan's Communist Party. The plot also bolstered the authority of the new Army Chief Ayub Khan, who would use the plot to justify reorganizing the army.

While Pakistan had been reducing tensions with many foreign countries, tensions with India continued to increase. On July 15, 1951, Liaquat announced that heavy concentrations of Indian troops were massing near Pakistan's border, and he responded by moving large numbers of Pakistani troops to confront them. Soon 200,000 Indian troops faced 70,000 Pakistani troops on the Indo-Pak border. It wasn't clear if Nehru was trying to intimidate Pakistan or was preparing for an invasion.[8] Fortunately the confrontation simmered down and soon heavy monsoon rains began making any Indian offensive impractical. By September, India's troops had withdrawn and the crisis had passed.

Pakistan lost another irreplaceable leader on October 16, 1951. Prime Minister Liaquat Ali Khan was preparing to address an unruly crowd of over 30,000 at Rawalpindi. He had barely uttered his first words when an assassin fired two bullets from his revolver, mortally wounding him. The crowd quickly subdued the man, and a nearby police officer fired five shots point blank at the assassin, killing him instantly. Whether the assassin had accomplices never would be determined, although the ease with which the assassin was able to approach the victim gave rise to several conspiracy theories.[9]

There were several repercussions to Liaquat's assassination. First, the deaths of Jinnah and Liaquat Khan were a stunning blow to the young nation. Their deaths left Pakistan without a respected national leader capable of unifying the country. The people would miss Liaquat, whom they had come to respect for his honesty, unselfishness and moderation. They would come to appreciate him even more when he was succeeded by self-serving politicians and military dictators. Also, without Liaquat's leadership and experience, the PML would further decline, leaving Pakistan without a credible national political party. Without a healthy, competitive political party system, the people would have no way to get their grievances heard and resolved. In addition, Liaquat's death would allow the army to increase its influence on Pakistan's civilian governments. The new military-dominated governments would tend to use force instead of diplomacy to handle provincial grievances, and this would eventually provoke provincial calls for secession.

4

Transition to Military Rule

During the seven-year period covered by this chapter (October 1951–October 1958), Pakistan would be led by two successive governor-generals. Each would be backed by the powerful Army Chief Ayub Khan. During the first four years, Governor-General Ghulam would dominate Pakistan by asserting his office's power to dismiss prime ministers. During the next three years, the newly appointed Governor-General Mirza also would control the government using the same dismissal power. Also during Mirza's tenure, Pakistan would adopt its first constitution. It provided for a powerful president—a position which was bestowed on Mirza himself. The chapter ends with Army Chief Ayub Khan overthrowing Mirza and becoming Pakistan's first military dictator.

Governor-General Ghulam Controls the Government

During the first five years after Liaquat's assassination, Pakistan would be dominated by three powerful men—Governor-General Ghulam Muhammad, Army Chief General Ayub Khan, and Defense Secretary Iskander Mirza.[1] Pakistan would retain its facade of being a parliamentary democracy by preserving the position of prime minister. However, prime ministers would have little power and would often be dismissed by the governor-general with the support of the army chief.

On October 17, 1951, Khwaja Nazimuddin became Pakistan's prime minister. He had been the governor-general, but he agreed to now serve as prime minister. He was selected as a temporary compromise candidate, even though he was slow-witted, naive and indecisive. Nazimuddin also was lazy, and instead of trying to solve problems he preferred to ignore them or put off solving them.[2]

While Pakistan's leaders had carefully debated Nazimuddin's appointment as prime minister, they spent surprisingly little time selecting Ghulam Muhammad as governor-general. They chose him to this ceremonial position as a reward for his long-dedicated career in the civil service. They also realized that the elderly Ghulam, who had suffered a stroke, was unlikely to challenge the prime minister.[3]

However, Ghulam Muhammad would surprise those who appointed him. Despite his age and physical infirmities, he was a decisive, strong-willed leader, and he had the backing of several powerful men—including Army Chief Ayub Khan. Ghulam refused to play a ceremonial role under the weak Prime Minister Nazimuddin. Furthermore, Ghulam soon decided to dominate and bypass the weak prime minister and take control of the central government.[4] However, Ghulam's declining health would adversely alter his personality and mental faculties. As time went on, he would become more impatient and abusive toward those he contacted. Ghulam particularly despised politicians—persons he considered to be selfish opportunists—and so he relied heavily on civil service bureaucrats to run the country. Ghulam constantly would undermine the authority of prime ministers, whose frequent dismissals would make a mockery of parliamentary democracy.

As this period began, Pakistan faced several major problems. First, Sunni Islamists had become more bold and intolerant toward other Muslim sects and other religions. Their growing intolerance and violence would threaten the country's fragile unity. Also, the central government was unrepresentative and unstable. The country was run by a troika which included governor-generals who arbitrarily dismissed prime ministers. The politicians were selfish and so wouldn't join together in opposing these dismissals despite their questionable legality. In addition, there was a growing divide between Pakistan's two wings. The East wing (East Pakistan) resented the West wing, which was more prosperous and better represented in the central government. The East wing's resentment would grow as the central government ignored East wing demands for more funds and fairer representation in the government.

The rift between Pakistan's West and East wings soon widened. On February 21, 1952, Mujibur Rahman's recently formed Awami League (AL) Party led an East wing protest to promote making Bangla a national language. The student demonstrators were joined by many others, and during the riot that followed the overwhelmed police finally fired live rounds into the crowds.[5] The police killed three East wing student demonstrators, and this day would be celebrated every year thereafter in the East wing as "Martyrs' Day." The

4. Transition to Military Rule 41

Martyrs' Day incident marked the start of continuing widespread East wing protests and demonstrations.

The growing intolerance of Pakistan's Sunni Muslims turned violent with protests against the Ahmadis—a Muslim minority sect whose religious beliefs and practices differed from those of mainstream Sunnis. On February 27, 1953, Islamist groups and religious parties organized anti–Ahmadi demonstrations in Punjab Province. The weak Prime Minister Nazimuddin delayed suppressing the rioters. While the Punjab provisional government yielded to the protesters, this inaction emboldened the agitators, who soon overwhelmed the police.[6]

On March 6, the prime minister finally declared martial law in Punjab Province, dismissed the provincial government, and had the army suppress the rioters. By the time the rioting ended, over 1,500 Ahmadis had been killed and the province's infrastructure was in ruins.[7] It would take years to repair the damage, and investor confidence in Punjab never would be completely restored. Before the army departed, it took the initiative to conduct a "Cleaner Lahore Campaign," during which squads of laborers widened Lahore's streets and beautified its parks and public buildings.

The central government's calling on the army to stop the rioting set a dangerous precedent. Army leaders noted how effortlessly they had stopped the rioting. They also noted how appreciative the civilians had been of the army's Lahore cleanup campaign. These successes would encourage the army to continue stepping into the government's role of keeping order and providing services. Army leaders also began to question how the country could survive in the hands of civilian politicians.

Pakistan's commitment to democracy was tested on April 17, 1953. In a shocking development, Governor-General Ghulam Muhammad suddenly dismissed Prime Minister Nazimuddin. Ghulam dismissed him partly because Nazimuddin had acted so slowly in stopping the Punjab rioting. The government was still operating under the Government of India Act, which didn't expressly give governor-generals this dismissal power. However, there was no public outcry, and the courts didn't strike down Ghulam's dismissal. Despite the doubtful legitimacy of Nazimuddin's dismissal, governor-generals would continue to dismiss prime ministers. The issue wouldn't be resolved until three years later when Pakistan's first constitution was adopted—which abolished the governor-general's office.

Governor-General Ghulam's dismissal of the prime minister had a number of repercussions. It was a setback for democracy since it seemed to violate the law and allowed the arbitrary dismissal of an elected official. However, there was no groundswell of protests against the dismissal, partly because the country still honored the inherent power of the governor-general with its majesty of viceregal tradition.[8] The dismissal would encourage later arbitrary removals of duly elected prime ministers. Also, the move weakened the authority and resolve of all prime ministers, who would hesitate to make controversial decisions for fear that they might lead to their dismissals.

Governor-General Ghulam Mohammad selected Mohammed Ali Bogra as the new prime minister on April 17. The carefree Bogra was chosen because he didn't seem to have the desire or ability to challenge the military-bureaucratic leaders who now really ran the country. Bogra also was chosen because the army's leaders desperately wanted access to American weapons. The generals believed that Bogra could secure these weapons, since he had made friends with key American officials while serving as Pakistan's ambassador to the United States.

The Korean War ended on July 27, 1953, with a cease-fire agreement. Pakistan's economy, already reeling from the damage to Punjab's infrastructure, now suffered further as the wartime demand for Pakistan's products ended. Pakistan soon began suffering from unemployment, food shortages and inflation.

A major political development occurred in the East wing on March 8, 1954, when elections began for the East wing's provincial assembly. The PML (Pakistan Muslim League) was opposed by a "United Front" of opposition parties. The United Front soundly defeated the PML, which won just ten seats in the 300-seat Provincial Assembly. The Front's success was largely due to its denunciation of the central government for having mistreated the East wing.

There were several repercussions to the United Front's crushing East wing victory over the PML. First, the PML's defeat revealed its total loss of political power in the East wing. Pakistan now had no major national political party representing all of Pakistan's diverse regions. Now Pakistan had only provincial parties, which represented only narrow provincial interests. Also, the United Front's overwhelming victory in the more populous East wing concerned West wing leaders. They rightly worried that the East wing, with its larger pool of voters, might one day take control of Pakistan's central government.

India Begins Absorbing Kashmir

With India's support, Sheikh Abdullah (the "Lion of Kashmir") had been ruling the Indian-controlled Indian Jammu and Kashmir (IJK) government in Kashmir for over five years. Abdullah was more popular than ever in the Kashmir Valley, and he would forever be their hero. He had freed the Kashmiris from Maharaja Hari-Singh's brutal rule, and he had freed them from serfdom by giving them land. However, the sheikh had become so popular and powerful that Indian leaders now looked on the sheikh as a threat since he had become too popular and powerful. Also, the sheikh was demanding the right of Kashmiris to control their own government.[9] Therefore, on August 9, 1953, Indian authorities suddenly dismissed the sheikh as IJK's prime minister and jailed him.

India's removal of the popular "Lion of Kashmir" was met with violent protests throughout Kashmir's IJK. Abdullah would remain in jail for the next 22 years except for three brief spells of freedom.

India's abrupt dismissal of Sheikh Abdullah was a turning point in the history of Indian-controlled IJK. First, his dismissal marked the start of India's campaign to absorb IJK into India. Also, the sheikh's dismissal marked the beginning of a series of Indian-controlled IJK puppet governments. India began appointing brutal and corrupt prime ministers to govern IJK, and these ministers would provide the Kashmiris with no real representation and would loot public funds. India's leaders, having ousted the popular Sheikh Abdullah, then appointed Bakshi Ghulam Mohammed as IJK's new prime minister—a position that he would retain for ten years. Indian Prime Minister Nehru was pleased with Bakshi's selection, since the pliable figurehead Bakshi would "legitimate" Indian rule by staying in office through a series of rigged bogus elections. India would allow Bakshi to run a corrupt, unaccountable government in return for Bakshi facilitating IJK's "voluntary" integration into India on Indian terms.[10] Bakshi, his ministers, and the bureaucrats plundered public funds, while his police and unruly gangs suppressed the slightest dissent.[11]

However, Bakshi became so hated by the Kashmiris in IJK that on October 3, 1963, Indian Prime Minister Nehru forced him to resign. Nehru had Bakshi replaced by another pliable figurehead, G.M. Sadiq, who would rule as IJK prime minister for seven years. During Sadiq's rule, the process of coercive integration of IJK into India would reach its peak. India would declare that India's president could impose dictatorial "presidential rule" on IJK in any emergency. India also had IJK's submissive legislature create the powerful position of an Indian-appointed IJK governor. IJK's prime minister would henceforth be called "chief minister," as in the Indian states. Finally, India declared that Kashmir was an integral part of India. While these integration moves were bitterly opposed by Kashmir Valley inhabitants, India was able to suppress their mass protests utilizing large-scale arrests.

America Starts Arming Pakistan

Pakistan's persistent requests for American arms finally paid off on May 19, 1954, when a U.S.-Pakistan Mutual Defense Assistance Agreement was signed. This accord was the first formal bilateral security agreement between the two countries, and it provided the legal basis for future military aid to

Pakistan. Over the next six years, the United States would give Pakistan $425 million in military aid and $855 million in economic assistance. The military aid would allow Pakistan to create a new armored division and to arm and equip five and a half infantry divisions. The United States made it clear that the agreement was not a military alliance, and that the weapons were to be used only for internal security and self-defense.

There were several repercussions to Pakistan's receiving this American assistance. First, Pakistan's small weak army began transitioning into a larger, better-trained army equipped with modern weapons. This transition boosted the army's confidence in itself. It also reinforced the army's belief that it was the country's "guardian" and should dominate the country. Also, as the army grew stronger, it would overestimate its own strength and become emboldened to take reckless actions—provoking Indian retaliation. In addition, Pakistan's leaders would come to depend so heavily on American aid that they wouldn't feel the need to make peace with India or make Pakistan's economy self-sufficient.[12] Pakistan's growing dependency on American aid eventually would even erode its self-esteem and would add to Pakistan's growing anti–American sentiment.[13]

Both Pakistani and American leaders soon became disappointed with the arms agreement and how it was being carried out. Pakistan's leaders complained that arms shipments were smaller and slower than expected.[14] At the same time, the Americans soon realized that despite receiving the arms shipments, Pakistan's army never would become strong enough to send large numbers of troops to Middle East trouble spots to support America in a crisis. However, despite their mistake, America's leaders wouldn't reverse their decision, probably because they didn't want to admit their mistake.

Pakistan's central government continued alienating leaders in the East wing. The East wing's first provincial government had been in place only three months when on May 30, 1954, Governor-General Ghulam dismissed the East wing chief minister. Ghulam justified the dismissal on grounds that the provincial government had been unable to provide security for its citizens, and that the chief minister had made some remarks in support of East wing freedom.[15] Then Ghulam appointed Iskander Mirza as the East wing's governor. Mirza imposed dictatorial rule throughout the East wing and deployed 10,000 troops to enforce it. While Mirza and the army managed to subdue the violent demonstrations that erupted after this intrusion, the takeover of the East wing's government soon after its first popular election stoked East wing anger at West wing interference in its affairs.

Governor-General Ghulam Muhammad was enjoying his dominant position in the central government, including his ability to dismiss prime ministers. However, Prime Minister Bogra now boldly challenged that power. On September 21, 1954, Bogra prompted the Constituent Assembly to adopt four

4. Transition to Military Rule

amendments to the Government of India Act of 1935. These amendments sharply curtailed the governor-general's powers and took away his power to dismiss prime ministers.[16] Ghulam was furious at these amendments, and he quickly put down this challenge to his authority with the support of Army Chief Ayub Khan. Ghulam and Army Chief Ayub pressured the Constituent Assembly to rescind the amendments.

Then on October 24, again with the army chief's support, Governor-General Ghulam declared a state of emergency and dissolved the Constituent Assembly. The courts backed the governor-general's state of emergency on the novel grounds that although the move had been unlawful, "necessity" made its lawful. The courts would use this new "doctrine of necessity" in the future as justification for approving military takeovers when civilians were unable to control violence. Ghulam's declaration of an emergency set back attempts to create a representative system of government.

Governor-General Ghulam now asked Prime Minister Bogra to form a new cabinet. Bogra was scared and contrite after his failed attempt to curtail Ghulam's powers, and he now suddenly became a submissive figurehead.[17] Ghulam selected most of Bogra's cabinet members and this new "Cabinet of Talents" included many of the nation's most powerful officials. In a disturbing precedent, Army Chief General Ayub Khan was named as defense minister— the first military officer ever appointed to a Pakistani government post.

Pakistan Secures More Allies

On January 19, 1955, Pakistan officially joined SEATO—the South East Asia Treaty Organization. While Pakistan had been pressured to join this Western defense pact by its American arms supplier, once it joined it became a content SEATO member. Pakistan's army would become stronger for joining because SEATO members were entitled to officer training and increased military aid. However, Pakistan's entry into this western defense pact damaged Pakistan's relations with the Soviet Union and Communist China.

In another move to gain foreign support, Pakistan sent representatives to the First Afro-Asian Conference in Bandung, Indonesia. The eight-day "Bandung Conference" convened on April 18, 1955, and was attended by delegates from 29 nations, including China and India. The landmark conference gave the representatives a feeling of self-importance and solidarity which reduced their feeling of inferiority that had developed during their prolonged subservience to colonial powers. This solidarity encouraged these nations to work together in the United Nations.

Pakistan continued to seek outside military assistance. On September 23, 1955, it formally joined the Baghdad Pact (later called CENTRO), joining pact members Britain, Iraq and Turkey. Pakistan joined with considerable enthusiasm, since CENTRO's members were mainly Muslim countries. There were several repercussions to its joining this pact. First, it further aligned Pakistan with the United States, and helped persuade the Americans to give it more military and economic aid. Also, joining CENTRO enabled Pakistan's military and civilian officials to enjoy regular contact and interaction with their counterparts in other member countries. Finally, Pakistan's joining both CENTRO and SEATO angered both India and the Soviet Union.

Governor-General Mirza Takes Charge

Pakistan still didn't have a constitution. Then on May 10, 1955, the Federal Court declared that the governor-general had the power to dismiss the First Constituent Assembly (First CAP) and convene a Second CAP.[18] Relying on this new authority, Governor-General Ghulam dismissed the First CAP, since its members hadn't been able to enact a constitution in seven years. Then Ghulam called for elections to a Second Constituent Assembly (second CAP), hoping that the newly elected members could agree on the wording of a constitution. Voters selected members to the second CAP, and this CAP convened on July 7, 1955. Its first job was to select a new governor-general, since the elderly Ghulam Mohammad had resigned for mental health reasons. The Second CAP selected Iskander Mirza to replace Ghulam, and Mirza would serve as governor-general for over three years.[19]

Mirza had several strengths. He was an intelligent and decisive leader and he would abide by the provisions of the new Constitution when it was enacted six months later. He also had many years of experience as a senior civil service official. However, he also had some weaknesses. First, he had no interest in transitioning Pakistan to a genuine representative government. He disliked and mistrusted politicians, and he had dictatorial leanings. He would dismiss prime ministers in rapid succession, thereby further destabilizing the country. In addition, Mirza didn't seek independent advice, but instead chose advisers who agreed with him.

A week later, the Second CAP selected Chaundhri Muhammad Ali as prime minister. The quiet, kindly, soft-spoken Chaundhri had been an outstanding civil servant, and he was reluctant to accept the appointment.[20] However, he did accept and he would remain in office for only 13 months. His was the first in a series of four short-lived weak coalition governments which would follow each other in rapid succession. However, during his short tenure, he would make several major contributions to the country.

Pakistan faced severe economic problems when Mirza and Chaundhri took over the government. In some regions there were widespread food shortages due to floods, droughts and pests. In other regions, crops were plentiful, but unscrupulous merchants hoarded food and criminals smuggled cheap food out of the country.[21] The crisis continued since the government didn't punish the hoarders, smugglers and tax evaders.[22] Instead, the government purchased food from abroad, and that in turn depleted Pakistan's scarce foreign exchange funds, which were needed to pay for machine parts and other critical imports.

On September 30, 1955, the Second CAP passed the One Unit Bill, which set up a "One Unit" voting system. The army helped steamroll the One Unit Bill through parliament by threatening to take over the country if the bill were defeated.[23] This voting system acquired its "one unit" name because the West wing's four provinces became considered a single unit, while the East wing was considered one unit. Each wing was allotted half the seats in the National Assembly. Also, each wing would have its own governor and chief minister.[24]

The adoption of the "One Unit" voting system angered the East wingers, since it gave the West wing voting parity with the more populous East wing. The East wingers also were upset with how the West wingers had steamrolled the One Unit Bill through the Second CAP over strong East wing opposition.

Governor-General Mirza had gained more power with the adoption of the One Unit voting system, since it strengthened the voting power of his West wing base. Mirza's West wing power grew further when the Republican Party was formed in October 1955. Mirza supported the new party, which drew many PML members to its ranks. These PML defectors disliked that the PML had become beholden to Muslim religious leaders, had refused to accept non–Muslims into its membership, and hadn't tried to work with the East wing.[25]

Pakistan Adopts Its First Constitution

On February 29, 1956, the second CAP adopted Pakistan's first constitution. Prime Minister Chaudhri had pushed the newly elected members of the Second CAP to write the Constitution in just six months by prodding the Assembly to meet in almost continuous session.[26] Pakistan had taken over eight years to adopt a constitution—more time than taken by any other newly formed country. The creation of a constitution was extremely important, since it created a system of government based on written laws rather than on the whims of its rulers. Rulers who violated the Constitution would face the possibility that Pakistan's Supreme Court would overturn their decisions, or even remove them from office.

The Constitution provided for a central government consisting of an executive branch (with a president and prime minister) and a legislative branch (the National Assembly). National Assembly members would be elected under the "One Unit" system of voting, with each wing having the same number of seats. The position of governor-general disappeared and was replaced by a powerful president. The president's substantial powers were offset by the national and provincial assemblies, whose members would form an electoral college which would elect the president.[27]

However, once the president took office for his five-year term, he would dominate the government. He was given the power to dismiss the National Assembly and to veto its legislation. The president also was given the power to remove a prime minister if he believed the prime minister had lost majority support in the National Assembly. The president also would select the governor of each province. Urdu and Bangla were declared to be Pakistan's official languages.

Pakistan's religious leadership, led by the JI religious party, managed to insert some significant Islamic provisions into the Constitution. Even Pakistan's secular leaders had to support some Islamic language in the Constitution since the survival of the state rested on the belief that Pakistan's central purpose was to protect Islam.[28] The Constitution described the country as the "Islamic Republic of Pakistan"—the first Muslim country to use Islam in its name. The Constitution also required Pakistan's president to be a Muslim and provided that laws must not conflict with Islamic teachings.

On March 23, 1956, the Constitution took effect, with Mirza becoming Pakistan's first president. The Second CAP dissolved itself since it had served its purpose by adopting a constitution, and its legislative functions had been taken over by the National Assembly. President Mirza retained Chaudhri Mohammad Ali as prime minister. The new National Assembly would be more active than the rubber-stamping Federal Assembly had been, and it would debate important bills. President Mirza would dominate the government and he often would dismiss prime ministers and thereby force new Assembly elections.

Prime Minister Chaudhri already had played a key role in getting the Constitution written. He now performed another valuable service to his country. On May 16, 1956, Chaudhri announced Pakistan's First Five-Year Plan. The Plan gave priority to improving agricultural production. He hoped the Plan would end food shortages and would produce farm income needed to purchase Pakistani factory products.[29] While the agricultural production goals would not be met, issuing the plan in itself set a healthy precedent. Future governments would issue five-year plans, and the plans would help increase the country's economic growth.

President Mirza and His Short-Serving Prime Ministers

On September 8, 1956, after only eleven months on the job, Prime Minister Chaudhri resigned. He quit because he had become exhausted and depressed by political infighting, and he had lost the support of his own PML Party.[30]

There were several reasons why President Mirza would be able to dispose of four successive prime ministers in rapid succession—usually by dismissing them. First, the new Constitution gave the president the power to dismiss a prime minister if he had lost majority support in the National Assembly. Also, the new national political parties didn't have popular programs that might attract mass support. Therefore, most political parties could secure its needed majority of assembly seats only by forming a coalition government with its rivals. These coalitions were fragile because coalition partners often deserted for trivial reasons. When there was a desertion, Mirza had reasonable justification for dismissing the prime minister on grounds that he may have lost the needed majority of seats in the National Assembly.

President Mirza reluctantly invited the popular, independent-minded East wing leader Suhrawardy to form a new government and become prime minister. Suhrawardy would spend just 13 months in office (September 1956 to October 1957). This was the second in a series of four short-lived, weak coalition governments.

Prime Minister Suhrawardy had several strengths. First, he was a polite, wise veteran politician, and was an unselfish political servant. He was the only major leader with nationwide acceptance, and he had a sense of Pakistan's past and future.[31] He was dynamic and had exceptional oratorical and organizational skills. However, he also had some weaknesses. He did not get along well with President Mirza. Also, Suhrawardy's control over his coalition government was tenuous. His Republican Party coalition partner had twice as many Assembly seats as Suhrawardy's own AL Party, and it would force him to make many concessions.[32]

Prime Minister Suhrawardy soon faced a problem over how to respond to the Suez Canal crisis. Britain had controlled the canal for decades, even though the canal was located in Egypt. When Egyptian President Nasser nationalized the canal, Britain and France landed troops at the canal on November 5, 1956, to reassert Western control. Pakistan's government and people were outraged at the British and French invasion of Muslim Egypt, and anti-invasion demonstrations erupted all over the country. Most Pakistani political parties demanded that the country quit its Western SEATO and CENTRO alliances. Pakistan's Prime Minister Suhrawardy handled the crisis skillfully. He allowed the people to freely vent their outrage, while he didn't sever relations with the West. The crisis ended with the Americans and Soviets exerting such great pressure on the British and French that they voluntarily withdrew their troops from the canal. However, Suhrawardy's retention of relations with Britain and France had damaged his popularity, and so President Mirza began searching for his replacement.

On January 5, 1957, American President Eisenhower promised American military or economic aid to any Middle Eastern county needing help to resist communist aggression (the "Eisenhower Doctrine"). Pakistan welcomed this new American commitment, believing that it might lead to it receiving more American assistance. However, Eisenhower had come to realize that it had been a "terrible error" to arm Pakistan, since it had become clear that Pakistan's army never would be strong enough to confront a Soviet military threat.[33] Eisenhower therefore started to reduce arms shipments to Pakistan.

Pakistan was upset at this reduction in American military assistance. It was even more upset when the United States began increasing its assistance to its enemy India. A major escalation in Indian aid began on June 15, 1957, when the United States learned that India would not be able to meet the goals it had set in its second five-year plan. The United States responded by tripling its economic aid to India, which soon began receiving twice as much American aid as Pakistan. This massive American aid to its rival India led some of Pakistan's leaders to question the value of aligning Pakistan with the United States, and to look for support from non–American sources.

While the East wingers still had major grievances against the central government, there was no political movement to strongly champion their cause. While Suhrawardy's Awami League (AL) Party had dominated the East wing, it hadn't openly challenged the central government's discrimination against the East wing. This changed on July 25, 1957, when dissidents broke away from the AL Party and formed the National Awami Party (NAP). The NAP focused on securing more East wing benefits, eliminating the "One Unit" voting system, and terminating western alliances. With two strong political parties now in the East wing, the PML Party's strength in the East wing was greatly reduced.

On October 17, 1957, President Mirza forced Prime Minister Suhrawardy to resign, exercising his constitutional power to dismiss prime ministers. Mirza dismissed Suhrawardy for having dared to challenge Mirza's authority. While the president made the dubious claim that Suhrawardy had lost majority support in the National Assembly, he refused to convene the Assembly to support this claim. This was the third in a series of four coalition governments to fall in rapid succession. Army Chief Ayub Khan was becoming concerned how Mirza was constantly replacing prime ministers and choosing their successors.

4. Transition to Military Rule

The same day that Suhrawardy was dismissed, Ibrahim Chundrigar was sworn in as prime minister at the head of a PML-Republican Party coalition. Chundrigar would retain his office for only two months. His term was cut short when the fickle Republican Party suddenly withdrew from the coalition for minor reasons. On December 11, Chundrigar resigned since without the Republican Party, he could not find enough coalition partners to control a majority of seats in the National Assembly. Two days later, President Mirza called on his friend Feroz Khan Noon to form a new government. This would be the fourth in the series of four short-lived coalition governments to succeed each other.

Feroz Khan Noon was sworn in as prime minister on December 16, 1957, and he would remain in office for just nine months. His Republican Party-led six-party coalition government was very fragile because it contained so many coalition parties. Noon tried desperately to keep his coalition members content by giving many members seats in his cabinet. This made his cabinet so large that it had difficulty maintaining discipline, reaching decisions, and checking corruption.[34]

Pakistan's rapid succession of weak coalition governments had led to unprecedented instability, calling into question the ability of civilian politicians to govern. Their inability to govern was highlighted on September 20, 1958, when a riot broke out inside the provincial assembly chambers in Lahore. The rioting began when the opposition tried to physically remove the Speaker from the chambers because he had made a ruling they disliked. Three days later there was more brawling in the chamber and someone threw a heavy object which hit the Deputy Speaker in the face. He died of his injury two days later.[35]

Pakistan's central government faced another challenge the following month in Baluchistan Province. The province's nominal leader, the Khan of Kalat, had defied the central government by seizing a fort and replacing the Pakistani flag with his own standard.[36] This was Baluchistan's second revolt against the central government. This new challenge to Noon's weak central government left his government so helpless that military intervention was required. On October 6, 1958, the army removed the Khan, stripped him of his titles, and seized his lands.

General Ayub Khan's Coup

It seemed clear to all that something had to be done to control the country's growing discord and violence which Prime Minister Noon's weak government was unable to control. So when President Mirza proposed imposition of martial law, Army Chief Ayub Khan agreed to support him.

On October 7, 1958, Mirza declared martial law throughout the country, suspended the Constitution, and dismissed the central and provincial governments. Mirza immediately appointed Army Chief Ayub Khan as Chief Martial Law Administrator (CMLA). Ayub Khan seized key government buildings, and transportation and communication facilities throughout the country. Ayub Khan was often called just "Ayub" because of the commonality of his last name. The military's seizure of the government was so well-executed that it probably had been months in the planning.[37]

President Mirza had several reasons for declaring martial law. First, he was concerned that the quick succession of weak coalition governments had been destabilizing the country. He also realized that the country's politicians had become incapable of enacting meaningful laws. They had stopped serious discussions and debates and instead just shouted criticisms at each other. Moreover, Mirza was concerned that the army might be preparing to overthrow his civilian government and he hoped to preempt a coup by declaring martial law in partnership with the army.

For a few weeks, President Mirza desperately tried to hold onto his presidency. He wanted to organize a new government, end martial law, and assert control over the army. However, General Ayub Khan had no intention of returning to the status quo. Ayub wanted a long period of martial law, which he claimed was needed to bring the country back to good health.[38] Mirza tried to lure Ayub into joining in a Mirza-Ayub "partnership," and so on October 14 he appointed Ayub as his Prime Minister. When Mirza asked Ayub to sign an oath of office for the new prime minister pledging to discharge "such duties as the president may assign me," Ayub refused to sign.[39]

President Mirza's "partnership" with Army Chief Ayub Khan lasted just 20 days. On October 27, 1958, Ayub sent three generals to Mirza's home with an ultimatum—Mirza could step down or be killed. Mirza immediately announced his retirement from the presidency and left for permanent exile in England. This regime change occurred without a single shot having been fired, since the army fully backed their popular army chief.

Ayub Khan decided to remove Mirza mainly because Mirza seemed to be making preparations to replace him. Also, Ayub and army generals wanted to preserve the army's dominant position in the country, and they worried that Mirza might cut the army's budget and leave the alliance with America—Pakistan's main arms supplier.[40] Most Pakistanis supported Mirza's removal since he had failed to resolve the food shortages, economic turmoil, and the violence that had broken out during his three years as governor and president.[41]

So began Pakistan's first military takeover—with full popular support. But how long would the army want to run the government, and how long would it be able to retain the people's support?

5

General Ayub Khan's Military Rule

During the ten-year period covered in this chapter (October 1958–March 1969), General Ayub Khan would rule as Pakistan's first military dictator. Ayub would build a huge complex in Islamabad to house the country's new capital. Ayub would send tribal raiders into Kashmir in an attempt to seize Kashmir for Pakistan. This intrusion would precipitate the First Indo-Pakistan War. The chapter ends with Ayub Khan turning over the government to General Yahya Khan.

Ayub Khan Sets Up His Military Regime

On October 27, 1958, 41-year-old General Ayub Khan seized power and Pakistanis began living under a prolonged military dictatorship. The general immediately declared martial law, assumed the position of president, and abolished the office of prime minister—a post which would remain vacant for 13 years. He also abolished the 1956 Constitution and dissolved the national and provincial assemblies. While he didn't retain his position as army chief, he would later assume the new military rank of "Field Marshal." He took this exalted rank to impress upon everyone that he was the pre-eminent leader of the country. Ayub would rule Pakistan for over ten years with a strong hand—under martial law during his first three and a half years.

The people greeted the army's seizure of power with considerable approval. The army had become a popular institution and the people were tired of the self-serving politicians who had done little to help them. The people hoped that Ayub could restore security and stability, and return the country to normalcy. Even the Supreme Court upheld Ayub Khan's seizure of power.

On the same day he seized power, Ayub Khan named his friend General Muhammad Musa as his successor as army chief. Ayub selected Musa because Musa was loyal and lacked a support base within the army—making it unlikely that he could overthrow Ayub. Musa would remain army chief for over seven years. However, Musa was a poor army chief. He became bogged down on managing the details of paperwork, and he abolished the important post of chief of staff. Under Musa, undeserving officers were promoted and training was inadequate.

Although Ayub Khan had abolished the position of prime minister, he nevertheless decided to form a "cabinet" to help him administer the government. His cabinet would be dominated by himself and three other generals. Ayub retained the portfolios of Defense and Kashmir Affairs. In addition, Ayub appointed to his cabinet several competent civilian ministers, including the 29-year-old Zulfikar Bhutto as minister of commerce. This began Bhutto's eight-year apprenticeship under Ayub Khan. While Bhutto was relatively inexperienced, he was intelligent, industrious and a quick learner. Ayub Khan would increasingly rely on him for advice.

Ayub Khan had a number of strengths. First, he was intelligent and rational, and his long distinguished military career had made him self-confident. Also, the general was Pakistan's first leader since Jinnah to act on a vision of the future of Pakistan. He had a strong desire to make Pakistan more unified, modern and economically strong. While he didn't believe that Pakistan was ready for a full-blown democracy, he recognized that civilians must eventually govern the country. Also, he was cautious and very patient, and so he would proceed methodically in choosing and implementing the reforms that he would pursue. In addition, Ayub was open-minded and flexible. He surrounded himself with competent young persons (like Bhutto) whom he encouraged to express their views. Also, while Ayub would demand loyalty and obedience, and while he suppressed his opponents, his punishments were not vengeful or overly harsh. He largely embarrassed his critics, or threatened them with fines and jail time. Those opponents that he did jail weren't tortured or executed. Most were soon released, and heavy fines were never recovered.[1]

Ayub Khan also had a number of weaknesses. First, he was a career military officer who had no experience in government, politics or economics. He was not inclined to learn.[2] Also, he had no interest in soon transitioning the country back to civilian rule. He considered politicians self-serving, narrow-minded, and ill-suited to lead the nation. Instead Ayub believed that protracted martial law was needed to return the country to stability and normalcy. He would retain martial law for four years.

5. General Ayub Khan's Military Rule

He would set up a highly centralized, army-dominated government which would make all the key decisions. He would defer to the bureaucrats to implement these decisions. In addition, Ayub believed that he was infallible and indispensable to the country.[3] He was arrogant, contemptuous and dismissive toward politicians and religious leaders, whom he deliberately alienated. In addition, he favored quick, simplistic solutions to problems, without having studied all sides of complex issues. In addition, when Ayub encountered strong resistance from vested interests to needed reforms, he often would cancel those reforms. Also, Ayub appointed mediocre officers to senior military positions just because of their loyalty. This system of promotions led him to appoint some unqualified generals, while bypassing those more experienced, talented and daring. His promotions of mediocre generals would weaken the army's senior leadership for decades to come. In addition, Ayub promoted Islam, hoping to unify the country around his dictatorship. However, his criticism of Hindus and other minority religions would encourage Islamist groups to criticize minorities and discriminate against them.[4]

The military's seizure of control of Pakistan's government had a huge adverse impact on Pakistan. First, from this time forward, Pakistan's army leaders assumed that they were the ultimate power in the country. They believed that they had the right to remove civilian governments whenever they challenged the military on matters of national security or interfered with military personnel decisions.[5] Also, the army takeover would make it more difficult for a system of civilian government control to return. During periods of military rule, politicians would be denied the experience of campaigning, compromising and legislating. At the same time, the people would be denied the experience of selecting candidates and voting. In addition, the army takeover damaged the commitment of the generals to their jobs. Military dictators gave the generals state lands and allowed them to form and operate their own businesses. The generals began focusing more and more on managing their businesses and less and less on preparing the army for war.[6]

Pakistan had a number of serious problems when Ayub took control of Pakistan. First, Pakistan still had an immense refugee problem. It still had to shelter and feed millions of Muslim refugees from India who had not yet found employment. Also, Pakistan's government was riddled with corruption, which had grown during previous governments. In addition, Pakistan's economy was very fragile. Food production was down because absentee landowners didn't cultivate all their land and small farmers couldn't afford to buy fertilizer. Finally, many Pakistanis couldn't find jobs. Those that had money had to pay high prices for food and medicine, which often had been adulterated.[7]

Ayub Khan the Reformer

Ayub Khan methodically set about to institute reforms to improve the country. He listed the problems faced by Pakistan in order of gravity. Then he set up some fifteen investigative commissions and committees to recommend reforms that might solve these problems. Ayub gave these bodies wide discretion, and for several years Ayub would follow most of their recommendations.

Ayub used his martial law powers to mandate some bold and needed reforms—especially in areas in which politicians had been reluctant to venture. He also began enforcing laws that had been universally ignored.[8] His first reform sought to reduce government corruption by demoting or firing many corrupt and incompetent bureaucrats and police.[9] Ayub also created training schools for civil servants to assure higher ethical standards.[10] Also, Ayub sought to improve government tax collections. He seized and audited the books of several prominent companies and imposed taxes on them. He also took steps to stop smugglers from bringing consumer goods into Pakistan without paying import taxes, and to stop them from selling these goods on the black market without paying sales taxes. In addition, Ayub sought to strengthen the economy. He increased food production by having state-owned lands and uncultivated lands rented out to farmers at low rents. He also instructed farmers in the use of fertilizers and irrigation.[11] He also imposed price controls on foodstuffs and textiles. He helped industrialists by deregulating the economy, by lowering their taxes, and by making foreign exchange available for importing machinery, spare parts and raw materials. Ayub also sought to improve the lives of the nine million refugees who still lived in poverty. He replaced slum dwellings with refugee housing, and made land available to those in rural areas. He compensated refugees from India with cash and land for property they had left behind in India.[12] In addition, Ayub sought to help factory workers. His regime pressured management to offer higher pay, shorter work hours, and improved worker safety. He also improved labor-management relations, which raised worker productivity and reduced the outbreak of strikes.[13] Ayub also sought to improve the legal system. To reduce the long delays in the courts, he set up special courts for speedier trials. In addition, he protected women by requiring that marriages and divorces be registered. He promoted laws setting minimum ages for marriage, restricting the husband's right to divorce his wife, and safeguarding women's property rights. Also, Ayub sought to improve the country's educational system. He instituted free compulsory education, set standardized curriculums, and paid subsidies to students who attended college and vocational schools. Finally, Ayub worked to control the country's high population growth. He called for setting up hundreds of clinics to dispense birth control information and devices.

5. General Ayub Khan's Military Rule

On February 7, 1959, Ayub Khan attempted to reform the archaic feudal system of land ownership by issuing a modest land reform regulation. Under the feudal system, wealthy feudal landowners living in distant cities exploited their sharecroppers by demanding half or more of the crops they produced.[14] Also, many feudals didn't bother cultivating all their land, thereby stunting Pakistan's food production.[15] Ayub's reform limited landownership to 500 acres of irrigated land and 1,000 acres of non-irrigated land. Landowners had to sell to the government lands which exceeded these ceilings, with the state selling the excess to cultivating tenants in easy installments. However, Ayub never intended that his land reforms would seriously harm the feudal landowners. After all, he depended on these "feudals" to maintain law and order in their regions, and to control the votes of farmhands and tenant farmers living on their lands. Therefore, his regulations contained several loopholes which allowed the feudals to retain most of their lands.[16] However, Ayub's modest land reform did serve as a precedent, and inspired his successors to implement more meaningful land reforms.

While General Ayub Khan was imposing his reforms to strengthen the country internally, he also sought to protect Pakistan from outside threats. On March 5, 1959, Pakistan signed two agreements that increased its ties with the United States. One agreement was a Bilateral Agreement of Cooperation, which provided for American assistance if Pakistan were a victim of foreign aggression. The same day, Pakistan leased some of its Badaber air base near Peshawar to the United States for ten years. The Americans would use the base as an NSA communications intercept facility and as a base for its U-2 reconnaissance planes.

Ayub Khan's "Bogus Democracy"

General Ayub Khan wanted to silence those civilian politicians who opposed his military takeover. He hesitated to issue an outright ban on all politicians, since that could make him unpopular with the masses. So instead he decided to let the courts do this work for him. On August 7, 1959, Ayub Khan decreed the Elective Bodies Disqualification Order (EBDO). This provided that current and former elected officials suspected of "misconduct" could choose to retire from public life or be tried by special courts. Those tried and convicted would be banned from holding public office for seven years. Ayub used the order to remove thousands of opposition politicians from politics. This deprived the main political parties of their leaders.[17]

Ayub Khan decided to give his dictatorship a taste of democracy by giving the people a slight input in his government. On October 26, 1959, Ayub Khan set up a "Basic Democracy" system. His scheme had two parts. One part created an indirect voting system for presidential elections. It provided for groups of some 1,500 voters at the local level to select a total of 80,000 "Basic Democrats" (BDs), who would serve as an electoral college. These BD electors would choose Pakistan's president.[18] This electoral college system strongly favored Ayub Khan, since he had been responsible for setting up the BD system which had given the BDs their new positions. A second part of the BD system was a four-tier administration composed of persons largely chosen by the BDs. These persons were given responsibilities over some local government functions, such as village sanitation and roads. Ayub claimed that this part of the BD system would train future leaders and provide for village decision-making. This delegation of some local governance was part of his desire to reach out to the populace and encourage them to think of themselves as members of a single nation.[19] Pakistan's traditional politicians weren't interested in seeking BD seats, since the positions didn't come with any power or opportunities to make money. These politicians were angry at Ayub for setting up the new system, which Ayub actually had developed to marginalize them.[20]

Ayub claimed that his BD system was intended to give genuine input into his government. However, he may have created the BD system to neutralize opposition and delude the people into thinking that they had some significant input into running the country.[21] The BD system would remain in effect for eleven years—until Ayub's successor abolished it. By that time, the people were ridiculing Ayub's BD system as "bogus democracy."

General Ayub Khan sought to further Pakistan's ties with the United States by inviting President Eisenhower to visit Pakistan. On December 7, 1959, Eisenhower arrived in Pakistan—the first American president ever to do so. Ayub Khan gave Eisenhower a warm welcome, and 750,000 flag-waving Pakistanis lined his parade route. Ayub pressed Eisenhower for more military aid, claiming that China was threatening Pakistan. Eisenhower was so impressed by Ayub that three months later the United States approved the sale of aircraft for Pakistan's first F-104 jet fighter squadron.

General Ayub Khan, having set up his "Basic Democracy" system, now sought to use it to prove his popular support. On February 14, 1960, he conducted a nationwide referendum which asked the BDs if they "had confidence" in his regime. According to the referendum's official results, 75,084 of the 80,000 BDs voted in the affirmative. Ayub hailed the referendum as a mandate for him to continue ruling and to write a constitution. Three days later, Ayub Khan was sworn in as the country's "first elected president," based on the affirmative referendum vote.

Pakistan faced a major international crisis on May 1, 1960, when the Soviets shot down an American U-2 reconnaissance plane over the Soviet Union. The American pilot, Gary Powers, had taken off from Pakistan's

Badaber airbase near Peshawar, and the Soviets threatened to attack Peshawar if another U-2 were launched from Pakistan. President Ayub Khan claimed to the Soviets that he hadn't been aware that the Americans had been using the rented space at its airbase for U-2 flights over Russia.[22] He sent a formal protest to the Americans about the flights. However, Ayub didn't waiver in his friendship with the Americans and he didn't even forbid future American U-2 flights.

There were several repercussions to the downing of the U-2 plane. First, the Americans decided to stop launching and retrieving U-2s from Pakistan, although they continued using the base as a listening post for Soviet communications. Also, Pakistan's leaders became concerned about the Soviet threat. They worried that if the Americans provoked the Soviets into attacking Pakistan, that the distant United States might not be able or willing to defend their country.[23]

To improve the country's economy, President Ayub Khan on July 1, 1960, introduced Pakistan's Second Five-Year Plan. The plan's goals were to increase Pakistan's agricultural and industrial output, to develop its private sector and to hasten development in the East wing. The plan turned out to be very successful due to Ayub's support, World Bank loans and American funds and expertise. Most of the plan's goals would be met or exceeded, and GNP would grow at an impressive 6.2 percent a year. This outstanding growth was called "Pakistan's Miracle," and it ushered in the "Golden Age" of Pakistan's economic development.

Pakistan's agricultural development secured another big boost when the Indo-Pak dispute over the subcontinent's massive Indus River system was resolved. The river flowed through both countries. On September 19, 1960, the two nations signed the Indus Waters' Treaty, calling for a 10 to 13-year transitional period during which an extensive system of dams and canals would be built. Then the three eastern rivers in the water system would be used exclusively by India, while the three western rivers would be used just by Pakistan. The United States and World Bank were heavily involved in mediating the agreement and financing the irrigation system.

Pakistan's expansion in agricultural production was also so impressive during this period because of the country's "Green Revolution." During this time, agricultural production grew rapidly due to improved hybrid seeds, improved irrigation and the use of more fertilizer.[24] The Green Revolution led to Pakistan's becoming self-sufficient in food production, and even enabled it to begin exporting wheat. The Revolution not only benefited large feudal landowners, but also helped the industrious owners of middle-sized farms. These latter farmers for the first time became prosperous, and their new wealth enabled them to challenge the political monopoly of the feudal landowners.[25] However, Pakistan's Green Revolution would falter after 10–15 years due to a decline in land fertility, the government's failure to repair irrigation canals, and farmers' abandonment of modern farming techniques.

Pakistan's relations with the United States showed signs of fraying when John F. Kennedy became America's president on January 20, 1961. Kennedy believed that the populous democracy of India was best suited to standing up to Communist China. He believed that Pakistan's hatred of India detracted from its usefulness as an ally against China and the Soviet Union. Ayub's adviser Zulfikar Bhutto would persuade Ayub that Pakistan should compensate for America's shift toward India by strengthening its ties with China.

President Ayub Khan traveled to Washington on July 11, 1961, to meet President Kennedy and try to improve Pak-American relations. He was given a warm welcome and was even invited to address a joint session of Congress. Ayub asked Kennedy to pressure India to leave Kashmir, but Kennedy explained that he had no such influence over India. Ayub warned that if the United States began arming India, Pakistan might have to seek Communist China's "protection." To console Ayub, Kennedy promised him that he would consult with Pakistan before ever giving military aid to India.[26] Ayub's state visit marked the high point in Pak-American relations.

The Second Constitution and the End of Martial Law

When General Ayub Khan had taken over the country in a military coup, he had suspended Pakistan's first Constitution. Now, seeking to provide a constitutional facade for his dictatorship, Ayub used his martial law powers to decree for the country a second Constitution—with minimal public input. This Constitution of 1962 was announced on March 1, 1962. It provided for a strong president, which office Ayub Khan was to initially fill on account of his having won the referendum.[27] There was no provision for a prime minister. The president was given the right to declare a state of emergency, during which he had absolute power. The president also dominated the National Assembly, which he could dismiss at will. His assent was required for every bill—unless the National Assembly overruled his lack of consent by a two-thirds vote. Laws passed by the Assembly could not be questioned by any court.[28] Pakistan would have a federal system of government with two provinces—East and West Pakistan. The 80,000 "Basic Democrats" (BDs) would elect the president and National Assembly members. The two wings would each have an equal number of Assembly seats, thereby preserving the "one unit" voting system. The Constitution discarded the word "Islamic" that had been inserted in the first constitution, and it renamed the country the "Republic of Pakistan." There was no public celebration over the new Constitution since Ayub had imposed it on the country without public discussion or approval.

The first election for the National Assembly under Ayub's new Constitution was held on March 28, 1962, with 80,000 Basic Democrats voting for candidates whose party affiliation was not identified on the ballots. While those elected were forbidden to form parties, they soon joined together in informal groups based on personal and provincial loyalties. These groups soon acted like political parties, and they voted in blocs.[29]

Having strengthened his presidential powers in the Constitution that he had imposed, President Ayub Khan felt comfortable enough on June 8, 1962, to announce the lifting of martial law. While he still exerted considerable power as president, he no longer could dictate decisions by martial law decree.

There were several repercussions to the lifting of martial law. First, Ayub became less confident and less comfortable, knowing that he had to work with politicians. He came to depend more and more on his ministers and the bureaucrats for advice and support—including his young protégé Zulfikar Bhutto. Ayub's reliance on Bhutto would increase over the years as Ayub's other advisers died or retired. Also, the politicians, who had been silent during martial law, suddenly reappeared. They had resented Ayub for having silenced them. Now they ridiculed him whenever possible, describing him as a self-serving dictator. Ayub never would be able to overcome his image as an oppressive dictator.[30]

President Ayub Khan soon realized that the new National Assembly members were forming de facto political parties, which he still hated. However, when on July 15, 1962, the National Assembly enacted a law authorizing the formation of political parties, Ayub's adviser Zulfikar Bhutto persuaded him not to veto the bill. The aging Ayub would begin to find himself increasingly on the defensive as political parties began forming and openly criticizing his regime. The Muslim League soon was reactivated, although it soon split into two parties—the Council Muslim League and the renegade Convention Muslim League (ConML).

The Sino-Indian Border Clash

India was so concerned with a series of minor Chinese attacks along its border with Communist China that it suddenly set aside its long-held policy of neutrality. On October 2, 1962, India asked the United States for military assistance against China. The United States immediately began airlifting weapons and ammunition to India, fearing that China might soon launch a full-scale invasion. The United States began arming India without even notifying Pakistan in advance—despite President Kennedy's promise to Ayub to give such a warning. On October 20, India foolishly sent troops into the Indo-Chinese border region, causing a powerful Chinese force to brush aside the Indian troops and occupy most of the disputed region.

On November 19, 1962, India's nervous Prime Minister Nehru wrote President Kennedy, requesting additional American military assistance. Nehru now requested that American fighter squadrons be deployed to India to protect India's cities.[31] The crisis ended two days later when China unilaterally declared a cease-fire and withdrew its troops from the disputed region.

There were several repercussions to the Sino-Indian border clashes. First, the clashes improved Pakistan's relations with China, since now both countries had fought Indian troops. China would go on to develop a long-lasting "all-weather friendship" with Pakistan. China also committed to help Pakistan become stronger economically and militarily in order to counter India's growing strength. China soon would become Pakistan's largest arms supplier. Also, American leaders were delighted that neutral India at last had stood up to communist aggression, and the Americans continued sending India large amounts of weapons. However, Pakistan was upset with the United States for having rushed arms to Pakistan's enemy India without even notifying Pakistan in advance as promised.[32] Pakistan's leaders also resented that during the border crisis, the Americans had pressured Pakistan to abstain from attacking Indian troops in Kashmir while its troops were tied up on the Chinese border.[33] To console Ayub Khan and allay his fears that America was arming India against Pakistan, President Kennedy quietly committed the United States to come to Pakistan's aid if India were to attack it.[34]

China soon began honoring the pledges it had made to Pakistan after the Sino-India border crisis. On January 5, 1963, a Sino-Pak commercial treaty was signed. This treaty was followed on March 2 by signing of a Sino-Pak Boundary Agreement that Pakistan had been seeking for some time. American officials were furious that Pakistan had made these agreements with Communist China.

Pakistan's relations with Communist China improved even more after June 15, 1963, when President Ayub Khan appointed Zulfikar Bhutto as foreign minister. Bhutto took over this important post from Mohammad Ali Bogra, after Bogra died unexpectedly. Bhutto always had favored closer relations with China, and with Bhutto now foreign minister, Sino-Pak relations would improve to its best ever. Bhutto also began urging Ayub to be more aggressive in pushing India out of Kashmir, which he believed was a good emotional issue that would increase Ayub's popularity.[35] Bhutto also would verbally attack India, and this won him popularity inside Pakistan.

Bhutto would use his new foreign minister position to gain popularity and power. His new position gave him the opportunity to work more closely with Ayub Khan, and Bhutto soon came to believe that Ayub's survival depended solely on himself. Also, as foreign minister, Bhutto regularly consulted Pakistan's senior generals, which allowed him to strengthen his ties with these military leaders. In addition, Bhutto promoted a bold new foreign policy which gave him substantial news coverage and popularity. He promoted a "Trilateral Policy," which sought equidistant relations with the United States, China and Russia. Pakistan soon followed up on this policy by signing a Sino-Pak air transport agreement in August and a Sino-Pak barter agreement in September.

President Ayub Khan's crowning achievement would be the construction of a new capital city in Islamabad. He conceived the idea of building a government complex on a plateau at Islamabad to serve as Pakistan's new capital. He wanted to move the capital to a more defensible position—further into the interior and closer to army headquarters in Rawalpindi. On October 25, 1963, after two years of construction, the first group of government workers moved from the old capital buildings in Karachi to the site of the partially completed new capital in Islamabad. When completed three years later, the new capital city would cover 351 square miles and house 750,000 residents.

President Ayub Khan hoped that Pakistan's relations would improve when Lyndon Johnson became America's president on November 22, 1963, following Kennedy's assassination. President Johnson wanted to improve relations with Pakistan and he expressed great confidence in Ayub Khan. However, Johnson soon would turn away from Pakistan. He would become preoccupied with the Vietnam War and he was angry when Pakistan refused to send troops to help the Americans there. Also, Johnson was upset that Pakistan continued to support Communist China even though China would assist the North Vietnamese in Vietnam. A frustrated Johnson eventually would give up trying to work with Pakistan.

During this time, a death in the East wing led to an increase in tensions between Pakistan's two wings. The Awami League (AL) had developed into a major East wing political party, and under its dynamic leader Hussain Suhrawardy, it had won seats in the National Assembly by championing East wing grievances. On December 5, 1963, Suhrawardy died, and his lieutenant Mujibur Rahman (better known as "Mujib") became the AL's principal spokesman. Mujib would increase the AL's demands for more East wing rights, increasing the AL's popularity in the East wing. The radicalized AL came to depend more on radical students to demonstrate for the AL's programs, and these students would assume a larger role in AL decision-making.

There soon was another major change in Pakistan's political landscape. President Ayub Khan had initially opposed allowing political parties to operate. However, he had come to realize that having the support of a political party could strengthen his own democratic credentials. Therefore, on December 24, 1963, Ayub accepted the presidency of the Convention Muslim League (ConML). He would remain the ConML's president for the rest of his rule and ConML membership would grow dramatically.

There were several repercussions to Ayub's becoming President of the ConML. First, he was becoming more like a politician and less like a military dictator. The personal attacks on him by rival politicians would grow. Also, Ayub came to depend even more on the young Zulfikar Bhutto. The brilliant Bhutto was far more adept at politics than Ayub. Ayub brought Bhutto into his inner circle, and after several years began to confide in him and seek his advice. Bhutto also became indispensable to Ayub because his youth, magnetism and persuasive oratory made him very popular with university students—a group which Ayub was having difficulty attracting.[36]

While Pakistan had been led by many leaders since its founding, India always had been led by Prime Minister Jawaharlal Nehru. Nehru's death on May 27, 1964, ended his 16-year domination of India's government, and his death brought a temporary relaxation in Pak-Indian relations. However, in the long run his death would reduce the likelihood that India would offer Pakistan a fair settlement on Kashmir. While Nehru had possessed the prestige and confidence that had allowed him to make peaceful gestures to Pakistan, none of his successors would possess such qualities. They didn't dare make concessions or even offer conciliatory remarks to Pakistan for fear of offending India's extremists.

India swore in its new Prime Minister Lal Bahadur Shastri on June 2, 1964. Pakistan's leaders believed that the small-sized, nervous Shastri would be too timid and indecisive to lead a strong resistance to a Pakistani offensive in Kashmir. Therefore, Pakistan's leaders decided to push for a military solution in Kashmir, and they even largely ignored his public statements.[37] However, Shastri turned out to be a tough adversary, and he was determined to show the Indian Army and his people that he could stand up to Pakistan.

Ayub Khan Elected President—Again

President Ayub Khan was expected to win the presidential elections that were scheduled for January 1965. However, Ayub's main challenger was 71-year-old Fatima Jinnah—the sister of Pakistan's founder Mohammed Jinnah. Fatima was a formidable opponent. She possessed her brother's oratorical skills and strong moral character. She had become the symbol of Pakistan's democracy. The main election issue had been whether the people wanted to be governed by Ayub Khan's one-man rule or by a parliamentary democracy. Fatima Jinnah would run as the candidate of the new Combined Opposition

5. General Ayub Khan's Military Rule 65

Party (COP)—an umbrella of six parties united for the purpose of defeating Ayub.

However, Ayub had many more advantages. During his time in office, he had exhibited strong leadership skills and had a record of solid accomplishments. He led the well-organized and well-funded ConML Party. He also controlled the media and the debates seemed stacked against Jinnah and exposed her inexperience.[38]

The election was held on January 2, 1965, and President Ayub Khan won 49,951 (63 percent) of the 80,000 Electoral College BD votes. However, while Ayub won a majority of votes, his narrow margin of victory wasn't impressive, especially since his ConML Party had been much better organized and better funded than his opponent.

There were several repercussions to Ayub's unimpressive victory. First, it exposed a weakening of his popular support and destroyed Ayub's aura of invincibility that he had nurtured. Also, it emboldened Ayub's opponents to criticize him more. The people were upset with the rampant corruption which had infected his ministers, the bureaucrats and his family.[39] In addition, Ayub became concerned about his waning popularity. He began relying more and more on Zulfikar Bhutto for advice.

President Ayub Khan reappointed Zulfikar Bhutto as his foreign minister, and Ayub began implementing the Bhutto-promoted Trilateral Policy— seeking good relations with China, Russia and the United States. On March 2, 1965, Ayub arrived in China for an eight-day state visit. During his visit, Ayub was warmly welcomed and he had several meetings with Chinese Premier Chou En-lai. The two leaders issued a friendly joint communiqué. The visit made Ayub more committed than ever to further strengthening Pakistan's ties with China.

A month later, on April 3, 1965, Ayub Khan arrived in Moscow for a seven-day official visit—the first visit ever by a Pakistani head of state to the Soviet Union. While in Moscow, Pakistan and the Soviet Union signed agreements on trade, economic cooperation and cultural exchange. However, Ayub's attempt to improve relations with all three of the world's major powers was risky and largely unsuccessful. His two visits to two major communist countries in two months risked Pakistan's losing all American assistance. Also, while Ayub's visit to the Soviet Union slightly improved Pak-Soviet relations, the Soviets continued to strongly support Pakistan's enemy India.

While Pakistan was improving relations with China and Russia, a border dispute broke out with India in the disputed border region of the Rann of Kutch. The Rann ("marsh") was a desolate, barren, marshy region between Pakistan's Sindh Province and India's Gujrat state. On April 8, 1965, Pakistan launched a preemptive strike to prevent Indian troops from capturing a key fort in the area. Pakistani troops decisively defeated Indian forces in several small-sized actions. The Indian troops withdrew because Pakistani troops controlled the dry ground north of the Rann, and India's troops risked being cut off since the Rann usually flooded during the rainy season. Pakistan's leaders were thrilled at this limited victory, but wrongly concluded that Pakistan's army could defeat the Indian army in a full-scale war. Foreign Minister Bhutto persuaded many senior army officers that the time was right to seize Kashmir before the Soviets gave more arms to India. With so many generals recommending an attack on Kashmir, even the cautious Ayub came to support such an attack.[40]

On July 1, 1965, Pakistan launched its Third Five-Year Plan. Under the plan, the government gave extraordinary incentives to businesses by cutting taxes and offering subsidies, loans and land grants. At the same time, the government didn't adequately regulate these businesses. Businesses took advantage of these government incentives by greatly expanding their production and moving into new profitable sectors. In contrast to this support for businesses, the government increased the burden on the downtrodden masses by raising sales taxes and other indirect taxes. It also cut funding for services desperately needed by the poor, including public schools, medical clinics and low-income housing.[41]

A Stolen Relic and the Second Indo-Pak War

When India seized Kashmir's capital Srinagar in 1947, it took over a nearby shrine which housed an irreplaceable Muslim relic—hair from the Prophet Muhammad's beard. On December 26, 1963, the sacred relic was stolen. The Kashmiris, already resentful of recent Indian moves to integrate Kashmir into India, were furious at the theft. They blamed India for having stolen the relic or having failed to prevent the theft. Kashmiri Muslims responded by attacking Hindus and Indian security forces, and rioting soon spread beyond Srinagar. The relic eventually was returned, and the identity of the thieves would never be discovered. However, the hatred that the stolen relic had generated against India remained.

Pakistan's leaders had carefully followed the growing hatred of Kashmiris over Indian rule in Indian-controlled IJK Kashmir. They concluded that the pent-up hatred had grown to the point that Kashmiris were ready to rise up in revolt against Indian occupation forces. They believed that a full-blown revolt would result if Pakistan were to send a few thousand raiders into IJK to lead a mass uprising.

However, Pakistan's plan to provoke a Kashmir rebellion was based on several erroneous assumptions. First, the planners assumed that the Kashmiris were ready to risk their lives by rising up in massive armed resistance

5. General Ayub Khan's Military Rule

against the Indian occupiers.[42] Also, they assumed that the new, inexperienced Indian Prime Minister Shastri wouldn't dare risk a general war with Pakistan just to put down a rebellion in Kashmir.

On August 8, 1965, pursuant to Ayub's plan, Pakistan sent 2,000–2,500 volunteers in six raiding parties from Pakistani-controlled AJK into Indian-controlled IJK. During this "Operation Gibraltar," the poorly trained tribesmen enjoyed some initial success largely due to surprise. However, the tribal invaders soon ran into trouble. India soon learned of Pakistan's invasion plans from captured prisoners.[43] Also, the Kashmiris didn't rise up against the Indian occupiers as Ayub had expected. In addition, on August 16, Indian troops launched a counteroffensive by crossing the Kashmir cease-fire line into Pakistan-controlled AJK, and moved to within striking distance of the AJK capital of Muzaffarabad. Indian troops would capture or kill most of the raiders during the next three weeks.

The fighting escalated on September 1, 1965, when regular Pakistan Army troops attacked the Indian troops who had entered Pakistani-controlled AJK. The Second Indo-Pak War had begun—the second time that the dispute over Kashmir had led to a general Indo-Pak war. Within three days, Pakistan's offensive was stopped by Indian troop reinforcements and air attacks. When Pakistan's troops began taking heavy casualties and began experiencing serious ammunition and fuel shortages, Ayub Khan decided to end the fighting. However, before a cease-fire could be arranged, Indian troops crossed into Pakistan itself.

On September 6, 1965, India's army invaded West Pakistan—but avoided invading East Pakistan because of China's warning not to attack it. India's well-led army was larger than Pakistan's army, and it launched a well-planned, three-pronged campaign aimed at capturing the city of Lahore—just 15 miles inside Pakistan. Two days later, the United States terminated arms shipments to both Pakistan and India in order to add weight to the United Nation's call for a cease-fire. The end of weapons' shipments affected Pakistan much more than India, since the former was almost totally dependent on American weapons and ammunition.

On September 23, 1965, the Second Indo-Pak War ended when a U.N.-sponsored cease-fire came into effect. The leaders of both countries agreed to the cease-fire on the advice of their military commanders. Each side had suffered heavy casualties and neither side had "won" the war by achieving its goals. India had failed to capture Lahore, while Pakistan had failed to force a resolution of the Kashmir dispute. Pakistanis were shocked at the cease-fire news. State media had fed them false stories that Pakistan was winning the war.[44]

There were several repercussions to the Second Indo-Pak War. First, the war had a sobering effect on leaders of both countries. India no longer considered it obvious that it could defeat its smaller neighbor—especially since China might intervene on Pakistan's behalf. At the same time, Pakistan's leaders no longer feared that Pakistan could lose its independence through an Indian invasion. Also, the war frustrated American President Johnson, since both his allies had fought using American-supplied weapons. Johnson largely would give up intervening in the Indian subcontinent. In addition, Pakistan was bitter at America's stoppage of arms shipments in the middle of the war. It also was disappointed that no Muslim nation had offered to send troops to help stop the Indian offensive. Pakistan would turn to China as a more reliable ally. China had condemned the Indian invasion, had warned India not to invade East Pakistan, and had played a major role in arranging a cease-fire. Also, Ayub Khan's prestige had declined. He was criticized for leading the country into war with an unreliable American ally and for mishandling the army. He also was criticized for allegedly selling the country out by not demanding tough terms from India after supposedly winning the war. In addition, Ayub's self-confidence had been damaged as he realized that he had some responsibility in approving the army's ill-conceived plans which resulted in losing the war.[45] Also, the war had further damaged relations between the East and West wings. The East wingers had noticed that the central government had focused on defending the West wing, while leaving the East wing unguarded. The West wing seemed ready to write off the East wing should India ever invade it.

While a cease-fire had ended the fighting in the Second Indo-Pak War, a peace treaty was needed to prevent a recurrence of hostilities. Soviet Premier Kosygin persuaded President Ayub Khan and Indian Prime Minister Shastri to hold peace talks in neutral Tashkent, Uzbekistan. The Tashkent Peace Conference convened on January 4, 1966. Kosygin "saved" the talks from collapsing by persuading the sickly, weary, and demoralized Ayub Khan to abandon Pakistan's traditional hardline position on Kashmir. Under heavy Soviet pressure, Pakistan and India signed the Tashkent Declaration on January 10, which formally ended the Second Indo-Pak War. The peace terms called for returning all troops to their pre-war positions. Kashmir was not even mentioned.

The signing of the Tashkent Declaration was followed by a period of blame assignment. Pakistan's people and Foreign Minister Bhutto blamed Ayub for having signed the agreement without having received any concessions on Kashmir. Ayub tried to deflect this blame by criticizing the United States for having suddenly "betrayed" Pakistan by withholding crucial weapons and ammunition at the height of the fighting.

To protest Ayub's having signed the peace agreement, Bhutto immediately submitted his resignation as Foreign Minister. Ayub delayed accepting his resignation, hoping that Bhutto might still support his regime. However, since Bhutto knew that Ayub would eventually dismiss him, he largely abandoned his ministerial duties so he spend his time strengthening his political future. He began criticizing the Tashkent Agreement, and even suggested that there might have been some secret Tashkent understandings that Ayub was hiding.[46] Bhutto also expressed support for the many university students who were promoting riots against the Tashkent Agreement. Ayub eventually would accept Bhutto's resignation as Foreign Minister five months later.

On January 11, 1966, Indian Prime Minister Shastri died—just days after the peace treaty had been signed. Shastri's death ended what little prospect there might have been that the two leaders might work together in implementing the peace agreement. Eight days later, Shastri was succeeded by Indira Gandhi—the daughter of India's late leader Jawaharlal Nehru. Prime Minister Indira Gandhi would become an accomplished politician and a daring leader who was willing to confront Pakistan.

Mujib's Six-Point Plan

On February 12, 1966, AL leader Mujibur Rahman ("Mujib") presented his Six-Point Plan for East wing autonomy. Mujib's plan demanded that Pakistan restore parliamentary government and adopt a strong federalist system, with the central government's authority limited to defense and foreign affairs. The plan would give the East wing the power to raise its own militia and retain all taxes raised in its territory. Mujib's Six Points would win widespread support in the East wing, where it soon acquired revered status. However, President Ayub Khan and his junta vehemently opposed Mujib's plan, which would transform the country into a confederation. Ayub reacted to the plan by labeling Mujib a "secessionist," razing Mujib's headquarters, and jailing Mujib for over two years. Ayub's harsh treatment of Mujib triggered riots and strikes in Dacca and other East wing cities.

General Muhammad Musa had served as army chief for over seven years. He had been in charge of the army when it had been defeated by Indian forces. On June 17, 1966, Ayub Khan dismissed Musa, partly to distance himself from the army's defeat in that war. Ayub replaced Musa as army chief with General Yahya Khan. Ayub chose Yahya because he was loyal and he seemed preoccupied with women and partying—with no interest in politics.[47]

Growing Support for Ayub's Resignation

President Ayub Khan decided to try to revive his sagging popularity by holding celebrations to highlight his regime's accomplishments. The celebrations began on October 27, 1967. However, his extravagant 12-month "Decade of Development" celebrations backfired because most Pakistanis were angry at Ayub's costly self-serving propaganda celebrations. Also, most Pakistanis didn't believe Ayub's extravagant claims of success, and realized that his economic "successes" had largely benefited the wealthy.[48] Moreover, the focus on ten years of Ayub's successes reminded people that he had been in power for a very long time. Zulfikar Bhutto joined the critics of Ayub's celebrations and he also denounced Ayub's regime for its corruption and suppression of free speech.

As President Ayub Khan's popularity continued to fall, left-leaning intellectuals formed a new opposition party. On December 1, 1967, they formed the Pakistan Peoples Party (PPP)—Pakistan's first political party with a socialist manifesto. The PPP quickly gained the support of the downtrodden masses with its simple slogan: "Bread, Clothing and Shelter." PPP founder J.A. Rahim persuaded Zulfikar Bhutto to lead the PPP, desiring to utilize his charisma and enormous popularity. Bhutto accepted the offer as the best way to advance his own political career—even though he had come from a wealthy feudal landowner family and never had shown any interest in social reforms.[49] Bhutto began giving a series of speeches to publicize the new PPP. He posed as a champion of the masses—a crusader against poverty and government corruption.

While Bhutto was on his PPP speaking tour, Ayub Khan's health declined. The 61-year-old Ayub suffered a serious heart attack. On January 29, 1968, soldiers set up a protective ring around his residence while Ayub spokesmen told the press that Ayub was just suffering from pneumonia. However, Ayub was so ill that he was unable to perform his presidential duties for six weeks. Army Chief Yahya Khan temporarily assumed control of the country, while the government largely ran on inertia. Even when Ayub resumed his official duties he was so feeble that he only could endure a restricted work schedule. Furthermore, he became depressed when some of his loyal supporters, sensing that Ayub was losing his grip on power, began abandoning him and maneuvering for power. Ayub, realizing that he couldn't stop the momentum that was building up against him, began planning to resign and turn over leadership to others.

While Ayub Khan was recovering from his illness, he decided to cut a key link with the United States. On April 7, 1968, Pakistan served notice on the Americans that it would not renew the Badaber Air Base lease. For years, the Americans had been leasing space on this Pakistan base, which it still was using for intercepting Soviet communications. On receiving the vacate notice, the Americans quickly and willingly vacated the base, since its space satellites now could perform the needed communication intercepts. Yet the Americans still were angry that its ally had terminated the lease, which had been the only valuable asset that Pakistan ever had given them in return for billions of dollars in aid. With the lease terminated, America's interest in Pakistan dropped precipitously.

Ayub Khan discovered a plot in which some East wing nationalists were allegedly planning to overthrow his government and set up an independent nation in the East wing (the "Agartala Conspiracy").[50] Ayub charged over 50 East wing officials of conspiring in the plot, and he even named the popular East wing politician Mujib as a conspirator. Ayub claimed that Mujib had been directing the plot from his jail cell. The Agartala Conspiracy trial began on June 19, 1968, with Ayub hoping to send the troublesome Mujib to jail for many years. However, the trial backfired on Ayub, since the highly publicized trial provided Mujib with a wonderful public platform to promote his Six-Point Program. The trial would make Mujib a hero of the East wingers, who believed that he was being persecuted by West wing leaders simply for trying to redress East wing grievances.

The merits of the trial went badly for the state prosecutors, who had great difficulty proving how Mujib could have planned a coup from his jail cell. The case would be dismissed before the end of the year for lack of evidence, and it had greatly bolstered Mujib's popularity in the East wing.

The Last Gasps of Ayub Khan's Dictatorship

Zulfikar Bhutto continued his relentless attacks on President Ayub Khan even though the elderly Ayub was still quite ill. On September 21, 1968, Bhutto viciously denounced Ayub's dictatorship, focusing on its corruption, nepotism and incompetence. This tough speech started a new anti–Ayub Movement. While Ayub didn't openly suppress Bhutto's campaign against him, he secretly tried to stop him—even trying to kill him.[51] However, Bhutto continued to speak out against Ayub, and people continued to risk arrest just to hear the charismatic Bhutto speak. Finally, on November 13, Ayub had Bhutto arrested, and Bhutto would remain in jail for three months. However, Bhutto's imprisonment only added to his popularity, and it inspired students, lawyers and women to demonstrate for his release. A wave of strikes paralyzed factories, and strikers and students even set up barricades on the streets of Pakistan's largest cities. The demonstrators demanded Bhutto's release and called for Ayub to step down.

Resistance to Ayub Khan became more organized when on January 6, 1969, the Pakistan Democratic Movement (PDM) was formed. Members of this anti–Ayub coalition included the ConML and the East wing AL and NAP parties. The PDM called for the immediate end of the state of emergency, the release of political prisoners and direct elections using adult franchise. The

PDM warned Ayub Khan that it would boycott the forthcoming elections unless its demands were met. Three days later, radical East wing students held a massive anti–Ayub rally attended by 100,000 students and city workers.

The desperate President Ayub Khan, realizing that opposition to his rule was becoming a mass movement, suddenly decided to appease his opponents. On February 17, 1969, he ended the state of emergency, and five days later he released Zulfikar Bhutto from his three-month house arrest. However, Bhutto regarded Ayub's concessions as a sign of weakness, and he was emboldened to resume his vicious anti–Ayub speeches.

Pakistan's armed forces chiefs warned Ayub Khan on February 20, 1969, that he must find a political solution to the disorders facing the country.[52] The generals no longer were willing to order their troops to confront and fire on unarmed demonstrators. This warning was a turning point, since Ayub knew that the police couldn't control the huge anti–Ayub demonstrations without army assistance.

President Ayub Khan still tried to reach a last-minute resolution to East wing grievances by convening "Round Table" conferences. However, in these conferences the East wing leaders demanded more East wing autonomy and concessions than Ayub was willing to allow.

Therefore, on March 25, 1969, Ayub Khan succumbed to pressure from Army Chief Yahya Khan and resigned as president. The 62-year-old Ayub decided to no longer resist calls for his resignation because he was physically and mentally fatigued, he was being viciously attacked by his former supporters, and he had lost the army's support.

Pakistan's Constitution provided that upon a president's resignation, that the National Assembly's Speaker should become acting president. However, instead, Ayub Khan turned over the government to his trusted Army Chief Yahya Khan. A number of generals had been grooming Yahya to succeed Ayub, knowing that he privately disagreed with many of Ayub's decisions.[53] Yahya's taking office demonstrated just how firmly the army controlled Pakistan.

Ayub Khan left an impressive legacy, having been one of Pakistan's most constructive rulers. During his ten-year rule, he had strengthened and improved the country, and he had constructed a new capital city at Islamabad. He had started the process of modernizing the country by promoting industrialization and by introducing modern farming techniques. During his tenure, Pakistan's average annual GDP had increased 7 percent, and the middle class had expanded.

However, Ayub Khan's legacy also had some disappointing features. Ayub had failed to convert his military dictatorship into a representative system of government. Instead he had set the precedent for a series of military coups and dictatorships—each initiated by the army chief with the backing of his generals. His economic development reforms had widened the gap between the wealthy and the poor. They had allowed a few giant businesses to grow without any restrictions, while he had cut back government services to the masses. He also had failed to listen to the East wingers who had demanded equal treatment and more autonomy, and instead he had branded them disloyal secessionists. Also, he had tolerated corruption by government officials and his family.

6

General Yahya Khan and Civil War

During the two years and nine months covered in this chapter (March 1969–December 1971), General Yahya Khan would rule the country through a military junta. Yahya would terminate the "One Unit" voting system, thereby allowing the more populous East wing and its AL Party to win a majority of seats in the National Assembly. Due to this victory, the AL would demand that it be allowed to take over Pakistan's new government. However, Yahya's military junta would refuse to allow the country to be ruled by the AL East wingers, and it would dispatch the army to the East wing to seize control. Indian troops would invade East Pakistan to help the East wingers secede, and they would defeat Pakistan's forces. The East wingers would form the independent nation of Bangladesh. The chapter ends with Yahya Khan resigning and civilian Zulfikar Bhutto being selected as Pakistan's new leader.

General Yahya Khan Sets Up His Military Government

On March 25, 1969, Army Chief General Yahya Khan began his military dictatorship. He immediately abolished the Constitution, declared martial law, and became the powerful Chief Martial Law Administrator (CMLA). He divided the country into western and eastern zones, with a Martial Law Administrator (MLA) in control of each zone and acting as governor.

6. General Yahya Khan and Civil War

Yahya Khan had several strengths. First, the easy-going Yahya was sociable and well-liked. He was a relatively benevolent dictator who didn't jail, torture or murder his political opponents. He also was more realistic than most of his military colleagues, and he realized that he must make major concessions to the East wing if Pakistan were to remain intact. His initial impulse would be was to solve the East wing disturbances through concessions and negotiations.

Yahya Khan also had several weaknesses. First, he was a happy-go-lucky man who enjoyed partying and heavy drinking—which would increasingly impair his judgment. He also tended to make impulsive decisions using a minimum of facts, thought or analysis. He wouldn't tolerate disagreement with his views.[1] Also, Yahya would find the daily chores of governing boring, and so he left his work to key administrators. He left major decision-making to the three-man junta. There he chose to be just an equal member, and he would allow himself to be swayed by his more conservative junta colleagues.

There were several reasons why Yahya Khan was able to quickly end the violence that had plagued his predecessor. First, the main target of the violent protests had been his predecessor, and Ayub had resigned. Also, few Pakistanis dared violate the martial law which Yahya imposed and strictly enforced. Also, Yahya quickly addressed some of the people's grievances. He immediately promised factory workers and farm laborers a fair deal, and he would follow up by introducing meaningful labor reforms. He also would dismiss many high-level civil service officials for corruption.[2] In addition, Yahya ended Ayub's "Basic Democracy" indirect voting system, and gave each adult the right to vote for national leaders. He even proposed greater autonomy for the East wing and promised to end the "One Unit" voting system which had diluted East wing voting strength. There was a sense of relief as daily life returned to normal.

General Yahya Khan took several measures to give the illusion that he was running a civilian government. First, on March 31, 1969, he added the title of president to his military titles, although the real ruler of the country continued to be his military junta. Also, Yahya formed a cabinet as civilian leaders would do. However, this shadow cabinet was created just to provide cover for the junta and was filled with generals.[3] In addition Yahya decreed the creation of a parliamentary system of government. There was to be a 313-member National Assembly, with 163 seats (52 percent) reserved for the East wing.[4] This seat distribution ended the "one unit" voting system which had unfairly restricted the East wing to just half of the Assembly seats.

Yahya Khan had promised the workers relief, and so on July 4, 1969, he announced a series of meaningful labor reforms. They were designed to resolve labor conflicts in the mutual interests of both labor and management.

The reforms gave unions the right to collectively bargain and strike, while limiting the length of the strikes.⁵

Yahya Khan and his military junta were anxious for the restoration of American arms shipments, which had been cut off for four years. They looked forward to the scheduled visit of the recently elected American President Richard Nixon who had pledged to improve relations with Pakistan. When Nixon arrived in Pakistan on August 1, 1969, Yahya Khan warmly received him. Nixon told Yahya that Pakistan's arms needs were under consideration by his administration and Congress. During the visit, Nixon also asked Yahya to help set up a secret meeting with Chinese leaders to try to open relations between the United States and Communist China. Yahya welcomed this chance to serve as a liaison between these two adversaries.

An Election with an Ominous Outcome

On January 1, 1970, President Yahya Khan announced that political parties could start campaigning for the national and provincial parliamentary elections scheduled for October 5. Candidates would be elected directly by all adult voters rather than indirectly by an electoral college. Yahya realized that there was some risk in holding direct elections, but Yahya's generals and the ISI predicted that in these elections, with 25 parties seeking 300 electable seats, no single political party would win a controlling majority of National Assembly seats. In that case, the winning party would need to form a coalition government—which the generals were confident they could control.

During the long nine-month campaign, Bhutto's PPP and Mujib's AL overshadowed all the other parties in terms of capable leaders, party organization, and grassroots support. These two parties had been transformed into unstoppable mass movements in their respective wings. Bhutto's PPP Party gained massive support in the West wing by advocating for the poor and downtrodden. At the same time, Mujib's AL Party emerged as the dominant party in the East wing by denouncing the central government and by demanding East wing autonomy.

Several danger signs emerged during the election campaign. First, neither the PPP nor the AL even bothered launching a credible campaign in the wing dominated by the other party. This guaranteed that whichever party won would not have strong backing in both wings. Also, during the long campaign the opposing PPP and AL parties bitterly attacked each other and hardened their positions. The angry parties would be reluctant to compromise if disagreements emerged after the election. In addition, Yahya announced that the newly elected Assembly would have the right to amend the

6. General Yahya Khan and Civil War 77

Constitution by a simple majority vote. This meant that the party securing a majority of National Assembly seats could radically change the Constitution despite protests from the opposition.

In the middle of Pakistan's parliamentary election campaign, the East wing suffered the worst natural disaster in its history. On November 12, 1970, a massive cyclone with 120-mile an hour winds struck the East wing's low-lying coast, killing at least 230,000 people. Yahya's regime was slow to recognize the enormity of the disaster, slow to show sympathy for the victims, and slow to provide emergency relief. The relief that was offered by the government was dwarfed by that given by international agencies. East wing politicians denounced Yahya's regime for its slow and modest disaster relief, and claimed that it confirmed that the central government didn't care about East wingers.[6] The East wing NAP Party would protest by not running candidates in the next month's national elections.

Pakistan's National Assembly elections were held on December 7, 1970. There was a huge voter turnout, since Election Day had been declared a public holiday and since it was Pakistan's first national election with direct, mass voting. The quiet and orderly election was Pakistan's fairest election ever. Since Bhutto's PPP ran candidates only in the West wing, while Mujib's AL ran candidates only in the East wing, it was as though two different countries were holding two different elections.

The election results were predictable. Mujib's East wing AL party secured a majority of National Assembly seats by winning 167 seats in the 313-member legislature. Bhutto's PPP won 81 seats. The AL won largely because there were two million more voters living in the East wing than in the West wing, the PPP hadn't run any candidates there, and the NAP boycotted the elections. Also, Mujib had been a charismatic campaigner and he had focused on the issue of West wing's mistreatment of the East wing. However, the AL hadn't won a single seat in the West wing where Bhutto's PPP dominated.

Several serious problems resulted from the election results. First, no national political party had emerged with strong support in both wings. This problem was compounded by the refusal of Yahya's military junta to accept the right of Mujib's AL party to govern the whole country through its control of the National Assembly. The junta wasn't willing to accept East wing rule, since that risked the army's losing its preeminent position in the country and losing its large cut of the national budget.[7] Also, the possibility of the crisis being resolved peacefully was slim, since the PPP and AL detested each other after the long and bitter election campaign. In addition, Bhutto and Mujib had large egos, disliked and mistrusted the other, and refused to submit to the other's leadership. They both were consumed by a desire for power, and both lacked a commitment to keep the country united.[8] Finally, both sides could challenge the election's questionable legitimacy. The election had not been authorized by any constitution, since no constitution had been in effect at the time. It had simply been decreed by Yahya under martial law.

President Yahya Khan was the sole West wing official interested in negotiating with the East wing. He initially made a genuine effort to reach a compromise with Mujib's AL Party in the East wing, and for a time it seemed that he and Mujib were headed for a compromise.[9] However, he began to realize that there could be no peaceful solution to the crisis given the stubbornness of both Bhutto and Mujib. Yahya finally gave up and he began deferring more and more to his conservative junta colleagues. On February 21, 1971, the junta conservatives took full control of decision-making. The junta began preparing for a military invasion of the East wing, on the assumption that the army would meet little opposition once it had arrested Mujib and the rest of the AL's leaders.[10]

The leaders of the two wings quietly made plans that guaranteed conflict. Mujib, emboldened by his party's election victory, planned to wait until the new National Assembly convened. Then his AL would take over the Assembly, have him named prime minister, and amend the Constitution to give the East wing much more autonomy. At the same time, the military junta planned to keep the new National Assembly from ever meeting by continually postponing its opening session. In the meantime, the junta had the army prepare to invade the East wing, and some 1,700 troops were flown to the East wing to reinforce its garrison there.[11] The junta expected that after arresting Mujib and destroying the AL, it could cow the East wingers into submission.

Prelude to Invasion

The crisis came to a head on March 1, 1971. Yahya made an address in which he postponed the National Assembly's meeting scheduled for two days later, without setting a new meeting date. Yahya claimed that the postponement was necessary to allow the political leaders to reach an understanding. Huge East wing mobs reacted by looting and burning, and rampaging through the streets—demanding full independence. Pakistan Army troops in the East wing declared a curfew, which was largely ignored. The mobs overwhelmed the soldiers, who retreated to the safety of their barracks. The next day, a Mujib-called six-day strike began in the East wing's city of Dacca and soon spread throughout the wing. Yahya's junta hadn't realized the depth of East wing discontent and hadn't anticipated how quickly disorders would spread.

Yahya Khan and the military junta responded to Mujib's demonstrations by moving up their East wing invasion timetable. The junta stalled

6. General Yahya Khan and Civil War

for time to allow the army to deploy more troops to reinforce its weak East wing garrison in preparation for the attack. As part of this stalling, the junta had Yahya and Bhutto meet several times with Mujib, pretending that they were genuinely interested in negotiating a settlement. Yahya still hoped that Bhutto and Mujib would reach a last-minute agreement. However, while Mujib was willing to compromise, Bhutto refused to genuinely negotiate. He had come to think that the East wing wasn't worth saving—especially since the secession of the East wing and its AL Party would enhance his own political future in the West wing.[12] Had Bhutto been more humble and patient, and accepted Mujib as prime minister, the bloody Civil War might have been avoided.

On March 4, 1971, Mujib began setting up a separate government in the East wing and began issuing policy directives from his home. He would call his new government "Bangladesh." He urged an indefinite strike in East wing government offices and courts, and he ordered his new government to start collecting its own taxes and stop sending revenues to the West wing.[13] Bangladesh flags replaced Pakistani flags and Dacca Radio stations began playing revolutionary Bengali songs. The East wing had in effect seceded from Pakistan.

On the eve of the army's invasion, the army had a number of advantages over the East wingers. First, the army initially deployed 16,000 combat troops in the East wing, and this number would grow to 34,000 well-armed, well-trained regular troops. They faced some 27,000 untrained and poorly armed Bengali fighters. Also, there would be no West wing public opposition to the invasion, since most West wingers supported the invasion against the shorter, darker-skinned Bengalis (the "Bingos") due to racial prejudices.[14] In addition, Pakistan wouldn't face criticism from the United States for the invasion, since the pro–Pakistan Nixon would call the invasion "an internal Pakistani matter."

However, the East wing Bengalis also had some strengths. First, they were highly motivated and united by their long-standing hatred of the central government. They were justifiably angry that the central government's leaders had refused to honor the results of their election victory and were trying to terrorize the East wingers into submission. Also, the East wing had a population of 70 million, whereas Pakistan had only 34,000 troops deployed against them. The army would have difficulty subduing so many hostile East wingers. In addition, if the defenders could prolong the war using guerrilla tactics, the central government might eventually withdraw its troops. The East wing was an ideal location for a long guerrilla war since guerrillas could retreat to India and to their own vast jungle areas. They also could count on India to give them training and supplies. Finally, their enemy faced serious logistics problems. Pakistan had to airlift lots of their supplies to its troops in the East wing. Since India refused to allow Pakistani planes to fly over its territory, these planes had to fly over 2,500 miles to reach the East wing.

The Civil War Begins

Pakistan's Civil War progressed in four stages. The first stage (March–May 1971) began on March 26, 1971, when the Pakistan Army attacked AL leaders and the Bengalis in the East wing ("Operation Searchlight"). Pakistan's General Tikka Khan sent troops to arrest Mujib in his home and arrest or kill many other top AL leaders. Troops stormed Dhaka University, killed students in their dormitories, and rounded up professors, doctors and lawyers whom they executed.[15] General Tikka Khan had encouraged his troops to kill Bengalis, and during the first few weeks they would kill 34,000 or more relatively defenseless civilians.[16] The soldiers were so ruthless because of their racial hatred of the darker-skinned Bengalis and because the Bengalis had insulted them while waiting in their barracks. Also, the soldiers had been instructed to view the large East wing Hindu population as being opposed to Pakistan's unity and as enemies to their Islamic faith.[17] The soldiers responded by destroying whole Hindu neighborhoods. Tikka soon earned the new nickname: "the Butcher of Bengal."

Initially, resistance in the East wing crumbled. The army gained control of Dacca and all East wing cities, although Bengali guerrillas conducted small-unit warfare in the countryside. India wanted to help the Bengalis, because if the East wing broke off from the West wing, Pakistan would become a much weaker adversary.[18] Indian Army leaders would have preferred to immediately fight alongside the East wingers, but heavy monsoon rains prevented them from deploying troops there for six months. However, while waiting for the rains to stop, India provided East wing troops with sanctuary, weapons and training. Also, India assisted the Bengali rebels organize their forces (the "Mukti Bahini") inside India. Their ranks grew since many soldiers in Bengali Army units escaped capture and fled to India with their weapons. On April 17, 1971, Bengali AL leaders in exile declared East wing independence and established the Peoples Republic of Bangladesh in Calcutta, India. India began allowing a Bangladesh radio station to operate within its borders.

On May 15, 1971, the civil war entered its second stage (May–July 1971). During this period, there was a lull in the fighting. Pakistan's army was confident that it had crushed organized East wing resistance, and so it didn't press its offensive. At the same time, the East wing's Mukti Bahini troops in India still were busy being trained by the Indian Army, and they refrained from raiding Pakistan Army troops in the East wing.

On July 9, 1971, during this lull in the fighting, American Secretary of State Henry Kissinger arrived in Pakistan for a visit during his tour of Asian capitals. As planned, during his visit he secretly traveled to China for his first of two meetings with Chinese leaders. Kissinger had lengthy talks with Chou En-lai and his colleagues, which would lead to Nixon's own triumphant visit to Peking on February 21, 1972. President Yahya Khan's key role in arranging Kissinger's secret trip to China earned him the gratitude of his American and Chinese allies. President Nixon was so beholden to Yahya for this liaison assistance that he not only refused to criticize Pakistan's invasion of the East wing, but he also pressured India not to invade Pakistan's West wing while Pakistan's army was bogged down in the East wing.

In August 1971, the civil war entered its third stage (August–September 1971). During this stage, the newly trained East wing Mukti Bahini guerrillas in India began crossing into the East wing and attacking power stations, lines of communication, and ships in their berths loaded with army supplies. The Mukti Bahinis' goal was to send as many guerrillas as possible into the East wing to force Pakistan's army to spread their forces and make possible later attacks on isolated army units. Pakistan's army responded with house-to-house searches and floggings of suspects, which further alienated the East wingers.

The civil war entered its fourth stage when the monsoon rains ended (October–November 1971). The end of the monsoons allowed the Bengali guerrillas to expand their activities. They seized many border posts and destroyed railroad bridges. In the face of these attacks, the army's East wing troops became an exhausted and disillusioned force. A stalemate developed, since Pakistan's army was unable to destroy the guerrillas, while the guerrillas weren't able to force Pakistan's army to withdraw.

The Third Indo-Pak War

Pakistan's civil war would turn into the Third Indo-Pakistan War when Indian troops crossed into East Pakistan. India had several reasons for invading the East wing. First, it wanted to allow the East wing Bengalis to secede from Pakistan—thereby depriving its rival of half its population.[19] Also, India wanted to soundly defeat Pakistan's armed forces there—but not to permanently seize any Pakistani territory. In addition, India wanted to end the stalemate in Pakistan's civil war so that the millions of East wing refugees who had fled to India would return home and thereby relieve India of this burden.

On December 4, 1971, the Third Indo-Pakistan War began in earnest when India launched a massive air, sea and land offensive against Pakistan's East wing. India claimed it was responding to Pakistani air raids which had attacked a few Indian airfields the day before. It was confident that it could overwhelm the Pakistan Army's forces in the East wing, since its invasion force enjoyed a three-to-one numerical troop superiority there. Also, the Indian Army had excellent senior leadership, had highly motivated troops, and enjoyed air supremacy.

Pakistan's army had serious handicaps. General Niazi had replaced General Tikka Khan as commander of troops in the East wing, and he had limited leadership skills. Moreover, the army's High Command had ordered Niazi to undertake tasks that could not be carried out by the forces that he had available.[20] Also, Pakistan's infantry was ill-trained and poorly equipped.[21] In addition, Niazi dispersed his forces in the East wing by having them defend many "fortresses."[22] This left his army with no strong troop concentrations in reserve. Finally, Indian warships soon began blockading East wing ports, thereby preventing the resupply by sea of Pakistan's troops in the East wing.

India's offensive in the East Wing went well. India quickly neutralized Pakistan's smaller air force. Then with overpowering numbers, Indian troops quickly overran the dispersed Pakistani defenses, lay siege to its "fortresses," and marched on Dacca. General Niazi was forced to withdraw his exhausted troops into a triangle around Dacca. While Pakistani army forces in the West counterattacked by invading India, this counteroffensive wasn't strong enough to force the Indian Army to call off its East wing offensive. No country intervened in Pakistan's behalf—not China, not America, and not any Muslim nation.

A desperate President Yahya Khan asked former foreign minister Zulfi Bhutto to travel to the United Nations in New York to represent Pakistan. Bhutto hadn't held government office since Ayub had let him go five years before, but Bhutto accepted the assignment. However, he accepted only after Yahya had agreed to form a new civilian government—with Yahya president and Bhutto foreign minister.

On December 11, Foreign Minister Zulfikar Bhutto arrived at United Nations headquarters in New York City. He realized that India's army would prevail in the East wing, and the three defiant speeches that he delivered were partly designed to bolster his own popularity at home. He concluded his final speech by claiming: "We will fight to the last man." He tore up papers lying on his desk, threw them in the air, and strode defiantly out of the room.

However, on December 16, General Niazi formally surrendered the 56,000 surrounded Pakistani troops in Dacca. In the face of intense American and Chinese pressure, India's Prime Minister Indira Gandhi offered a cease-fire. She made it clear that India would not make Pakistan's East wing part of India, but that it would recognize the East wing's right to independence.

On December 17, 1971, Pakistan's government accepted India's cease-fire, thereby ending the Third Indo-Pak War. India would retain as POWs the 56,000 surrendering troops, along with 22,000 West wing paramilitary troops

6. General Yahya Khan and Civil War

and 12,000 civilians—a total of some 90,000 prisoners. Pakistan's people were shocked and angry when its government announced that its troops had surrendered in Dacca, since Yahya's state-controlled media had been feeding the people false stories claiming a series of Pakistani victories. Pakistan lost its East wing, which would become the independent nation of Bangladesh.

There were several repercussions to Pakistan's dismemberment. First, Pakistan suddenly had become a much weaker nation, since it had lost over half its population. Also, its armed forces had been severely weakened during the war, having lost a third of its army, half of its navy and a quarter of its air force. Also, the prestige of the army junta and senior generals had been shattered. They had blundered into a war that they couldn't win, when the junta could have negotiated an agreement allowing the East wing to peacefully secede without killing over 26,000 unarmed East wing civilians. In addition, Pakistanis blamed Yahya Khan for the army's defeat and for his having fed the people false stories of victories throughout the fighting. Also, India's invasion of the East wing made Pakistanis more angry and fearful of India, which had helped the East wingers secede from their country. Pakistani leaders also saw the need to cultivate Islamic identity as a way to unify the country against further Indian aggression.

Part Two—Pakistan After Dismemberment

7

Zulfikar Bhutto's Missed Opportunity

During the six-year period covered in this chapter (December 1971–November 1977), Pakistan would be led by Zulfikar Bhutto's civilian government. Bhutto's first two years would be the closest Pakistan would ever come to true democratic rule. He would prod the National Assembly to enact Pakistan's Third Constitution. However, Bhutto would squander away an opportunity to create a truly representative government by his growing desire to accumulate more power. His lieutenants would engage in massive ballot rigging in the 1977 national elections, and Bhutto wouldn't be able to resolve the crisis. The chapter ends with Zia overthrowing Bhutto's government.

Civilian Rule Resumed Under Zulfikar Bhutto

Even though Pakistan's army had lost the war with India, President Yahya Khan and his senior generals wanted to keep ruling the country. However, many middle-level army officers wanted to turn the government over to civilians. These officers were mad that Yahya Khan had started a war with India which the army was unprepared to win. They seethed with anger at the poor leadership of General Yahya Khan and his senior generals, which had led to their comrades' imprisonment or death. Brigadier Ali and six other mid-level officers took command of a large contingent of army troops and tanks. They demanded that Yahya and his senior generals resign or else Ali's troops would march on army headquarters.[1] Brigadier Ali's discontent was shared by many other mid-level officers who confronted senior generals at army headquarters and bluntly revealed their discontent.

The senior generals gave in to this groundswell of discontent and agreed to turn over the government to civilians. The generals quickly agreed that Zulfikar Bhutto should take the job, since his PPP had won the most votes in the West wing the year before, and he was the most popular politician in the country.

On December 20, 1971, General Yahya Khan resigned as president due to the mini-mutiny within the army, and he immediately transferred power to Zulfikar Bhutto. Bhutto was sworn in as president and Chief Martial Law Administrator (CMLA)—the first civilian to hold the latter position. The office of prime minister would remain vacant. Bhutto was the first civilian politician to rule Pakistan in over 13 years, and the first native of Sindh Province to become Pakistan's leader. Bhutto would remain president for over six years. At first, everyone wanted Bhutto to succeed, since his success meant the survival of the newly dismembered country. Bhutto took office at an opportune time to revitalize the country. He had a popular mandate from his PPP's victory inside the West wing during the National Assembly elections 12 months before. Also, the army was dispirited and tired of governing.

The 44-year-old Zulfikar Bhutto had many strengths. First, he was young, a charismatic speaker, and possessed supreme confidence in his leadership ability. He was able to get the people behind him, since he was Pakistan's first leader to address the needs of the downtrodden masses. He always felt he could count on the poorer classes to back him. Also, Bhutto was intelligent and a brilliant politician. He would secure grassroots support by putting his PPP Party into thousands of communities across the country. In addition, Bhutto's university education in the West had exposed him to democratic practices, and this would lead him to push for a widely acceptable constitution. In addition, Bhutto was adept at foreign affairs, having acquired diplomatic experience while serving as Ayub Khan's foreign minister. Finally, Bhutto could count on the army's support. Army leaders had learned to trust him while he had served as Ayub Khan's foreign minister. Bhutto would be able to win over these senior generals by listening to their views, satisfying their needs, and winning them over with his reasoning and rhetoric.

However, Bhutto also had many weaknesses. First, Bhutto believed that he had been born to lead Pakistan due to his extraordinary abilities.[2] He was arrogant, scornful of others, and came to believe in his own infallibility. Bhutto would demand blind obedience and fawning loyalty from his advisers and subordinates, and therefore he wouldn't receive honest feedback. Also, Bhutto didn't want to develop a political system which would allow rival politicians to succeed each other through fair elections. Instead, his overall goal was to create a personality cult and permanent majority that would allow him to remain the nation's leader for the indefinite future.[3] To secure control, Bhutto favored using force over negotiating alliances, and so he relied on the ISI and his own paramilitary forces to control the opposition. Bhutto would create an ISI Internal Security Wing which he would have bug the phones and offices of both his own ministers and his opponents.[4] He even would create his own FSF paramilitary force to serve as his own private army. In addition, Bhutto was a poor administrator. The tireless Bhutto tried to do everything himself instead of delegating his work. He also would do an extremely poor job selecting people to important posts, and he would choose most candidates just for their professed loyalty. In addition, Bhutto was not committed to the PPP and its socialist values, and he just used it to give him legitimacy.[5] He would weaken his own PPP party by driving out the PPP's idealist founders and veterans and replacing them with self-serving newcomers.[6] In addition, Bhutto would weaken the civil service system—whose nonpartisan professionalism had been one of Pakistan's greatest strengths. He would make entry and promotions dependent on loyalty to himself.[7] Finally, Bhutto would constantly interfere with provincial governments to insure that they remained under his control. He would keep provincial leaders weak by appointing cautious and submissive men as governors and chief ministers. He also would take over provincial governments when they challenged his authority.

President Zulfikar Bhutto took over a country which had several big problems. First, Pakistan's fragile economy had suffered during the war with India. Pakistan's businessmen and investors had lost confidence in the country's economic future, and so there had been a sharp decline in investments. Also, the people's morale had declined since the country had been humiliated by military defeat and dismemberment. Pakistan was isolated and spurned by the international community for its having brutally killed tens of thousands of unarmed East wing civilians.

Fortunately, Bhutto's ability to solve some of these problems had improved due to dismemberment, since Bhutto would be governing a smaller, more homogeneous population. There were 60 million Muslims living in the dismembered Pakistan out of a total population of 62 million. Also, the army could defend the country better since it had a shorter border to protect and no longer had to defend the distant and vulnerable East wing. In addition, Pakistan no longer would be weighed down by the East wing's recurrent food shortages, which were being brought on by droughts, floods and its rapidly expanding population.

Bhutto's First Six Months in Office

On December 20, 1971, President Zulfikar Bhutto gave an uplifting speech on national radio which helped lift the fallen spirits of millions of his countrymen. He admitted that Pakistan's army had been defeated by India, and he recognized that Pakistan faced an economic crisis. However, he promised to rebuild Pakistan and lead it to prosperity. He said that he disliked the martial law which he had "inherited," and he pledged to end it as soon as possible. He promised to return control of Pakistan to the people through elections, and he promised amnesty to all political prisoners. Bhutto followed up with a whirlwind tour of Pakistan in order to rally the shattered nation. His speech and tour made Bhutto very popular.

On the same day as his speech, President Bhutto appointed Gul Hassan Khan as army chief. General Hassan accepted his appointment only on condition that Bhutto would lift martial law and not interfere in army affairs. Bhutto soon would decide that he really wanted an army chief who would help him politically, and he would remove Hassan within two months.

Bhutto took several steps to secure the support of army leaders. First, he made sure that the army received adequate funding, and its funds would substantially increase during Bhutto's term in office. Also, he would offer the sale of choice farmland at cheap prices to both senior and junior officers.[8] In addition, he would patiently and skillfully negotiate for the return of the 90,000 Pakistanis languishing in Indian POW camps. Also, he would promote the creation of Pakistan's own arms industry, which would make the army more self-sufficient in securing weapons and ammunition.[9] Finally, Bhutto would publicly denounce former Army Chief Yahya Khan, claiming that he was solely responsible for the loss of the East wing. Making Yahya the scapegoat not only deflected blame from Pakistan's soldiers, but also resonated with the middle-level officers who deeply resented Yahya's senior generals for their role in the army's defeat.[10]

President Zulfikar Bhutto's foreign policy was based on improving relations with the United States, China and (temporarily) India. First, Bhutto wanted Pakistan to depend less on the United States and more on China—its new main arms supplier. However, he still needed American arms to re-equip Pakistan's defeated army. Pakistan also needed American economic assistance and needed American help in dealing with the IMF and the World Bank. In addition, Bhutto had both short-term and long-term goals in dealing with India. In the short-term, he wanted to stabilize relations with India, since its troops were still on Pakistan's border and Pakistan's army was too weak to repel another invasion. He also wanted good relations with India so it would release the 90,000 Pakistanis that it held inside India. However, in the long-run, Bhutto wanted to replace all the weapons lost in the recent war with India and to avenge the army's defeat.[11]

President Bhutto began three years of bold economic changes while he still had martial law powers. However, his reforms were not well thought out. First, while the centerpiece of his economic reforms was nationalizing private companies, his government never seriously discussed whether nationalization would be best for the country.¹² Also, Bhutto failed to set up a central development plan, and so Bhutto and PPP leftists approved different expensive projects—more than the government could afford. Many of these development projects were meant to benefit Bhutto's supporters, even if they weren't best for the country's overall growth.

President Bhutto selected Finance Minister Mubashir Hassan to oversee the nationalizations of private companies, and the first in a series of nationalizations was approved by the submissive National Assembly without serious debate. On January 2, 1972, Hassan announced the nationalization of over thirty large companies in ten major industries. The submissive National Assembly had approved these nationalizations without serious debate. The government took over the management (but not ownership) of the nationalized companies, and the owners weren't compensated for their loss of control. While the nationalizations were intended to improve the economy, they also were intended to reduce the power of the industrialists since they were exploiting their workers—a key PPP constituency.¹³

There were several reasons why Bhutto's nationalizations would fail to improve the economy. First, Bhutto's planners didn't consult Pakistan's technocrats about the nationalizations, and so they made many mistakes—including nationalizing some unprofitable companies and some companies that had no assets. Some company owners had anticipated the takeovers, and just before their companies were nationalized had dismissed their key employees and had sold their best equipment.¹⁴ Also, the government nationalized companies with little warning, and so businessmen put off innovations and modernizations of their factories for fear of sudden nationalizations. Also, investors stopped placing their funds in Pakistani enterprises. In addition, the nationalized companies performed poorly because they were now managed by government bureaucrats with no business experience.¹⁵ Many of these businesses would fail to make a profit and had to be subsidized by the government. Also, Bhutto nationalized the Ittefaq Foundry, which was the heart of the industrial empire of Bhutto's rival Nawaz Sharif and his family. This attack on Sharif's foundry touched off decades of feuding between Pakistan's powerful Sharif and Bhutto families.¹⁶

President Zulfikar Bhutto had to resolve the problem of what to do with the former East wing leader Mujib, who was languishing in a Pakistani jail. On January 8, 1972, Bhutto released Mujib after pressuring him to promise to help Bhutto unite Pakistan and Bangladesh, and jointly rule the two countries as a confederation. However, after Mujib was released, he broke his coerced promises.

Bhutto had always wanted to improve Pakistan's military capability, so one of his first acts was to develop plans to accelerate Pakistan's nuclear bomb program. On January 24, 1972, he convened a meeting of Pakistan's most eminent scientists. He gave an inspiring speech and had the scientists endorse his plan to build an atomic bomb in just three years. He wanted the bomb primarily to deter India from ever invading Pakistan.[17] Bhutto also reasoned that if he were to develop a bomb and control it, he would gain leverage over the army. He also believed that developing a "Muslim Bomb" would restore Pakistan's leadership in the Muslim world.

To strengthen Pakistan's economy, President Bhutto and Finance Minister Hassan undertook some far-reaching labor reforms. On February 10, 1972, Bhutto announced a series of the most comprehensive labor laws ever introduced in Pakistan. This "New Deal" for labor mandated workplace safety standards, higher minimum wages, job security and company pensions. Also, employees could bring complaints against their employers before newly created labor courts. However, the cost of implementing these labor reforms made most of the nationalized companies unprofitable, and the reforms emboldened workers to launch a series of strikes and lock-ins which reduced industrial output.[18]

Bhutto followed up his labor reforms with land reforms, which he announced on March 3, 1972, during a televised address. They included reducing the ceilings on individual land ownership to 150 acres of irrigated land and 300 acres of non-irrigated land. However, these land reforms brought little relief to the landless peasants, since most feudal landowners kept their best land using falsified deeds and transfers to relatives.[19] The feudal landowners continued to prosper since they paid no income taxes and took large shares of the harvests from their sharecroppers.[20]

On the same day, Bhutto announced that General Gul Hassan had resigned as army chief. Bhutto had pressured him to resign since Hassan wouldn't use the army to suppress anti–Bhutto demonstrations.[21] Bhutto replaced Hassan with General Tikka Khan. Bhutto chose him because Tikka was willing to follow all of Bhutto's orders, and he deemed the "Butcher of Bengal" to be too unpopular within the army to be capable of carrying out a coup.[22]

Bhutto continued with his social reforms by improving the public school system. Educational reforms clearly were needed, since only 45 percent of school-age children were attending school. Most poor children were staying out of school because their parents depended on their earnings to support the family. On March 15, 1972, Bhutto's government announced that school attendance would be mandatory up to middle school, and that 3,000 private educational institutions would be nationalized.

On April 17, 1972, Bhutto terminated martial law. He had been promising to lift it ever since taking office four months before, and the Supreme Court and his supporters had been pressuring him to take this step. While

Bhutto would miss being able to issue unilateral decrees with his martial law powers, he still retained considerable presidential powers which allowed him to bully opponents into submission.

Pakistani businessmen had grown to dislike Bhutto for his nationalization of businesses. Their dislike of Bhutto grew when on May 11, 1972, Bhutto had Pakistan sharply devalue its currency—a condition set by the IMF and World Bank for their rescheduling of Pakistan's debts and granting further loans. However, devaluation had a devastating effect on those Pakistani businessmen who had borrowed heavily from foreign lenders, since devaluation made repaying their loans more costly.

While the Third Indo-Pak War had ended with a cease-fire, the two countries still had not signed a formal peace agreement. This was remedied on July 3, 1972, when India and Pakistan signed the Simla Accord. Bhutto had come to the Simla bargaining table with little leverage, but peace terms were worked out since both countries wanted to reach an agreement. The Accord called for a withdrawal of all Indian troops from Pakistan's soil in return for Pakistan's agreeing to solve future disputes through peaceful bilateral negotiations. There was no progress in resolving the Kashmir dispute, and Bhutto wisely didn't revive Pakistan's demand for a Kashmir plebiscite. Given Pakistan's weak bargaining position, Bhutto had achieved remarkably favorable terms. Pakistan's National Assembly quickly approved the Accord.

President Zulfikar Bhutto had become immensely popular. In just six months, he had rekindled his people's spirits, had ended martial law, and had bought precious time to rebuild the army. He had started programs of economic development which promised to lead to long-term economic growth. At Simla, he had won back all Pakistani territory lost to India during the war.

Bhutto had accomplished so much during these first six months because he was able to use his martial law powers, and his PPP Party would face no genuine opposition during his first three years in power. However, soon he would face criticism from within his own PPP party, since many members were deeply committed to social issues which Bhutto more and more ignored. Also, Bhutto's popularity and strength would fade in time, and if he made mistakes, the army might use them to justify another military takeover.[23]

President Bhutto was a native Sindhi, and he sought to strengthen the PPPs political base in Sindh Province by supporting Sindhi as the official provincial language. The PPP also supported a Sindhi anti-mohajir campaign to end mohajir dominance in Karachi.[24] The mohajirs now made up 30 percent of the province's population and controlled Karachi's commercial and banking center. The mohajirs angrily accused Bhutto of being a "Sindhi President."

The Sindhi language issue came to a head on July 7, 1972, when a Bhutto-promoted Sindhi language bill was passed by the provincial legislature. The law made Sindhi the province's official language, and made it a compulsory language course in schools from grades four to twelve. The mohajir refugees in Sindh Province strongly opposed this law which pressured them to speak an unfamiliar language. The mohajirs organized large demonstrations to protest the new law, and mobs on both sides of the issue looted, burned and killed. These Sindhi-mohajir disturbances would burden Bhutto for the rest of his rule.

Another Baluchistan Insurgency

On October 5, 1972, Law Minister Mahmud Ali Qasuri resigned from Bhutto's government. He left because he opposed Bhutto's policies, and Bhutto no longer even listened to his input. This was the first of a series of resignations by PPP leaders who were disturbed by Bhutto's growing distrust of them and his ignoring their views. Each resignation further distanced him from his PPP base.

President Zulfikar Bhutto began taking steps to increase his power, and these power grabs would further alienate his supporters. His most blatant power grab was his formation of his own "private army"—the Federal Security Force (FSF), which he created on October 11. Bhutto wanted his own paramilitary force that he could totally control, so that he wouldn't have to depend on the army to suppress anti–Bhutto elements—even within his own party. Bhutto had been able to create the FSP partly because the army's officers had become divided over the army's defeat by India, and so initially weren't united in opposition to the FSP.

Bhutto appointed Masood Mahmood as the FSF chief—an arrogant and sadistic police officer. Mahmood recruited veterans, ex-policemen and criminals who he would order to harass and intimidate Bhutto's critics. The FSF would also beat critics, seize their properties and sometimes kill them.[25] The FSF expanded their victims to include attorneys and journalists. Bhutto's opponents responded in kind. Political murders and assassinations became routine.[26] While Bhutto didn't always order individual acts of violence, he did little to stop them. Within two years, this para-military group of would grow into a well-armed, 13,000-man force, causing the army to become concerned with this threat to its pre-eminent position.

Pakistan's government always had trouble working with rebellious Baluchistan—Pakistan's largest-sized but sparsely populated province. Bhutto now intervened because he was paranoid about the possibility of losing Pakistan's largest province to secession so soon after losing the East wing.[27] Baluchistan had been traditionally organized by tribes, and governed by regional "sardars." Bhutto wanted his central government to control the region, and so he decided to destroy the power of the sardars.[28]

7. Zulfikar Bhutto's Missed Opportunity

On February 15, 1973, Bhutto removed Baluchistan's Governor Bizenjo and his chief minister—leaders whom Bhutto himself had appointed. Bhutto believed that Bizenjo was plotting secession. Bhutto claimed that immediate action was necessary because a weapons shipment had been seized inside the Iraqi Embassy in Islamabad, and Bhutto assumed that the shipment must have been destined to support Baluchistan's secessionists.[29] Bhutto's takeover of Baluchistan's government was a huge mistake, and the seized arms most likely had been intended for anti-Iranian guerrillas—not for Baloch secessionists.

Bhutto took draconian measures to gain total control in Baluchistan. He appointed Governor Bizenjo's rival Akbar Bugti as the province's new governor, and he declared "President's Rule" throughout the province. Bhutto also had Army Chief Tikka Khan (the "Butcher of Bengal") deploy over 80,000 troops to Baluchistan to suppress any resistance that might develop. The Baloch tribes resisted the army's intrusion, and so began the "Fourth Baluchistan Insurgency." General Tikka Khan conducted a ruthless and bloody campaign which earned him the new nickname "Butcher of Baluchistan." While he suppressed the outnumbered and poorly armed rebel forces, the survivors fled into the hills and began a guerrilla war. During the four-year insurgency that followed, 6,000 Baloch and 3,000 Pakistani soldiers would be killed.

There were several repercussions to Bhutto's military intervention in Baluchistan. First, Bhutto's refusal to allow his appointed governor and chief minister to run the province set back democracy in all of Pakistan. Also, the army's arrests and killing of civilians totally alienated all Baloch. In addition, Bhutto's calling on the army to intervene helped accustom army leaders to remove elected civilian governments whenever they seemed too weak to suppress anti-government protests.

The military intervention in Baluchistan wasn't Bhutto's only intervention in the provinces. Bhutto removed the governments in the NWFP and Sindh Province, and placed these two provinces under his control as well. Bhutto insured that he personally controlled these two provinces by selecting loyalists as governors, and then routinely rotating the governors to prevent any from developing a strong base which might be used to challenge him.

In addition to handling challenges from the provinces, Bhutto also had to deal with a plot by middle-ranking military officers to overthrow him. Military Intelligence had uncovered the plot. On March 30, 1973, Pakistan's army arrested a number of discontented junior army and air force officers who were planning a military coup (the "Attock Conspiracy"). These officers were angry at Bhutto's retention and promotion of incompetent senior generals who had mishandled the Third Indo-Pak War.[30] The conspirators also were concerned that Bhutto seemed to be creating a civilian dictatorship, and they disliked Bhutto's use of the army to suppress his political opponents. General Zia Ul-Haq was selected as president of the court martial, and Zia ingratiated himself with Bhutto during the regular trial briefings that he gave to Bhutto.[31] This Bhutto-Zia contact would convince Bhutto later to select Zia as the new army chief. The conspirators were tried by a military tribunal and many received long prison sentences.

Pakistan Adopts Its Third Constitution

Pakistanis already had lived under two constitutions—the Constitution of 1956 and the Constitution of 1962. These constitutions had been abolished by military dictators. Prime Minister Zulfikar Bhutto now promoted the idea of a brand-new constitution supported by a strong consensus of all political parties. Bhutto wanted the new constitution to provide for a strong central government. He skillfully led the campaign in the National Assembly for a new constitution, and both his PPP delegates and the opposition compromised on the terms. Bhutto compromised by settling for a parliamentary system rather than a presidential one. On April 10, 1973, Pakistan's National Assembly unanimously adopted Pakistan's Third Constitution. Overseeing the creation of this Constitution of 1973 was one of Bhutto's greatest achievements. This Constitution still governs Pakistan today.

The Constitution was the first to concentrate the entire executive power in a prime minister. The prime minister would be elected by a majority vote of the National Assembly, and would hold office for up to five years or until a vote of "no confidence" was passed. The president would be relegated to a figurehead "head of state." For the first time, there would be a two-chamber national legislature—a National Assembly and a Senate. The National Assembly could amend the Constitution by a two-thirds vote. The prime minister could dissolve the National Assembly. The prime minister would appoint the provincial governors, who were required to act on the advice of their chief ministers—who would really run the provinces. The Constitution also provided that every five years, the president would appoint a National Financial Commission (NFC) which would decide on a formula of resource-sharing between the central government and each of the provinces. The Constitution provided that no judge could be removed except by a vote of the Supreme Judicial Council.[32] The Constitution declared that Pakistan was to be called the "Islamic Republic of Pakistan," and declared Islam to be the country's religion. Only a Muslim could become President. It provided for a Council of Islamic Ideology (CII), which was to recommend to parliament which laws should be enacted (or should be repealed)—depending on whether they conformed to Islam.

7. Zulfikar Bhutto's Missed Opportunity

The Third Constitution would be more durable than its two predecessors, because it had been adopted in a fair manner by elected representatives, and it was supported by all political parties. It would become the bedrock of Pakistan's future governments.

Having succeeded in getting parliament to pass a new constitution, Zulfikar Bhutto now turned to securing another difficult goal—persuading India to release the 90,000 POWs still in its custody. Bhutto realized that getting the POWs released would require delicate handling, since India was adamant that it wouldn't release the POWs until Pakistan first recognized Bangladesh. He also knew that most Pakistanis were firmly opposed to recognizing this new nation which had once been Pakistan's East wing.

Bhutto patiently began carrying out a long-range, two-part plan to free the POWs. The first part of the plan was to persuade the National Assembly to pass a resolution giving him discretion to recognize Bangladesh whenever he deemed the time to be appropriate. This part of the plan was achieved on July 3, 1973, when the Assembly gave Bhutto that discretionary authority. Bhutto decided to delay carrying out the second part of his plan—recognizing Bangladesh—until such time as he believed that Pakistan's people were more receptive to recognizing Bangladesh.

On August 14, 1973, Zulfikar Bhutto was sworn in as prime minister under the new Constitution, and he anticipated governing Pakistan for many terms. He would gradually increase his powers by having the National Assembly enact constitutional amendments which would slowly chip away at the constitution's checks and balances. He would implement many of his reforms through ordinances, which the National Assembly willingly passed with little discussion. The Opposition expressed its dissatisfaction with Bhutto's reforms by criticism, walkouts and street demonstrations.[33] He would govern Pakistan with such firmness that he would be nicknamed the "Imperial Prime Minister."

Having been appointed prime minister under a constitution, Bhutto knew he could rest easy on his democratic credentials for at least a year or two. He felt that with his new powers and with the support of the adoring masses, he no longer needed the support of the PML, NAP or other opposition parties. He soon began refusing to cooperate with his opponents, and he even began needlessly insulting them in public.

On January 1, 1974, Bhutto's regime continued its nationalizations of Pakistani businesses. This time it nationalized Pakistan's banks, petroleum distributors and maritime shippers. Nationalizing banks was particularly risky, since the bureaucrats who took over their management had no banking expertise, were mainly interested in making a profit, and weren't adequately regulated.[34] This new wave of nationalizations further convinced Pakistan's major corporate owners that the country was not a safe place to conduct business. Many investors and large corporations departed to other countries, causing Pakistan's economic growth to further stagnate.

Prime Minister Zulfikar Bhutto now believed that the time had come when the people would finally be willing to accept the reality that Bangladesh was an independent nation. Therefore, on February 21, 1974, Bhutto announced that Pakistan officially recognized Bangladesh—exercising the authority given to him by the National Assembly. Bhutto had Pakistan recognize Bangladesh's independence only as a means to secure the release of Pakistan's POWs. Pakistan's recognition of Bangladesh independence was soon followed by the return to Pakistan of its 78,000 soldiers and paramilitary personnel and 12,000 civilians. Most of the released army POWs returned to military service, and so the Pakistan Army's strength returned to its pre-war 300,000 level. Bhutto's popularity improved with the POW release, since he had persistently and skillfully worked for their release. With the return of the POWs, Bhutto saw less need to be deferential with India, and he began focusing his attention on trying to recover all of Kashmir.

On February 22, 1974, a worldwide Islamic Summit Conference convened in Pakistan's city of Lahore (the "Lahore Conference"). Bhutto had organized the conference in order to improve Pakistan's stature in the Muslim world. It was attended by 30 leaders from Muslim countries—the largest gathering ever of Muslim world leaders. The delegates exuded confidence and a new spirit of Muslim solidarity. They were united in condemnation of Israel, and they were optimistic since Muslim oil-producing countries in OPEC now were setting world oil prices.

While Prime Minister Bhutto had been instrumental in enacting the Constitution of 1973, within a year of its passage he began amending that Constitution in order to increase his own powers. He was able to amend the Constitution because he controlled two-thirds of the votes in the National Assembly needed to approve constitutional amendments. On May 8, 1974, the Assembly enacted the First Amendment to the Constitution. This allowed the federal government to ban political parties "operating in a manner prejudicial to the sovereignty or integrity of Pakistan." The vague wording of the amendment could be used by Bhutto to justify his banning any political party, and it set a dangerous precedent. Bhutto would continue amending the Constitution to enhance his own power, although each amendment would weaken the strength of the Constitution itself.

Bhutto Moves to the Right

On July 3, 1974, Prime Minister Zulfikar Bhutto abruptly removed J.A. Rahim from his cabinet for having vehemently accused Bhutto of destroying

7. Zulfikar Bhutto's Missed Opportunity

party identity and morale.[35] Rahim had been one of the PPP's founders. The angry Bhutto dismissed the elderly Rahim from the meeting. Later he sent an FSF unit to his home to deliver a message. A scuffle developed during which Rahim was savagely beaten.[36] Bhutto's crude dismissal and beating of the elderly PPP founder prompted many PPP leaders to resign. The PPP never would be the same.

Bhutto's removal of Rahim marked the start of his shift to the conservative right and the start of a decline in his popularity. He no longer would support progressive reforms to benefit the masses. Bhutto would continue dismissing PPP leaders until all six PPP founders had been dismissed or pressured to resign. He replaced them with wealthy landowners, whom he could count on to secure the votes of farmhands and sharecroppers who worked on their lands.[37] In addition, Bhutto also tightened his control over the PPP by personally appointing all PPP Party office holders.

The PPP broke into several factions, with each having its own leader—each protected by his own personal security detail. With the PPP weakening, AL leader Wali Khan, the leader of the Opposition in the National Assembly, stepped up his public criticisms of Bhutto and his demands for holding elections. Wali Khan further embarrassed President Bhutto by having the opposition walk out of the Assembly whenever the president rose to speak. Wali Khan also organized public meetings during which he strongly attacked Bhutto, and which police and FSF units routinely broke up.[38]

Bhutto also ended his commitment to leading a tolerant secular government. He supported the enactment of the Second Amendment to the Constitution of 1973, which the National Assembly passed on September 7, 1974. This amendment targeted the unpopular Ahmadi Muslim sect. While not mentioning the Ahmadis by name, it defined a non–Muslim as one who didn't believe in the absolute finality of the Prophet Muhammad, or who recognized a prophet after Muhammad. Since the Ahmadis were followers of a man who claimed to be a later prophet of Islam, Ahmadis legally became non–Muslims. They no longer legally could observe Muslim rituals or hold government or military positions.[39] Bhutto took other measures to appease the Islamists, including government funding of religious schools, standardizing the printing of the Koran, and subsidizing the travel of Pakistan's Muslim pilgrims to Saudi Arabia.[40]

Bhutto's turn to the right led to more PPP veteran resignations. On October 22, 1974, Mubashar Hassan resigned as Bhutto's finance minister. Mubashar had led the PPP ultra-leftist faction, which had pushed through nationalizations and other progressive economic reforms. With Mubashar gone, Bhutto's government made economic decisions with no central planning. Instead, for the next three years, his regime spent its development funds haphazardly, with no single person or agency overseeing overall spending.[41]

Bhutto officials authorized projects, while Bhutto personally supported his own "grand projects" to gain voter popularity. The government couldn't afford all the development programs that were being started, and it soon would borrow great sums from abroad to complete them.[42]

Bhutto's suppression of his critics turned more and more violent. He was particularly annoyed by public criticisms of his regime made by the gadfly politician Ahmad Raza Kasuri. On November 10, 1974, assassins ambushed the car of this anti–Bhutto gadfly—the third attempt on his life. While the shooter missed hitting the young Kasuri, a bullet from an automatic weapon struck and killed his aged father who had been sitting beside him. The young Kasuri went to the National Assembly, accused Bhutto of having ordered the ambush, and waved his father's bloody shirt for all to see. Many believed that Bhutto had ordered his FSF thugs to assassinate Kasuri.[43] Years later, after Bhutto had been removed from office, Bhutto would be prosecuted for having conspired to murder the elderly Kasuri.

Bhutto's violent suppression of political opponents continued. On February 8, 1975, Bhutto's trusted lieutenant Sharpao was assassinated when plastic explosives detonated under his lectern while he was delivering a speech. Bhutto suspected that Wali Khan and his NAP party might have been involved. Bhutto used this killing as a pretext for arresting Wali Khan and NAP leaders, banning the NAP, and seizing its assets.

Pakistan's Breakthrough in Atom Bomb Development

In May 1974, India surprised the world by conducting a hot underground nuclear test, making it the world's sixth nuclear power. The Indian test shook Pakistan's confidence in its own defenses. The United States was upset with India for its unauthorized nuclear test, but didn't impose sanctions on India. Bhutto gained popularity by immediately declaring that Pakistan would not succumb to India's "nuclear blackmail," and that it would develop its own "Islamic bomb" to deter an Indian invasion.

President Zulfikar Bhutto had become disappointed at the lack of progress that Pakistan's scientists had been making in enriching uranium for use in building a nuclear bomb. These scientists had been using the plutonium method for enrichment, while involved reprocessing spent nuclear fuel from nuclear power plants. However, Bhutto's spirits revived when he met Pakistani A.Q. Khan in mid–December 1974. Khan had been working for the Dutch FDO company, which was part of a URENCO multi-national project to enrich uranium using centrifuges. A.Q. Khan had been stealing the latest designs for constructing centrifuges, which was a quicker way of enriching uranium than the plutonium method. A.Q. Khan convinced Bhutto to use his stolen enrichment secrets to accelerate Pakistan's uranium enrichment, and use the enriched uranium to make a nuclear bomb. Bhutto asked Khan to return to the Netherlands to steal more plans.[44] A.Q. Khan returned to work for his Dutch employer.[45]

On December 15, 1975, A.Q. Khan departed the Netherlands for the last time. He took with him his family and three large suitcases stuffed with centrifuge designs, instructions, manuals and supplier lists.[46] He immediately joined Pakistan's PAEC atomic energy agency. Bhutto now ordered the PAEC to continue its plutonium enrichment program in full view. However, at the same time he authorized A.Q. Khan to secretly proceed with the centrifuge method of uranium enrichment using his stolen technology. This method not only would produce enriched uranium more quickly, but also would be easier to conceal from foreign inspectors.

Pakistan's atomic bomb program began in earnest on July 31, 1976, when Bhutto signed a secret order establishing A.Q. Khan's centrifuge enrichment program ("Project 706"). Khan began constructing a facility in isolated Kahuta, 40 miles southwest of Islamabad. Army Chief Zia Khan would help build the facility and would provide security once the site was completed. Khan proved to be an excellent manager and taskmaster. He recruited excellent foreign scientists and technicians to come to Pakistan by offering unmatched salaries and good working conditions.[47] To secure centrifuges and parts, A.Q. Khan initially relied on lists of suppliers that he had stolen from URENCO, and he soon set up an impressive procurement network. His procurement efforts were indirectly assisted by greedy private foreign companies, their governments and lax customs officials—whose obsolete rules didn't even forbid shipping centrifuge parts.[48] To speed up uranium enrichment, Khan connected centrifuges together into "cascades," with each centrifuge producing a higher grade of enriched uranium. After running and rerunning the uranium through enough cascades, weapons grade enriched uranium was finally produced.

The Lull Before the Storm in Kashmir

Despite the seriousness of the Kashmir fighting which had provoked two Indo-Pak wars, India had continued with its provocative moves to fully integrate into India the territory that it had seized in Kashmir. To soften these moves, on February 25, 1975, India brought back the popular Sheikh Mohammed Abdullah (the "Lion of Kashmir") to rule IJK as chief minister. India allowed Abdullah to take office only after he had agreed that IJK was part of India. A period of stability in IJK set in and there followed several years of fragile peace in the IJK. Sheikh Abdullah would retain his office for seven more years until his death.

This fragile peace in the IJK was threatened when Sheikh Abdullah died of a heart attack on September 8, 1982. Abdullah had been the dominant political leader in Kashmir for 50 years and had personified Kashmir's independence movement. The Sheikh's eldest son Farooq (the "Lion Cub") succeeded his father as IJK's chief minister and took over the Kashmir independence movement. However, Farooq never would be as popular or powerful as his father. He was regarded by many to be a lightweight political dilettante. However, Farooq and a new generation of young Kashmir activists did keep alive the independence movement in IJK, and thereby forced India to keep 100,000 troops deployed inside IJK to guard its Kashmir territorial claims.

The "Lion Cub" Farooq would remain IJK's chief minister for a year and a half. Then Indian Prime Minister Indira Gandhi had the "Lion Cub" dismissed in July 1984 for meddling in India's politics. However, Indira Gandhi was assassinated in October 1984, and her son Rejiv Gandhi succeeded her as prime minister. In November 1986, Rejiv allowed Farooq to return as IJK's chief minister after Farooq agreed to be more cooperative with India.[49] Farooq's sudden return as IJK's chief minister in exchange for his acceptance of Indian control subjected him to widespread scorn in the Kashmir Valley inside IJK. Many Kashmiri anti–Indian insurgency groups condemned Farooq as a cowardly Indian puppet, and they took control of the anti–Indian insurgency in Kashmir. Some of the insurgent groups would even try to assassinate the hated "Lion Cub."

Choosing a New Army Chief

Prime ministers had authority to choose the leader of Pakistan's army—the "Army Chief." This was always a critical appointment since an army chief was in an excellent position to lead a military coup if he wanted. So when General Tikka Khan's term as Army Chief expired, Bhutto carefully vetted senior generals when filling the vacancy. On March 1, 1976, Bhutto selected General Zia Haq to be his new army chief. He chose him because Zia appeared to be a harmless, obedient sycophant with no political ambitions. Zia seemed to want to focus on modernizing the army. Bhutto also chose Zia because he believed that Zia would be so grateful for his having appointed him over eight more senior generals that he would strictly carry out his orders. In addition, Zia had made a good impression on Bhutto during the Attock Conspiracy court-martial.[50]

At first it appeared that Zia had been a good choice. Zia followed Bhutto's orders and largely didn't question his actions. Zia's humble and obsequious deference to Bhutto led Bhutto to lower his guard. However, it turned out that Zia had secret ambitions and a ruthlessness which he cleverly hid behind a mask of civility and cooperation. Zia would end up leading a coup to overthrow Bhutto.

To bolster his chances of success in the upcoming elections, Prime Minister Bhutto continued with his nationalization programs. On July 17, 1976, Bhutto took over the management of some 4,000 privately owned businesses in the agricultural sector, such as rice mills and cotton-ginning plants. Bhutto claimed that these "middlemen" were exploiting the people and were responsible for the struggling economy. However, since Bhutto turned over the management of these mills to wealthy landowners, these nationalizations primarily benefited these landowners instead of the people.[51] The program also was economically impractical, since taking over thousands of tiny rice mills (some in people's backyards) proved to be unworkable. Thousands of these relatively poor entrepreneurs joined the anti–Bhutto opposition.

Pakistan's good relations with China suffered a setback on September 9, 1976, when China's leader Mao Tse-Tung died. Mao had been China's strongest supporter of Pakistan, and after his death, Sino-Pak relations never would be the same. However, China still remained a good Pakistani ally, and it honored the commitments that Mao had made to Pakistan.

Zulfikar Bhutto continued to try to broaden the PPP's popularity in preparation for the upcoming elections by enacting more labor reforms. On January 4, 1977, he announced some modest reforms, including increasing worker salaries. The next day Bhutto announced dramatic new land reforms, which further reduced the amount of land that a Pakistani could own from 150 acres of irrigated land to 100 acres. He said that the excess land would be distributed to tenants and other landless farmers.

Bhutto Wins a Rigged Election

Prime ministers had the power to schedule national elections, providing that at least two-months' notice were given. Using this power, on January 7, 1977, Prime Minister Zulfikar Bhutto suddenly announced that National Assembly elections would be held in just two months. Bhutto wasn't required to call elections at that time, but he did so because he was confident of victory, he hoped to catch his opponents off guard, and he wanted to secure a fresh mandate to reverse his declining popularity. He wanted an overwhelming victory to show that he was Pakistan's undisputed leader of the entire country.[52] He also hoped to win two-thirds of the seats in the National Assembly, which would allow him to increase his powers through new constitutional amendments.

Bhutto had good reason to be confident of victory. First, his scheduling the elections on short notice gave Bhutto a big advantage. While the opposition would have trouble finding suitable candidates on such short notice, Bhutto had quietly been preparing hard for his reelection. Also, Bhutto was Pakistan's dominant leader and he had an experienced campaign organization. He had jailed most of the opposition leaders and he controlled the media. In addition, the economy had recovered and his recent labor and land reforms had given the poorer classes even more reason to support him. Bhutto encouraged his lieutenants to take strong (but unspecified) measures to ensure a landslide victory in every province.[53]

Bhutto's opponents were indeed ill-prepared by Bhutto's surprise election announcement. However, they hurriedly formed an ad hoc Pakistan National Alliance (PNA) of all major anti–Bhutto parties. The PNA was able to run a credible campaign because its members were highly motivated. They realized that Bhutto wanted to secure two-thirds of National Assembly seats so he could amend the Constitution to further enlarge his powers.

The first sign that Pakistanis had that the election would be fraudulent came on January 19, 1977—the deadline for candidate filing for office. Bhutto claimed that PPP candidates already had won 18 National Assembly seats because they faced no opposition.[54] The public couldn't believe that the PNA would have neglected to file for any of these seats, and in fact Bhutto's regime had forcibly prevented some opposition candidates from running for office.[55] Bhutto's claims of 18 default victories discredited the whole election even before the campaigning had begun.

On March 7, 1977, Pakistan began its two-day National Assembly elections, during which 17 million voters cast ballots out of 31 million eligible voters. The vigorous PNA campaign and the lack of opinion polls had misled the PPP into thinking that it would be a very close election. Therefore, Bhutto's eager lieutenants, without informing Bhutto, engaged in massive election-day misconduct to assure a comfortable Bhutto victory.[56] The evidence of massive election fraud was obvious to everyone. There were numerous reports of people voting multiple times, and pre-marked ballots were found in the streets. Some polling places had closed for hours while ballot boxes were removed at gunpoint. Furthermore, election returns showed huge PPP victories even in some PNA strongholds.[57]

The final vote tally showed the PPP winning 136 seats in the National Assembly, compared to just 36 seats for the PNA. This gave Bhutto more than the two-thirds majority of Assembly seats he needed to amend the constitution. He probably would have won handily in a fair election, and the people probably would have accepted a PPP election victory had it been by a reasonable margin. However, the people were unwilling to tolerate such obvious massive rigging.

Bhutto Mishandles the Rigging Backlash

There were several reasons why Zulfikar Bhutto wouldn't survive the uproar that the massive vote rigging had provoked. First, for years Bhutto had been offending the opposition parties with his insults and with his refusal to work with them. They were in no mood to work out a settlement. Also, Bhutto would mishandle the backlash to the massive rigging. Instead of quickly admitting the fraud and offering the opposition a reasonable settlement, he delayed his offers in the hope of securing better terms. Finally, Bhutto's FSF paramilitary force declined to forcibly suppress the anti-Bhutto rioting. This reluctance to face the rioters was likely because the FSF troops were not being fully paid, and because army infiltrators into the FSF had persuaded many to abandon their posts.[58]

The day after the election results were announced, the PNA declared that it rejected the results. It demanded that Bhutto resign and that new elections be held under neutral oversight. While Bhutto refused to resign, he did offer to give the PNA 35 to 40 more seats in the National Assembly to compensate for the seats that Bhutto's lieutenants confided that they had rigged.[59] However, the PNA rejected this offer and refused to compromise. There is some evidence that Zia and the ISI may have secretly given conflicting advice to Bhutto and the PNA in order to prevent the two sides from reaching a compromise.[60] The PNA believed that millions of voters, disgusted by the massive rigging, might change their votes if a totally new election were held. The PNA announced a boycott of the provincial assembly elections which were scheduled to take place two days later. Bhutto's refusal to postpone these provincial elections was a mistake, since these elections also were massively rigged, and they further discredited the elections.

Bhutto's troubles increased when on March 11, 1977, a PNA-called nationwide strike began to protest the election fraud. The PNA followed up with a series of rolling strikes and demonstrations. Bhutto was unable to suppress these nationwide disorders since the police and Bhutto's FSF paramilitary troops initially were unwilling to shoot unarmed demonstrators.

Bhutto kept making more mistakes in handling the rigging's backlash. First, he refused to hold totally new elections because he was too proud and stubborn to surrender to the PNA demands.[61] Also, Bhutto was exhausted and he dreaded the prospect of conducting a whole new election campaign. Instead of compromising, on March 25 Bhutto had the PNA president and some 10,000 PNA protestors arrested. This was a turning point in the PPP-PNA conflict, since the arrests provoked larger and more violent demonstrations. The police—forced to confront larger and more violent crowds—began firing live rounds into the crowds to protect themselves. Several demonstrators were killed.

On April 22, 1977, Prime Minister Zulfikar Bhutto imposed "limited martial law" in five cities and asked Army Chief Zia to regain control in these cities. Bhutto knew there were risks in taking these measures, but he was confident that he could control the obedient Zia and the army. Zia fully complied with his call for help. Once these five cities were under military control the protests subsided. Subsequent PNA calls for new massive demonstrations were largely ignored.

By now, both Bhutto and the PNA had become tired of the deadlock and had become concerned that over 300 innocent civilians had died in the violence. They were also concerned that some 30,000 PNA supporters were in jail and that soldiers controlled most major cities. Therefore, after meeting with Zia, Bhutto ordered the release of the PNA leaders whom he had jailed. The PNA suspended their protests. On June 3, 1977, Bhutto and PNA leaders began negotiating in earnest. On June 15, a tentative agreement was reached calling for new elections, with details to be worked out by subordinates.[62] However, in the middle of these negotiations, Bhutto suddenly left on a five-nation tour of Muslim countries before a final agreement was reached.

On June 23, 1977, Bhutto returned from his overseas tour, and on July 3, the PPP-PNA negotiators reached a final agreement. However, Bhutto delayed signing the agreement, despite warnings by military leaders that he should sign immediately. This was a huge mistake.

On July 4, 1977, Army Chief Zia called a meeting of senior army officers. He disclosed to them a plan to overthrow Bhutto's government. Zia had not developed this plan. Rather it was the army's mid-level officers of colonels and majors who had been planning to remove Bhutto, who they claimed was dividing the nation for his own selfish purposes. They also resented Bhutto's use of the army to suppress political opposition. These officers pressured Zia to join their plot. Zia realized that these officers would carry out their coup with or without him. He realized that if he didn't join them, he would be removed too and the army's integrity and chain of command would suffer.[63] Zia also may have been influenced by Bhutto's having reportedly embarrassed and insulted Zia in public for years.[64]

On July 5, 1977, at 1:30 a.m., General Zia Haq seized control of the government from Zulfikar Bhutto. Zia sought to justify his coup on grounds that the PPP-PNA talks had broken down and so the country was moving toward civil war. However, actually the PPP and PNA had been within hours of signing an agreement.

Zulfikar Bhutto's rule was over, but during his rule he had left an impressive legacy. First, when he first had taken office, he had lifted the battered nation's spirits right after its crushing defeat by the Indian Army and Pakistan's loss of its East wing. He had skillfully arranged the return of the 90,000 troops in Indian POW camps. Also, he was Pakistan's first leader who

7. Zulfikar Bhutto's Missed Opportunity

had ever championed Pakistan's downtrodden masses, and he had made these groups aware of their voting power. In addition, he had developed Pakistan's first grassroots popular political party, and he had initiated the first sustained period of democratic rule. Also, Bhutto had skillfully persuaded the diverse political parties to join in writing Pakistan's only constitution that had been approved by representatives of the people. In addition, he had greatly advanced Pakistan's atomic bomb development by recognizing A.Q. Khan's unique abilities and placing him in charge of uranium enrichment using centrifuges.

However, Bhutto's legacy had been tarnished during the later years of his rule by his growing desire to increase his own power. First, he had squandered a real opportunity for Pakistan to develop a true democratic tradition. He had abandoned the PPP's lofty goals of helping the downtrodden and creating a democratic system. He had turned to the right and had restored the dominance of wealthy landowners. Also, he had suppressed the political opposition and had treated them so badly that they had little interest in compromising with him. In addition, he had failed to allow the provinces to govern themselves, and he had seized control of several elected provincial governments. Also, his lack of central control over development projects had led to so much government spending that the national debt doubled.

8

General Zia and the Death of Bhutto

During the two and a half years covered by this chapter (July 1977–December 1979), General Zia worked hard to eliminate his key rival, Zulfikar Bhutto. Zia would have Bhutto prosecuted, convicted and executed for conspiracy to murder. Then Zia would set up a system of "local bodies" to give his regime the illusion of democracy. The chapter ends with the Soviet invasion of Afghanistan.

General Zia Sets Up a Military Dictatorship

On July 5, 1977, General Zia-ul-Haq overthrew Prime Minister Zulfikar Bhutto's civilian government and imposed martial law. Zia retained his position as army chief and he also became the powerful Chief Martial Law Administrator (CMLA). He dissolved the national and the provincial assemblies, and fired all federal and provincial governors. To give the illusion that he was operating within the law, he only "suspended" the Constitution instead of abolishing it. He also retained Fazal Chaudhry as president, allowed political parties to operate, and allowed the Supreme Court to continue to function. He wasn't worried about the Supreme Court's challenging him since he had retained the power to dismiss and appoint the justices. Zia immediately placed Bhutto under house arrest and abolished the office of prime minister—which would stay vacant for the next eight years. He shut down Bhutto's FSF paramilitary force and arrested its leader. Zia would pressure them to divulge their most deplorable acts and implicate Bhutto in most of them.

8. General Zia and the Death of Bhutto

Pakistan would be run by a Zia-led military junta of senior officers, surrounded by active and retired officers and civilian specialists in the federal ministries. The military would run the country through the junta command headquarters.[1] Over the years, Zia gained the respect of the junta due to his hard work, his austere lifestyle, and his pious Muslim practices. Zia would become the buffer that the junta needed to protect itself, and so Zia gradually took over the junta's leadership.[2]

Zia gave his first speech to the nation on the day he seized power. He told the people that the army had stepped in "temporarily" because the civilian political coalitions had failed to compromise and so were moving the country into chaos. He stated that my "sole aim is to organize free and fair elections" and to introduce an Islamic system to Pakistan. He assured his audience that new national elections would take place within three months. However, whatever may have been his initial intentions, Zia soon decided that he would rule the country by himself. While Zia continued to schedule elections, he would continually postpone them. He would claim that the postponements were necessary to give the military time to unite the country by transitioning it to a new Islamic order.[3]

Zia had several strengths. First, he had a quick, intelligent mind and he would be very inventive in trying to solve problems. He was reasonably well-informed. Also, he was very cautious, patient and politically gifted. Also, Zia had a quiet, polite, self-effacing manner. He would live in a modest residence on a military base for most of his rule. The people initially were impressed with this "simple" humble soldier, who seemed reluctant to hold power and seemed only interested in restoring national unity and stability. In addition, Zia was a good administrator who knew how to delegate responsibility. Also, Zia was genuinely religious. The public knew that he prayed often and scrupulously observed Islamic rituals. This image helped him gain the support of Islamic fundamentalists.

However, Zia had many weaknesses. First, he had no experience in politics or running a government. He had no training or interest in economics, and he would blindly reverse Bhutto's economic socialist policies merely because Bhutto had adopted them. Also, Zia would prove to be a coldly calculating, ruthless, widely disliked man. He would severely regulate political parties and would refuse to allow elections. In addition, while Zia himself wasn't corrupt, he would ignore the rampant corruption of his officials, relatives and close friends. Also, Zia hated India, and his refusal to make peace with this neighbor weakened Pakistan's ability to strengthen its own economy. Finally, Zia would have no interest in helping the downtrodden masses improve their well-being. He claimed that the government didn't need to do more for the poor, since they could be taken care of by the voluntary Muslim zakat taxes collected for the needy.[4]

General Zia used a number of techniques which would allow him to rule Pakistan for 11 years—the longest rule of any of Pakistan's military dictators. First, he would work hard to gain the support of Pakistan's generals. He would run the country as head of a military junta which he constantly consulted. He also would give his senior generals money and land of unprecedented value—leading to a new crop of millionaire generals.[5] He also would make sure that the military received a large share of the national budget. In addition, he would maintain firm control over these generals through his authority as army chief. He would appoint the generals to fixed terms and rotated their job assignments and duty stations to prevent any from accumulating excessive power. Also, Zia didn't initiate any reforms which might antagonize large segments of the population.[6] Also, Zia would make sure that the country's powerful industrialists retained their privileged position. He would return to private ownership many of the companies that Bhutto had nationalized. He also would arrange for large, low-interest loans for a few favored wealthy businessmen—loans which were not expected to be repaid.[7] In addition, Zia would exploit the religious susceptibilities of the masses. He claimed that his regime was Islamic and that opposing his "Islamic government" in itself would be un-Islamic. Also, Zia would exercise tight control over the media—mainly by threatening anti-Zia journalists and editors. He also would prosecute hostile journalists in special courts and would subject some to public floggings and torture.[8]

At first, the people enjoyed Zia's rule since he had restored peace and stability. Pakistanis could relax—as long as they didn't engage in politics. Most Pakistanis didn't regret the disappearance of the discredited civilian politicians, whose only goal seemed to be to win office without bothering to try to solve the country's problems. Also, the people had lived under military rule several times before and so easily made the adjustment. However, the people eventually would turn against Zia as he became the most repressive dictator in Pakistan's history.

Two Persons, One Grave

Zia spent his first two years in power trying to secure cover for his illegal seizure of power and to deal with his rival Zulfikar Bhutto. When Zia overthrew Zulfi Bhutto, he immediately placed him in a special cottage under "protective custody." When Zia met with Bhutto on July 12, he had not yet decided how to deal with Bhutto. He wouldn't decide to have Bhutto killed until he determined that his rival remained a serious challenge to Zia's rule.[9] At this meeting, Zia continued to treat the former prime minister with deference, and implied that he might soon set Bhutto free. Bhutto was still taken in

8. General Zia and the Death of Bhutto

by Zia's deceptive submissive manners, and Bhutto unwisely maintained his arrogant and threatening manner toward Zia.[10]

General Zia released Bhutto from the rest house on July 28. He believed that Bhutto's PPP had lost so much support due to the recent election rigging scandal that the pro-army PNA could defeat him in the upcoming elections. However, once Bhutto was released, Bhutto immediately went on a triumphant tour, attracting wildly cheering crowds. He told the crowds that he would punish Zia for his misdeeds. Zia was shocked at Bhutto's defiance, and he quickly realized his mistake in releasing Bhutto. Zia concluded that Bhutto remained a formidable rival as long as Bhutto lived. As some put it, there were "two persons and one grave."

Zia now began planning how to permanently eliminate Bhutto while making it appear that Zia had nothing to do with his death. Zia's plan was to have a court convict Bhutto of conspiracy to murder, let Bhutto's inevitable appeals run their course, and then refuse to commute the death sentence. The whole process could last several years, but the patient Zia was willing to wait.

Zia moved cautiously with his plan. On September 3, 1977, Zia had Zulfikar Bhutto arrested on the charge of conspiracy to murder the father of the gadfly Kasuri, whose car had been ambushed three years earlier. The prosecution's charge may have been justified, since Bhutto had been ruthless in dealing with his enemies and may have ordered Kasuri's assassination. However, ten days after his arrest, Bhutto was released on bail by the civilian judge.

Zia was angry at Bhutto's release, and on September 17, he had Bhutto rearrested—this time under martial law authority with no possibility of bail. Bhutto was charged again of having conspired to murder Kasuri's father. He was placed in a tiny dark cell and Bhutto for the first time realized that Zia never would allow him to go free.

Zia took several measures to insure that Bhutto would be convicted, sentenced to death and executed. First, Zia arranged to have the case heard by pro–Zia judges without a jury.[11] Zia also had the ISI pressure the judges hearing the case to rule against Bhutto, and witnesses were pressured to testify against him.[12] Also, Zia would pack the Supreme Court with loyalists, to prevent it from overturning Bhutto's inevitable lower court conviction. Finally, while the trial was pending, Zia would conduct an extensive publicity campaign exposing Bhutto's misconduct while he had been in office—hoping this would reduce the public's anger after Bhutto had been executed.

With Zulfikar Bhutto secure in jail, Zia decided to hold national elections. He authorized national elections to be held on October 18. However, when the election campaigning began on September 18, Zia was startled when

Zulfikar Bhutto's wife Nusrat, and his daughter Benazir, began campaigning on behalf of the jailed Zulfikar. The two Bhuttos were attracting huge crowds. Therefore, on October 1, fearful that Bhutto's PPP might win, Zia postponed the elections. He claimed that the country needed more time to repair the damage that had been done during Bhutto's rule. This was Zia's first of many election postponements, and Zia, who held the position of CMLA, would become known as "Cancel My Last Announcement Zia." Zia would keep postponing elections throughout his rule.

On October 24, 1977, Zulfikar Bhutto's non-jury trial began in Lahore. During the five-month trial, the prosecution's key witness was Bhutto's former FSF chief General Masood Mahmood. Mahmood had been granted immunity in return for his agreeing to testify that Bhutto had ordered him to assassinate the gadfly Kasuri. The pro–Zia trial judges convicted Bhutto on the conspiracy to murder charge. Bhutto appealed the conviction to a Lahore High Court panel of judges, which upheld the trial court's decision and sentenced Bhutto to death. The panel reached its conclusion despite the prosecution's having only offered weak evidence to prove his guilt.[13] Bhutto appealed that decision to the Supreme Court.

While Bhutto's appeals were being decided, Bhutto's supporters filed a lawsuit challenging Zia's declaration of martial law. Zia was confident of success when the Supreme Court took up this case, since he had appointed many loyalists to that court. Therefore, nobody was surprised when on November 10, 1977, the Court upheld Zia's imposition of martial law. The Court based its decision on the "law of necessity"—reasoning that it had been "necessary" for Zia to impose martial law in order to avert a civil war following Bhutto's rigged elections.

On January 1, 1978, American President Jimmy Carter visited India, but didn't stop in neighboring Pakistan. Carter's failure to visit Pakistan reflected Carter's condemnation of Zia's human rights abuses and his condemnation of Pakistan's nuclear weapons program. Carter's refusal to visit Pakistan marked a low point in Pak-American relations.

President Carter's concerns over Zia's human rights abuses were justified. On January 2, Pakistani troops attacked striking workers at the Colony Textile Mill in Multan—a mill owned by one of Zia's friends. Zia ordered the strike crushed when he heard a rumor that the strikers planned to attack a wedding reception scheduled soon for the mill owner's daughter.[14] The soldiers locked the mill's gates and fired down from the roof on the trapped workers below, killing over 200 of them. Many of the wounded died because the soldiers refused to let them be taken to a hospital for immediate treatment. The strikers had been planning to join the anti–Zia "Day of Democracy" scheduled for three days later.

When the PPP-called "Day of Democracy" was held on January 5,

8. General Zia and the Death of Bhutto

1978, Zia had thousands of PPP supporters arrested. Many were whipped for displaying PPP flags or for shouting "Long Live Democracy." Zia's harsh suppression of the protests made it clear that while Zia hadn't banned political parties, he wasn't going to allow them to openly demonstrate against him.

General Zia soon faced a crisis in neighboring Afghanistan. On April 27, 1978, communist military officers seized power from President Daoud and killed him and his family. Communist leader Noor Taraki took over Afghanistan's government. The communist takeover alarmed Pakistan's leaders, and so the ISI revived its "Afghan cell." The cell's primary function was to assist the Afghan anti-communist resistance, and it soon began training to attack Taraki's regime.

General Zia had been ruling Pakistan through his army junta, while allowing the pliable Chaudhary to serve as the figurehead president. When the elderly Chaudhary resigned on September 16, 1978, after his term had expired, Zia used his martial law powers to declare himself the new president. He would retain that position until his death, hoping that this position would add to the illusion that he headed a democratic government. However, Zia would continue to wear his army uniform, and his real power derived from his positions as army chief and CMLA.

Zia's plan to have Zulfikar Bhutto judicially executed moved ahead. On February 6, 1979, the Supreme Court upheld the Lahore High Court's decision that Bhutto was guilty of conspiracy to murder. The Supreme Court's 4-3 decision held that all the "errors" and "illegalities" in Bhutto's trial had been "irrelevant." However, the three dissenting judges rejected the evidence relied on as being "absurd." The Supreme Court unanimously recommended that Bhutto's death sentence be commuted to life imprisonment. However, in a major departure from precedent, Zia refused to commute the sentence.

President Zia finally eliminated his rival Zulfikar Bhutto on the night of April 4, 1979. Bhutto was executed just after his daughter Benazir visited his jail cell and promised to carry on his mission for a new Pakistan. After the execution, Zia gleefully announced to his colleagues: "the bastard's dead!" For many years thousands of Bhutto's supporters would walk long distances to the Bhutto family graveyard to pay him their respects.

There were several repercussions to Zulfikar Bhutto's execution. First, with his only serious rival dead, Zia now fully grasped his full powers and became convinced that it was his destiny to keep ruling Pakistan. Also, Bhutto's execution crippled the hopes that the military might allow a transition to civilian rule. In addition, Bhutto's death was followed by a steady decline in Zia's popularity. Bhutto's many supporters were angry that Zia had orchestrated the execution of their hero. Even Bhutto's enemies were appalled at Bhutto's unfair trial and Zia's refusal to commute his death sentence. Also, Bhutto's execution made Zulfikar Bhutto a martyr, and the Bhutto family name would continue to haunt Zia. Zulfikar Bhutto's daughter Benazir would carry on her father's fight against Zia. Bhutto's son Murtaza went into exile and formed the Al-Zulfikar (AZO) anti–Zia resistance group, which would try to assassinate Zia. The AZO received training from India's RAW and Afghanistan's KHAN intelligence agencies.[15]

Zia's Islamization of Pakistan

While Zia felt more confident after Zulfikar Bhutto's death, he still was concerned that the people might object to his denying them any input into his regime's decisions. However, he didn't want to risk offering direct elections, since the PPP party still might win elections despite Zulfi Bhutto's death. Zia decided that he would solve this dilemma by offering an indirect system of voting to give the masses the illusion of democracy. He set up a system of local council ("local bodies"). The local bodies would have no power in the junta-controlled government, although they were given limited responsibilities in local governance. For example, the 50,000 local councilors were given responsibility for local education, health, sanitation and agricultural production.[16]

On September 29, 1979, voting for "local bodies" began. Zia had forbidden candidates to identify their party affiliations on the ballots, in order to prevent the PPP from showing its strength. However, the PPP managed to reveal its power by describing each of its candidates as a "friend of the people." The PPP's ability to identify its candidates made Zia realize that it was too risky for him to allow direct elections.

Therefore, on October 16, Zia postponed Pakistan's national and provincial elections indefinitely. This began a new phase, with Zia's junta no longer acting as a temporary body which tolerated the politicians. Instead, Zia banned all political parties, strikes and public gatherings. He prohibited anyone from criticizing the army in any way. He also began requiring newspapers to submit pre-publication proofs for his regime's approval. Zia jailed Zulfi Bhutto's widow Nusrat and her daughter Benazir, and he wouldn't release them for seven months.

Having failed in his attempt to win support of the masses through elections, Zia turned to gaining their support by making Pakistan more "Islamic." He would encourage Pakistan's Muslims to observe Islamic practices more strictly. Zia hoped that his "Islamization" program would increase his credibility among the people and would divert their attention from their poverty. Zia claimed that returning Pakistan to Islamic practices was necessary

8. General Zia and the Death of Bhutto

to restore the nation's moral fiber. He even claimed that Allah had given him the mission to Islamize Pakistan. He hoped that by mingling Islam with his regime, few would challenge his regime's legitimacy.

Zia's Islamization program would have many elements. First, Zia declared Pakistan to be an Islamic state, and he promoted Sunni Islam to the status of an official state ideology. Also, he appointed thousands of Islamists to government posts. He gave to tens of thousands of JI religious party members low-level government and judicial jobs, which would allow Zia's Islamist agenda to survive long after his death. In addition, Zia created a new legal code based on Islamic law—the "Hudood" ordinances. The ordinances restored strict Islamic offences and punishments, including public lashings for consuming alcohol, hand amputation for theft, and death by stoning for adultery.[17] Zia also decreed changes to Pakistan's penal code by broadening the definition of "blasphemy" to include defiling the Koran and making defamatory remarks about Muslim clerics.[18] Also, Zia had public school textbooks rewritten with a pro–Islamic, anti–Indian, anti–American historical slant.[19] In addition, Zia funded the building of thousands of new conservative religious schools (madrassas). Zia also replaced secular professors with JI religious party members in Pakistan's higher education institutions. In addition, Zia facilitated Islamists in becoming army officers by turning down for office training applicants who had weak religious beliefs.[20] He gave preference in army promotions to devout Islamist officers, regardless of their competence. Finally, Zia placed Islamist journalists in influential positions in state-controlled media, and assisted them in launching new Islamist newspapers and magazines.

Zia had hoped that his Islamization program would unite the country behind him, while keeping the religious leaders from gaining too much influence. For several reasons, these hopes would not materialize. First, most Pakistanis never accepted the government's intrusion into their daily religious life, and many were bitter at the conservative dress codes and public lashings for minor offenses. The women especially resented laws forbidding widows and other single women from holding jobs.[21] Women protested in the streets against Zia's harsh laws, and these protests began a battle for women's rights which would become a major part of an anti–Zia movement. Finally, Zia's Islamization didn't unify the country, but instead encouraged Sunnis and Shiites to mistrust each other.

Iran's Challenge to Pakistan

On November 6, 1979, Muslim cleric Ayatollah Khomeini seized power from Iran's provisional government in Iran and turned Iran into an Islamic state (the "Iranian Revolution"). Iran became the only Shiite Islamic state in the world. Iran's leaders wanted to spread the Shiite faith to neighboring Sunni Muslim states like Pakistan.[22] It also became the main protector and supporter of Shiites in Pakistan, Iraq, and other countries with significant Shiite populations.

The Iranian Revolution had several repercussions in Pakistan. First, Iran's mission to protect Shiite minorities overseas emboldened Pakistan's Shiites to resist Zia's Sunni laws which were marginalizing Shiites in the country. Also, Iran began funding Pakistan's Shiite political parties, mosques and madrassas. This Iranian support made Pakistan's Sunnis feel threatened by the Shiites. Sunni extremists began criticizing and attacking Pakistan's Shiites, setting up a deadly Sunni-Shiite conflict within the country.[23] In addition, with the removal of Iran's pro-western Shah, the United States lost its main ally in the region. Pakistan's leaders worried that since the United States had failed to prevent Iran's Shah from being overthrown, that America might be powerless to prevent a similar overthrow of Pakistan's government. Also, Khomeini's overthrow of the Shah convinced Muslim extremists that they could seize control of any country—even if that country were backed by a strong ally.

President Zia soon faced another crisis—this one involving the United States. On November 21, 1979, at noon, a group of radical Pakistani students spearheaded an attack on the American Embassy in Islamabad. The student attack had been organized by the Islamist JI religious party. The JI was reacting to a false rumor (spread by Zia) that Americans had been behind the recent attack on the Grand Mosque in the holy Saudi city of Mecca.[24] The JI bused over 600 students to the embassy. The student-led mob broke into the embassy, causing the embassy staff to lock themselves inside a steel communications vault. The mob, now joined by over 4,000 civilians, wrecked cars in the parking lot and set them on fire using gasoline drained from the vehicles. The mobs set fire to the compound's buildings.[25] Despite frantic calls for help from the trapped staff, Zia didn't order the army to rescue the trapped Americans until four hours later—after the embassy had burned to the ground. Four people died in the embassy fire, including two Americans. The United States was furious that Zia didn't seem to care whether the embassy burned down with its staff inside.[26] He was more worried about Islamist retaliation against him if he had the mob suppressed. While Zia later apologized to the Americans for the incident and funded the construction of a new embassy, Zia refused to punish the JI for its role in the attack.

There were several repercussions to the embassy attack. First, American relations with Pakistan reached an all-time low. Zia's idly standing by while the American Embassy burned destroyed America's image of Pakistan as a friendly ally. It also showed the Americans that Zia didn't have the desire to rein in Pakistan's Islamist extremists. Also, Zia's support within Pakistan's army plummeted, since army leaders were appalled that Zia had been unwilling to use force to keep order inside the capital.[27] Finally, the embassy burning and the feeble American protests which followed, demonstrated America's eroding power in the Muslim world.

9

The Soviets Invade Afghanistan

During the five-year period covered in this chapter (December 1979–February 1985), Soviet troops invaded Afghanistan. Zia would give substantial support to the Afghan Muslim mujahideen who fought the Soviet troops occupying their country. Zia would offer the mujahideen sanctuary and training, and he would cooperate with the Americans by delivering CIA weapons to the Afghan rebels. The chapter ends when Zia became Pakistan's president.

Brezhnev's "Christmas Present"

On December 25, 1979, Soviet troops invaded Afghanistan to stabilize Afghanistan's communist government and prevent it from being overthrown. Soviet leaders recently had installed Barbak Karmal to head the communist government in Kabul, and worried that anti-communist forces might remove him. They feared that an overthrow of the Afghan communist regime would encourage more countries to defect from the Soviet bloc.[1] Soviet Premier Brezhnev naively thought that a short Russian military intervention would prevent Islamic groups from overthrowing the struggling communist regime. The Soviets deployed 85,000 troops into Afghanistan—mainly in the Kabul region.

President Zia saw the Soviet invasion as a threat to Pakistan. First, it was a threat because if the Soviets took control of Afghanistan, they might invade neighboring Pakistan next. Also, Soviet control of Afghanistan would deprive Pakistan of a friendly Afghan government on its border. Zia believed that a friendly Afghan government was essential to Pakistan's protection, since it would provide it with "strategic depth" on its western border to counter India's threat on its eastern border.

Zia also considered the Soviet invasion as an opportunity—a "Christmas present" from Brezhnev. Zia predicted that if he supported a jihad ("holy war") against the "infidel" Soviets, he would gain popularity with Muslims at home, win American aid and gain international respect as a frontline state in the struggle against Soviet expansion.[2] He hoped to transform his image abroad from that of a brutal dictator into that of a "benevolent leader" who helped defeat the communist invaders.

President Zia's support was so critical to the Afghan mujahideen fighters that the Afghan-Soviet War would become known as "Zia's war." Zia supported the mujahideen in several ways. First, Zia would allow Pakistan to act as the prime conduit through which outside weapons could be distributed to the mujahideen. America's CIA would arrange for weapons to be shipped into Pakistan, and then Pakistan's ISI would transport them to the mujahideen inside Afghanistan. Zia would insist that he control the number and type of CIA-purchased weapons that entered Pakistan, since he worried that uncontrolled arms shipments might provoke Soviet leaders to carry out their threat to retaliate by invading Pakistan.[3] Zia would allow enough weapons shipments to the Afghan mujahideen to "keep the pot boiling," but not so much that the pot would "boil over." Also, Zia allowed Pakistan's western border regions to serve as a sanctuary for the Afghan mujahideen, with their headquarters in the NWFP capital of Peshawar. The mujahideen would use this secure base to rest, regroup and undergo ISI training.[4] In addition, Zia would allow over three million Afghan refugees to enter his country to escape the fighting. Also, Zia would construct hundreds of new religious schools (madrassas) in Pakistan. These schools attracted poor, unemployed and bored young Afghan boys from refugee camps, and offered them free room, board and a crude education. Many madrassa schools taught Islamist jihadist ideas, and many graduates would go to Afghanistan to fight the Soviets. In addition, Zia would allow Muslim volunteers from all over the world to come to Pakistani camps to train to fight the Soviets.

The United States also supported the Afghan anti–Soviet mujahideen in order to prevent a feared Soviet southwards expansion. The Americans also wanted to pay back the Soviets for their having supported North Vietnam during the Vietnam War.[5] On December 29, 1979, American President Carter approved a broad program of secret CIA assistance to the Afghan mujahideen. The CIA would ship weapons and ammunition for the muhjahideen, and would make monthly cash payments to individual mujahideen commanders.[6] However, during the initial years of the Afghan-Soviet War, the Saudis provided far more assistance to the mujahideen than the Americans did.

Zia realized that his bargaining position with the United States had vastly improved because of the Soviet invasion, and he took advantage of it. Therefore, when President Carter on October 17, 1980, offered Pakistan a $400 million aid and economic package, Zia rejected the offer and held out for a larger package. Zia ridiculed Carter's offer as "peanuts"—too small to justify the huge risk that Pakistan was being asked to take, since aiding the mujahideen might provoke a Soviet invasion of Pakistan itself.

Zia Amasses More Power

General Zia, as army chief, had nominal control of Pakistan's army. He wanted to acquire more influence over the military, and he found justification for taking more control when he discovered that some disgruntled generals planned a coup. On March 15, 1980, Zia announced the arrest of retired General Hussain Malik and other conspirators for having plotted to assassinate him and overthrow his government. With the jailing of these generals, and the resignations and retirements of others, Zia became the undisputed leader of the armed forces after just two years in power.

General Zia had begun implementing his "Islamization" program to increase his popularity and power. However, Islamization also had increased the power of the country's religious leaders, who had assumed responsibility for interpreting and enforcing Islamic laws. To take over this power from the clerics, Zia on May 26, 1980, announced the creation of a Federal Shariat Court. This court would hear cases involving Islamic law, such as violations of the Hudood ordinances and the Blasphemy law.[7] This court would oversee district Shariat courts in the villages. Zia claimed that the Shariat court system was not intended to replace the regular civil courts. Instead he said they were meant to offer the masses in the villages with legal help if they didn't have the assistance of secular lawyers.[8]

Zia soon took over even more powers from the Muslim clerics. Sunni clerics had been collecting a voluntary Zakat alms tax of 2.5 percent of every Sunni Muslim's annual household savings, and had been distributing it to the poor. On June 20, 1980, Zia took over this responsibility for collecting the tax. He required banks to deduct 2.5 percent from each customer's savings account and send it to the government for distribution.[9] The mandatory tax led to widespread protests. The Shiites were especially upset about the zakat taxes, since the taxes never had been part of the Shiite religious tradition. The Shiites bitterly protested the tax, and after a group seized a federal building for three days, Zia relented and exempted Shiites from paying these taxes.

There were several repercussions to the imposition of the zakat taxes and the protests which followed. First, the success of the Shiite tax protests

9. The Soviets Invade Afghanistan

made the Shiites realize that by uniting in protests, they could win greater concessions. Also, the zakat tax and protests rekindled the Sunni-Shiite rivalry by reminding members of the two branches of their differences. Sunni and Shiites began criticizing each other.

On January 20, 1981, Ronald Reagan became president of the United States, and Pak-American relations improved considerably. Reagan believed that Pakistan deserved far more support than his predecessor Carter had offered it. Reagan would increase military and economic aid to Pakistan until it would become the world's third largest recipient of American foreign aid. Due to this increased American aid (and the theft of some of the best weapons intended for the Afghan rebels), Pakistan's army would expand to 450,000 troops with more modern weapons.[10]

American President Ronald Reagan was so pleased with Zia's help in distributing arms to the Afghan mujahideen that he dropped America's objections to Zia's military dictatorship and his human rights abuses—declaring them to be Pakistan's "internal problem." Also, Reagan knew that Pakistan was building a nuclear bomb, but he and Zia reached an unwritten agreement. Reagan would pretend that Pakistan's nuclear program didn't exist. In return, Pakistan must refrain from actually constructing a nuclear bomb, must not transfer nuclear technology abroad, and must not publicize its nuclear weapons program.[11]

Zia's amassing of power led to growing opposition to his rule. The most successful opposition came from the Movement to Restore Democracy (MRD), which was formed on February 6, 1981. The MRD was an ad hoc alliance of the PPP and seven other banned political parties. The MRD's stronghold was in Sindh Province, where the Sindhis hated Zia for his "judicial murder" of the popular Zulfi Bhutto—a Sindh Province native. The MRD demanded the lifting of Zia's ban of political parties, the restoration of the 1973 Constitution, and an end to discrimination against religious minorities and women.

President Zia initially was able to blunt the MRD's popular uprising against him by diverting the country's attention. Zia had the state media give extensive coverage to the hijacking of a Pakistani airliner. Terrorists hijacked the plane on March 2, 1981, and forced it to fly to Damascus, Syria. The hijackers were from the Al-Zulfikar Organization (AZO) which had been formed by the late Zulfi Bhutto's son Murtaza to overthrow Zia's regime. Zia falsely claimed that Zulfi Bhutto's daughter Benazir was a conspirator in the hijacking. On March 8, Zia's police arrested Benazir and over 6,000 PPP supporters and other Zia opponents. Zia's regime confined Benazir Bhutto alone in a bare cell and failed to provide her with adequate medical treatment—perhaps hoping that she would die in jail.[12] Zia refused to release her because she refused to promise to stay out of politics.

President Zia also increased his powers by expanding his control over the judicial system. On March 23, 1981, Zia issued a Provisional Constitution Order (PCO), which allowed him to declare that civil courts had no jurisdiction to review any martial law orders or sentences. The PCO also required Supreme Court and other appellate court judges to take a fresh oath of submission to Zia. One-fourth of Pakistan's appellate judges were removed for refusing to take the humiliating oath.

On December 24, 1981, Zia declared the formation of the Majlis-i-Shoora. Zia called it a temporary parliament. Since Zia would choose all of its 287 members, critics criticized it as just a junta tool.[13] It had very limited powers, since it could only recommend laws that the junta should enact.

Zia also strengthened his powers on September 23, 1982, by issuing a martial law regulation which broadened crimes punishable by death. It authorized the death sentence for anyone committing an offense "liable to cause insecurity" or "despondency among the public." Also, anyone found guilty of failing to inform the authorities that such an offense had been committed could be sentenced to death.

Sunnis and Shiites had lived peacefully together for centuries, but now Pakistan's Sunni extremists and hardline clerics provoked violence between them.[14] Sunni hard-liners clamored for a declaration that Shiites were non–Muslims. The Muslim Sunni-Shiite rivalry was becoming more pronounced and more violent. On January 29, 1983, Shiites and Sunnis clashed in Karachi, injuring 30 or more persons. The Karachi rioting soon spread to the rest of Sindh Province. While the junta-imposed curfew forbade any form of assembly, and arrested hundreds of demonstrators, the rioters continued their indiscriminate attacks. Soon wide areas of Karachi were ablaze.

The Sunni anti–Shiite rivalry would become even more deadly as the rival branches formed well-armed militias which began fighting each other. Sunni extremists formed the anti–Shiite SSP 21 months later. When the SSP began attacking Shiites in Punjab Province, the besieged Shiites formed the Sipah-e-Mohammed Pakistan (SMP) to counter the SSP.[15] Over 1,000 Punjabis would die in this sectarian fighting. The military junta warned Zia that too many religious decrees might provoke so many violent demonstrations that the army might not be able to control them. The growing sectarian clashes and the army's warning led Zia to slow down his Islamization program.

On August 1, 1983, the inventive Zia presented an outline of the junta's new political order for Pakistan. The Majlis-i-Shoora would be dissolved and a national ombudsman would be created to redress individual grievances. Then the 1973 Constitution would be revived and amended. It would provide for a strong president who would be elected by the combined vote of the national and provincial assemblies. The president would be the head of the country's military forces and he would have the power to dissolve parliament.

The office of prime minister would be restored, but he would be appointed by the president and subordinate to him. National and provincial assembly elections would occur in 19 months, without the participation of political parties.[16] Then martial law would be lifted. Under the junta's new political order, Zia as president would have such unrestricted power that he would almost become an absolute ruler. This declaration of a new political order was followed by protests and street demonstrations.

Zia Accelerates the Nuclear Weapons Program

Before seizing power, Army Chief General Zia had worked closely with A.Q. Khan on Pakistan's nuclear bomb program, helping build the Kahuta uranium enrichment facility. Upon seizing power, Zia told Khan that Zia would give him all the funds he needed and that he would allow Khan to proceed without government oversight. Zia secured some of the funds for the nuclear program by diverting to it substantial CIA funds intended for arming the Afghan mujahideen.[17] Six years later, on March 11, 1983, Pakistan ran its first "cold test" of a nuclear device. A cold test involved testing the trigger of a nuclear device, while substituting conventional explosives for highly enriched uranium—thereby avoiding the huge explosion of a nuclear chain reaction.[18] The test went perfectly. Since Pakistan had produced weapons grade uranium, for all intents and purposes it had an atomic bomb.

American President Reagan soon became aware of the secret test, since the CIA had an informer inside the Kahuta facility. The CIA even had a floor plan of the facility and a scale model of Pakistan's atom bomb.[19] Pakistan would follow up by cold-testing over a dozen nuclear devices over the next years. Reagan did nothing to stop these secret tests, since he was so pleased with Zia's cooperation with the Americans against the Soviets. He prevented information about the tests from reaching Congress, for fear that Congress would end the flow of weapons to the Afghan mujahideen.[20]

President Reagan's plan to conceal Pakistan's nuclear weapons program from Congress would become increasingly difficult as more publicity was released about the program. The first major publicity came from Pakistan itself. President Zia had become worried that India might launch a preemptive air strike against Pakistan's Kahuta nuclear facility. To prevent such an attack, Zia arranged for A.Q. Khan to hint to the Urdu-language press that Pakistan might already have achieved a nuclear breakthrough.[21] Zia hoped that India (but not the West) would read the interview coverage. Following Zia's directive, A.Q. Khan gave an interview which was picked up by a Pakistani urdu-language newspaper on January 16, 1984. The boastful Khan then gave several more interviews in which he implied that Pakistan actually had an atom bomb. One of these interviews was picked up by Pakistan's English-language press, and this was picked up by the Americans. President Reagan was angry when he learned of this disclosure, since he had assured the American public that he would not allow Pakistan to produce weapons grade uranium needed for a bomb.

This disclosure also troubled American Senators. They responded by passing the Solarz and Pressler amendments to the Foreign Assistance Act, which were signed into law on August 8, 1985. They provided that military and economic assistance to Pakistan would end unless America's president certified in writing that Pakistan didn't possess a nuclear device. Presidents Reagan and G.H. Bush would sign false certifications year after year, even though they knew that Pakistan already had a nuclear bomb.

Zia Keeps the Afghan Pot Boiling

In spite of President Zia's harsh suppression of his opponents, the Movement for the Restoration of Democracy (MRD) refused to submit to his rule. A showdown began on August 14, 1983, when in defiance of martial law, the MRD launched its second mass protest to restore democracy. Mass protests began in Sindh's capital of Karachi, and spread to Sindh Province's rural areas. Large crowds burned government buildings and vehicles. To crush the rebellion, Zia ordered three army divisions into Sindh Province, and the soldiers killed civilians, destroyed crops and burned whole villages. Many previously uncommitted Sindhis joined the MRD rebellion—the only sustained rebellion against Zia's rule. Zia had become the most repressive ruler in Pakistan's history.

There were several reasons why Zia was able to hold onto power despite the growing MRD opposition. First, General Zia, through his martial law powers, had a firm grip on power. Few dared to demonstrate against him since he suppressed dissent with excessive force. He was able to blunt the MRD's protests by arresting, jailing and exiling most of the MRD's key leaders. Also, MRD support was mainly confined to Sindh Province, and the middle classes in Punjab Province continued to back Zia. In addition, most Pakistanis liked Zia for his support of the Muslim Afghan mujahideen who were fighting the Soviet "infidel" invaders.

While Zia succeeded in suppressing dissent inside Pakistan, he was unable to stop criticism abroad. Benazir Bhutto was still in jail and so her protests could not be heard. However, she had developed a severe ear infection which had grown progressively worse since her jailers had refused to treat it. Finally, Zia felt obliged to do something, and so on January 10, 1984, he allowed Benazir to fly to London for treatment. When Benazir arrived in

9. The Soviets Invade Afghanistan

London (where many exiled PPP members were living), she underwent ear surgery. Two months later she flew to the United States where she tried to debunk Western media's portrayal of Zia as a "benign dictator." She reported how Zia had jailed most of his political opponents.

Despite Zia's ruthless suppression of his opponents, the United States kept working with him to deliver CIA-supplied weapons for distribution to the Afghan mujahideen. In January 1984, Texas Congressman Charlie Wilson arrived in Pakistan and held private meetings with President Zia. The two already had agreed that if Wilson could greatly increase American foreign aid to Pakistan, Zia would allow the CIA to escalate its arms shipments to the Afghan mujahideen.

After this latest meeting with Wilson, Zia agreed for the first time to allow the CIA to send Pakistan heavy machine guns and mortars for distribution to the Afghan mujahideen. However, at the same time, the Soviet Army began a series of large offensives, relying more on helicopter-borne special forces troops. While the Soviets inflicted heavy casualties on the mujahideen, the Soviets themselves would suffer 4,000 casualties during the year—the highest Soviet losses of any year of the war.

While the Afghan-Soviet War roared on, the Sindh-mohajir conflict also grew more violent. In March 1984, the mohajirs (refugees) in Sindh Province formed the Mohajir Qaumi Mahaz (MQM) Party. The MQM quickly grew since it was the only party which criticized the central government for ignoring mohajir concerns. The MQM's growth was also initially supported by ISI funding.[22] The MQM soon took control of the municipal governments in Karachi and Hyderabad. Native Sindhis countered by forming the ANP and other groups to meet the MQM threat. The MQM and ANP soon were fighting pitched battles for control of Karachi.[23]

Adding to Pakistan's troubles was the breakout of an Indo-Pak conflict on the Siachen Glacier. The 34-mile long glacier in Northern Kashmir was remote, barren and uninhabitable. Since the glacier was uninhabitable, Pakistan and India never had bothered settling the Indo-Pak border in that region. However, India sent troops to the glacier intending to set up a permanent base there. Pakistan responded by sending its own troops to remove the Indians, and fighting broke out on April 25, 1984. Soon each country had 3,000 troops fighting over possession of the useless glacier. The fighting would go on for several decades, causing the deaths of some 800 Indians and over 200 Pakistanis. Most of the casualties were caused by sub-zero weather, blizzards and avalanches on the high mountain peaks.

The United States and Saudi Arabia now increased the funds they were committing to the Afghan mujahideen in the Afghan-Soviet War. On October 11, 1984, CIA director Casey proposed to the Saudi government that each country provide $250 million in funding for the mujahideen the next year. The Saudis agreed and the funding for the mujahideen suddenly tripled. Texas Congressman Charlie Wilson persuaded Congress to fund the $250 million American share, and this American-Saudi match would continue for years.

President Zia realized that opposition to his dictatorship was growing. He decided to remedy this by "civilianizing" his regime. He didn't dare hold direct presidential elections, so he settled on a referendum. Zia pledged that if the referendum passed, he would lift martial law and restore the office of prime minister.

When Zia's referendum passed on December 19, 1984, Zia claimed that passage entitled him to serve another five years as president. However, the referendum "victory" actually had proven little. First, the referendum wasn't a real mandate for five more years of Zia's rule, since it didn't expressly ask whether Zia should serve another term.[24] Instead it had been worded in such a way that it implied that a "no" vote was a vote against Islam. Also, even Zia was embarrassed by the very low referendum voter turnout, which was only approved by between 10 to 30 percent of registered voters. In addition, Zia had to rig the election results even to justify his claim that the referendum had passed. Zia's generals were disappointed that Zia had held a referendum instead of direct elections.

On January 8, 1985, President Zia reluctantly scheduled elections for the national and provincial assemblies for the end of February. He scheduled the elections due to army pressure, and in order to preserve his claim that he headed a civilian government. Zia was confident that he would win the elections since political parties still were banned and candidates were prohibited from revealing their party names or symbols on the ballots.

Voting for the 200-seat National Assembly began on February 25, 1985. Turnout exceeded 50 percent since this was the first opportunity for Pakistanis to directly vote for legislators in eight years. Many of Zia's candidates were defeated, including seven ministers in his own cabinet. However, despite the poor showing of Zia-backed candidates, Zia still retained a firm grip on power since he retained his martial law powers.

10

Zia's Last Years

During the three and a half years covered in this chapter (March 1985–August 1988), President Zia would restore the office of prime minister. Then Zia would have the Constitution amended to give himself (as president) the power to dismiss prime ministers. Zia would lift martial law. He would continue supporting the mujahideen in the Afghan-Soviet war, and the Soviets would decide to withdraw from Afghanistan. The chapter ends with Zia's death in a mysterious plane crash.

Zia Restores the Office of Prime Minister

On March 23, 1985, General Zia was sworn in as president on the basis of his having won the referendum three months before. Zia surprised everyone by retaining his position as army chief. However, Zia did allow the restoration of the office of prime minister—which he had terminated seven years earlier. The National Assembly unanimously ratified Zia's candidate Muhammad Khan Junejo as prime minister. Zia was confident that he could control this soft-spoken politician who didn't have his own following. Zia certainly never intended for the docile Junejo to really share power with him. Instead, Zia intended to use Junejo to civilianize his regime and help him transition from martial law and implement Zia's new political system.[1] However, nothing really had changed, since Zia still maintained control though his positions as president, army chief and CMLA head of the martial law apparatus.

The awkward power-sharing arrangement between President Zia and Prime Minister Junejo didn't work well for Zia because Junejo soon developed surprising independence. First, Junejo conducted himself as the head executive of a duly elected government, and he became the final authority in the government's day-to-day operations. He controlled finances and he gained supporters by using his power to appoint government officials. Also, Junejo would gain the support of most members in the National Assembly, and Junejo and the Assembly sometimes refused to support Zia's decisions. In addition, Junejo gained popularity by calling for the revival of political parties, the end to martial law, and an end to the Afghan-Soviet War.

President Zia decided to exert more control over how the CIA-supplied arms would be distributed to the Afghan mujahideen. To this end he arranged for the formation of the "Peshawar Seven" Islamic alliance on May 16, 1985. The alliance was composed of the seven Peshawar leaders who dominated the major Afghan mujahideen commands. Zia pressured all mujahideen to join one of these seven commands as a condition for continuing to receive CIA weapons. Hundreds of Afghan mujahideen groups would join one of these seven groups.[2] This new system of distributing CIA arms was more orderly and efficient than the previous system.

The ISI's Afghan Bureau was in charge of transporting and distributing the CIA-supplied arms. The bureau had its headquarters at an 80-acre complex at the Ojhri Camp, where it stored most of the CIA arms bound for Afghanistan. When it distributed arms to these seven commanders, the ISI gave the most weapons to fundamentalist Muslim Sunni groups, which consequently increased their membership and strength. While the Sunnis grew stronger, the Shiites grew weaker, since the latter largely avoided fighting in Afghanistan. They didn't want to fight beside the Sunnis—who were oppressing and killing them inside Pakistan.[3]

President Zia now pressured parliament to expand his presidential powers. On November 11, 1985, Pakistan's Senate passed the Eighth Amendment to the Constitution, which transformed Zia's position as president from a figurehead into a powerful government official. The amendment gave the president the power to remove prime ministers, and this dismissal authority would remain in effect for the next 12 years. The president also was given the power to dissolve parliament. The president was to be elected by an electoral college of the two houses of parliament and the four provincial assemblies. The amendment also validated as legal all Zia's ordinances and orders issued since he had taken power, and provided that their validity couldn't be challenged by any court.

Zia now had so much authority as president that he felt he could end martial law and rule as a "constitutional dictator." On December 17, 1985, he even had the National Assembly enact a law allowing the return of political parties in order to bolster the democratic facade of his regime.

Martial Law Ends and Nuclear War Narrowly Averted

On December 30, 1985, President Zia finally terminated martial law, which he had used for nine years to control the country. Zia claimed that he was returning the country to true civilian rule. Zia's powers did in fact diminish somewhat since political parties now had the right to exist and public political meetings could resume. Also, as military courts disbanded, civilian courts recovered their powers. Moreover, lifting martial law encouraged Benazir Bhutto to return to Pakistan to challenge Zia's dictatorship.

On April 10, 1986, Benazir Bhutto returned to Pakistan after having spent two years in London. She was greeted by a crowd of over one million supporters, and this warm welcome gave fresh impetus to the movement for Zia's removal. Benazir began campaigning across Pakistan denouncing Zia and demanding that he resign. Zia was caught off balance by the huge demonstration of Bhutto's popularity, and he quickly moved to stop Benazir and her PPP election campaign.

Pakistan now came very close to a nuclear war with its arch-enemy India. The crisis began on February 21, 1986, when India's army began a series of massive "Brass Tacks" war games that would continue for 13 months. India never fully informed Pakistan's leaders of its plans to hold the war games.[4] India's hawkish General Sundarji would conduct the war games in four phases, with the first three involving mainly discussions, maps and sand models. However, the fourth phase would involve massing troops close to Pakistan's border. While General Sundarji informed India's Prime Minister Rajiv Gandhi of the general scope of Brass Tacks, he didn't reveal the massive number of troops that would be involved in the fourth phase. General Sundarji began the fourth phase on November 28, 1986, and started to move 400,000 Indian troops to within 100 miles of the Indo-Pak border. President Zia feared that India might be staging its troops near the border as a jumping off point for an actual invasion of Pakistan. In response, Zia ordered three of his corps to the border opposite the Indian buildup.

On January 20, 1987, Indian Prime Minister Rajiv Gandhi learned for the first time about his generals' massive troop buildup close to the Pakistan border and learned about Pakistan's counter moves. Prime Minister Rajiv, realizing that the Brass Tacks deployment might provoke a nuclear war, immediately took over India's military decision-making. Rajiv met with General Sundarji and a few senior bureaucrats and during the meeting the group rejected a proposal for a preventative strike against Pakistan's nuclear facilities and military targets. The group realized that Pakistan probably had nuclear weapons that could strike Indian cities.[5] Three days later, Pakistan proposed urgent talks with India, and the dormant phone hotline between the two countries was reactivated. Talks began on January 31, and on February 4, India and Pakistan agreed to withdraw their troops, thereby ending the crisis.

Soviet Setbacks in the Afghan-Soviet War

Soviet troops in Afghanistan had been losing a slow war of attrition. The war suddenly tipped further against the Soviets when the CIA began providing the Afghan mujahideen with American Stinger shoulder-fired anti-aircraft missiles. The first mujahideen Stinger attack took place on September 26, 1986, when a mujahideen commander shot down three Soviet HIND attack helicopters.[6] Arming the mujahideen with Stingers was a major factor in turning the balance against the Soviets, since it deprived the Soviets of their ability to fly their planes and attack helicopters at low altitudes. The Soviets now began flying so high to avoid the Stingers, that the mujahideen began calling the Soviet pilots "Cosmonauts."

Partly because of the Stingers, the Soviets on November 20, 1986, secretly decided to withdraw their troops from Afghanistan. The Soviet army immediately stopped offensive operations and ordered its troops to fight only when attacked or when supporting Afghan Army troops. However, Soviet leader Gorbachev wanted to leave a communist-dominated "coalition" government in charge in Kabul before completing the withdrawal. He began negotiating with Afghan and Pakistani leaders for concessions in return for a Soviet withdrawal.

On December 17, 1987, Benazir Bhutto improved her political credentials by marrying Asif Zardari, a wealthy businessman from Karachi. Being married was important for a woman in the conservative, male-dominated country. Unfortunately, Zardari's reputation for shady business dealings would make him a liability.

On April 10, 1988, there were two massive explosions at Pakistan's huge Ojhiri arms depot located between the twin cities of Islamabad and Rawalpindi. The explosions killed a hundred people, collapsed buildings in both cities, and destroyed 8,000 tons of arms and munitions. It never would be determined whether the explosions had been accidental or caused by sabotage.[7] The ISI officers in charge of the arms depot were severely criticized for having haphazardly stored munitions in the huge depot next to a civilian neighborhood. Prime Minister Junejo angered Zia by demanding that Zia's protégé, former ISI chief Rahman, be fired for his mismanagement of the arms depot.

The Afghan-Soviet War virtually ended when the Geneva Accords were signed on April 14, 1988. The accords were bilateral agreements

10. Zia's Last Years

between Afghanistan and Pakistan. The Americans and Soviets signed as interested parties and guarantors. Zia had opposed the signing of the accords, but Junejo instructed his foreign minister to sign anyways.[8] The Soviet troops started withdrawing the next day, and completed their withdrawal ten months later.

The Geneva Accords did not stop Pakistan from intervening in Afghanistan, which still was ruled by a communist government. Pakistan's ISI and the Afghan mujahideen began planning how to defeat the communist Afghan Army and overthrow the government. The ISI advised the mujahideen to rely primarily on the forces of the Afghan Islamist HiH leader Hekmatyar to lead the attack on Kabul's communist government. This was a mistake, since Hekmatyar was a ruthless commander who was murdering rival mujahideen commanders who threatened his leadership. The ISI pressured mujahideen commanders to join Hekmatyar, threatening that otherwise the ISI would stop shipping them arms and ammunition.

On May 29, 1988, President Zia suddenly dismissed his independent-minded Prime Minister Junejo for having threatened his authority. Junejo had taken over Pakistan's foreign policy decision-making, had recommended cuts in military spending, and had demanded an investigation of the Ojhiri munitions depot explosions.[9]

There were several repercussions to Zia's dismissal of Junejo. First, Zia's unilateral decision to dismiss Junejo offended several of Zia's generals. They were becoming increasingly alienated by Zia's one-man dictatorship which increasingly operated without consulting them.[10] Also, Junejo's dismissal made it clear that Zia wasn't willing to share power with civilians. This provoked a new groundswell of discontent with Zia's dictatorship. Finally, Zia became more depressed and isolated than ever. Fearing assassination, he went into virtual seclusion inside his military residence in Rawalpindi.

Zia didn't really want to hold elections for a new prime minister to replace Junejo. However, the Constitution required him to call for National Assembly elections within 90 days. Therefore, on July 20, 1988, Zia announced that national and provincial elections would be held on November 16. However, he insisted that no party names or symbols could appear on the ballots. This restriction was designed to hurt the PPP, since the illiterate masses could only identify PPP candidates if a PPP symbol appeared next to their names on the ballot.

Zia's Last Flight

On August 17, 1988, President Zia was returning to Islamabad after having witnessed a tank demonstration. As usual, three C-130 military transport planes were standing by, and one was chosen at random at the last minute to carry Zia.[11] The plane made a normal takeoff, with 31 senior officials on board. Zia's Vice-Chief, General Aslam Beg, should have been sitting next to Zia, but Beg took off in his own plane shortly after Zia's departure, either at Zia's suggestion or at Beg's request.[12] Zia's plane climbed to 5,000 feet and then began pitching and rolling uncontrollably. After two minutes, the plane crashed—killing Zia and everyone on board. The victims included 15 of Zia's senior generals and the American ambassador to Pakistan. Zia's close supporters mourned his passing and many attended his funeral. However, instead, most Pakistanis celebrated his death by buying sweets and honking their car horns.

The cause of the crash never would be determined. Some believed that the crash was accidental—caused by hydraulic flight control failure or a rearward shift in the plane's center of gravity.[13] However, many suspected that sabotage had been involved, especially since Zia had stopped insisting on strict security checks on his planes.[14] Many theories were put forth as to how sabotage might have been carried out, including that the gift crate of mangoes that had been loaded aboard just before takeoff had contained a disabling poison gas.[15] Those who believed that sabotage had been involved couldn't agree on who had been responsible, since Zia had so many enemies.[16] Both Pakistani and American authorities stifled independent investigations of the crash and seemed to prefer that the assassins, if any, never be identified.[17] At first, America's leaders feared that the downing of Zia's plane might be the start of a series of attacks to destroy Pakistan. Therefore, the United States sent warnings all over the world making it clear that America would launch an attack on any country that made further attacks on its Pakistani ally.[18]

During his eleven years in power, Zia had weakened Pakistan. First, he had made no attempt to transition the country toward a system of representative civilian rule. Political parties had been denied the experience of campaigning, compromising and legislating, while the people had been denied the experience of voting. Also, Zia's Islamization program had accentuated sectarian differences between religious groups (including Muslim Sunnis and Shiites), and had led to increasing sectarian violence. In addition, Zia had weakened the army's senior leadership by promoting generals on the basis of their loyalty and Islamic devotion rather than on their competency. Zia also had given his senior generals houses and land, which caused them to divert their attention away from training the army.

However, Zia also had improved Pakistan in some ways. First, Pakistan's economy developed at an impressive pace during his rule. Pakistan had transitioned from a poor to a middle-class nation, and the standard of living of all classes had improved.[19] Also, Zia had increased the size of Pakistan's military forces. He provided the army with more modern weapons, partly by skimming off some of the most sophisticated weapons intended for the Afghan mujahideen.[20] In addition, Zia had moved Pakistan's nuclear weapons program forward with great persistence.

11

Benazir Bhutto's First Term

During the two-year period covered in this chapter (August 1988–August 1990), Benazir Bhutto was elected prime minister. The military would limit her powers by dominating the three-person troika which ruled the country. Her powers also would be limited because the president had the constitutional power to dismiss prime ministers at any time. During her short term, the Soviets would complete their withdrawal from Afghanistan.

Civilian Rule Returns

Right after Zia's August 17, 1988, plane crash, Army Vice-Chief General Aslam Beg safely landed in his own plane in Rawalpindi. That afternoon, Pakistan's surviving generals met at army headquarters. They accepted General Beg's recommendation that the elderly senior bureaucrat Ghulam Ishaq Khan, the president of the Senate, become Acting President as provided for in the Constitution. Ishaq didn't believe that Pakistan was ready for independence, and he didn't trust politicians. He focused on stabilizing the country and he identified with the military.[1] Ishaq immediately appointed General Aslam Beg as Army Chief, largely because most of the senior generals had perished when Zia's plane crashed. The generals believed that the people wouldn't tolerate yet another period of military rule, and some officers were tired of the army being used to keep a military dictator in power. The generals were confident that they could control whatever civilian politicians were elected to govern. Ishaq announced that general elections would be held in three months.

11. Benazir Bhutto's First Term

Pakistan's interim government soon faced a serious outbreak of ethnic violence in Sindh Province. On September 29, 1988, several dozen hooded Sindhi nationalists riding motorcycles and in cars randomly killed 186 civilians in Hyderabad—a stronghold of the mohajirs and their MQM Party. When news of the massacre reached Karachi, angry mohajir mobs took to the streets and retaliated by killing native Sindhis. This "Hyderabad Massacre" marked the start of a more violent period inside Sindh Province and its capital Karachi. The army was called in and did a remarkable job suppressing the violence—simply by patrolling the streets in the two cities and acting even-handedly against all mobs.

Army chief Beg and other generals who had supported Zia were worried that the popular PPP leader Benazir Bhutto might win the forthcoming elections. They feared that if Bhutto were elected, she might seek revenge against army officers who had stood by while Zia had her father executed. Therefore, to oppose Benazir's election, ISI chief Hamid Gul in September secretly organized the Islami Jamhoori Ittehad (IJI)—a Sharif-led coalition of eight pro-army, right-wing parties.[2] The ISI assisted the IJI by giving it funds and advising its candidates how to run a dirty election campaign.[3]

The National Assembly election campaign was dominated by two groups—Benazir Bhutto's PPP party and Sharif's new ISI-formed IJI coalition. During the campaign, the PPP promised democratic government and promised change after 11 years of Zia's military rule. The Sharif-led IJI coalition questioned Benazir's fitness to be prime minister, on grounds that she was a woman, had little governing experience, and was pro–American.

Pakistan's National Assembly elections were held on November 16, 1988. Voter turnout was low, partly because interim president Ishaq Ghulam had required a National Identification Card to vote—which few rural residents possessed. Benazir Bhutto's PPP won 94 of the 217 seats in the National Assembly, while the IJI coalition won 54 seats. The PPP had won because the voters wanted a change after 18 years of military rule and they wanted to repay Zia for having the popular Zulfikar Bhutto executed. Also, Benazir Bhutto had earned voter respect by her stints in Zia's jails and by her being the daughter of the martyred Zulfikar Bhutto.

However, Benazir Bhutto's PPP hadn't won enough seats on its own to achieve majority control of the National Assembly. Tradition called for the party which had won the most seats to ask other parties to join in a coalition which could control the needed majority of seats. However, instead, Ishaq consulted both PPP and IJI leaders before asking Bhutto to try to form a coalition.[4] When the PPP announced that it had formed a coalition with the MQM, Ishaq called on Benazir to try to form a coalition—but only after she had reluctantly agreed to accept some army-imposed conditions. She agreed to retain Ishaq as president, General Beg as army chief, and

General Gul as head of the ISI. Bhutto also agreed to maintain existing levels of military spending and retain military perks. She pledged not to interfere with the country's defense strategy, its nuclear weapons program, and military promotions. Benazir accepted these conditions because she was worried that otherwise the army might return the country to a military dictatorship.[5] After agreeing to these conditions, Benazir formed a fragile coalition with the MQM Party.

Provincial assembly elections were held three days after the National Assembly elections. The pro-army IJI defeated the PPP in Punjab Province by a slight margin. Sharif won by cornering the independently elected members and isolating them until election day. The IJI set up a Punjab provincial government with ISI help, with Benazir's rival Nawaz Sharif as the powerful provincial chief minister. Sharif would become the opposition leader to Bhutto's national government.

Benazir Bhutto Begins Her First Term

On December 1, 1988, 35-year-old Benazir Bhutto was sworn in as Pakistan's prime minister. The Constitution provided that she would serve for five years or until she lost majority control of the National Assembly—whichever came first. Benazir was the first female leader of a Muslim nation and the world's youngest prime minister.

Benazir Bhutto had a number of strengths. She was young, vigorous and very attractive. She was intelligent, well-educated and an inspiring speaker. She had great courage, which allowed her to keep fighting, even when she was most depressed.[6] Also, she was very popular with the masses, since she carried the legacy of her enormously popular martyred father Zulfi Bhutto. Her imprisonment had made her a symbol of resistance to dictatorial rule. In addition, Benazir was too young to have witnessed the horrors of partition with India, and so she didn't hate India. She would be willing to improve relations with that neighbor. Also, Bhutto believed in human rights, and her human rights record would be the best in Pakistan's history. She would grant amnesty to all political prisoners and she would lift Zia's ban on student and labor unions. She would give all political parties regular uncensored access to the state media.

However, Benazir also had some weaknesses. First, she was a female leader in a country traditionally run by men. Pakistan's ISI and religious leaders didn't believe that any woman should run the country. From her first day in office, ISI head General Hamid Gul began undermining her, and waited for her to make a misstep that would justify removing her from office.[7] Also, Bhutto was young and inexperienced. She came from a privileged, wealthy family, had never held a paying job, and had never contacted many ordinary citizens. Therefore, she had trouble understanding the country's problems and had little idea of how to solve them. In addition, Bhutto had trouble focusing on the most important issues, and she changed her mind excessively.[8] Also, she was arrogant, reluctant to take advice and dismissive of those who disagreed with her. She had the illusion that only she had the right and ability to govern the country. She also still had strong personal feelings against the deceased Zia, who had her father executed. This lingering hatred of Zia and her feelings of irreparable loss of her father was one reason why she couldn't seem to cooperate with those who had supported Zia in having her father executed.[9] In addition, she never had held a government position before, and she didn't really believe that democracy would work in Pakistan.[10] Therefore, she decided to try to destroy her rival Sharif—before he would destroy her. In addition, she was unable or unwilling to select competent advisers and key officials—often choosing candidates just because they had served her father or had spent years in jail. Also, Bhutto had absorbed some of the selfish beliefs of her feudal family upbringing, such as protecting the privileged and relying on force to solve problems.[11] Also, she would weaken her own PPP party by having party officers appointed instead of elected.[12] She would alienate party loyalists by abandoning the PPP's socialist platform and by allowing wealthy landowners and other opportunists to enter the party. In addition, Benazir would be unwilling or unable to control the corruption within her own government and family—including her own husband. Under Bhutto, corruption would grow to unbelievable levels.[13] Finally, Bhutto would be plagued by a highly publicized scandal within her own family (the "Battle of All Mothers"). Her mother Nusrat had turned against her—resenting that Benazir had become the PPP's head instead of herself. Nusrat also would help her son Murtaza return to Pakistan, form a rival PPP Party, and win a seat in parliament. He publicly denounced Benazir and her husband Zardari.[14]

For several reasons, Prime Minister Benazir Bhutto would have just a precarious hold over the government. First, Pakistan really would be run by a junta of General Beg (leader of the army), Benazir Bhutto (leader of the government), and President Ishaq (leader of the bureaucracy). Bhutto was the weakest troika member, while Army Chief Beg was the strongest—since his army could remove Bhutto by force at any time. General Beg supported Bhutto and sheltered her from criticism, and the two shared a dislike for the ISI head General Gul (who was trying to remove them both).[15] President Ishaq also was stronger than Bhutto due to his constitutional power to dismiss her. Ishaq disliked Bhutto and he used his contacts in the bureaucracy to obstruct her—such as by having all communications sent to him before going to Bhutto.[16] Also, Bhutto lived under the shadow of the Constitution's Eighth Amendment, which provided that Zia's orders and ordinances were part of the Constitution. Therefore, Bhutto couldn't reverse any order or ordinance that Zia had issued except by passage of another constitutional amendment. Finally, Bhutto headed a very fragile coalition government. Her MQM and ANP partners would both soon desert her.

Pakistan faced many problems when Benazir Bhutto took office. First, criminals and terrorists were everywhere and they possessed lethal weapons which had flooded into the country during the war. Pakistan had over one million heroin addicts, and drug lords were too wealthy and powerful for the government to suppress.[17] Criminals engaged in bribery and smuggling, while terrorists assassinated government and security officials. Karachi was a particularly dangerous city, with 1.5 million squatters living in a city of 7.0 million people. Also, Pakistan's economy was in terrible shape. The government had few sources of revenue, since Pakistan's citizens and businessmen went to extremes to evade paying taxes. Also, sales taxes and customs duties were low, because many consumer goods were smuggled into the country and then sold on the black market.[18] The government's modest revenues were overwhelmed by huge military expenditures and the government's obligation to pay off the huge national debt. In addition, Pakistan still sheltered millions of Afghan refugees who were reluctant to return to their dangerous homeland. They were frustrated with their dead-end lives in the refugee camps, where they had little prospect of securing employment.

Prime Minister Bhutto realized that she was in a precarious position. Therefore, she initially acted cautiously to prolong her stay in office. First, she was careful not to openly antagonize the army's leaders, and she promised to work toward building a strong professional army. However, Army Chief General Beg quickly realized from bugged phone conversations that Bhutto didn't trust him and that she favored reducing military spending.[19] Also, Bhutto followed Zia's economic policies—rather than trying to restore her father's socialist reforms. In addition, while Benazir didn't promote Islam and didn't strongly support Islamist extremist groups, she still made concessions to these groups. For example, she wore a head scarf, didn't criticize religious parties, and included JUI religious party members in her coalition government.

Bhutto was primarily interested in domestic policy, and considered foreign policy of secondary importance. While she did have several foreign policy goals, she would be unable to achieve many of them due to obstruction by her junta colleagues and the ISI. First, she was a strong supporter of the United States, partly because of her pleasant college experiences in that country. Her success in improving Pak-American relations would be one of her major achievements. Also, she desired peace with India. However, the junta would pressure her to take a hawkish position on Kashmir, and so she never would be able to greatly improve Indo-Pak relations. Finally, Bhutto wanted to remove the Afghan communist regime that still controlled Afghanistan's government.

Hope for peace between Pakistan and India revived when India's Prime Minister Rajiv Gandhi visited Pakistan—the first trip by an Indian premier to Pakistan in over 24 years. The visit began on December 13, 1988, and during the visit, Gandhi and Bhutto agreed to establish a hotline between their military headquarters and agreed not to attack each other's nuclear facilities. They also agreed to improve cultural relations. There was great hope that the two young leaders might be able to start a new era of improved relations. However, the Bhutto-Gandhi peace initiative never would gain momentum, partly because the two leaders each depended on keeping tensions high in order to retain popular support at home.[20]

The ISI resumed its campaign to discredit Prime Minister Bhutto. It chose to rile up Pakistan's Islamist extremists about Salman Rushdie's novel *The Satanic Verses*—a novel which had parodied the Prophet Muhammad. It had been published a year before by a British-Indian author, and it had been banned by Pakistan's government as blasphemous. The ISI was disappointed that the book had scarcely been noticed inside Pakistan. In order to stir up anger and embarrass Bhutto, the ISI sent a copy of the book to Pakistan's Islamist extremist groups with the offending passages highlighted.[21] On February 12, 1989, Islamist extremists responded by inciting a Pakistani mob to lay siege to the USIA building in Islamabad. The demonstrators burned books and an American flag, and police killed five demonstrators while trying to protect those inside the building.

The "Lost Decade of Democracy" Begins

Benazir Bhutto's inauguration as prime minister began a decade of uninterrupted civilian rule, during which Pakistan would be ruled alternatively by prime ministers Benazir Bhutto and Nawaz Sharif. During this "Lost Decade of Democracy," elected civilians controlled the government and had the opportunity to work together, win mass support, and strengthen democratic institutions. Had they done so, they would have made it difficult for the army to justify another military takeover. However, instead, Bhutto and Sharif would fight each other and mismanage the country, thereby giving army leaders justification for resuming military rule.

There were several reasons why neither leader was able to establish a durable civilian government. First, prime ministers Bhutto and Sharif refused to cooperate. When one was elected prime minister, he spent most of his time suppressing his opponent. The opponent spent all his time trying to remove the prime minster. This lack of cooperation alienated the masses. Also, the civilian president didn't cooperate with the prime ministers, but instead dismissed them—sometimes under army pressure. The frequent dismissals didn't allow either prime minister to remain in office long enough to build up the mass support needed to diminish the army's dominance over their civilian governments. In addition, the army and ISI often intervened in the National Assembly elections to support or oppose candidates. Also, both prime ministers were heavily engaged in corruption.[22] They even tried to weaken each other's family businesses by changing income tax laws and import duties. Finally, during these ten years both Bhutto and Sharif mismanaged the country's economy. Both leaders recruited businessmen to join their parties, and these businessmen secured more government building contracts than the government could afford. When the government borrowed funds to pay for these contracts, Pakistan's national debt soared.[23]

The Soviets Leave Afghanistan

On February 15, 1989, the Soviets officially completed their withdrawal from Afghanistan. The Afghan-Soviet War had adversely affected Pakistan in many ways. First, during the war thousands of Pakistani Muslim jihadists had received guerrilla experience. After the war, these veterans returned home with nothing to do, and many turned to fighting the Indian troops in Kashmir. Pakistan's leaders encouraged this activity—partly to divert these dangerous jihadists from striking targets inside Pakistan.[24] Also, Pakistan's ISI intelligence agency had greatly increased in strength and independence during the war and it had grown to over 15,000 operatives. Many ISI officers had adopted Islamist extremist ideals while working with the Afghan mujahideen. In addition, Pakistan had become more dangerous during the war since large numbers of cheap deadly weapons had flooded into the country. Men toting automatic weapons were everywhere and so no one felt safe at home or in public—the "Kalashnikov culture."[25] The easy availability of inexpensive weapons led to an increase in deaths from drug wars and sectarian violence. Also, during the war a huge drug trafficking trade had developed, with Afghan opium poppies being processed into heroin and shipped to Pakistan. Many Pakistani youth had become drug addicts and had turned to crime to support their addictions.[26] The government had been unable or unwilling to prosecute major drug dealers, partly because the drug barons had bought the support of many politicians.[27] In addition, the war had forced over three million Afghans to seek refuge in Pakistan. Most would remain there for years after the Soviet withdrawal, since Afghanistan was still too dangerous to live in. Afghan farmers were reluctant to return to their farms, since their fields had become unworkable due to years of neglect, and the presence of millions of land mines that still littered the countryside.[28] Finally, during the war the number of religious schools (madrassas) had significantly increased, and many promoted intolerance of other religions.

Pakistan Tries to Overthrow the Communist Afghan Government

Pakistan's army and ISI leaders weren't satisfied with just the Soviet withdrawal from Afghanistan. They also wanted to remove Najibullah's communist Afghan government that the Soviets continued to prop up with arms. This would prove to be a difficult task for several reasons. First, the Soviet Union continued sending large amounts of weapons to the Afghan Army, which still defended the communist Afghan government. Also, Pakistan's army decided to defeat the Afghan Army using their Afghan mujahideen proxies instead of Pakistani troops. These proxy fighters lacked the unity, training, and experience needed to seize heavily fortified Afghan cities.

To overthrow the communist government and defeat the Afghan Army, Pakistani army and ISI leaders developed a three-step plan. The first step would be to set up a pro–Pakistan Afghan Interim Government (AIG). The second step would be to have mujahideen proxy fighters seize the Afghan city of Jalalabad and make it an AIG base and interim capital. The third step would be to launch attacks from its AIG base and drive Najibullah's communist government from Afghanistan.

The first step was achieved with relative ease. Pakistan's ISI head Hamid Gul convened a meeting of the Peshawar Seven mujahideen chiefs. On February 24, 1989, these commanders declared the formation of an Afghan Interim Government (AIG).[29] However, the AIG was located in Pakistan. It controlled no Afghan territory and had no military forces.

The second step would take several years to achieve. It began on March 6, 1989, when some of AIG's proxy mujahideen fighters began attacking Jalalabad—a heavily fortified city defended by well-armed, Soviet-trained Afghan Army troops. Pakistan's ISI chief General Gul directed the attack, using Hekmatyar's Islamist Afghan HIH group as its main striking force. The mujahideen attackers were supported by a few Pakistan Army units, ISI supplies, and ISI and CIA advisers. The Afghan Army defenders fought hard against the mujahideen attackers, partly because they feared they would be murdered if they were overrun or surrendered. In contrast, the mujahideen attackers had weaker motivation, since they fought mainly for the booty and the prestige they might gain if they prevailed.[30] Also, they had no training in attacking heavily defended positions.

The mujahideen were unable to break through the city's strong defenses, and so General Gul decided to lay siege to the city and starve out the defenders. However, several large supply convoys managed to break through the mujahideen blockade and reach the city.[31] Six months later, the mujahideen abandoned their siege after having lost 4,000 fighters.

The failure of the mujahideen to capture Jalalabad boosted the morale of Kabul's communist government and its Afghan Army. At the same time, the failure to capture the city weakened the standing of the ISI generals who had overseen the attack. Najibullah would remain in power in Kabul for two more years—until the Soviets stopped supplying his army with weapons.

Prime Minister Benazir Bhutto had been growing frustrated with how General Hamid Gul had been undermining her ever since she had taken office.[32] Using Gul's failure to seize Jalalabad as an excuse, Bhutto on May 31, 1989, removed Gul as ISI chief and replaced him with Shamsur Rehman Kallu. Bhutto and army chief Beg both wanted to remove Gul (who was trying to remove them both), but her appointment of Kallu over army opposition greatly disturbed army leaders, who never would tolerate civilians interfering in military affairs.

Prime Minister Bhutto was having difficulty maintaining control of the National Assembly, which had become so divided that it often couldn't even raise a quorum needed to conduct business. On June 4, 1989, sensing an opportunity, Sharif's PML (N) and other opposition parties formed the Combined Opposition Party (COP). The COP leaders decided to try to remove Bhutto from office by securing a "no-confidence" vote in the National Assembly. The COP brought the no-confidence motion with the support of the president, the army chief, the ISI and al-Qaeda leader Osama bin Laden.[33] Bhutto and the Sharif-led COP both campaigned hard to secure votes for and against the crucial motion, and there was widespread vote-buying, intimidation and "kidnapping" of Assembly members.[34] On November 1, the "no-confidence" motion was narrowly defeated. It had been the first "no confidence" motion ever brought in Pakistan.

Facing growing opposition at home, Prime Minister Bhutto decided to try to bolster her credentials by traveling to the United States. On June 5, 1989, Bhutto arrived in Washington for her first official visit. The beautiful young graduate of an American college was warmly greeted as a symbol of her country's transition from dictatorship to democracy. She was given a rare invitation to address a joint session of Congress. During her address she pledged to drive the remnants of the communists from Afghanistan, and she claimed that Pakistan was not trying to acquire a nuclear weapon. During her visit, she was genuinely shocked when American intelligence officials briefed her in detail on Pakistan's actual nuclear program. They even showed her a mockup of Pakistan's atomic bomb.[35] Nevertheless President George H. W. Bush agreed to certify one last time that Pakistan didn't possess a nuclear weapon, and thereby avert imposing sanctions on that country. Bush also agreed to give Pakistan large amounts of economic and military aid.

Kashmir's Mass Uprising Sparks Another Nuclear Confrontation

While the native Jammus and Kashmiris seethed with anger at India's taking steps to integrate IJK into India, they never had become so angry that they were willing to risk their lives by taking up arms against the Indian occupiers. That was about to change.

The Kashmiris in IJK recently had been suffering under the Indian puppet government of IJK Chief Minister Farooq Abdulla (the "Lion Cub"). However, India still backed the unpopular Farooq during his reelection campaign. During that campaign, Farooq intimidated opposition candidates, and when the elections were held on March 23, 1987, Farooq engaged in massive vote rigging. Farooq claimed that he had won the election, although his opponent clearly had received far more votes.[36] When Farooq resumed his position as chief minister, he virtually deserted his governing duties while spending his time as a playboy—living up to his nickname: the "disco chief minister." Farooq's regime resorted to widespread repression in a vain effort to stifle growing discontent. More young Kashmiri men crossed the Line of Control into AJK to secure ISI weapons and combat training, and when they returned, many joined the native Kashmiri JKLF anti–India terrorist group.[37] The JKLF began assassinating IJK government officials.[38]

The spark that really set off the explosive Kashmir mass uprising occurred on January 19, 1990. On that day, India dismissed Farooq Abdullah (the "Lion Cub") as IJK chief minister on grounds that he had been unable to control the JKLF terrorists. While Kashmiris had hated Farooq because he was an Indian puppet, they were even more outraged by India's arbitrary dismissal of this native Kashmiri. The next day, India brought the IJK under Governor's rule and appointed the brutal Jagmohan as IJK's new governor.

Two days later, on January 21, 1990, Kashmiri armed resistance to India's occupation forces exploded into a mass uprising ("the Intifada"). Mass anti–Indian demonstrations broke out in Srinagar, and for three days Indian paramilitary forces fired into unarmed crowds, killing some 300 Kashmiri protesters. The entire Kashmiri population rose up against the Indian occupiers and demanded IJK independence. This mass resistance would last for five years. The Kashmiris had given India more than a fair chance to give IJK some form of representative self-government. They finally had enough of India's bogus IJK elections, and Indian-controlled corrupt and oppressive puppet governments.

India quickly took firm action to put down Kashmir's mass uprising. On February 19, 1990, it dissolved the IJK's Legislative Assembly, which would not meet again for nine years. India began deploying 220,000 troops to IJK to contain the uprising. On April 11th, Pakistan's Army Chief Beg said that he was ordering the army to counter this massive Indian troop deployment, and he put Pakistan on nuclear alert. While Pakistan had not yet conducted a hot test of its nuclear bomb, it knew it could detonate a real nuclear bomb by simply inserting an enriched uranium core into one of the bombs that it already had successfully cold tested. The American intelligence detected Pakistani preparations for a nuclear strike against India.[39]

To prevent an Indo-Pak nuclear war, American President Bush dispatched his deputy National Security Adviser Robert Gates to the area. Gates arrived in Pakistan on May 20, 1990, and met with President Ishaq Khan and Army Chief Beg. Gates then traveled to India and met Indian Prime Minister V.P. Singh. Gates' intervention helped avert a nuclear war by his reporting to India that Pakistan had just pledged to close its terrorist training camps.[40]

While the danger of an Indo-Pak nuclear war subsided, the mass uprising in Kashmir continued. On July 19, 1990, India imposed dictatorial President's Rule in the IJK, which would continue for over nine years. The mass uprising was centered in IJK's Muslim-dominated Kashmir Valley. The JKLF spearheaded the uprising, and at first received ISI assistance. There was great enthusiasm and hope of success among the Kashmir Valley Muslims.

However, India was able to suppress the Intifada uprising by saturating the Kashmir Valley with Indian Army and paramilitary troops. The army built bunkers on many street intersections in Valley cities and towns. They imposed curfews, set up checkpoints, and rounded up all young men in towns and villages in "crackdowns."[41] During these crackdowns, those identified as suspected terrorists by masked informants were taken to camps where they were harshly interrogated. Many were tortured and some never were heard from again.[42]

The Kashmiri-based terrorist JKLF group which spearheaded the insurgency began suffering heavy losses. The Indian Army began killing over a thousand JKLF fighters each year, and the JKLF lost its ISI support. The ISI began supporting the JKLF's rivals, including the Pakistan-based HuM. The HuM was the military arm of Pakistan's JI religious party, and it soon dominated all militant groups in Kashmir. To secure its supremacy, the HuM even betrayed JKLF hideouts to the Indians and began directly attacking JKLF forces.[43] The HuM became hated by Kashmiris for collaborating with India in destroying the native-led JKLF and for terrorizing Kashmiri citizens into supporting HuM.

Benazir Bhutto Removed from Office

While Prime Minister Bhutto was monitoring the uprising in Kashmir and trying to avoid a nuclear war, a new crisis developed in Karachi—Sindh Province's capital. The Karachi crisis began on February 8, 1990, when an anti–Bhutto MQM strike turned into a day of violence. Police traded gunfire with gunmen among the looting demonstrators, and over 55 persons were killed. The police were unable to control the Karachi violence, and criminal gangs began kidnapping wealthy businessmen for ransom. On May 27, 1990, Sindh's provincial government had Sindhi police enter the MQM-controlled Pucca Qila fort area in Hyderabad—the center of MQM power. The police claimed they entered to seize illegal weapons at the fort, but they also conducted house-to-house searches using police lists of suspects. The MQM resisted this intrusion and 31 women and children were killed.[44]

The Karachi violence increased as terrorist attacks added to the mayhem. On May 31, 1990, terrorists attacked a bus in Karachi, killing 45 persons and injuring 33 more. Army Chief Beg offered to deploy the army to Karachi, but only on condition that he be given authority to set up military courts there and be authorized to arrest both MQM and PPP agitators. Prime Minister Bhutto refused to give Beg these emergency powers, fearing that a strong military intervention would alienate her supporters in this main PPP political base in her native province.[45] So troops wouldn't be deployed in Sindh Province for another two years. This disagreement between Bhutto and General Beg over how to handle the Karachi violence marked the beginning of the end of the solid relationship between the two leaders.[46]

A major international crisis now suddenly broke out in the Middle East. On August 2, 1990, Iraqi dictator Saddam Hussein's army invaded and occupied Kuwait. Saddam realized that by seizing Kuwait's vast oil fields, Iraq would greatly increase its power in the region. The United States reacted by organizing a multi-country coalition to force the Iraqis out of Kuwait. Benazir Bhutto authorized sending a Pakistani brigade to join the coalition to "guard the Holy Places" inside Saudi Arabia. Later Pakistan would dispatch 3,000 more troops with orders to operate exclusively within Saudi borders.

Prime Minister Benazir Bhutto and her successor Nawaz Sharif had several reasons for joining the coalition against Saddam Hussein. First, Pakistan was beholden to the Saudis for their years of generous financial support, and the Saudis were genuinely afraid that Saddam might invade Saudi Arabia next. Sharif also hoped that by joining the American-led coalition, the United States might lift its sanctions and restore aid to Pakistan.

However, even this token support to the American-led coalition was widely criticized by Pakistan's people, who sympathized with Saddam Hussein for his daring defiance of the powerful United States. Pakistan's

Islamists took to the streets in support of Saddam Hussein, and the forthcoming American attack on Saddam's forces would strengthen Pakistan's anti–American sentiment.

Iraq's invasion of Kuwait hurt Pakistan's economy since it led to a rise in world oil prices, causing Pakistan's oil import costs to double. Also, Iraq's invasion caused Pakistanis working in Kuwait to flee and return home. This exodus led to a US$300 million per year loss to Pakistan in remittances that were being sent home by these workers to their families.

Army Chief General Beg had tried to undermine Benazir Bhutto soon after she had taken office. His dislike for her had grown as she had interfered with army promotions, had refused Beg's offer to send troops into Karachi and had tried to slow down Pakistan's nuclear weapons program.[47] Beg wanted Bhutto dismissed, and he worked with President Ishaq Khan to arrange for her ouster.[48] So on August 6, 1990, President Ishaq Khan dismissed Benazir Bhutto as prime minister—using his constitutional power as president to dismiss prime ministers. Ishaq cited corruption as the main justification for removing Bhutto, and Bhutto's administration had indeed been unusually corrupt. Army Chief Beg allowed Ishaq Khan to stay on as president. Bhutto was unrepentant and denied that her regime had been unusually corrupt or that she had made any mistakes. She charged that top military leaders had removed her simply because she represented democracy.

Benazir Bhutto left a mixed legacy from her short 17 months in office. On the positive side, she had focused attention on human rights—especially the rights of women. She had taken action against drug dealers, terrorists and bandits in the countryside.[49] On the negative side, she had been so preoccupied with maintaining power that she seldom had acted in the national interest. During her term, not a single piece of meaningful legislation had been passed by the National Assembly. She hadn't even tried to push through needed reforms for fear of losing support among powerful landowners and Islamist religious leaders. Also, she had made no attempt to work with other politicians to strengthen democratic institutions. She had spent much of her time attacking her main rival Nawaz Sharif.

12

Sharif's First Term

During the three-year period covered in this chapter (August 1990–October 1993), Nawaz Sharif was elected Pakistan's prime minister. While he nominally headed a civilian government, a military-dominated junta would really control the country. The junta constantly would monitor Sharif's activities. The chapter ends with the army pressuring Sharif to resign.

Sharif Takes Office

After President Ghulam Ishaq Khan dismissed Benazir Bhutto as prime minister on August 6, 1990, Ishaq declared a state of emergency and dissolved the national and provincial assemblies. Then President Ishaq appointed Mustafa Jatoi as interim prime minister to lead a two-month caretaker government. President Ishaq Khan and Jatoi's caretaker government took measures to insure that Bhutto would not win the upcoming elections. The government initiated corruption investigations of Benazir Bhutto and her PPP colleagues. The government-controlled media accused Bhutto of misconduct but refused to report her denials. These attacks on Bhutto made it impossible for her to meaningfully compete in the upcoming elections.

Pakistan had been relying on American military aid for over three decades. However, during the last several years, it had been warning Pakistan's leaders that if Pakistan kept developing a nuclear bomb, America would stop this assistance. Pakistan's leaders ignored these threats, since the Americans never had carried out past threats. However, newly elected President George H. W. Bush wasn't willing to issue a false certification that Pakistan didn't possess a nuclear bomb, partly because Pakistan had lost its strategic value to America once the Soviets had left Afghanistan. Therefore, on October 1, 1990, the United States terminated assistance to Pakistan.

Pakistan's leaders were in a shocked state of disbelief at America's aid cut off. They had been confident that the Americans never would carry out its threats that sanctions would be imposed. They also were shocked at the enormity of the sanctions. Pakistan went from being the world's third largest recipient of American foreign aid to receiving almost nothing. The caretaker government sent its foreign minister to Washington to try to work something out. However, Pakistan's leaders chose not accept the tough conditions for dropping the sanctions, which included destroying its nuclear bomb cores. Most Pakistanis felt betrayed by the United States, which had used their country to drive the Soviets from Afghanistan and then suddenly cut off all aid. With the loss of American military funds, the army began developing its own independent sources of revenues, including the sale of nuclear technology and equipment abroad.

The National Assembly elections were held on October 24, 1990. Nawaz Sharif's PML(N) party and its IJI nine-party coalition won an absolute majority of Assembly seats. There were several reasons for the IJI victory. First, the voters felt that during her term, Benazir Bhutto had cheated them out of a representative government—just as her father had done before her. The voters also were disappointed that Bhutto had tolerated high levels of corruption in her government. Also, Sharif's IJI campaign had been better organized, and his campaign workers had worked harder than Bhutto's workers. In addition, the army and ISI had backed Sharif. The ISI had directed the IJI's campaign and had collected millions of dollars in a slush fund which they distributed to anti–Bhutto politicians.[1] The ISI also had manipulated the election results.[2]

Nawaz Sharif was sworn in as Pakistan's prime minister on November 6, 1990. He would remain in office for just two years and six months. During this short time, Pakistan was again really controlled by a three-man junta of the army chief, president and prime minister. The army chief and president once again would dominate the prime minister. Sharif lifted the state of emergency and promised a government totally committed to serving the country. These selfless statements were followed by a brief "Era of Good Feelings," during which even the violence in Sindh Province temporarily subsided.

Sharif had a number of strengths. First, he had some experience in government administration, having served as chief minister of Punjab Province. Also, his Sharif-led IJI coalition had won a clear election victory. Sharif would have the support of Pakistan's businessmen, partly because he was a businessman from a family of Lahore industrialists. He was the first national leader who relied on the backing of the business and commercial classes, in contrast to prior leaders who had been backed by feudal landowners. In addition, he

12. Sharif's First Term

had a secure power base in the crucial Punjab Province, where he was immensely popular and backed by the same urban middle-class that had supported Zia. In addition, Sharif had good relations with Pakistan's military leaders who had helped him come to power. He worked well with the powerful military-controlled junta.

Sharif also had a number of weaknesses. First, Sharif's position was very fragile. President Ishaq Khan had the constitutional authority to dismiss him at any time by claiming that Sharif had lost majority support in the National Assembly. Since Sharif headed a large nine-party IJI coalition government, he would struggle to keep this coalition together. Also, Sharif had no experience in public finance, economics or foreign affairs. In addition, he wasn't even conscious of his limitations, and he believed he could simply apply business principles to solve the country's economic, political and social problems.[3] Also, Sharif was a poor administrator. He would fill key posts with relatives and business friends instead of competent advisers. His choosing businessmen instead of economists for advice on Pakistan's economy would have negative consequences.[4] He would make important decisions without careful consideration, without setting priorities and without examining long-term consequences. Also, Sharif would focus on strengthening his own political power, and so he wouldn't work with his rival Bhutto to pass meaningful reforms. Instead he suppressed the opposition by reinstating press censorship, blocking the opposition from using the media, and banning student unions. Also, Sharif would support the demands of Islamists to further limit the rights of non–Muslims, and this would lead to an upsurge in religious-based intolerance.[5] In addition, Sharif was beholden to army and ISI leaders for their having supported his election. To repay them he would give them a free hand in national security matters, and thereby weaken his ability to make peace with India.

On May 9, 1990, Prime Minister Sharif announced his new conservative economic policy which called for promoting private business by reducing government regulations. However, with government regulatory oversight removed, most companies chose to maximize profits by lowering their workers' wages and by raising the prices of their products. The plan would result in the country's larger aggressive companies making huge profits, without needing to hire new workers.[6] Companies in the food industry began hoarding food, hoping that prices would rise. Many companies also adulterated the food that they sold.[7]

Sharif also returned to private management those companies that Zulfi Bhutto had nationalized. Sharif even privatized some public service monopolies that always had been state-owned, including those controlling telephones, highways and canals. Sharif made privatizations with little thought of the consequences, and so the country would rotate between support of private and public enterprises, depending on who was in power.[8] He privatized most national banks, which now began making more risky loans with low interest rates, minimal security, and small down payments—loans which often never would be repaid.[9] Sharif's privatization program failed to revive the already weak economy, and critics labeled his so-called "reforms" as "loot and plunder." At the same time, Sharif reduced public school funding and closed women's health clinics and population control offices.

It now came time for the American-led military coalition to forcibly remove Saddam Hussein's Iraqi troops from Kuwait. The United States had assembled a large, multi-national coalition on Saudi soil, and on February 24, 1991, these troops struck Saddam's troops in Kuwait (the "First Gulf War"). The allied coalition would liberate Kuwait in just three days, and after pursuing Saddam's forces into Iraq, signed an armistice on March 3. However, coalition forces hadn't destroyed Saddam's retreating elite Republic Guard divisions and had left Saddam's regime intact.

Pakistan's Islamic clerics were angry at Sharif's support of the American-led attack on the Muslim Iraqi troops. To conciliate the angry clerics, Sharif urged the National Assembly to enact the Sharia Act—legislation long sought to Islamists. On May 16, 1991, the Assembly enacted this law, which declared the Koran and Sunnah to be the law of the land—not just guidelines for legislation. This opened the way for courts to base decisions on Islamic law instead of secular law. The act also declared that laws repugnant to Islam were null and void. However, the passage of the act didn't fully satisfy the Islamic fundamentalists, who now insisted that the act's provisions be inserted into the Constitution.

Army Chief Aslam Beg had presided over the military juntas which had undermined both Sharif's and Bhutto's governments by secretly supporting their opponents. So when Beg retired after three years in that post, Prime Minister Sharif chose a replacement who he was sure would not interfere in politics. On August 16, 1991, Sharif appointed General Asif Nawaz as the new army chief. Nawaz was a strong, no-nonsense, incorruptible leader who would seek to reintroduce professionalism and quality training to the army. He had a strong commitment not to involve the army in politics, and his declaration of neutrality in the Sharif-Bhutto rivalry would disappoint Sharif.

A major shift in world power occurred on December 9, 1991, when the Soviet Union (USSR) broke up into many independent nations. Russia was the largest of the former Soviet states, but it was smaller than the former USSR. The United States suddenly became the world's sole superpower. The Soviet breakup affected Pakistan in several ways. First, Pakistan's leaders became more friendly toward the United States—not wanting to risk offending the world's sole superpower. Also, Soviet aid to the communist Afghan

Army stopped, and this would severely diminish its ability to protect Najibullah's communist government in Kabul. In addition, the Soviet breakup heralded the end of the Cold War, and thereby ended Pakistan's role as an anti-communist American ally.

Prime Minister Sharif still was committed to privatizing Pakistan's economy. He now came up with an unusual plan to privatize public transportation. On February 11, 1992, he announced a government loan program to enable individuals to borrow money to purchase taxis, buses and trucks (the "Yellow Cab Scheme"). The program's goal was to allow the unemployed to buy and drive these vehicles and thereby improve the public transportation system. The program jammed city streets with small taxis. It was immensely popular and widened Sharif's base of supporters. However, it also was widely abused. While many borrowers did use the loans to buy cabs, many hired others to drive them, or allowed their relatives to use the vehicles for pleasure.[10]

Prime Minister Sharif still wanted to show that he supported the Islamist clerics. Therefore, when the position of ISI chief became vacant, Sharif on March 14, 1992, selected Islamist extremist General Nasir as the new ISI chief. The appointment of this bearded "born again" Muslim extremist was a big mistake. During his 14 months in office the maverick Nasir would transform the ISI into a poorly organized, non-professional organization which focused on promoting Islamist jihadist operations in Bosnia, China and the Philippines.[11] Pakistan's military leaders became concerned with Nasir's far-flung radical activities, and how the ISI was losing its ability to gather intelligence needed to protect Pakistan from a surprise enemy attack. In response to army pressure, Nasir would be removed as ISI chief 14 months later. Nasir's successor would be Javed Ashraf Qazi. The army chief instructed Qazi to reorganize the ISI and return it to an intelligence-gathering agency. Qazi would purge many Islamist extremists from his ISI.

Civil War in Afghanistan

For three years, Pakistan had quietly supported the mujahideen campaign to defeat communist forces in Afghanistan. After the failure to seize Jalalabad, the Northern Alliance had emerged as the strongest mujahideen group in Afghanistan. With the Soviet Union's collapse and the end of Soviet arms shipments to Kabul, the Afghan communist regime was doomed. On April 16, 1992, as Northern Alliance fighters closed in on the Afghan capital Kabul, communist leader Najibullah fled from the city.

With the overthrow of the Afghan communist government, Pakistan quickly intervened in the selection of a new Afghan government. On April

24, Prime Minister Sharif had most of the Afghan leaders-in-exile sign the "Peshawar Accord." The accord called for a series of rotating interim Afghan presidents. Mojadiddi was to rule for two months, followed by Rabbani for a four-month term. Mujahideen commander Hekmatyr refused to sign the accord since he wanted to become Afghanistan's sole ruler. He raced to Kabul to stake out his claim, but Northern Alliance forces under Rabbani beat him to the capital city. Rabbani helped set up the rotating leadership plan provided for by the Peshawar Agreement, and he soon would take over full control of Afghanistan's new government.

A four-year Afghan civil war began when mujahideen commander Hekmatyr began shelling Kabul with the aim of overthrowing Rabbani's interim Afghan government. Initially the fighting was just between the forces of Hekmatyr and Rabbani's government. However, this local fighting soon turned into a multi-sided contest between many warring mujahideen groups who competed for power, territory and spoils. The civil war would continue for four years, until the Islamist Taliban seized Kabul and set up its own government.

Meanwhile, Pakistan was again experiencing its own violence in Sindh Province. Provincial officials and businessmen in the province had been requesting army intervention for years to stop the highway robberies in rural Sindh and the kidnappings in Karachi. To put an end to this violence, Army Chief Asif Nawaz planned to deploy 60,000 troops to Sindh Province. The soldiers began arriving on June 19, 1992, and they soon had the 2,000 bandits (daicots) in the countryside on the run. Then, on its own initiative, the army began suppressing the violent MQM militants in Karachi who were responsible for much of the city's violence.[12] This new campaign upset Prime Minister Sharif, since the MQM was a strong Sharif supporter.

On January 8, 1993, Army Chief Asif Nawaz died of a heart attack. President Ishaq Khan and Sharif quarreled over the procedure for appointing the new army chief, and this quarrel ended Sharif's ability to work with the President.[13] Four days later, President Ishaq Khan appointed General Abdul Waheed as Nawaz's replacement. General Waheed would serve in that post for three years. He was one of the rare, selfless, incorruptible army chiefs who put Pakistan's national interests above everything else. He also would allow civilians to run the country without army interference.

Pakistan's Risky Game of Supporting Terrorists

On February 26, 1993, terrorists detonated explosives packed inside a van in the parking garage beneath the New York City's World Trade Center, killing six persons. The FBI would conclude that Pakistani Ramzi Yousef had been behind the attack. In response to this terrorist attack on American soil by Pakistani terrorists, the United States demanded that Prime Minister Sharif shut down ISI's terrorist camps. The ISI didn't comply, but it did move the locations of the camps. The CIA director advised President Clinton that Pakistan was on the verge of becoming a terrorist state, and already the United States had placed Pakistan on its watch-list of nations suspected of supporting terrorism.

Pakistan also was implicated in a terrorist attack inside India. On March 12, 1993, terrorists detonated bombs at the stock exchange in Mumbai, India, killing over 250 people. Pakistan's bearded Islamic extremist ISI chief Nasir had collaborated with Indian Muslim criminals in the attack.

With Pakistan being linked to two high-profile attacks in foreign countries, Sharif felt obliged to take a public stance against terrorism. On April 1, 1993, Sharif's government announced that it was beginning a "crackdown on Islamic extremists." For the next decade, Pakistan would repeatedly promise to prevent Islamist militant groups from openly operating in Peshwar and other bases inside its territory. After each promise, Pakistan would take just enough limited measures to prevent America from declaring it a state sponsor of terrorism—a declaration that would have led to extremely harsh sanctions.[14] Pakistan's leaders tried to create the impression that they were doing everything possible to destroy the extremists—a task which they claimed was proving extremely difficult.

The instability of Pakistan's government structure became clear when President Ishaq Khan used his presidential power to dismiss prime ministers a second time. On April 18, 1993, he dismissed Prime Minister Nawaz Sharif, claiming that Sharif no longer controlled a majority of seats in the National Assembly. He also claimed that Sharif had been engaging in corrupt activities. However, the president's real reasons for dismissal was that Sharif had been threatening the president's power, denouncing the president on television and interfering in army affairs.[15] The public was disturbed with President Ishaq's second dismissal of an elected prime minister, and crowds of Sharif's supporters lined the railway tracks as a train took him home. The president appointed a caretaker government to run the country until elections would be held three months later.

However, this time President Ishaq's dismissal was challenged in court. On May 26, 1993, the Supreme Court made an unusual decision. It reinstated Sharif as prime minister on grounds that the president's dismissal had been illegal, since there had been no proof that Sharif had lacked majority support in the National Assembly—as required by the Constitution. President Ishaq was shocked that the court had reversed his dismissal, since the same court had upheld his dismissal of Benazir Bhutto just a few years before. The Court may have reached this courageous decision partly because it was trying to salvage its reputation from a disclosure that a former army chief had influenced the Court in an important case.[16]

While Sharif had been reinstated as prime minister, the Sharif-Ishaq power struggle continued. The struggle was highly publicized and was destabilizing the country. While army leaders had been supporting Ishaq, even they had to recognize that he now seemed willing to destroy his enemies in a paranoid rage, regardless of the consequences.[17] Several months later, Army Chief Waheed felt obliged to resolve the public power struggle. He convinced both Prime Minister Sharif and President Ishaq to resign for the good of the country.

On July 18, 1993, Moeen Qureshi was immediately sworn in as Pakistan's interim prime minister. The non-political Qureshi was an excellent choice, since he was an honest, dedicated and competent civil servant. The sincerity of this retired World Bank official led most military and civilian leaders to give him their total support. He would use his three months in office to undertake some long overdue financial reforms demanded by the World Bank to bring the country's huge budget deficit under control. He devalued the rupee, imposed a temporary tax on agricultural income, and he reduced government expenditures. He pressured borrowers to repay government loans by publishing their names in newspapers.[18]

The October 6, 1993, election for a new National Assembly was relatively fair, and free from ISI interference. Pakistan seemed to have moved toward a two-party system, since the election was dominated again by Benazir Bhutto's PPP and Nawaz Sharif's PML(N).

Benazir's PPP party won the most seats as many voters overlooked the corruption that had marred her first term. However, the PPP won just 86 out of 207 National Assembly seats, while the PML (N) won 72 seats. Since the PPP hadn't won a majority of seats on its own, Bhutto had to cobble together a coalition government which would control such a majority. The PML assumed the role of the opposition in the National Assembly. A two-party system seemed to have developed, with the two mainstream and moderate PPP and PML parties alternating control of the government.

A.Q. Khan: Nuclear Weapons Proliferator

Pakistan's A.Q. Khan had stolen centrifuge uranium enrichment secrets from his Dutch employer, and then had supervised the construction of Pakistan's first nuclear bomb. A.Q. Khan now decided that he would secretly take uranium enrichment technology and equipment from Pakistan's Kahuta nuclear facility and sell them to other countries. He was able to transport the equipment to his buyers using military aircraft because Khan (the "Father of

12. Sharif's First Term

the Bomb") had such great prestige that he was largely untouchable. Also, the proceeds of the sales went largely to the Kahuta facility and the army.[19]

A.Q. Khan had several reasons for selling the nuclear weapons secrets and devices. He wanted to allow Muslim and other non–Western countries to break the Western monopoly of atomic weapons. He also wanted to raise money for Pakistan and himself. By taking kickbacks from the sales, A.Q. Khan would become extremely wealthy, and he would use his illegal earnings to buy houses, businesses, and clubs.[20]

A.Q. Khan's first venture into nuclear proliferation was the sale of nuclear technology and devices to Iran. These sales were noted in a secret February 1, 1993, American report.[21] The following year, Khan helped Iran assemble its first 50 uranium-enriching centrifuges.

A.Q. Khan's proliferation would continue during Benazir Bhutto's second term as prime minister. When he learned that Bhutto planned to visit North Korea, he asked her to assist him. A.Q. asked Bhutto to ask Korean President Kim Il-Sung to sell Pakistan blueprints of the latest version of the No-Dong missile that could carry a nuclear warhead. During her December 29, 1993, visit, Bhutto met Il-Sung and purchased the blueprints.[22] A.Q. followed up by trading Pakistan's uranium enrichment secrets for North Korean missile technology and devices.[23] During the next years, Khan would provide nuclear technology to North Korea, Iran and Iraq. He also visited Muslim nations like Libya, Syria, and Saudi Arabia, trying to persuade their governments to buy Pakistan's nuclear secrets.[24] Then in May 1998, Pakistan conducted its first hot testing of some of its nuclear bombs.

13

Benazir Bhutto's Second Term

During the three years covered in this chapter (October 1993–February 1997), Benazir Bhutto had her second chance at governing the country as prime minister. Toward the end of her second time in office, the Afghan Taliban would be founded, and 20 months later it would seize the Afghan capital of Kabul. The chapter ends with the president dismissing her from office.

Benazir Begins Her Second Term

On October 19, 1993, Benazir Bhutto was sworn in as prime minister of Pakistan for a second time. Benazir began her second term with great promise, and for several reasons she was expected to serve out the five-year limit on a prime minister's term. First, her old foe Ishaq Khan was gone—the president who had dismissed her during her first term. The newly elected President, Farooq Leghari, not only was a former PPP member, but he also promised never to use his constitutional power to dismiss prime ministers. Also, a two-party political system seemed to have emerged, with PPP and PML(N) governments alternating in office after fair elections. Pakistanis were becoming accustomed to voting in successive elections, and they tended to vote for moderate candidates. In addition, Bhutto had reached an understanding with Pakistan's army leaders, who no longer would obstruct her at every turn as they had during her first time in office. Realizing that she needed the army's leaders on her side, she decided to defer to the army chief and ISI director on sensitive foreign policy and security matters. Also, Bhutto decided not to interfere with Pakistan's nuclear program, since she realized that she was powerless to stop that army-supported program. In addition, Bhutto would issue more presidential ordinances instead of trying to persuade the National Assembly to enact desired programs.

However, Benazir's hopes for a long, peaceful term in office were quickly dashed when her main rival Sharif immediately began viciously attacking her and the PPP. She responded with equally vicious counterattacks. Encouraged by her husband Zardari (her principal adviser), she used her government authority to investigate the Sharif family businesses and even arrested Sharif's ill and aged father and Sharif's closest associates.[1] This vendetta would sap her strength and divert her attention from governing.[2]

When Benazir Bhutto began her second term in office, Pakistan faced enormous problems. First, Pakistan's economy was in terrible shape. Government revenues were modest because of widespread tax evasion and smuggling. Most of the national budget was dedicated to paying huge military expenditures and making payments on the immense national debt. Also, Pakistan's agricultural output had declined due to floods and disease, and most of Pakistan's cotton, rice and sugar cane crops had been destroyed. In addition, Sindh and Punjab provinces continued to suffer from violent sectarian conflict. Finally, over 2,500 well-armed foreign fighters tied to al-Qaeda resided in Peshawar, in Pakistan's NWFP. They were a constant threat to Pakistan's government itself.

Bhutto adopted many of the foreign policy goals of her predecessors. First, Bhutto would try to achieve Pakistan's long-standing goal of manipulating the installation of a friendly, pliable government in Afghanistan. In furtherance of this goal, once the Afghan Taliban had been formed, she would assist it with its military campaign to seize all of Afghanistan. Also, Bhutto supported the Kashmir insurgency against India. Bhutto would allow Islamist groups to openly raise funds and recruit fighters for the Kashmir jihad. She also would allow the ISI to train and arm these recruits. Finally, she sought to restore good relations with the United States, which had reached a new low under Sharif's government.

Prime Minister Benazir Bhutto focused on staying in power by not offending influential groups. However, she would restore some of the reforms that she had set in place during her first term—which Sharif had dropped. She would build public schools, set up health and family planning clinics, and promote a polio immunization program.[3] She also would improve sanitation and the water supply in all the provinces.

While Bhutto had always stood up for the rights of women and other oppressed minorities, she was unable to stop the rising violence against religious minorities. These minorities were increasingly being accused of blasphemy and other violations of religious ordinances. The violence against non–Muslims turned more deadly on April 5, 1994, when three SSP gunmen attacked three Christians just after they had left a Lahore courthouse in a blasphemy case. One defendant was killed and two were wounded. This attack marked a transition from mob attacks on non–Muslims to attacks carried out by terrorists and well-armed militias. Pakistan's central government wouldn't adequately protect these minorities.[4]

While Prime Minister Bhutto was trying to promote the virtues of her civilian government, the reputation of all Pakistan's civilian governments was damaged by the "Mehrangate" scandal. The scandal became public on April 7, 1994, when Mehran Bank owner Yunnus Habib was arrested. Habib's Mehran Bank had been giving gifts, bribes and low-interest loans to high-ranking members of both Bhutto's and Sharif's governments. Army Chief Beg and the ISI also had used the bank for improper purposes.[5] President Leghari also was implicated in the scandal.

President Leghari, wanting to preserve his tarnished reputation, began to distance himself from Prime Minister Bhutto. He had become concerned with Bhutto's growing use of intimidation, assaults, and arrests of her political opponents. Bhutto seemed to be seeking total power, and she even began packing the courts with loyalists.[6]

The Birth of the Afghan Taliban

Pakistan's leaders became very interested when the Taliban was formed in neighboring Afghanistan, and developed into a national movement. The Taliban movement began on September 20, 1994, when Mullah Mohammed Omar rescued some children who had been kidnapped by local warlords on the outskirts of Kandahar, Afghanistan.[7] Mullah Omar's rescue convinced a local committee to pick Omar to lead a group to defend locals from similar abuses[8] Mullah Omar began recruiting to his group students (talibs) from local madrassas and mosques, and the group began carrying out vigilante attacks against local warlords. Mullah Omar called his group the "Taliban."

Pakistan soon established good relations with Mullah Omar's Taliban movement, partly due to the Taliban's rescue of a Pakistan Army convoy inside Afghanistan. On October 29, 1994, a Pakistan Army "goodwill" convoy of 30 trucks left Quetta, Pakistan, loaded with food and medical supplies, and headed to the Afghan border. The purpose of the convoy was to try to open up a trade route between Pakistan and Turkmenistan to the west.[9] The convoy had been organized by Pakistan's Interior Minister and was led by several ISI officers. When the convoy was intercepted inside Afghanistan by a local warlord, Mullah Omar rescued it.[10] The thankful ISI immediately began supporting the Taliban, and the rescue began decades of Taliban-ISI cooperation.

13. Benazir Bhutto's Second Term

Pakistan hoped that the Taliban could end the Afghan civil war, and hoped that the ISI could control any Afghan Taliban movement that might emerge.

The Taliban movement soon took over most territory in Afghanistan, largely because most of its "conquests" were won by threats, bribes and negotiations rather than fighting. Also, the ISI would secretly supply the Taliban with ammunition, fuel and food. On November 5, 1994, the Taliban seized Kandahar—Afghanistan's second-largest city. The Taliban had taken the city in just two days of fighting—partly because the Taliban had bribed a commander inside the city.[11]

This easy seizure of Kandahar led the Taliban to secretly plan the conquest of the whole country.[12] The seizure also enabled the Taliban to attract to its ranks over 10,000 highly motivated young students from Pakistan's religious schools, who swarmed into Kandahar to join the Taliban.[13] Pakistan's army and ISI would keep expanding their support to the Taliban with every province that the Taliban seized on its march to Kabul.

While the Taliban was seizing control of Afghanistan, Pakistan's government was trying to suppress the violence in Karachi. The army and police had engaged in a futile two-year operation to control the city, but their ruthless tactics had only provoked further violence. The police had even resorted to extrajudicial killings, since Karachi's judges were slow, corrupt and easily intimidated. The army finally gave up trying to restore order, and on November 30, 1994, it suddenly withdrew from the city. After the army's departure, bombings, assassinations, and murders in the city rose to new levels.

Prime Minister Bhutto now took some bold action which greatly impressed the United States. She learned that terrorist Ramzi Yousef had been living in an Islamabad rooming house for two years under ISI protection. Bhutto believed that Yousef had twice tried to assassinate her, and that he also was the primary suspect in the garage bombing of New York City's World Trade Center. Bhutto had supporters in the ISI seize Yousef on February 7, 1995, and the next day had him extradited to the United States. She wasted no time because she feared that a delay might give extremists in the ISI a chance to free him.[14]

India Triumphant in Kashmir

The mass uprising (intifada) in Indian-controlled Kashmir (IJK) ended on May 11, 1995, with an Indian defeat of Kashmiri insurgents—the last major battle between the two adversaries. After this battle, there was a noticeable reduction in guerrilla activity in Kashmir, and mass anti–Indian demonstrations ceased.

There were several reasons why India had been able to put down the mass uprising in IJK. First, India had shown great stamina and commitment in retaining control over IJK, and it had saturated the Kashmir Valley with army and security forces. At the same time, despite thousands of deaths, the Kashmiris had no more autonomy, and the Indians still occupied all of IJK. Kashmiris no longer were willing to risk more lives in a futile battle against overwhelming Indian forces. Also, India had been receiving substantial support from guerrillas who had quit the rebellion and enlisted as auxiliaries in India's war on the insurgents. These "renegades" had been helping India by identifying terrorists and disclosing their hideouts.[15] In addition, the mass uprising had fragmented between the Kashmiri insurgents (led by the Kashmiri-based JKLF), and outside militants (dominated by the Pakistan-based HuM).

The Indian suppression of the Kashmiri mass uprising was followed by a four-year period of Kashmir demoralization and inaction. The Kashmiris retained a simmering hatred for the Indian occupiers, but they largely kept to themselves their hatred and desire for independence. The Indians responded to this superficial return to normalcy by reducing the number of their bunkers and checkpoints.

Indian leaders didn't use this lull in the fighting to take any long-term measures that might have resolved the grievances of the IJK residents. Instead, India continued imposing corrupt puppet governments on the IJK. On October 9, 1996, India had Farooq Abdullah (the "Lion Cub") reinstated as IJK's chief minister. His Indian-backed government was widely detested, since Farooq was incompetent, corrupt, and supported India's counter-insurgency campaign.

The Taliban Overthrows Afghanistan's Government

Prime Minister Benazir Bhutto continued to encourage Pakistan's army and the ISI to assist the Afghan Taliban in its conquest of Afghanistan. On September 5, 1995, the Taliban seized the western Afghan city of Herat with help of ISI military advisers and supplies. Afghan President Rabbani was furious at this Pakistani support for the Taliban who were trying to overthrow his government. The day after Herat fell, a pro–Rabbani mob set fire to Pakistan's embassy in Kabul in retaliation for Pakistan's interference in Afghan affairs. Rabbani may have instigated the burning.

Despite Bhutto's support for the Kashmir insurgency, some impatient Islamist army officers planned a coup to immediately make Pakistan an Islamic dictatorship. Bhutto discovered the plot and on September 26, she had plot leader General Zahir Abbasi arrested, along with 35 other officers.[16] The plotters had been preparing to storm a corps commanders conference, kill

13. Benazir Bhutto's Second Term

the generals meeting there, and set up an Islamic dictatorship. The Islamist influence in the army had been growing because the army had begun recruiting more soldiers from cities—where boys had grown up in conservative Islamist families.

The Taliban campaign to seize control of Afghanistan concluded on September 27, 1996, when it seized Kabul from Rabbani's coalition government. The quiet, reclusive Taliban leader Mullah Omar chose to rule Afghanistan from his home city of Kandahar rather than from the traditional capital in Kabul. This mysterious mullah would dominate the country like a medieval lord, dispensing cash to his loyal followers from a large box in his office.[17] The Taliban still didn't control all of northern Afghanistan, and it soon launched a military campaign against its Northern Alliance rival.

The Taliban's seizure of Kabul affected Pakistan in several ways. First, the Afghan Taliban became much more independent from Pakistan now that they had set up its own Afghan government. Also, jihadist groups became emboldened. They began operating openly in Pakistan, and spread religious intolerance and terrorism throughout the country.[18] In addition, with new territory under their control, the Taliban expanded their smuggling operations into Pakistan, which became their main source of income. The smuggling of more opium and heroin into Pakistan led to more Pakistani leaders becoming involved in drug trafficking and added to Pakistan's growing heroin addiction problem.[19]

After the Taliban's seizure of Kabul, Pakistan expanded its support of the Taliban. Pakistan became the first government to officially recognize the Taliban's new government. Also, Pakistan provided the Taliban with additional funds to beef up its military forces which were trying to destroy the Northern Alliance.[20] Pakistan even repaired Afghan power stations and installed a modern Afghan phone system, and helped rehabilitate Afghan olive orchards.[21]

The Taliban now received a boost from another source with the arrival of al-Qaeda leader Osama bin Laden. Bin Laden had been living comfortably in Sudan, where he had been inciting others to violence but had refrained from terrorist activities himself. However, the United States had pressured Sudan's government to expel bin Laden for inciting terrorism. On May 6, 1996, the stateless bin Laden flew into western Afghanistan, and two weeks later moved to Jalalabad in eastern Afghanistan. Bin Laden met Taliban leader Mullah Omar, who allowed him to remain in Afghanistan.[22] Bin Laden and Mullah Omar would reach an agreement whereby bin Laden could stay in Afghanistan and recruit foreign fighters—mainly Uzbeks and Chechens.[23] In return, bin Laden promised to keep a low profile, not antagonize America, and use his foreign fighters to help the Taliban fight its Northern Alliance enemy.[24]

While in Afghanistan, Osama bin Laden would strengthen terrorist groups in the region. The wealthy, well-connected bin Laden would give funds to the Taliban and to the pro-Taliban Haqqani terrorist network based in FATA. He also would set up terrorist training camps for the Taliban and foreign fighters at which trainees would be indoctrinated in his vision of global jihad—which included overthrowing pro-Western Muslim governments like in Pakistan.[25]

Benazir Bhutto Removed from Office

On January 12, 1996, President Leghari appointed General Jahangir Karamat as the new army chief. He appointed Karamat because he was the army's most senior general, and he was a competent and respected officer supported by the army's High Command. His appointment boosted army morale by ending the recent appointments by civilian leaders of their favorite junior generals, which was intended to give the civilians more control of the army.[26] President Leghari also made permanent appointments to the Supreme Court and provincial High Courts which restored the independence and prestige of these institutions.

President Leghari's moves to strengthen the independence of the army and appellate courts were a welcome change. The President had transitioned from being a PPP supporter and Bhutto protector to being a bold leader committed to acting in the country's best interests.[27] However, Leghari's commitment to make the country's institutions stronger and more independent conflicted with Bhutto's desire to increase her own power. A showdown between the two leaders was inevitable.

Prime Minister Benazir Bhutto's popularity was declining due to unprecedented corruption in her government and family. Newspapers were calling her regime "Alice in Plunderland."[28] Her popularity further declined when on July 31, 1996, she appointed her husband Asif Zardari as Minister for Investment. Zardari had a history of corrupt dealings, and he had acquired the nickname "Mr. Ten Percent" for the commission he reportedly demanded in return for approving government construction projects. Bhutto's opponents also attacked her for her support of the United States and for her friendly gestures toward India.

Bhutto's popularity also was declining because of adverse publicity over the feud within her own family. Benazir's own mother and her brother Murtaza were still criticizing her in public. This family feud forever ended on September 20, 1996, when a heavily armed police force confronted her brother Murtaza and his bodyguards outside his home after he returned from an anti-Benazir rally. In the shootout, Murtaza and seven of his bodyguards and supporters were killed. Murtaza was shot in the jaw and left untreated

13. Benazir Bhutto's Second Term

in the street to die of his wounds.[29] The police would claim that Murtaza and his bodyguards fired the first shots.[30] The policeman who shot Murtaza was himself killed shortly thereafter, raising suspicions that Murtaza's death had been part of a high-level plot. Many believed that the ISI had worked with police to assassinate Murtaza, due to his former leadership of the Al-Zulfikar terrorist group. The ISI hated the Al-Zulfikar group since it had received help from India's RAW intelligence group and had tried to assassinate Zia.[31]

President Leghari suspected that the Bhutto regime might have been behind Murtaza's death. Leghari concluded that Bhutto's regime, with its violent suppression of its opposition, must be removed. The President even met with Bhutto's rival Sharif to discuss the lawlessness of Bhutto's regime.

Bhutto's main rival Nawaz Sharif decided that with Bhutto's popularity declining, it was time to promote his own return to office. He organized a whistle stop train tour, during which he sharply criticized Bhutto and her government. He also called for a nationwide work-stoppage to dramatize the widespread dissatisfaction with her government. When the work-stoppage began on October 11, 1996, it semi-paralyzed the country. Then on October 29, Sharif convened a meeting of all major opposition parties, and the parties decided to hold street protests throughout the country until Bhutto's government fell.

The massive Sharif-led protests that followed would give President Leghari the justification he needed to remove Bhutto. On November 4, 1996, Leghari dismissed Bhutto and dissolved the National Assembly. He justified these actions on the grounds of her regime's corruption, her ruthless suppression of opponents, and her inability to control the widespread violence. Her government had lasted just three years, and this was the third in a series of prime ministers dismissed before reaching their five-year term limit. President Leghari appointed a caretaker government and called for fresh elections in three months.

There was no public outcry over Bhutto's dismissal since most Pakistanis had become indifferent to the quarrels between selfish politicians. During these three months, President Leghari led the new caretaker government in a campaign to remove many of Benazir's associates.

The two main competitors in the upcoming National Assembly elections would be Bhutto's PPP and Sharif's PML (N). Benazir Bhutto decided to take a gamble. Instead of preparing for the upcoming elections, she would devote her time to getting her dismissal reversed by the courts. She was sure the Supreme Court would declare her dismissal illegal—as it had declared Sharif's dismissal illegal three years before.

Benazir Bhutto lost her gamble. On January 29, 1997, the Supreme Court held that President Leghari had possessed the legal authority to remove Prime Minister Bhutto on national security grounds. This adverse ruling made it unlikely that she could win the election, since she had not campaigned yet and the election was just five days away.

On February 3, 1997, Pakistan held its national elections. The elections were relatively fair but the 32 percent voter turnout was a record low. The people had become weary of corrupt politicians serving short terms without helping the people. Sharif's PML (N) won 134 seats out of the 217 seats in the National Assembly. Sharif's PML (N) easily won because Bhutto hadn't campaigned and many voters had been disappointed with her uninspiring performance during her first term in office. The army's leaders were glad that the pro-army Sharif had prevailed, but they were disappointed that Sharif had won such an overwhelming victory. They realized that Sharif would have been much easier to control if he had been required to form a coalition government with some of his rivals.

14

Sharif's Second Term

During the two years and eight months covered in this chapter (February 1997–October 1999), Nawaz Sharif would serve his second term as prime minister. Pakistan would conduct its first hot nuclear bomb tests in reaction to India's second series of nuclear tests. Sharif would appoint General Musharraf as army chief, and Musharraf would infiltrate troops into Kashmir—precipitating the Third Kashmir War and a fourth war with India. The chapter ends with Musharraf removing Sharif in a military coup.

Sharif Quickly Expands His Powers

The pro-army Nawaz Sharif was sworn in as prime minister for a second non-consecutive term on February 17, 1997. President Ahmad Leghari retained his position as president. Sharif began his second term in an enviable position. His overwhelming election victory gave his PML(N) party an outright majority of General Assembly seats, and he had the support of the army and the business community.

During the first year of his second term, Sharif greatly expanded his powers. His PML(N) dominated both the National Assembly and the Senate, and this parliament would enact major constitutional amendments and laws that would significantly enhance Prime Minister Sharif's powers. On April 1, 1997, the National Assembly enacted the Thirteenth Amendment to the Constitution, which repealed the president's power to dismiss prime ministers.

Sharif strengthened his powers again on July 3, 1997, when the Sharif-controlled parliament adopted the Fourteenth Amendment. This amendment allowed political party leaders to expel from the National Assembly any party member who had voted or spoken out against their party's official position. The amendment made it unlikely that Sharif would ever be dismissed by a "no confidence" vote, since now he could expel any PML(N) member who voted for that motion.

Sharif enlarged his powers once again by having the National Assembly enact the controversial Anti-Terrorist Law on August 13. This gave his police and security forces the right to "shoot to kill" as long as the shooting had been done in "good faith." Some police would use this law to give them cover to murder LeJ militants who had been issuing death threats to judges to intimidate them from presiding over their criminal trials.

Sharif strengthened his powers further by arranging for the removal of his rival President Leghari. On December 2, 1997, Sharif pressured Leghari to resign by threatening to otherwise have the National Assembly impeach him. Then Sharif had Leghari replaced as president by Sharif's close relative and friend, Mohammed Rafiq Tarar.

Prime Minister's Sharif's accumulation of power made him the most powerful prime minister in Pakistan's history. But the more he strengthened his powers, the more he undermined the legitimacy that he had acquired from his landslide election victory. His power grabbing also had antagonized virtually all political groups in Pakistan. Even Pakistan's military leaders were becoming troubled that Sharif's growing powers were weakening the army's influence over his government.

Dueling Atom Bomb Tests

Prime Minister Sharif developed several foreign policy goals. First, Sharif sought American backing for his government, since he believed that this would protect him from a military coup. Also, Sharif sought the support of the Afghan Taliban. He believed that the Taliban could unify and stabilize neighboring Afghanistan, and become a friendly neighbor. In addition, Sharif continued Pakistan's support for the anti–Indian Kashmir insurgency.

Pakistan Army leaders were growing restless, since they had been out of power for almost a decade. They began looking for justification for seizing control of the government. This justification came when Sharif's government had to call on the army to help it perform basic government services. The first call came when Sharif asked the army to take a national census, which the army began conducting on March 7, 1998. Sharif's second call for army help came in November when Sharif brought in the army to manage the affairs of the Water & Power Development Authority. These calls by Sharif for army assistance set a precedent that the army would be called upon when the civilian government couldn't perform basic tasks. These transfers of civilian functions to the army led the generals to ask themselves why they shouldn't just take over the entire government.

Prime Minister Sharif faced a new crisis with India on March 19, 1998, when India detonated three nuclear devices and two more devices two days later. These were called "hot tests," because the bomb core had contained highly enriched uranium, which caused a huge chain-reaction explosion when triggered. India had hot tested nuclear devices 24 years before, but Pakistan viewed India's new tests as a further threat. Pakistan had already cold-tested its own nuclear device 15 years before. A "cold test" involves triggering a nuclear device whose core contains only natural uranium, thereby avoiding the chain reaction and nuclear explosion.[1] Pakistan knew it could detonate its own nuclear device in a "hot test" by simply inserting enriched uranium into its bomb cores. Sharif debated with his top officials whether to respond with Pakistan's own hot test, while President Clinton phoned him four times urging him not to test.

On May 28, 1998, Pakistan hot-tested five nuclear devices by detonating nuclear devices in a cemented tunnel at a Baluchistan test site. Pakistan's people were proud that their country had developed the first "Islamic bomb" and had become the world's seventh nuclear power. People danced and sang in the streets and worshiped A.Q. Khan—the "Father of the Bomb."

There were several repercussions to Pakistan's hot nuclear tests. First, Pakistan's leaders were emboldened by its new nuclear status to expand its proxy war against India. They believed that India wouldn't dare retaliate against Pakistan for these limited attacks, since they would risk provoking a Pakistan nuclear response. At the same time, Pakistan's generals warned the people that despite Pakistan's possession of a nuclear bomb, India still might try to destroy Pakistan.[2] Therefore, the army successfully requested funds to build a stockpile of nuclear bombs and delivery systems. The army now wanted to achieve parity with India in both nuclear and conventional forces, and so military expenditures would increase.[3] In addition, the decades-old Indo-Pak dispute over Kashmir now became one of the world's most potentially dangerous conflicts. The major world powers became much more committed to defusing this conflict for fear that it could develop into the world's first nuclear war. Also, the United States responded to Pakistan's test by imposing severe economic sanctions, which led to a Pakistani economic meltdown. The army, facing a loss of government funding, increased its sale of nuclear technology and equipment overseas. Finally, Pakistanis were angry at how the Americans seemingly sanctioned Pakistan more than India for its nuclear testing. This perceived unequal treatment added to decades of Pakistan's animosity toward the United States.

Al-Qaeda Strikes American Targets from Its Afghan Base

Osama bin Laden had been forced out of his Sudan sanctuary in May 1996, and had set up his new base in Afghanistan. Afghan Taliban leader Mullah Omar had allowed him and his al-Qaeda fighters to remain in Afghanistan only if he kept a low profile and didn't antagonize the United States. But bin Laden would break this pledge by commencing major terrorist attacks against American targets. On August 7, 1998, his al-Qaeda suicide terrorists detonated two trucks filled with homemade explosives next to the American embassies in Kenya and Tanzania. The explosions destroyed the embassies and killed 224 persons.

The United States quickly discovered that al-Qaeda had been behind the two embassy attacks and it quickly responded. On August 20, President Clinton had over 50 cruise missiles launched against terrorist training camps in Afghanistan. The missiles struck two ISI-run terrorist training camps in Afghanistan, killing five ISI officers and some 20 ISI trainees. The strike also hit Osama bin Laden's Al-Badr camp, which Pakistan contractors had built with ISI funds, and which the ISI and the Haqqani network had been protecting.[4] Pakistan's army leaders were furious at these missile attacks, since they had received only a 10-minute warning of the missile launches.

There were several repercussions to the American cruise missile strike. First, the attack suddenly publicized the name of the previously unknown Osama bin Laden throughout Pakistan. Also, popular support grew in Pakistan for the Afghan Taliban's Muslim government, which was being attacked by the world's only superpower. Many Pakistani Islamist extremists traveled to Afghanistan to become the largest source of foreign fighters assisting the Taliban. In addition, Taliban leader Mullah Omar became worried when America attacked Afghan targets in response to al-Qaeda's attacks on the distant American embassies. Some of Omar's colleagues began questioning why Omar was giving al-Qaeda sanctuary in Afghanistan, since its attacks on American targets were provoking retaliatory attacks on Afghan targets. To meet Omar's concerns, Osama bin Laden took an oath of allegiance to Mullah Omar.[5] However, bin Laden had no intention of putting his al-Qaeda organization under Omar's control, and he went ahead with plans for attacking targets on the American mainland.

PPP leader Benazir Bhutto suddenly departed Pakistan for a long self-imposed exile overseas. She had been indicted on August 12, 1998, on charges of illegally awarding a government contract to a Dubai-based company. Her indictment induced her to leave Pakistan and live in her house in Dubai. She realized that she could be jailed if she were convicted by a

Pakistani court and still were living in Pakistan. She would remain in exile in Dubai and London for the next nine years.

Prime Minister Sharif continued his moves to strengthen his powers, and this time he sought to gain more control over the army. On October 7, 1998, he pressured Army Chief Karamat to resign because Karamat had refused to use the army for Sharif's political purposes. Karamat also had been criticizing Sharif's government. Sharif's removal decision was unwise, since Karamat never had posed a military takeover threat to Sharif's rule, and Karamat had avoided risky foreign adventures. Sharif compounded his dismissal error by appointing General Pervez Musharraf as Karamat's replacement. Sharif mistook Musharraf's mild manner as weakness, and he wrongly assumed that Musharraf could never develop strong support within the army.[6] Musharraf would remain army chief for nine years, during which time he would promote risky adventures inside Kashmir.

Prime Minister Sharif now took steps to improve relations with India. He invited Indian Prime Minister Vajpayee to come to Lahore for a ceremony celebrating the resumption of bus service between India and Pakistan. Vajpayee accepted the invitation and on February 20, 1999, he traveled by bus to meet Sharif in Pakistan—the first visit by an Indian prime minister in 11 years. This resumption of bus service was a confidence-building measure toward improving relations between the two countries. The next day, the two prime ministers issued the "Lahore Declaration," in which the two countries pledged to work toward peaceful and stable relations. The two leaders also agreed to engage in secret back-channel diplomacy, and nine secret rounds of discussions were held. However, these discussions would end abruptly a few months later after Pakistan infiltrated fighters into Kargil in Indian-controlled territory in Kashmir.

Kargil and the Third Kashmir War

During the first week of March 1999, Pakistani-based HuM militants, along with army troops disguised as jihadist volunteers, began slipping into the Indian-controlled Kargil region in northern Kashmir.[7] Army Chief General Musharraf had developed the plan largely on his own, and his insistence on tight secrecy had prompted him to avoid seeking input from either his military staff or Pakistan's diplomats. The army's plan called for seizing Indian positions in the desolate mountainous Kargil region which the Indian Army routinely abandoned over the winter. Musharraf naively hoped that seizing these positions would focus the world's attention on the need to resolve the Indo-Pak stalemate in Kashmir.[8] While the initial infiltration was small, gradually over 1,500 Pakistani soldiers moved into the

Indian positions without detection. The Pakistani troops occupied over 100 strongly constructed Indian bunkers on the top of steep approaches and stocked with Indian weapons, food and heating oil.[9]

Prime Minister Sharif wasn't briefed of the Kargil infiltration until May 17, 1999. At that meeting, he approved the operation, but he may not have been told then that Pakistan Army troops were involved.[10]

India's military leaders discovered the full extent of the Pakistani incursion on May 21. India's army reacted by moving troops, heavy weapons, and planes into the Kargil region to retake their bunkers, and the subsequent fighting in Kargil became the "Third Kashmir War" (also known as the "Fourth Indo-Pak War"). India was furious that Pakistan had violated the spirit of the peace process which had recently begun with the signing of the "Lahore Declaration." The Indian Army would gradually retake fourteen of the bunkers in hard-fought fighting, and both sides suffered heavy casualties and supply shortages. Both sides soon concluded that a cease-fire was desirable.

America's leaders became very concerned that the Kargil infiltration might develop into a general Indo-Pak war. Therefore, on June 19, 1999, President Bill Clinton wrote a secret letter to Prime Minister Sharif, strongly urging Pakistan to withdraw from Kargil. Sharif traveled to Washington, hoping that Clinton would help him withdraw from Kargil without his having to lose face. Clinton was worried about the possible Indo-Pak nuclear war. He asked Sharif if he knew that his military was preparing nuclear-tipped missiles.[11] On July 4, Sharif signed a pullout agreement in Clinton's presence (the "Washington Agreement"). Sharif agreed to immediately pull back Pakistan's troops to Kashmir's Line of Control (LOC), honor the sanctity of the LOC and resume the Lahore peace process with India.

There were several repercussions to Pakistan's Kargil infiltration. First, the Kargil fiasco weakened Prime Minister Sharif, since he had eventually supported it and had signed the humiliating withdrawal agreement. The public criticized him for ordering the withdrawal of army troops from their strong defensive positions in Kargil without having received any Indian concessions in return. Also, the Kargil incident increased the hostility between Sharif and Army Chief Musharraf. Sharif became angry when Musharraf began blaming Sharif for the entire Kargil incident, even though Musharraf had planned and promoted the operation. Musharraf also hadn't raised serious objections to withdrawing the troops. In addition, Indian resentment against Pakistan grew, and whatever Indo-Pak trust that had been built up now had been destroyed. Finally, Pakistan's image in the world had been tarnished by its ill-considered, reckless Kargil adventure, which had almost led to a full-scale war. Pakistan had acquired the reputation as an aggressive and unpredictable state which could not be trusted.

General Musharraf's "Countercoup"

Army Chief Musharraf sensed that Prime Minister Sharif wanted to dismiss him for his blaming Sharif for the Kargil infiltration. To prevent this, before Musharraf left Pakistan for a visit to Sri Lanka, he put in place a contingency plan to prevent Sharif from dismissing him while he was overseas. Musharraf's precautions proved to be justified.

The showdown began at noon on October 12, 1999, when Musharraf boarded a commercial airliner in Sri Lanka for a scheduled six-hour flight home to Karachi. While the flight was airborne, Sharif put into effect his plan to replace Musharraf as army chief with a Sharif loyalist. Troops loyal to Sharif seized the control tower at Karachi's airport. As the plane entered Pakistan's airspace, the airport's control tower notified the pilot that the airliner couldn't land in Karachi—or at any other airport in Pakistan. Musharraf reacted by trying to contact his military colleagues at home by cell phone to carry out his contingency plan. There was a tense standoff as the airliner waited for tower permission to land, while Musharraf ordered the pilot to demand permission to land at Karachi. After the airliner had been circling the airport for nearly an hour, the tower gave the pilot permission to land at a town 100 miles north of Karachi. Soon afterwards, pro-Musharraf troops seized the airport tower, which now granted it permission to land. The plane turned around and landed in Karachi with just seven minutes of fuel remaining.[12]

The next day, on October 13, 1999, General Pervez Musharraf seized power from Sharif's civilian government. Musharraf would call his takeover a "countercoup" to emphasize his claim that he was simply reacting to Sharif's reckless attempt to remove him. Musharraf also removed Sharif for his having used the army to perform civilian duties, for his inability to control the country's violence, and for his having failed to fix the country's struggling economy.

15

General Musharraf Takes Control

During the two years covered in this chapter (October 1999–September 2001), General Musharraf secured total military control over the country. He would institute a system of elections to "local bodies" to try to give the illusion of democratic rule. The chapter ends with Osama bin Laden's al-Qaeda terrorists hijacking airliners and crashing them into New York's World Trade Center and the Pentagon.

Musharraf Sets Up His Military Dictatorship

When Musharraf seized control of the country on October 13, 1999, he kept his powerful position as army chief, while abolishing the post of prime minister. The latter office would remain vacant for three years. He immediately named Mahmoud Ahmed as the new ISI chief—the loyal general who had seized the airport tower and permitted Musharraf's plane to land.

Pakistanis cheered in the streets at the return to military rule. They had a genuine respect for the army, and they were willing to give Musharraf a chance. The people had become disillusioned with their civilian leaders during the "Lost Decade of Democracy." Bhutto and Sharif had refused to work together for the country's benefit, and both had tolerated major corruption within their governments. They both had engaged in heavy government spending which they had financed by massive foreign borrowing. During the decade, the country's foreign debt had doubled.

General Musharraf had several strengths. First, he was intelligent,

15. General Musharraf Takes Control

amiable and polite. Also, his military rule was far more tolerant than Zia's had been, and he didn't kill his civilian predecessor as Zia had done. Also, Musharraf was not a deeply religious man, and he had no interest in continuing Zia's Islamization of the country.

Musharraf also had weaknesses. First, he had contempt for all civilian politicians and he had no intention of returning the country to democratic rule. Also, he was impetuous and he sometimes would take overly bold and ill-considered actions without deep thought. He often wouldn't follow up on his dramatic statements and policy initiatives. In addition, he would select mediocre and incompetent advisers. He would become increasingly intolerant of those who disagreed with him, and so few would dare to offer opposing views.[1] Also, Musharraf's regime would be even more corrupt than his civilian predecessors had been. Finally, Musharraf would try to resolve foreign problems using military force instead of diplomacy. He hated India and he would not try to make peace with this powerful neighbor.

General Musharraf would take a number of actions which would allow him to survive in office for a very long time. First, he took unprecedented steps to secure the support of his senior generals. He consulted his nine corps commanders before making any strategic decisions, and these decisions usually were immediately approved.[2] Musharraf also expanded the practice of giving generals large tracts of state-owned lands, and allowing the generals to operate large farms and military businesses ("Milbus"). He also appointed over 1,000 active and retired generals to lucrative government and university posts. Also, Musharraf would use the ISI to spy on Pakistan's citizens. The ISI created a huge network of informers who would give scraps of conversation and other information to their ISI handlers.[3] In this way, Musharraf determined who opposed his regime. In addition, Musharraf secured the support of Islamist religious groups by giving them funds, arms and training for their jihadist activities in Afghanistan and Kashmir.

Musharraf also would try to gain the people's support by making his regime seem more civilian. First, he assumed the novel and innocuous-sounding title of "Chief Executive." Also, he allowed the Sharif-chosen President Rafiq Tarar to remain in office. In addition, Musharraf didn't impose martial law— although he did continue the "state of emergency." He "suspended" the 1973 Constitution instead of abolishing it. Also, Musharraf imposed only limited control over the press.[4] In addition, he retained the civil judicial system, although he required judges to take an oath of allegiance to him if they wanted to remain on the bench. The Supreme Court Chief Justice and six of his colleagues resigned rather than take the humiliating oath.

Pakistan faced several major problems when Musharraf took control of the country. First, Pakistan's economy was weak and showed little sign of improving. The government's annual deficit had grown to over $33 billion—primarily due to debt servicing (45 percent of the national budget) and military spending (26 percent). Also, Pakistan had become home to over a dozen armed religious jihadist and sectarian groups. Sunni Islamists attacked Shias and other minority religious groups, and the Shias struck back. Finally, millions of dissatisfied, unemployed Afghan refugees still resided in Pakistani refugee camps, and dominated Peshawar and other Pakistani northern cities and towns.

Musharraf would adopt a two-prong foreign policy. First, he encouraged Pakistani-based jihadist proxy groups to attack Indian troops in Kashmir. Second, he had Pakistan support the Taliban's government in Afghanistan. Pakistan provided the Taliban with advisers and arms as they sent their troops northwards to try to destroy their Northern Alliance rival. This two-prong foreign policy antagonized the United States. America strongly supported India and therefore opposed Pakistan's support for terrorists attacking Indian troops in Kashmir. The Americans also had become disenchanted with the Taliban as they learned of the Taliban's rigid enforcement of Islamic Sharia laws and its mistreatment of women.

General Musharraf took significant measures to strengthen the government's finances and reduce the national debt. To generate more government revenue, he imposed a tax on farm income, services and electricity.[5] To cut government expenses, Musharraf abolished some government subsidies on wheat and petroleum products. On November 16, 1999, he issued an ordinance creating the National Accountability Bureau (NAB) to prosecute tax evaders and wealthy citizens who were refusing to repay loans to national banks.[6] While Musharraf would hamper the NAB's work by intervening on behalf of wealthy friends and supporters, the NAB would remain an effective institution for prosecuting white collar criminals.

Musharraf wasn't noted for initiating social reforms. While he did enact some reforms, many of these didn't succeed—such as his attempt to stop corruption, abolish bonded labor, and disarm private citizens.[7] Also, Musharraf abandoned reforms when they didn't immediately succeed, or when his supporters rallied against them.[8] For his habit of reneging on promised reforms he became nicknamed "double-talk Musharraf."

Musharraf's most disappointing reversal was reneging on his public promise to reduce the power of militant jihadists. When Musharraf proposed a reform to limit widespread abuses of the blasphemy law, he encountered widespread Islamist demonstrations, and so he withdrew that proposal. His reneging on this reform damaged his credibility and emboldened Islamist extremists to become even more assertive. Several of his cabinet ministers even reacted by resigning, while many educated and skilled Pakistanis left the country altogether.

The Kashmir Uprising Revives

India had successfully put down the Kashmiri mass uprising (intifada), and had been enjoying a four-year period of Kashmiri demoralization and inaction. India also had beaten back Pakistan's clumsy attempt to seize IJK territory by infiltrating soldiers into the Kargil region. However, the Kashmir fighting soon was revived by Pakistani-based LeT terrorists (and some LeM terrorists) who moved into Kashmir to confront the Indian occupiers. Pakistan's army supported them, hoping that the proxies would force India to withdraw from Kashmir, or keep so many troops tied up there as to "bleed" its armed forces and economy. At first, Pakistan's LeT proxies suffered heavy losses, since they boldly attacked the heavily armed Indians with frontal assaults.

The LeT soon abandoned their frontal assaults and in July 1999 transitioned to a fidayeen ("life-threatening") campaign. During this fidayeen phase, two-men, semi-suicidal terrorist teams raided targets in Kashmir and India. Their goal was to inflict maximum damage, and most of the raiders were killed during their attacks. Pakistan's army and ISI trained large numbers of LeT fidayeen recruits. The LeT's fidayeen campaign began on July 13, 1999, when two terrorists attacked an Indian security camp in the Kashmir Valley, killing six soldiers. During the next four years, the LeT and LeM launched raids against police stations, army camps and government installations in the Kashmir Valley, killing over 150 persons.[9]

The start of the fidayeen campaign was soon followed by a terrorist airliner hijacking. On December 25, 1999, five Pakistani-based HuM extremists hijacked an Indian Airlines plane and forced it to land in Taliban-controlled Kandahar, Afghanistan. The hijacking was a spectacular HuM victory, since HuM bartered the passengers' release for India's freeing three key Kashmiri terrorist leaders.

There were several repercussions to the hijacking. First, the hijacking increased India's hatred of Pakistan's government, whose leaders seemed to condone the hijacking and other terrorist attacks against India. India pledged not to resume a peace dialogue with Pakistan until it stopped supporting the Kashmiri insurgency. Also, Pakistani-based terrorists were emboldened by their government's seeming support for the hijackers. Finally, India released terrorist leader Maulana Masood Azhar as part of the hostage negotiations. Azhar soon would form the JeM group with the help of Pakistan's ISI.[10] The JeM quickly grew in strength after Azhar conducted a whirlwind recruitment tour inside Pakistan. The formation of JeM revived the demoralized Kashmir campaign, and the JeM soon would outnumber the Pakistan-based HuM terrorists fighting in Kashmir.

The JeM soon launched a series of attacks on Indian forces in Kashmir, using its new deadly suicide tactic. On April 20, 2000, a JeM suicide bomber detonated a car bomb at the entrance of the Srinagar headquarters of an Indian Army Corps, killing five soldiers. On October 1, 2000, a JeM suicide bomber drove a truck filled with explosives into the courtyard of Kashmir's state assembly building in Srinagar, killing 36 persons. India had some 500,000 troops and security personnel in Indian-controlled IJK, while Pakistan had 180,000 troops on Kashmir's Line of Control. Thousands of Kashmiris were being killed in the crossfire between the two huge foreign armies.

A period of quiet set in after the Indians installed the moderate Mufti Mohammad Sayeed as IJK's chief minister on November 2, 2002. During his three years in office, he allowed the Kashmiris to demonstrate against his regime without hindrance. While the Kashmir Valley became relatively peaceful, most of the IJK still resembled a huge prison camp dotted with checkpoints, bunkers and military camps.

On March 25, 2000, American President Bill Clinton made a five-hour "doormat visit" to Pakistan, after having just spent five days in India. Clinton made his visit so short due to the threat of an imminent terrorist attack on his life.[11] The Secret Service used decoy planes and a Clinton "look-alike" to protect the president. Musharraf was disappointed that Clinton's visit was so short, and that while they were talking, Clinton was condescending to him. During a two-hour meeting, Clinton urged him to rein in terrorist groups and end Pakistan's nuclear proliferation.[12] Clinton also urged Musharraf to spare the life of deposed prime minister Sharif.[13] Clinton humiliated Musharraf even more during a 14-minute address that he delivered on national television. He warned his Pakistani viewers about the dangers of extremism and terrorism and called for a return to civilian rule. After his address, Clinton sped off to the airport without even having shaken Musharraf's hand. Musharraf was furious at how Clinton had humiliated him.

While Clinton's visit had damaged Pak-American relations, it may have had one positive result. It seems to have helped Musharraf decide not to kill Sharif or jail him indefinitely. On April 6, 2000, a Musharraf-controlled court found Sharif guilty of hijacking Musharraf's plane, and sentenced him to two life sentences. However, Sharif would remain in jail for only one year before Musharraf gave Sharif a conditional pardon. The pardon allowed Sharif and his family to move to exile in Saudi Arabia—providing he remain there for ten years. Musharraf now would have little difficulty with political opposition, since Sharif and Bhutto, the leaders of Pakistan's two mainstream national parties, were both living in exile overseas.

Pakistan's Supreme Court once again sided with Pakistan's army and its military takeovers. On May 12, 2000, the Musharraf-packed Court ruled that Musharraf's coup seven months before had been legitimate—justifying its decision on the "doctrine of necessity." However, the Court did require

Musharraf to hold national elections within three years, and it forbid him from distorting the constitutional framework. Musharraf decided that he would comply with this three-year election mandate.

Musharraf's "True Democracy" System

General Musharraf desired to remove the feudal landowners, tribal leaders and politicians who dominated local governments. He would do several things to accomplish this. First, using the National Accountability Bureau (NAB) created in November 1999, he prosecuted top politicians for corruption. Then on August 14, 2000, he announced his intention to create a "True Democracy" system in which groups of 15,000 or more voters would elect local officials ("nazims"), who would act like mayors and assume some important duties in local administration. Musharraf intended that these nazims would replace the old feudal class at the local level and become his supporters. To insure that few of the traditional feudal elite would become nazims, Musharraf provided that nazim candidates must have attended a university.[14]

The anti–Musharraf PPP and PML(N) parties realized that Musharraf's "True Democracy" system was just a phony scheme to delay the restoration of real democracy. Therefore, on December 3, 2000, they joined together in a coalition called the "Alliance for Restoration of Democracy" (ARD). The ARD began organizing rallies protesting Musharraf's "True Democracy" scheme, and demanding that Musharraf relinquish his position as army chief. Musharraf responded by arresting thousands of ARD politicians and their supporters.

Despite this strong opposition to his "True Democracy" system, Musharraf went ahead with the elections for nazims. The elections began on December 31, 2000, and went on for seven months. While Musharraf had decreed that candidates not reveal their party affiliations, they found ways around this restriction.[15] He was disappointed in the low voter turnout and that the traditional PPP and PML (N) parties and powerful landowners won most of the seats.

On January 19, 2001, UN sanctions against the Taliban went into effect. The U.N. Security Council had imposed the harsh sanctions for the Taliban's refusal to close Afghan terrorist training camps and its refusal to extradite Osama bin Laden. Musharraf protested that the U.N. was sanctioning Pakistan's friendly neighbor. Furthermore, Pakistan's army and ISI continued advising and supplying the Taliban forces on their military operations against the Northern Alliance.[16]

American anger over Pakistan's support for the Taliban subsided once

G.W. Bush became America's president on January 20, 2001. President Bush ignored the warnings from outgoing President Clinton about the dangers of Pakistan, al-Qaeda and the Taliban's government in Afghanistan.[17]

General Musharraf strongly supported the Taliban partly because he believed that in return, Pakistan would gain considerable influence over its government in Kabul. However, Musharraf soon discovered how little influence Pakistan actually had over the Taliban when the Taliban announced that it planned to destroy the two giant Buddha statues carved into the cliffs overlooking Bamian in central Afghanistan. The Taliban decided to destroy these priceless Afghan national treasures on grounds that they were "non-Islamic." Although Pakistan's leaders pleaded with the Taliban to cancel their plans, the Taliban dynamited the two giant statues on March 10, 2001.

Musharraf Tries to Tame "The Father of the Bomb"

When General Musharraf took control of Pakistan from Sharif in his October 1999 coup, he was generally aware that A.Q. Khan had been engaging in some nuclear proliferation activities. Musharraf wanted the army to assume more control over the nuclear weapons program and so he quickly ordered an investigation of A.Q. Khan's nuclear proliferation activities.

Musharraf soon discovered that A.Q. Khan had been selling Pakistan's nuclear secrets and devices to foreign countries and had been amassing a personal fortune in kickbacks from the sales.[18] Musharraf started insisting on controlling Khan's activities, and he ordered him to start reporting all his travels overseas. When the defiant Khan refused to do so, Musharraf realized that Khan must be let go.[19]

Musharraf handled A.Q. Khan's termination delicately due to Khan's immense popularity as the "Father of the Bomb." He told Khan that he was being removed as director of the Kahuta nuclear facility, but that he would be allowed to leave gracefully. On March 10, 2001, A.Q. Khan was retired at an official ceremony during which Musharraf praised Khan profusely as a "hero" for his role in making Pakistan a nuclear power. Soon afterwards, Musharraf told Khan that he would be banned from entering the Kahuta facility ever again. With A.Q. Khan banned from Kahuta, Musharraf ordered an inventory of the facility, which reported that 40 canisters of highly enriched uranium were missing.[20]

A.Q. Khan's forced retirement and loss of access to Pakistan's nuclear facilities would stunt his nuclear proliferation activities. However, the irrepressible Khan would use his knowledge and contacts to continue nuclear proliferation on his own.

Al-Qaeda Prepares to Attack the United States

Musharraf decided to further enhance his powers. On June 20, 2001, he simply dismissed President Tarar and declared himself Pakistan's new president—adding the presidency to his powerful position as army chief. This was Musharraf's "second coup," and it removed Pakistan's last traces of democratic rule.

President Musharraf recognized the benefits of reaching a peaceful accommodation with India—which Pakistan couldn't defeat on the battlefield. Therefore, he accepted Indian Prime Minister Vajpayee's invitation to visit India. Musharraf arrived in India on July 14, 2001, for three days of peace talks (the "Agra Summit"). The two leaders were unable to agree on even a modest declaration, since neither leader was willing to resist pressure from their respective hard-liners over Kashmir. The conference concluded without even a joint closing statement. Extremists in both countries were glad that the peace talks had failed, since they thrived in an atmosphere of tension.

President Musharraf also had come to recognize that he needed to confront the Islamic extremists who were promoting Sunni-Shiite violence inside Pakistan. On August 14, 2001, Musharraf banned the key Islamist terrorist groups that were responsible for most of the Sunni-Shiite sectarian violence. He banned the Sunni SSP and Lej groups which were killing Shiites, and he banned the SMP which the Shiites had formed to retaliate against the Sunnis. However, the bans didn't stop the violence since most of the banned groups kept operating under new names.[21]

President Musharraf also tried to regulate Pakistan's religious schools (madrassas), since many were indoctrinating their students in religious intolerance. On August 18, 2001, Musharraf issued a law which standardized their curriculum and required them to disclose their funding sources. However, the law proved unworkable, since the madrassas were so numerous, were very uncooperative, and had strong political allies.[22]

The Afghan Taliban government was still providing sanctuary to Osama bin Laden and his al-Qaeda terrorists in Afghanistan. Bin Laden was preparing his 9/11 attacks on the United States and he realized that he would need Taliban support to oppose American troops who might enter Afghanistan to destroy al-Qaeda's sanctuary there. To gain favor with Taliban leader Mullah Omar, bin Laden on September 9, 2001, had al-Qaeda terrorists assassinate Ahmed Shah Massoud, the talented commander of the Taliban's arch-enemy—the Afghan Northern Alliance. Two assassins had gained access to Massoud's headquarters by posing as foreign journalists, and they detonated explosives hidden in a camera when they were ushered into Massoud's presence. Pakistan's ISI had assisted al-Qaeda in this assassination.[23]

PART THREE—PAKISTAN AFTER AL-QAEDA'S ATTACK ON AMERICA

16

Musharraf Joins America's War on Terrorism

During the 14-month period covered in this chapter (September 2001–October 2002), al-Qaeda destroyed America's World Trade Center in New York City using hijacked planes. When America's leaders learned that al-Qaeda leader Osama bin Laden had organized the attack from his sanctuary in Afghanistan, they would plan a campaign to capture and kill al-Qaeda's leaders and overthrow the Afghan Taliban government. Under great American pressure, Musharraf would offer to support America's invasion of Afghanistan by providing logistical support.

Al-Qaeda Attacks America's Mainland

On September 11, 2001, Osama bin Laden's al-Qaeda members hijacked four airliners and crashed them into New York City's World Trade Center towers and the Pentagon, the fourth plane crashing in rural Pennsylvania. The attack came as a complete surprise to the Americans, although Musharraf and the ISI may have known the attacks were coming without warning the United States.[1] Bin Laden had planned and organized this "Planes Operation," and he secretly carried out the plan even after al-Qaeda's Leadership Council had rejected it.[2] Bin Laden's goal was to make such a horrific attack that it would make al-Qaeda the most outstanding Islamic group in the world, and thereby attract more recruits. He also wanted to lure America into sending large numbers of troops into Muslim Afghanistan and thereby provoke a war between the West and the Muslim world.[3] He also believed that his Muslim jihadists could defeat the American troops who would invade Afghanistan.

Within hours of the attack, America's leaders concluded that al-Qaeda was responsible for the attack and that al-Qaeda still was based in Afghanistan. Most Pakistanis reacted with horror and shame that Muslims had carried out the attack against innocent civilians.[4] However, Islamist extremists applauded the attack as legitimate payback for American attacks on Iraq and other Muslim countries.

America's leaders quickly and bluntly demanded that Pakistan support the United States in retaliation against al-Qaeda, which was based in Afghanistan. On September 12, 2001, American Secretary of State Colin Powell phoned President Musharraf with a list of non-negotiable demands and Musharraf assured Powell of his country's cooperation. While Musharraf seemed receptive to fully complying with this ultimatum, he later would deny that he had accepted all these demands.[5]

Two days later, Musharraf discussed America's ultimatum with his nine corps commanders, who included three hardline, pro–Taliban generals. Musharraf had already made up his mind to support America's war on terrorism and during the seven-hour meeting he persuaded the reluctant generals to largely submit to America's ultimatum. His main arguments were that if Pakistan didn't submit to America's ultimatum, the United States would greatly strengthen its ties with India, and might even attack Pakistan's nuclear weapons facilities.[6]

President Musharraf asked ISI Chief General Mahmud to try to persuade Taliban leader Mullah Omar to hand over Osama bin Laden to the Americans, hoping to dissuade them from invading Afghanistan. Mahmud did travel to Afghanistan on September 17 and officially transmitted Musharraf's request to Mullah Omar (although Mahmud privately advised him not to surrender bin Laden).[7] Mullah Omar indicated to Mahmud that he would seriously consider surrendering bin Laden, but only to a neutral Muslim country.[8] The Americans rejected this condition. The Mullah also was against turning bin Laden over to the Americans because he doubted that the United States would invade Afghanistan just to capture bin Laden. Also, if Afghanistan were invaded, the Taliban would need bin Laden's tough foreign fighters to help it repel the Americans.[9]

On September 19, 2001, President Musharraf gave a nationally televised address seeking to justify his support for America's war on terrorism. He explained that if Pakistan did not join the United States, the Americans would enter an alliance with India. In reaction to Musharraf's speech, thousands of Pakistan's Islamist extremists demonstrated in the streets. They considered it heresy to support an American invasion of Muslim Afghanistan. In addition, over 10,000 Pakistanis would cross into Afghanistan to assist the Taliban in resisting the American invasion.[10]

American President G.W. Bush soon rewarded Musharraf for his commitment to support America's invasion of Afghanistan. On September 22, 2001, the United States lifted its sanctions against Pakistan, and soon American military and economic assistance resumed. Also, Bush pushed Congress to authorize sending Pakistan coalition support funds (CSF) averaging $1.3 billion annually for the next eight years. Bush also took steps to reschedule or forgive Pakistan's debt owed to the United States. Moreover, Bush pledged to Musharraf that he would take no action that would hurt him politically. Bush officials stopped criticizing Musharraf's human rights abuses and Pakistan's nuclear proliferation activities. President Bush believed that Musharraf could do no wrong, and Bush began referring to Musharraf as "one of my best friends." Pakistan's press dubbed the two leaders "Mush and Bush," and derisively gave Musharraf the nickname "Busharraf."

As part of President Musharraf's cooperation with the United States on its War on Terrorism, Musharraf changed the ISI's leadership. On October 7, 2001, Musharraf dismissed ISI chief Mahmud Ahmed—the hardline Islamist ISI chief who had been supporting the Taliban and al-Qaeda.[11] Musharraf wanted to create a new team which would back his new pro–Western policy. Musharraf chose the moderate General Ehsan ul-Haq as his new ISI chief. Musharraf ordered Haq to purge the most hardline Islamists from the ISI and Haq transferred many Islamist extremists back to the army.[12] Musharraf also instructed Haq to fully cooperate with the CIA in America's War on Terrorism.

With the American invasion of Afghanistan looming, Musharraf ordered all Pakistani military advisers and personnel in Afghanistan to return to Pakistan. He ordered this withdrawal to preserve his own army personnel. While this weakened the Taliban's military forces, the Taliban still could count on the assistance of over 9,000 Pakistani jihadist volunteers, and some 2,500 Central Asian fighters.[13]

The Northern Alliance Drives the Taliban from Afghanistan

The Taliban hadn't surrendered Osama bin Laden by America's deadline, and so the United States went ahead with its offensive to drive the Taliban from Afghanistan ("Operation Enduring Freedom"). The Northern Alliance–American offensive began on October 7, 2001, with a series of American air attacks on Taliban defenses, in preparation for an Afghan Northern Alliance ground offensive. The Northern Alliance (NA) was based in Northern Afghanistan and hoped to defeat the Taliban forces and replace the Taliban's government. The Americans also targeted Kandahar, where Mullah Omar and Osama bin Laden had just met. Mullah Omar was furious at bin Laden for having launched the "Planes Operation" without his approval, and for not even warning him when that operation would begin.[14] Mullah Omar realized that Bin Laden was risking the destruction of the Taliban's government and military forces by striking the American mainland.

The Northern Alliance (NA) ground offensive against the Taliban began when NA warlords Dostum and Atta carried out a two-pronged attack on horseback against the Taliban at the northern Afghan city of Mazar-e-Sharif. They captured this key city on November 9, 2001, with the help of American air strikes. Then on November 13, the NA captured the Afghan capital Kabul, which the Taliban had abandoned in the face of the NA offensive. The Americans wanted a pro–Western government to replace the Taliban's government, and they backed English-speaking Hamid Karzai as their candidate. On November 14, 2001, American helicopters infiltrated Pashtun leader Karzai into Uruzgan Province, along with a 17-man CIA/Special Forces team. The plan was for Karzai to generate anti–Taliban support in the province and then seize the Taliban stronghold in nearby Kandahar.[15]

The Karzai-American plan succeeded brilliantly. On November 16, 2001, Karzai and his American protectors entered Karzai's home town of Tarin Kowt—70 miles north of Kandahar. The next day, when a convoy of 50 Taliban troop-filled trucks tried to seize Karzai, they were turned back by devastating air strikes called in by Karzai's American protectors.[16] This Karzai victory convinced many Pashtuns to join Karzai's forces, and soon Karzai and the small American team began advancing on the Taliban stronghold of Kandahar.

While Karzai's force was advancing on Kandahar, the Taliban were fleeing eastwards to Kunduz. NA troops soon surrounded Kunduz, but delayed their attack. Musharraf had personally asked President Bush for permission to land Pakistani planes in Kunduz to evacuate officers and soldiers from Pakistan's ISI and Frontier Corps who were trapped there. Bush agreed and these evacuation flights began on November 15 (the "Great Escape"). Musharraf abused this trust by also allowing these flights to evacuate many top al-Qaeda and Taliban leaders.[17] Then on November 23, the Taliban in Kunduz surrendered to the NA commander. They were taken to warlord Dostum's massive fortress, where they staged a revolt. Many were killed by Dostum's troops.[18] By this time, most Taliban fighters had left the battlefield. Some 10,000 had been killed, some 20,000 had been wounded, and 7,000 had been taken prisoner.[19]

On December 5, 2001, the Bonn Agreement was signed in Germany by many Afghan groups, setting up a structure for an interim Afghan government. The Americans succeeded in getting Karzai named as head of the Afghan Interim Government (AIG).

16. Musharraf Joins America's War on Terrorism

The next day, on December 6, Karzai's forces entered Kandahar. The Taliban had given up Kandahar and were abandoned the fighting. Mullah Omar had offered to surrender his Taliban government to Karzai on certain conditions, but Karzai turned down the offer.[20] Mullah Omar got on a motorbike and disappeared into the desert.

The Taliban had largely abandoned the fight, leaving the disappointed Osama bin Laden and his al-Qaeda fighters to fend for themselves against the U.S.-backed Northern Alliance. Bin Laden and his foreign fighters moved eastwards to the mountains and caves of Tora Bora. It was in this mountain stronghold that Bin Laden had been able to hold out against Soviet troops decades before. The Americans hired two Afghan warlords as their proxies to seize Tora Bora. These warlords would attack al-Qaeda forces at Tora Bora in return for CIA funds, enhanced prestige, and the lure of booty. To oversee the warlords and call in air strikes, the Americans embedded among the warlords a few dozen CIA officers, air controllers and British commandos. At first, the warlords just advanced during the day and retreated to their bases at sunset—thereby giving up their daylight gains. Soon the Americans, who were better trained and wearing night-vision goggles, began holding onto the captured gains over night.[21] They soon were able to set up observation sites near the Tora Bora caves.[22]

The fighting at Tora Bora quickly moved to a conclusion on December 12, 2001, after American planes began striking the Tora Bora caves night and day. The planes dropped laser-guided bombs at the cave entrances. Direct hits killed all inside, while close hits forced the enemy into the open where they were quickly killed.[23] On December 15, Osama bin Laden transmitted a radio message to his followers to surrender if they desired, and some of his fighters began withdrawing. On December 17, 2001, the Northern Alliance dislodged the foreign al-Qaeda fighters from the Tora Bora caves—their last stronghold in Afghanistan. The Tora Bora battle had lasted only 16 days.

The Taliban and al-Qaeda were demoralized and in disarray. They had predicted a decisive victory over the Northern Alliance and the Americans, but instead their fighters had been routed in just three months. The Americans were ecstatic at their having routed their enemies with the loss of only 12 Americans. They also had captured or killed several thousand al-Qaeda and Taliban fighters. However, this turned out to be just a short-term victory since most of the Taliban escaped and would eventually return.

While Osama bin Laden and his al-Qaeda fighters were fleeing from Tora Bora, Pakistani-based terrorists launched a desperate attack inside India. During this December 31 attack, five ISI-backed JeM terrorists drove a car with official markings onto the grounds of India's parliament building in New Delhi, hoping to kill Indian government ministers inside. However, Indian security guards were able to block the terrorists from entering the building and killed them all. Indian leaders immediately blamed the Pakistani-based militant groups JeM and LeT for the attack, and assumed that the ISI must have been involved. India reacted by severing diplomatic relations with Pakistan and cutting rail and air travel between the two countries.

Al-Qaeda and Taliban Fugitives Find Sanctuaries

Most of Osama bin Laden's al-Qaeda fighters in Tora Bora fled to Pakistan—just 10 miles away. Most of the fighters escaped because Pakistan and the United States deployed too few soldiers to stop them. Over 1,000 al-Qaeda leaders and fighters would find sanctuary in Pakistan's cities and in FATA's North and South Waziristan. Many al-Qaeda leaders and bin Laden's family members (including Bin Laden's son Hamzi) found sanctuary in Iran. Iran would detain them as "hostages" for over five years.[24] Osama bin Laden himself initially hid in Afghanistan's Kunar Province. Khalid Sheik Mohammad (KSM), leader of al-Qaeda's military council, hid in Karachi, where he planned more terrorist plots.[25] Bin Laden and KSM communicated by couriers.

Most of the Taliban fighters who had fled after the fall of Kunduz and Kandahar returned to their homes and stopped resisting the conquerors. However, many senior Taliban leaders immediately fled to Pakistan, where they would live in Quetta and its vicinity. These top leaders left behind only mid-level leaders and foot soldiers. Those remaining in Afghanistan had trouble living there in peace. Karzai never offered former Taliban fighters a serious peace plan or amnesty, and without amnesty ex-Taliban had trouble making a living in Afghanistan. They didn't have any job experience or training.[26] They also began being harassed by Karzai's warlords and police.[27] The Americans killed and captured many in night raids after being falsely identified as al-Qaeda. Furthermore, some of Karzai's strongmen even jailed them until their families raised funds for their release.[28] Finding it impossible to live peacefully in Afghanistan, most of these ex-Taliban would find safety only by moving to Pakistan, or by rejoining the Taliban once it returned to Afghanistan.[29]

The Taliban who fled to Pakistan thrived in Pakistan's FATA tribal region for several reasons. First, Pakistan's Islamist extremist groups provided them with safe houses, food and false documents.[30] They were warmly welcomed because many of the Taliban and their relatives had lived in FATA for years—having married into local tribes and having enjoyed their protection.[31] Also, the local tribesmen honored the tribal custom of hospitality for guests. Moreover, the tribesmen admired the fugitives for their jihadist credentials and for their bravery in having stood up to the strong American forces which had invaded their country. Finally, for many years, Pakistan's central, provincial, and local governments would leave the Taliban fugitives alone—free to reorganize and operate in the Waziristans, and free to operate in Quetta and other Pakistani cities. The ISI would even set up a secret organization to provide these refugees with assistance.[32]

Pakistan After the Afghan Taliban's Rout

When the Northern Alliance overthrew the Taliban's Afghan government, Musharraf was disturbed that Pakistan no longer could count on a friendly Afghan government on its border to support it should India invade Pakistan. Musharraf became even more concerned when he discovered that Karzai was accepting some Indian assistance. India would implement a well-planned, very successful $500 million reconstruction program, which was well received by the Afghans.[33] However, instead of countering this with Pakistan's own economic assistance program, Musharraf just countered with an extensive ISI campaign misrepresenting India's intentions in Afghanistan. Musharraf also was disturbed that some 1,000 al-Qaeda fighters had fled to Pakistan after having been flushed out of their Tora Bora stronghold. He correctly feared that they would destabilize Pakistan. In Pakistan, these deadly fighters would convert many Pakistani extremists to their vision of global jihad against Muslim governments allied to the United States. Bin Laden even began giving Pakistan's extremist groups advice and funds for striking targets inside Pakistan—including Musharraf himself.

The overthrow of the Afghan Taliban government was followed by a period of excellent Pak-American relations. Musharraf was grateful to the United States for the billions of dollars given to Pakistan to reimburse its army for counterterrorism operations it was taking on America's behalf.[34] At the same time, the United States was grateful for the logistical support that Pakistan had provided for its campaign against al-Qaeda and the Taliban. America also would be grateful for Pakistan's assistance in locating and/or capturing al-Qaeda leaders in Pakistan, and turning them over to the Americans. The Americans were focused on destroying al-Qaeda, and in fact the mandate given to American troops was to destroy al-Qaeda (not the Taliban) and train the Afghan Army. Therefore, the Americans weren't disturbed that the Pakistanis weren't very helpful in ferreting out Taliban fugitives. The Americans soon had custody of so many al-Qaeda suspects that housing the prisoners in Afghanistan became an increasing problem.[35] So the Americans began shipping the most important al-Qaeda prisoners to its facility in Guantanamo Bay, Cuba. On January 11, 2002, the first batch of 20 al-Qaeda and

Taliban detainees arrived at "Camp X-ray" in Guantanamo Bay. Three days later, another batch of 30 arrived at the camp.

Musharraf's Two-Track Policy

President Musharraf continued Pakistan's traditional multi-goal foreign policy. First, Musharraf sought good relations with the United States since Pakistan depended on American military and economic support. Also, Musharraf continued to resist India's occupation of Indian-controlled IJK territory in Kashmir. To achieve this, he continued to support Pakistani-based Islamist extremist groups in attacking Indian forces in Kashmir.

Musharraf developed a secret two-track foreign policy.[36] His first track was to publicly support the United States in its war on terrorism, and he did this in several ways. First, he would allow American supplies to be transported by truck convoy to American forces in Afghanistan. Also, while he didn't allow American planes to take off from Pakistan's bases, he did allow American planes to fly over assigned Pakistani air space to reach Afghan targets. He also offered three Pakistani airfields for emergency landings. In addition, Musharraf instructed the ISI to cooperate with America's CIA and FBI. These American agencies would rely heavily on ISI human assets, and together they would apprehend hundreds of al-Qaeda terrorists.

Musharraf's second track was to secretly support the Afghan Taliban and other Islamist jihadist groups—some of which were killing American troops in Afghanistan. To conceal this support, a new secret organization was created outside the army and ISI to work with the jihadists.[37] Musharraf supported the Taliban because he reasoned that after the Americans invaded Afghanistan they would eventually withdraw. After the withdrawal, the Taliban might be able to return to Afghanistan and form a friendly, pro–Pakistan government in Kabul. So Musharraf supported the Taliban by providing them with a safe sanctuary in Pakistan, giving them food, arms, and medical care.[38] Musharraf also helped all Islamist extremists by greatly increasing the number of madrassas, and many of these taught religious intolerance and jihadism.

Musharraf was playing a dangerous double game by adopting his two-track policy, since it angered both sides. For one thing, Musharraf's public support for the Americans and his crackdown on Islamist terrorists would provoke al-Qaeda and its allies to attack his government and even try to assassinate him. Also, his two-track policy was dangerous because after a year, the Americans would discover that Musharraf had betrayed them by secretly supporting the Taliban.

Afghanistan After the Taliban's Rout

On December 22, 2001, Hamid Karzai was sworn in as President of the Afghan Interim Government (AIG)—a temporary position that he would hold for five months. Karzai had been selected for this post by several Afghan groups at a meeting in Bonn, Germany.

President Karzai initially had excellent relations with the Americans. American President G.W. Bush developed a close personal relationship with Karzai, and the two often held videoconferences with each other. Also, Bush sent the highly qualified Afghan-born Zalmay Khalilzad as his special envoy to Afghanistan. Karzai would trust Zalmay and often would seek his advice.[39] Bush later would appoint Zalmay as Ambassador to Afghanistan.

On December 23, 2001, NATO troops began arriving in Afghanistan, and eventually 21 NATO members would send troops to Afghanistan as part of NATO's International Security Assistance Force (ISAF). While ISAF troops initially confined themselves to providing security inside Kabul, they would gradually deploy throughout the country, and at one time would total 67,000 troops. However, the ISAF forces were weakened because each government imposed some of its own restrictions ("caveats") on what its troops could do.

Hamid Karzai's political authority in Afghanistan grew on June 19, 2002, when a national Emergency Loyal Jirga (tribal assembly) selected him to head a "Transitional Afghan Government." However, his foreign military backing began to weaken when in March 2003 the United States invaded Iraq and pulled many of its troops out of Afghanistan to fight in Iraq.

On January 4, 2004, a Constitutional Loyal Jirga approved an Afghan Constitution, which provided for a strong president with a five-year term. Pursuant to the Constitution, Afghanistan on June 9, 2004, held its first presidential election. There was an impressive voter turnout during this free and fair election, and Karzai won an impressive victory.

During President Karzai's first term, he would do a remarkable job keeping together the diverse ethnic groups in his fragile coalition government. He prevented Afghanistan from reverting to another civil war as had followed the Afghan-Soviet War. However, while Karzai himself was honest, many of his family members and officials engaged in unprecedented corruption, and he refused to allow them be prosecuted.

Also during Karzai's first term, he turned hostile to the United States. He genuinely sought to protect the Afghans, and he began criticizing the Americans when innocent civilians were killed during air strikes, and were humiliated and arrested during night raids.[40] He also was angry when Americans investigated his corrupt officials and family members, and tried to prosecute them.

Musharraf Turns Against Pakistan's Islamist Extremists

On January 12, 2002, Musharraf, under heavy American pressure, gave a landmark television speech denouncing religious extremism and terrorism. In his famous "address to the nation," he criticized Pakistan's Islamist extremists for claiming that their version of Islam was the only true one. He called on Pakistanis to live together peacefully and to respect each other's religious beliefs. He pledged that he would not allow terrorists to operate from inside Pakistan, even if they were supporting the Kashmiri insurgency. He announced that he was banning (and freezing the assets of) five Islamist extremist groups, including the JeM, HuM, and SSP.

Musharraf had several reasons for denouncing terrorism. First, he wanted to maintain good relations with the United States, which Pakistan depended on for military and economic assistance. His speech had been largely for international consumption. Also, Musharraf was trying to appease India, which was threatening to invade Pakistan if it continued to support terrorists who targeted India. Also, Musharraf was starting to realize that Pakistan's Islamist extremists were threatening his own regime. Finally, Musharraf wanted to show Pakistanis that he would try to protect them from the indiscriminate terrorist attacks which were killing innocent civilians. His promise to crack down on terrorists marked the highest point of Musharraf's popularity among his own people.

Pakistan's Islamist extremists pushed back on Musharraf's anti-Islamist declaration. First, the religious parties strongly criticized Musharraf for having dared to criticize Islamists and for having banned some Islamist groups. Also, to escape the ban, a number of the banned militant groups simply changed their names, and some moved to FATA and the NWFP, where they could operate more freely.[41] In addition, those Islamist terrorists who were arrested were never prosecuted, and they soon resumed operations after serving periods of house arrest. In addition, Musharraf's ban prompted many non-banned extremist groups to join or ally with al-Qaeda.

Musharraf followed up on his dramatic denunciation of Pakistani extremists by taking further steps to rein them in. First, Musharraf had teams of ISI operatives, working with CIA and FBI agents, capture or kill many al-Qaeda fighters in Pakistani cities. Most of the surviving al-Qaeda leaders and fighters fled the cities and joined the Afghan Taliban fugitives in their FATA sanctuary—mainly in North Waziristan where the Haqqani network became their main protector.[42] Also, Musharraf ordered the closing of some ISI-supported militant training camps. In addition, Musharraf tried organizing and arming tribal militias to defend themselves, and thereby stop al-Qaeda and its Uzbek allies from assassinating tribal chiefs. However, this effort would fail, since the terrorists attacked tribes that were trying to form militias, and many tribal militiamen who were given weapons deserted with their arms.[43]

There were several reasons why Musharraf's declared war on terrorism would have only limited success. First, Musharraf had issued his denunciation of terrorism mainly in reaction to international pressure, and he took only modest and temporary action against the terrorist groups that he had banned.[44] He sought to contain the terrorists in FATA rather than trying to destroy them. Also, his "ban" excluded the deadly LeT, Haqqani network and so-called "freedom fighters" who attacked Indian targets in Kashmir.[45] Musharraf and army leaders believed that these terrorists could be controlled and should be warehoused in case they were needed as proxy fighters in an emergency. In addition, Musharraf didn't carry out his promise to take action against the Islamist madrassas and mosques, and many continued to promote and spread hatred and violence. Finally, when Musharraf did order military offenses against the FATA militants, he deployed the poorly trained, lightly armed Frontier Corps. These troops were no match against the battle-hardened, heavily armed insurgents there.[46]

Islamist Extremists Attack Musharraf's Regime

While President Musharraf didn't strongly back up his call for a war on terrorists, his call was enough to provoke Islamist extremists to attack his regime and its supporters. Pakistan's Islamists first attacked Musharraf's American supporters. On January 23, 2002, a freelance jihadist kidnapper lured American *Wall Street Journal* reporter Daniel Pearl into a trap in Karachi by promising to arrange a coveted interview. The kidnaper turned Pearl over to an al-Qaeda leader, Khalid Sheik Mohammad (KSM). KSM personally beheaded Pearl as a means of deterring Musharraf from pursuing his campaign against terrorists. Musharraf was indeed deterred.[47] He didn't strongly condemn the murder and the kidnapers who were apprehended never were prosecuted. Musharraf even freed thousands of jailed militants. Musharraf's weak response to Pearl's murder was a devastating blow to his hollow claim that he was tough on terrorism.

The Pearl beheading was just the start of Islamist terrorist retaliation against Musharraf. Incited by al-Qaeda, Pakistani terrorists began attacking Pakistan's government officials and professionals—trying to show the people that Musharraf's regime couldn't protect them. Sunni hit squads killed some 500 Shiite doctors and other professionals in a campaign to "cleanse" Pakistan of its highly educated Shiite minority.[48] Karachi was particularly vulnerable to terrorist attacks, since the killers could easily hide in the slums of this 12 million-person city. The Karachi police had little success in stopping the killings, since most police were poorly trained and poorly equipped, and many were corrupt.[49]

On January 29, 2002, American President G.W. Bush delivered his annual State of the Union address to Congress. Bush declared that the United States was engaged in a "war on terror," which began with al-Qaeda. He asserted that Iraq, Iran and North Korea constituted an "Axis of Evil" which posed the greatest threat to America. Bush declared that "we must take the battle to the enemy." However, Bush did not even mention Pakistan as a threat, even though it was serving as a sanctuary and training center for so many terrorists.

Bush's Axis of Evil declaration was a major blunder. It provoked North Korea to resume its nuclear weapons program. It also led Iran's leaders to release al-Qaeda leaders that it had detained so they could fight the Americans in Afghanistan—instead of turning them over to the Americans as they had been preparing to do.[50]

To further undermine Musharraf, Pakistani Sunni extremists incited a Sunni-Shia war by attacking Shiite mosques, religious processions and Christian churches. On March 17, 2002, a JeM terrorist threw grenades into a Christian church located inside Islamabad's highly secured diplomatic enclave, killing five and wounding 41 more. On July 4, 2003, a Sunni suicide bomber killed 44 worshipers at a Shia mosque in Quetta. The Sunni and Shiite sects, through their respective militant wings, began sending suicide bombers to inflict maximum casualties on their rivals.[51]

The Americans were pleased with Musharraf's public declaration against Islamist terrorism. They also were pleased how Pakistani and American intelligence agencies were cooperating in capturing al-Qaeda leaders. The first major capture occurred on March 28, 2002, when 100 FBI and Pakistani intelligence agents captured an al-Qaeda leader, Abu Zubeida, in a raid on a house in Pakistan. Zubeida's capture was a serious blow to al-Qaeda, since he was the head of its overseas operations. His capture would further convince President Bush that Musharraf must not be criticized in any way.[52] The CIA's constant wall slamming and water boarding of Zubeida at a secret "black site" in Thailand would set a new standard for CIA's brutal "enhanced interrogation" techniques.[53] When these techniques were eventually publicized, they would turn more Muslims against the Americans.[54]

Al-Qaeda soon struck back at Zubeida's capture by helping Pakistani terrorists try to assassinate Musharraf. On April 26, 2002, Islamist HuM terrorists parked an explosive-laden vehicle on a street on Musharraf's convoy route. The assassination attempt failed only because the remote control timing device failed. The police arrested some of the plotters and Musharraf was alarmed when it was discovered that some soldiers had provided the terrorists with vital information on Musharraf's travel routes. Musharraf reacted by having the U.S. Secret Service accelerate its training of his 250-man security detail. However, Musharraf still refused to suppress all extremists, since he believed that some should be warehoused for a time to be called on in case of a future conflict with India.

Musharraf Tries to Improve His Legitimacy

President Musharraf recognized that his regime might survive longer if it appeared to have popular support. Therefore, on April 5, 2002, Musharraf announced that he would hold a national referendum to ask the people if they wanted him to extend his term. His referendum announcement was widely condemned since it conflicted with the constitutional requirement that presidents must be chosen by an electoral college of members of the national and provincial assemblies.

On April 30, 2002, Musharraf's national referendum was held. Musharraf had taken several precautions to insure an affirmative vote, including drastically reducing voting eligibility requirements, pressuring millions of soldiers and government workers to vote, and rigging the results.[55] Despite these precautions, the 15 percent voter turnout was embarrassingly low. However, Musharraf claimed that the referendum had passed and that it gave him a "heavy mandate" to serve five more years as president.

There were several repercussions to Musharraf's rigged referendum. First, his by-passing the Constitution's clear presidential electoral-college voting procedures in favor of a referendum greatly reduced Musharraf's legitimacy. It made it clear that he intended to rule indefinitely. Also, the low turnout for the referendum exposed how greatly his popularity had fallen.

Musharraf had made his public denunciation against terrorism with little intention of destroying Islamist extremist groups. However, he was gradually realizing that he must suppress some of these groups, since their attacks on Indian targets in Kashmir and India risked sparking a war with India. The May 14 terrorist attack in Kashmir was particularly vicious. On that day, terrorists attacked a bus and the family quarters at an Indian Army camp, killing 34 persons—mostly women and children. The terrorists almost succeeded in their goal of provoking an Indo-Pak war. India quickly put its troops on war alert and moved troops to forward positions on the Indo-Pak border. India warned that if Pakistan didn't stop infiltrating militants into Indian-held IJK territory in Kashmir, that India would invade Pakistani-held AJK territory— or even Pakistan itself.

Musharraf was desperate to prevent a war with India, which he doubted that Pakistan could win. American diplomats helped prevent a war by mediating between their leaders. This American intervention was critical, since the two countries hadn't installed an emergency hot line for communicating directly with each other during a crisis. On May 27, Musharraf pledged to India that all cross-border infiltration into Kashmir would end, and this pledge eased tensions and ended the stand-off.

President Musharraf finally ordered the army to conduct its first major offensive against foreign fighters in Pakistan's FATA. On June 22, 2002, Pakistan's army deployed 24,000 regular army troops against militants in FATA's South Waziristan ("Operation Al Mizan"). However, the army's massive deployment didn't destroy the foreign fighters. While the army showed an impressive commitment by continuing its campaign for two years, the army ended by concluding a peace agreement with the insurgents. This operation confirmed the presence of strong al-Qaeda and other foreign fighters in South Waziristan, who enjoyed substantial local support. Musharraf realized that he must take even stronger action to eliminate this foreign fighter presence in his country.

To give the Americans the sense that he was cooperating in their war on terrorism, Musharraf developed a carefully planned routine. He would arrest an important al-Qaeda leader every few months, and then give all other terrorists free rein until the next arrest.[56] As part of this campaign, on September 11, 2002, Pakistani police and intelligence agents captured al-Qaeda leader Ramzi bin al-Shibh after a three-hour shootout at a Karachi apartment building. This was a significant blow to al-Qaeda, since Ramzi had been leading al-Qaeda's military wing, and had been a key planner of the 9/11 attack on the World Trade Center.

President Musharraf now took two steps to further increase his strength. First, on August 20, 2002, he had his ISI supporters form his own right-wing political party. He adopted the old Pakistan Muslim League (PML), and called it the PML(Q). He hoped that this party would dominate elections and support his agenda. Most PML members left the PML and joined the PML(Q), since it offered greater patronage. Critics mockingly called Musharraf's PML(Q) party the "King's Party." The PML remnants renamed their PML party the PML(N)—to identify it with Nawaz Sharif.

The next day, Musharraf took a second step by issuing a Legal Framework Order (LFO). Musharraf's LFO decreed 29 amendments to the Constitution. These included making him president for the next five years and restoring the president's power to dismiss prime ministers and dissolve parliament.[57] On October 2, the Supreme Court stopped Musharraf's attempt to seize more power. It declared that he didn't have authority to amend the Constitution—only parliament did. Despite this setback, Musharraf would prevail a year later by pushing through parliament the

Seventeenth Constitutional Amendment, which would include most of the LFO's provisions.

Musharraf now allowed political parties to participate in the October parliamentary elections. This was a gamble for Musharraf, since the parties could now openly criticize his regime. However, by tampering with the election rules, Musharraf felt sure he could defeat Benazir Bhutto's PPP Party. First, he had election officials reject Benazir Bhutto's application to compete in the election on grounds that she had been convicted of a crime. Sharif withdrew to express solidarity with her.[58] He also had the ISI promote the formation of a MMA coalition of six Islamist extremist parties. The ISI would use strong-arm tactics to get politicians to support the MMA.[59] Moreover, the army prohibited the PPP, PML (N) and other secular political parties from holding processions or rallies. However, these campaign restrictions didn't apply to religious parties, and so they would do well at the polls for the first time.

Pakistan's elections for the National Assembly and Senate were held on October 10, 2002—elections which the Supreme Court had mandated that Musharraf hold within three years of his coup. The voter turnout was a very low 25 percent, since most people knew that the elections were being manipulated, and that ballot counting would probably be rigged. Musharraf's PML (Q) won 118 seats in the 342-seat National Assembly, while the PPP won 81 seats. The new MMA Islamic Alliance won 63 seats. This surprised everyone, including the ISI which had supported it. Since the PML (Q) Party hadn't won a majority of Assembly seats, it began weeks of trying to form a majority coalition with other parties.

There were several repercussions to the National Assembly elections. First, the election results once again exposed Musharraf's dwindling popularity, since over 60 percent of the votes went to parties opposed to his regime. Also, the Islamist Islamic Alliance (MMA) coalition for the first time secured for the religious parties substantial power in the National Assembly. The MMA had attracted many votes with its anti–American campaign.

The Islamist extremist MMA took control of the NWFP's provincial government and became a coalition partner in Baluchistan's provincial government. The radical MMA government in the NWFP would govern poorly. It would suffer from corruption, nepotism and incompetence.[60] It would focus on Islamizing the NWFP by enacting a law requiring strict compliance to its interpretation of shariat law, and it would close girls' schools, barbershops and video stores.[61] At the same time, the MMA would take no action against the Taliban, thereby allowing the Taliban to reorganize, gain strength and terrorize the NWFP. The Taliban soon would virtually take over a suburb in Baluchistan's provincial capital Quetta for its headquarters. From that base, they would attack provincial government and army personnel and facilities.

17

The End of Musharraf's Reign

During the five and a half year period covered in this chapter (November 2002–February 2008), Islamist terrorists twice would nearly assassinate Musharraf. There followed years of major army operations interspersed with peace agreements. Musharraf would have the army seize an Islamist center at the Red Mosque. The mosque seizure would provoke a major Islamist terrorist campaign to overthrow Musharraf. A terrorist would assassinate former PPP prime minister Benazir Bhutto. The chapter ends with the PPP winning the National Assembly elections.

America Invades Iraq

On November 16, 2002, Pakistan's National Assembly and Senate named General Musharraf as president for a five-year term—partly in deference to his winning his presidential referendum. Musharraf gave up his "Chief Executive" title. He revived the office of prime minister which he had abolished when he had seized power three years before.

On November 21, the National Assembly confirmed PML(Q) leader Zafarullah Jamali as prime minister—at the head of a weak coalition government. Musharraf had helped Jamali assemble a coalition after weeks of hard bargaining and vote buying. Jamali was a weak, unimportant, highly deferential politician. He had little power since Musharraf retained the powerful positions of president and army chief. Jamali would stay in office for only a year and a half, during which time he would take little interest in governing.

17. The End of Musharraf's Reign

On January 1, 2003, a CIA drone crashed inside Pakistan soon after take-off, making it impossible for Musharraf's regime to any longer deny that it knew about American drone attacks. The Pakistani people were angry at this confirmation of what they had long suspected—that Musharraf had been allowing American drones to attack targets inside Pakistan.

President Musharraf continued his modest campaign of capturing al-Qaeda leaders on an occasional basis to satisfy the Americans. On March 3, 2003, it was announced that ISI agents had captured Khalid Sheikh Mohammed (KSM) at a safe house in Quetta, Pakistan. KSM, the head of al-Qaeda's military wing, had masterminded the 9/11 World Trade Center attacks against the United States. American officials were extremely pleased that Pakistan had captured KSM and had quickly turned him over to them. Pakistan eventually would turn over to the Americans some 700 al-Qaeda and Taliban suspects.

On March 19, 2003, the United States invaded Iraq in order to remove Saddam Hussein from power (the "Second Gulf War"). This American invasion of Muslim Iraq was a huge mistake. While President G.W. Bush claimed that the invasion was necessary because Saddam possessed weapons of mass destruction, there was no solid evidence behind this claim, and no such weapons would be found. Also, the invasion drew the United States into a long unwinnable war. Hundreds of thousands of Pakistanis demonstrated against this invasion of a Muslim nation. These protests created a dilemma for Musharraf, who wanted to continue supporting the United States. In a delicate balancing act, he expressed sympathy for the people's anti–American anger. However, at the same time he quietly continued to cooperate with the Americans.

There were several repercussions to America's invasion of Iraq. First, the invasion increased the anger and mistrust of most Pakistanis toward the United States. They came to believe al-Qaeda's claim that the back-to-back invasions by the "infidel" Americans of Muslim Afghanistan and Iraq proved that America was "at war with Islam." This belief would help the Afghan Taliban regain a foothold in Afghanistan. Also, Pakistan's Islamist extremists became emboldened by the new anger of Pakistan's masses. They intensified their criticisms of Musharraf and denounced him as an "American stooge." In addition, the United States became preoccupied with its war in Iraq and redirected funds, troops and intelligence assets away from Afghanistan and into Iraq.[1] This preoccupation with Iraq largely ended America's counterterrorist operations in Pakistan and Afghanistan. Also, this transfer of focus caused Musharraf's generals to start thinking that the Americans would leave Afghanistan. This prospect led them to strengthen their ties with the Afghan Taliban. Finally, during the Iraq hostilities, al-Qaeda would develop suicide bombing into a deadly weapon against the well-armed Americans. It soon would introduce this deadly new tactic into Pakistan.

The Taliban Revives in Afghanistan

The Afghan Taliban leaders had thrived and regrouped in Pakistan's FATA, and now they decided to return to Afghanistan. On June 25, 2003, Taliban leader Mullah Omar created a ten-man Taliban leadership council in Quetta, Baluchistan (the "Quetta Shura"). The shura decided to return to Afghanistan, overthrow Karzai, and recover their control of the Afghan government. From their Pakistan sanctuary, the Taliban began their revival by conducting small sporadic cross-border raids against Karzai's Afghan government.

There were several reasons why the Taliban would be able to revive in Afghanistan and soon become a serious threat to Karzai. First, the Taliban had been founded by Pashtuns, and most of Taliban were Pashtuns. Since the Pashtuns were Afghanistan's largest ethnic group, this gave the Taliban a large support base. However, Karzai's government was dominated by Northern Alliance Tajik and Uzbek warlords—who were widely viewed as anti–Pashtun. Few Pashtuns would support a government that they viewed as dominated by and supported by their ethnic rivals.[2] The Taliban would be joined by many former Taliban fighters who still lived in Afghanistan, were being harassed on account of their ex-Taliban status, and who rejoined the Taliban for protection.[3] In addition, Pakistan's ISI intelligence agency provided the Taliban with weapons and medical treatment. The ISI also assisted the Taliban in drug smuggling, which was a major source of Taliban funding.[4] The ISI even hid Taliban leader Mullah Omar in an ISI safe house in Karachi during an illness.[5] Also, the Taliban was assisted by the Haqqani network based in North Waziristan, which provided sanctuary to the fugitives and facilitated the movement of fighters and illicit drugs across the Af-Pak border.[6] Finally, the United States had only 8,000 soldiers in Afghanistan when Karzai took office, and initially international peacekeepers didn't leave the capital.[7] The Bush administration missed an opportunity to strengthen Karzai's government during the first few years after Karzai took office when Pakistan was enjoying peace.[8] Bush not only refused to increase troop levels in Afghanistan, but he also failed to provide funds for Afghan reconstruction projects. Then President Bush turned his attention to invading Iraq, and began deploying to Iraq many of the limited American troops still stationed in Afghanistan.

However, the return of Taliban fighters to Afghanistan would be slow, since many ex-Taliban refugees living in Pakistan were reluctant to leave their peaceful sanctuary in Pakistan and resume fighting in Afghanistan. But Pakistan's ISI began threatening these ex-Taliban fighters to return to Afghanistan and fight NATO troops, or else be turned over to the Americans.[9]

Once the Taliban resumed major operations in Afghanistan, three main groups of militants emerged to fight NATO forces in Afghanistan. These groups were all situated in western Pakistan in areas adjacent to the Pak-Afghan border, and each group managed fighters in those Afghan provinces closest to them. One group was led by Mullah Omar and his Quetta Shura, from its base in Quetta, Baluchistan. This group sent fighters westward into South Afghanistan's Helmand and Kandahar provinces. A second group, further north, was the Haqqani Network based in FATA's North Waziristan. The Haqqani Network oversaw the fighting in Afghanistan's eastern provinces of Khost, Paktika and Paktya.[10] A third group, located even further north, was the TNSM militant group, based in FATA's northernmost Bajaur and Mohmand provinces. The TNSM sent fighters into Afghanistan's eastern Kunar and Nangarhar provinces.

A.Q. Khan's Post-Retirement Nuclear Proliferation Career

While A.Q. Khan (the "Father of the Bomb") had been forcibly retired as head of Pakistan's Kahuta nuclear facility, he was by no means through with his profitable nuclear proliferation activities. After Musharraf told Khan that he was being removed from his job—but before Khan was barred from access to the Kahuta nuclear facility—he made copies of the designs of the most advanced centrifuges, and had eight of the newest centrifuges shipped to his private headquarters in Dubai.[11] Khan chose to make Dubai his proliferation headquarters since it had become the world's center for trafficking illegal nuclear technology and equipment.[12] He would sell these blueprints and centrifuges to Iran so that they could manufacture more on their own.[13] Khan would use his worldwide contacts to purchase centrifuge parts and other material needed to complete the orders he had to fill from Iran and Libya.

Khan's major project was to construct a complete nuclear facility for Libyan dictator and terrorist Gadafi. His contract with Gadafi called for building a facility capable of both enriching uranium and building nuclear bombs. However, the British and Americans learned about this vast project through informers. Gadafi became worried. He knew how after the 9/11 attacks, the Americans had invaded Afghanistan, had quickly routed the Taliban forces, and had installed a pro–American government. Gadafi worried that his regime might be America's next target. Therefore, he began negotiating with the Americans and British to voluntarily give up his infant nuclear weapons program.[14] After a lull in negotiations, talks resumed when in October 2003, the Americans and British searched the ship "BBC China" bound for Libya. They found five huge crates of centrifuge components and parts sent by A.Q. Khan. With his nuclear weapons program exposed, Gadafi quickly made a deal with the United States.[15] In December 2003, Gadafi announced that Libya was abandoning its nuclear weapons program, was ending its contract with A.Q. Khan, and was sending its centrifuges to the United States.[16] In return, the United States promised not to attack Libya or sanction it. Gadafi's disclosure that A.Q. Khan was supplying most of the equipment and technology for its nuclear weapons program (including designs for a proven nuclear warhead) exposed Khan as a greedy and reckless nuclear weapons smuggler.[17]

With A.Q. Khan's private nuclear proliferation activities exposed, Musharraf took further action to end Khan's nuclear proliferation. Musharraf detained several of Khan's former Kahuta associates, who signed statements implicating their old boss. Then Khan was detained, shown these incriminating statements, and threatened with physical harm to himself and his family unless he admitted to his illegal proliferation activities.[18] Khan capitulated, and on February 4, 2004, he read his "confession" from a carefully scripted text. He accepted full responsibility for all of Pakistan's nuclear proliferation. He even gave the implausible story that neither the government nor the army had been involved.[19] The next day, Musharraf pardoned Khan. He didn't dare put the "Father of the Bomb" on trial for fear of a massive reaction among the people, and fear that the angry and impulsive Khan would implicate the army in his proliferation activities. Musharraf ordered that A.Q. Khan and some of his former colleagues be held under house arrest for a long period of time.

While A.Q. Khan had been rebuked by his government and was under house arrest, his worldwide nuclear procurement network remained. America's CIA and the UN's IAEA now cooperated in trying to dismantle it. However, dismantlement proved difficult, since Khan had hidden his vast network by using false invoices, front companies and multiple banks. While Pakistan offered only limited assistance, the American-IAEA team eventually was able to track down most of A.Q. Khan's suppliers with the help of the Libyans.[20]

A. Q. Khan had played a central role in spreading nuclear weapons throughout the world. During the early post-war proliferation period, five powerful nations had acquired a monopoly of nuclear weapons (the U.S., U.K., France, USSR and China). During a second period, A.Q. Khan helped make nuclear weapons available to smaller, less developed nations like Pakistan and North Korea. The five-nation nuclear monopoly had been broken.

17. The End of Musharraf's Reign

Pakistan's Extremists Turn Against Musharraf

Pakistan's Islamist extremists wanted to kill Musharraf. They were furious at him for his denouncing them in public, for his having supported the Americans, and for his having dismissed A.Q. Khan. During December 2003, Islamist terrorists twice would try to kill Musharraf using al-Qaeda explosives. During the first attempt on December 14, JeM terrorists detonated a 550-lb roadside bomb as his convoy was crossing a bridge. The explosion lifted his three-ton armor-plated car into the air, bursting all four tires. His car sped away on the tire rims. Musharraf escaped serious injury because the spotter didn't have a good view of the convoy.[21] Also, the FBI had a jamming device on his vehicle had delayed cell phone signals from detonating the explosives until a few seconds after his car had passed. During the second assassination attempt on December 25, suicide bombers drove two explosive-laden minivans into Musharraf's three-vehicle convoy. An alert police patrol car blocked one minivan heading for his vehicle. However, a second minivan then drove straight at the stopped convoy and detonated its explosives just a few feet away. Musharraf once again amazingly escaped serious injury.

Musharraf was very interested in identifying his attackers, and he ordered an investigation. Both crime scenes were sealed off. A thorough search revealed parts of cellphones, which revealed that the assassins were al-Qaeda and Islamist terrorists. Several soldiers from a nearby base also were involved.[22] The excellent investigation showed how Musharraf had the expertise to solve assassinations—when he wanted to.

There were several repercussions to the two assassination attempts. First, Musharraf soon improved his personal security by having the CIA and FBI further train and equip his Pakistani bodyguards. Also, Musharraf now realized that al-Qaeda and Islamist extremist groups had become such a serious threat to himself and his regime that they must be destroyed. In addition, Musharraf's narrow assassination escapes made American leaders worry that if Musharraf were killed, he might be replaced by an anti–American leader. Therefore, they eased back on public criticisms of Musharraf that might weaken his regime.

To further enhance his security and power, Musharraf made a deal with the six-party MMA coalition of militant Islamist parties. Under this December 24, 2003, agreement, Musharraf pledged to resign as army chief and to push for the official adoption of Islamic Sharia Holy Law. In return, the MMA agreed to support Musharraf's presidency and help him pass the Seventeenth Amendment to the Constitution.

With this newly acquired MMA support, Musharraf on December 30, 2003, had the National Assembly enact the Seventeenth Amendment by the required two-thirds vote. The amendment restored the president's power to dismiss prime ministers and to dissolve the National Assembly. Also, the amendment approved all the actions that Musharraf had taken since he had seized power. Finally, the president henceforth would be elected by an electoral college of the members of the National Assembly, Senate and four provincial assemblies.

On January 5, 2004, President Musharraf and Indian Prime Minister Vajpayee signed the "Islamabad Declaration" in order to start a peace process between the two countries. In the declaration, the two leaders agreed to try to resolve the Kashmir dispute through bilateral negotiations. The declaration marked a change in Musharraf's position, and he would come closer than any other Pakistani leader to reaching a peace agreement with India. However, the two countries would not normalize relations, primarily because both leaders would leave office before the Kashmir dispute could be resolved.

Army Probes Into South Waziristan

President Musharraf, reeling from the assassination attempts on his life, began taking new steps to control or destroy Pakistan's insurgents and their al-Qaeda supporters. On February 18, 2004, he delivered a nationally televised address in which he called on foreign extremists to leave Pakistan. Musharraf made his address partly because the Americans had discovered from a captured courier that al-Qaeda had established a large base in South Waziristan's Shakai Valley.

The Shakai Valley had indeed become al-Qaeda's largest command-and-control center in the world.[23] The base housed several hundred foreign fighters and was protected by local tribal leader Nek Mohammad. The Americans pressured Musharraf to have the army attack the base. On March 15, 2004, General Safdar Hussain, who commanded 7,000 Frontier Corp troops, sent 300 poorly trained and poorly equipped paramilitary troops against 2,000 al-Qaeda fighters and Nek Mohammed's tribesmen (the "Kaloosha Operation").[24] The defenders ambushed this small force in the mountains and surrounded the survivors. The army had to rush in over 5,000 regular troops to rescue the besieged force, and the army soon abandoned the disastrous operation. The army lost some 200 troops and scores of vehicles.

There were several repercussions to the army's failed Kaloosha Operation. First, Musharraf and his senior generals discovered the seriousness of the threat posed by the presence of large numbers of seasoned foreign fighters in FATA. Army leaders began planning how to remove or neutralize this menace. Musharraf authorized CIA drone strikes on TTP leaders in South Waziristan.[25] Also, the army tried (with limited success) to get the local tribesmen to evict the foreign fighters.[26] In addition, the failed army offensive in the Shakai Valley weakened the army's confidence, and led the government to start offering peace deals. The army didn't want to fight these tough adversaries.

After the failed Kaloosha operation, U.S. Secretary of State Colin Powell visited Musharraf. He gave Musharraf an ultimatum—send in regular troops to destroy al-Qaeda camps in South Waziristan or the Americans would do it for him. As an incentive, Powell promised that if Pakistan complied with his request, America would confer on Pakistan the coveted "Major Non-NATO ally" (MNNA) status, which would give Pakistan special access to American weapons.[27]

Peace Deals with the Taliban

President Musharraf initially would try to resolve the problem of foreign fighters and Islamist extremists in FATA by making peace deals with them. The first deal was signed on April 26, 2004, with Taliban leader Nek Mohammed, who was protecting al-Qaeda's base in South Wazirisitan. This "Shakai Agreement" was widely perceived as virtually a government surrender, and it didn't last long. Within weeks Nek Mohammed's fighters began attacking army posts, and six weeks later, the army would return to the Shakai Valley with a larger force of regular troops to remove the foreign fighters.

The government's Shakai Agreement began a three-year period of repeated partially successful army operations in FATA, relying heavily on poorly trained Frontier Corp troops. The army's operations gradually improved as the troops received better training and better equipment. However, even after successful operations, the army would negotiate "peace deals" with the insurgents and withdraw from the territory that it had seized.

These peace deals strengthened Pakistan's Islamist insurgents in several ways. First, the government negotiated the peace deals with the Islamist militant leaders rather than with tribal elders, thereby giving the militants new legitimacy. Also, the peace agreements rewarded the militants with funds to compensate them for the destruction that the army had inflicted on them. The militants would use these funds to buy arms in anticipation of the next army offensive. In addition, the militants used these intermittent lulls in the fighting to seize control of local governments by assassinating government officials and uncooperative tribal leaders.[28] They even set up parallel local governments which imposed a strict Sharia code on beards, clothing and entertainment.

President Musharraf had allowed Jamali to serve as his prime minister for 18 months. During that time Musharraf had gradually taken over the few duties that the subservient prime minister had been allowed to perform. Musharraf had even started taking personal control of Jamili's cabinet meetings. However, Musharraf wanted an even more pliable prime minister. Therefore, on June 26, 2004, he forced Jamali to resign and replaced him with a loyal favorite—Shaukat Aziz. The pliable figurehead Aziz would loyally serve Musharraf for over three years.

While Pakistan's army leaders had been supporting Pakistan's Islamist militants for decades, they began to realize that this had been a mistake as the militants began attacking army convoys and posts. The first militant attack occurred on June 9, 2004, when they ambushed a convoy in Karachi carrying a Pakistani army general. While the general escaped injury, his driver and seven of his guards were killed. That same day, Islamist militants struck two army posts, killing fourteen soldiers. The army soon responded to these attacks. It not only wanted to avenge the attacks but also sought to appease the Americans who were threatening to stop arms shipments if the army didn't take action.[29]

The army's first response came on June 10, when it sent 10,000 regular soldiers to attack Arabs, Chechens and Uzbeks in South Waziristan's Shakai Valley. The army killed 50 militants and seized nine militant compounds. The army also raided a massive cave which al-Qaeda was using as a base, training facility and propaganda office.[30]

To destroy the foreign fighters, Musharraf also started allowing the Americans to use drones against the South Waziristan militants. The Americans responded on June 17, 2004, by launching a CIA drone missile which killed tribal leader Nek Mohammed just after he answered a satellite phone to give a media interview. However, the death of this insurgent "hero" provoked a resurgence of Islamist guerrilla activity in South Waziristan. Thousands of young, radical FATA tribesmen converged on South Waziristan and joined the tribesmen in resisting the army's intrusion.[31] Also, Nek was replaced by Baitullah Mehsud as South Waziristan's Taliban leader. Baitullah soon created a loyal army of several thousand fanatical black-turbaned militia, who began attacking army targets and killing tribesmen suspected of collaborating with the army.[32]

Pakistan's army concluded its operations in South Waziristan on September 9, 2004, with a major attack against three foreign terrorist strongholds. The army sent in 10,000 regular troops, and killed over 70 terrorists. However, most of the terrorists escaped into North Waziristan.

The Baluchistan Insurgency Revives

The Baloch in Pakistan's sparsely populated Baluchistan Province already had rebelled several times against central government rule. Baluchistan's leaders demanded separation from Pakistan. This time they focused on claims that the central government was exploiting the province's natural resources. The Fifth Baloch Insurgency began on May 2, 2004, when Baloch insurgents killed three Chinese engineers in Gwadar. The Baluchistan Liberation Army (BLA) insurgents opposed the Gwadar port project (and the Sui gas development field project), claiming that these central government projects were seizing Baluchistan's natural resources without fairly compensating the province. They were particularly opposed the Gwadar port project because many Chinese were working on the project, and the Baloch feared that Chinese workers would settle there.

Baloch BLA insurgents struck again on January 9, 2005, and blew up pipelines in the Sui gas fields, which were providing 45 percent of the country's energy needs. The BLA also destroyed railway tracks, electricity pylons, and pipelines throughout the province. When the army rushed 2,500 troops to defend the Sui fields, the BLA initiated guerrilla operations across the province.

The Baloch insurgency grew when the army killed Baluchistan's BLA guerrilla leader Nawab Akbar Bugti. On August 26, 2006, Bugti was resting in a cave when an air attack flushed him out. Troops killed Bugti and 35 of his followers, seized his body and refused to turn it over to his family.[33] Bugti's death led to widespread anti-government protests, rioting and arson, which shut down Quetta and all major Baluchistan cities for a week. India may have been providing arms and funds to the Baluch insurgents.[34]

Bugti's death rekindled the Balulchistan insurgency, and his grandson took over as the BLA's leader. The central government responded to the protests and rioting with a "kill and dump" campaign, in which its security forces tortured and killed Baluch nationalists, and then dumped their bodies by the roadside. This brutality intensified the hatred that the Baloch felt toward the government.[35]

Trying to Reach Peace with India

President Musharraf realized that Pakistan no longer could compete with India militarily. He convinced army leaders that peace with India was needed so that Pakistan's economy could expand and thereby support Pakistan's large military expenditures.[36] Therefore, on September 24, 2004, Musharraf met with India's Prime Minister Manmohan Singh for the first time. After a friendly meeting, the two issued a joint statement reflecting a common desire to move the peace process forward. Two months later, Musharraf devised several innovative plans for peacefully resolving the Kashmir dispute, such as by declaring independence for sections of Kashmir's disputed territory.

Pakistan and India moved the peace process forward further by agreeing on a cease-fire in Kashmir. While fighting between the Pakistani and Indian armies had ended five years before, an official cease-fire agreement never had been signed. Now, on September 30, 2004, India and Pakistan finally agreed to a formal cease-fire line along the disputed 460-mile "Line of Control" (LOC) that separated Pakistani-occupied AJK from Indian-occupied IJK. This cease-fire line would hold for many years, although Pakistan never would accept the LOC as a permanent boundary. In contrast, India sought to make the LOC a permanent boundary, and even started building a tall, 340-mile electrified fence along the LOC with a system of motion sensors.

To further reduce tensions with India, Musharraf selected a new ISI chief. On October 7, 2004, Musharraf appointed the cautious, non-political General Ashfaq Parvez Kayani to that position. Musharraf ordered Kayani to reduce the ISI's traditional support for Islamist extremists and Kayani fired or transferred many ISI extremist officers.[37] However, Kayani had difficulty controlling low-level personnel, and many hardline ISI field officers refused to abandon the Islamic extremists who the ISI had been supporting for so many years.

President Musharraf had pledged to give up his post of army chief. However, on December 30, 2004, he declared that he would not surrender his army chief post after all. This reversal particularly angered the MMA coalition of militant Islamist parties which had been supporting Musharraf in return for his promise to give up his uniform. The MMA responded to this betrayal by conducting anti–Musharraf strikes and marches.

Pakistan's army had achieved some successes in its offenses against Islamist militants in South Waziristan. It still hoped that it could prevent the militants from expanding beyond FATA without further fighting. Therefore, on February 7, 2005, the army signed a second peace agreement with Islamist militants in South Waziristan. The agreement was signed with the new militant tribal leader Baitullah Mehsud in the town of Sararogha (the "Sararogha Agreement"). As usual, the army offered generous terms, including a promise to withdraw its troops from South Waziristan. Pulling out the troops virtually handed over control of the area to the militants. Baitullah soon violated the peace terms by attacking local pro-army government leaders and tribal elders.

President Musharraf and Indian Prime Minister Singh continued their peace initiative by implementing several confidence-building measures. They agreed to restart bus service between two towns on opposite sides of Kashmir's Line of Control, and this service resumed on April 7, 2005. Nine days later, Musharraf visited India on Singh's invitation to watch an Indo-Pak cricket game together. The two leaders had a productive meeting which included an in-depth discussion of Kashmir. The two leaders then issued a joint statement declaring that the peace process was "irreversible."

The Americans were pleased with Pakistan's efforts to make peace with India. They also were pleased with the success of the Pak-American campaign to destroy al-Qaeda's leadership. On May 2, ISI agents captured al-Qaeda terrorist Abu Faraj al-Libbi while he was riding a motorbike in the NWFP. Abu Faraj was al-Qaeda's chief of operations in Pakistan. Then on May 14, CIA drone missiles killed senior al-Qaeda leader Haitham al-Yameni in North Waziristan. North Waziristan had become the main target for CIA drone strikes after many terrorists had fled there to escape the army's South Waziristan offensives.

Pak-American Relations Start to Fray

While Pak-American relations had been improving, they deteriorated when the United States agreed to help India develop its civilian nuclear power industry. On July 18, 2005, American president G.W. Bush and Indian Premier Singh signed a joint statement which was the framework for an Indo-American nuclear power sharing deal. Under this agreement, India would separate its civil and military nuclear facilities and would place all its civil nuclear facilities under safeguards of the IAEA (the UN International Atomic Energy Agency). It allowed India to purchase nuclear fuel from the United States and other countries. While this framework would not lead to a formal agreement until October 2008, it angered Pakistan's leaders, who predicted that the nuclear fuel made available through the agreement would free up India's own stockpiles of peaceful uranium for use in making more nuclear bombs. Pakistan's leaders also would be disappointed that President G.W. Bush wouldn't make similar nuclear fuel available to Pakistan. The agreement also helped stoke an Indo-Pak nuclear arms race. Pakistan began building additional long-range nuclear warheads and began developing small, short-range nuclear-tipped missiles to meet a possible Indian ground attack.[38]

While the United States had been killing some al-Qaeda leaders with sporadic help from Pakistan's ISI, Osama bin Laden himself remained at large. He was still exercising such strong control over al-Qaeda that his American pursuers gave him the code name "Crankshaft"—reflecting his vital role over al-Qaeda's "engine." Unknown to the Americans, in August 2005, 48-year-old bin Laden secretly moved into a large compound in Abbottabad, Pakistan— just one mile from the Pakistan Army's national training academy. The main building in this compound had been specially built for him by two Kuwaiti brothers, and it would remain bin Laden's home for the next five years until his death. The compound was so much larger than other buildings in the neighborhood that the locals would call it the "Waziristan Palace." To conceal the inside, the building had high walls, and the residents barely left the compound. For security, Bin Laden didn't use cell phones, and instead he communicated with his lieutenants only by messages carried by trusted couriers.[39]

Pakistan's leaders suddenly refocused their attention on Kashmir when a devastating earthquake struck the mountainous region of Pakistani-controlled AJK. The October 8, 2005, quake killed over 86,000 persons and left 3.5 million homeless. Pakistan's army deployed 50,000 troops to the devastated area, and the government distributed some $350 million in cash payments to the survivors. The United States contributed military aircraft to help with the rescue effort. However, the survivors mostly appreciated the quick assistance provided by Islamist militant groups, which were able to respond quickly because they had nearby bases and training camps.

American Drone Missiles and Terrorist Suicide Bombs

American drone strikes against al-Qaeda leaders accelerated during this period. On November 30, 2005, a CIA drone's Hellfire missile killed Abu Hamza Rabia, al-Qaeda's chief of operations in Pakistan. This strike in North Waziristan was one of the first of many successful American drone attacks against al-Qaeda leaders in Pakistan's FATA region. Musharraf once again vigorously denied to the public that a drone had been involved in the attack. However, this time a local journalist reported that shrapnel found at the site proved that Rabia had been killed by an American drone-fired missile. Photos of pieces of the American missile appeared in newspapers around the world. The reporter who broke the story soon was murdered—presumably by the ISI.[40]

On January 6, 2006, the Taliban announced a suicide campaign against American and NATO forces in Afghanistan. Until then, the Taliban had used suicide attacks sparingly, but now they began using the suicides as a regular weapon. The Taliban set up suicide training schools in the Waziristans, and recruited young teenagers for suicide missions—especially illiterate, sickly, or mentally ill boys. Some recruits were normal boys thirsting for revenge over the death of family members. Their trainers motivated them with promises of a wonderful afterlife if they carried out a successful mission.[41]

On January 13, 2006, a second major drone attack occurred—this time in the northernmost FATA agency of Bajaur. American Predator drones fired missiles at three houses—hoping to kill al-Qaeda's number-two leader Zawahiri during a holiday feast. While Zawahiri had left just before the missiles struck, five senior al-Qaeda leaders were killed, including al-Qaeda's chief bomb maker. However, since the missiles also killed a number of women and children, Islamist extremist groups organized a large protest in Karachi—the largest anti-American rally in four years.

The success of the drone strikes encouraged the Americans to conduct more drone attacks in FATA. Al-Qaeda leaders began fearing the drone strikes above all else, and to limit their losses they began avoiding meeting in large groups. Pakistani Islamist groups tried to pressure Musharraf to forbid all drone attacks, but Musharraf continued to support the strikes.

American President G.W. Bush was becoming concerned over Musharraf's seeming wavering commitment to America's war on terrorism. So on March 4, 2006, Bush flew to Pakistan to ascertain Musharraf's true level of commitment. Bush showed Musharraf a list prepared by Afghan President Karzai's NDS intelligence agency, whose agents had been observing Taliban leaders living in Pakistan's cities of Quetta and Peshawar. Musharraf frustrated both Bush and Karzai by ridiculing the accuracy of the list.[42] Musharraf was following his policy of suppressing the Pakistan Taliban (who were attacking targets inside Pakistan) but opposing attacks on the Afghan Taliban (who were using Pakistan as a base for attacks on NATO troops in Afghanistan).[43]

Pakistan's own Sunni Muslim extremists began attacking rival religious sects inside Pakistan. They began by striking mosques, marketplaces and schools, killing many innocent civilians. One of the deadliest massacres in Pakistan's history occurred on April 11, 2006, when a suicide bomber attacked a Muslim religious gathering in a Karachi park. The explosion killed 47 persons, including the entire leadership of a moderate Sunni Muslim group. During the next three years, suicide attacks would increase ten-fold. Pakistan's civilians suffered greatly and many would turn against the Islamic terrorists.

Musharraf was concerned with these new attacks by Pakistani extremists against rival religious sects, since they could spark a major sectarian war inside Pakistan. He was even more concerned when Pakistani terrorists struck targets inside India, since they might provoke a general war with India. Musharraf was particularly concerned with the July 11, 2006, attack in Mumbai, India. During this brazen attack, terrorists detonated a series of seven pressure cooker bombs within 11 minutes on Mumbai commuter trains. The bombs killed 209 Indians. Indian investigators concluded that some of the terrorists belonged to a Pakistani terrorist group, and that the ISI had assisted in the attack.

Despite the increased threats from Islamist insurgents, Musharraf hesitated to destroy them, hoping that they could be contained inside FATA. He also was reluctant to turn on these "Muslim brothers" who had served as Pakistan's proxies in the fighting in Afghanistan and Kashmir. So Musharraf's regime kept signing peace agreements with them. On September 5, 2006, his regime entered into its third peace agreement with FATA insurgents (the "Waziristan Accord"). The government signed the agreement with Islamist extremist leader Baitullah Mahsud, the Haqqani network, and tribal leaders. Musharraf supported the agreement because the army lacked the ability or resolve to fight the jihadists there, and because he needed the troops to help put down the Baluchistan insurgency.[44] As usual, the army offered the insurgents generous terms. It agreed to confine army troops to their barracks, while the militants agreed to stop attacking the army inside Pakistan. Once again the militants used the lull in the fighting to recuperate from their losses, recruit new fighters, and kill uncooperative tribal elders. FATA had become the center of world terrorism.

Pakistan's Islamic extremists had been attacking Musharraf regime targets for some time, but had largely avoided striking military targets. However, a turning point occurred on November 9, 2006, when a suicide bomber wrapped in a shawl charged into the midst of exercising recruits at the army's Paramilitary School in Dargai in the NWFP. The attack killed some 42 soldiers and wounded 40 more.

The attack on the paramilitary school was a turning point in army-Islamist extremist relations, since this was the first time that Pakistani Islamist militants had attacked a military target inside Pakistan. Also, the attack convinced army leaders that they must stop negotiating peace deals with Islamist militants in FATA and the NWFP. In addition, the success of this single suicide bomber encouraged al-Qaeda and the Taliban to greatly expand their suicide bomber program, since suicide attacks had become such an efficient way to kill their enemies. Terrorist suicide attacks in Pakistan leaped from six in 2006 to 56 in 2007.

Islamist suicide bombers also continued attacking high-profile civilian targets. On February 6, 2007, a terrorist blew himself up in a parking lot as he tried to enter the Islamabad Airport. He died before he could claim any victims. This was the first suicide attack in Pakistan's capital and it demonstrated just how vulnerable the country had become to Islamist extremist attacks.

Musharraf Picks a Fight with Judges and Lawyers

President Musharraf had been losing the support of many of Pakistan's key leaders and groups as he had become increasingly arrogant, dictatorial and isolated. He made most of Pakistan's important decisions, relied on a smaller and smaller group of advisers, and listened less and less to anybody.[45] He even refused to acknowledge that he might be responsible for Pakistan's growing violence, and instead he spent millions on a campaign to improve his image at home and abroad.[46] As part of his campaign, he denounced hostile media, denied them lucrative government advertising, and refused to renew their operating licenses.

Musharraf would lose the support of more civilians by attacking Pakistan's judicial system. On March 9, 2007, he dismissed Supreme Court Chief Justice Iftikhar Chaudhry. Musharraf had appointed Chaudhry two years before, expecting that he would submit to the country's military rulers—as Supreme Court judges always had done. However, Chaudhry had an independent streak, and he had become a threat to Musharraf by demanding an accounting of missing Baloch insurgents who had been seized by Musharraf's security forces. Musharraf also feared that the independent Chaudhry might get the Supreme Court to declare that the Constitution barred Musharraf from serving a second presidential term. When Musharraf exerted pressure on Chaudhry to resign, Chaudhry surprised everyone by refusing to quit. Musharraf summarily dismissed him from office and placed him under house arrest.

The chief justice's dismissal galvanized Pakistan's lawyers to support Chaudhry, and it led to a two-year "Lawyers Movement." The day after the chief justice's dismissal, lawyers in every bar association in the country demonstrated for Chaudhry's reinstatement. They boycotted court sessions and marched in the streets. Soon the lawyers were joined by other professionals and by women's groups. Hundreds of thousands cheered Chaudhry's motorcade as it toured the country. Chaudhry became a national hero for standing up to Musharraf and for demanding that the government and the army follow the law.

Musharraf reacted to the "Lawyers Movement" challenge with brute force, and 42 were killed in the disturbances. Musharraf's violent crackdown enraged the lawyers even more, who now began demanding that Musharraf resign and hold free and fair elections. This "First Lawyers Movement" ended on July 20, 2007, when the 13-member Supreme Court declared that Chaudhry's dismissal had been illegal and restored Chaudhry as chief justice. Musharraf didn't immediately respond to Chaudhry's reinstatement. Chaudhry's restoration was greeted with widespread celebrations throughout the country. However, this was only a partial victory because Musharraf didn't accept the Supreme Court's decision, and he would dismiss Chaudhry again four months later.

The Seizure of the Red Mosque

On July 3, 2007, on Musharraf's orders, police and an elite army commando brigade surrounded the Islamabad Red Mosque, which had become a center for Islamist militancy. The huge mosque complex was being run by the two radical Ghazi brothers, and it housed thousands of male students and a girls' seminary. During the previous six months, the Ghazi brothers had been secretly stockpiling weapons and digging tunnels in the basement to defend against a possible attack by government forces.[47] Also, the extremist students from the complex had been imposing strict sharia law on nearby residents and shopkeepers using verbal abuse and sticks. Musharraf finally demanded that the Ghazi brothers leave the mosque and surrender their weapons. When the brothers refused, Musharraf reluctantly ordered the army to lay siege to the mosque and seize it.

On July 9, 2007, Musharraf ordered a full-scale assault on the Red Mosque after the 1,100 extremists remaining in the mosque complex refused to negotiate and shot at the army siege forces.[48] The defenders fiercely resisted the assault using machine guns, grenades and suicide explosive vests. The bloody assault was televised. Army commandos fought room-to-room against the heavily armed militants who had retreated into the basement. The army seized the mosque after three days of fighting, during which 93 defenders were killed—including one of the two Ghazi brothers.

There were several repercussions to the seizure of the Red Mosque. First, it exposed how years of ISI support of Islamic extremists had backfired. Many extremists no longer believed that the ISI supported them, and many no longer obeyed their ISI handlers. Some Islamist extremists even began attacking ISI offices.[49] Also, Musharraf lost much public support for his failure to carry out his promise to stop Islamist extremism and for his inability to peacefully resolve the Red Mosque crisis. In addition, the deaths of so many defenders provoked a wave of public sympathy for the mosque "martyrs." It also united many scattered Islamist extremist groups and motivated them to attack government and military facilities. These groups included the "Punjabi Taliban," which was a network of members of banned militant groups who had been hiding in southern Punjab Province. While these Punjabis had no militant base, they would assist other groups with intelligence and logistics when the other groups attacked targets in Punjab Province.[50] The number of terrorist killings of civilians each year would double in five years to 3,000 victims.[51]

The first jihadist attack in revenge for the Red Mosque seizure took place on July 17, 2007. A suicide attack struck an army convoy in FATA's North Waziristan, killing 24 soldiers. A second attack took place on August 30, when Taliban forces surrounded an army convoy in South Waziristan. The convoy's 266 soldiers surrendered without firing a shot. This was widely regarded as the Pakistan Army's worst humiliation ever involving fighting inside the country. A third attack occurred on September 13, when two suicide bombers penetrated the army's base at Tarbala and killed 25 troops.

The Islamist terrorists also continued attacking innocent civilians in order to show the people that Musharraf couldn't protect them. In Islamabad, government workers and residents in upper-class neighborhoods began surrounding their homes and job sites with concentric circles of police checkpoints, barricades and barbed wire.[52] Most foreigners fled from the capital.

Two Exiled Leaders Return Home

President Musharraf recognized that his grip on power was weakening. To remedy this, he offered a deal to former Prime Minister Benazir Bhutto, which would allow her to end her exile overseas and reenter Pakistani politics. On July 27, 2007, Musharraf agreed to allow Bhutto to return home, but insisted that she not return until after the National Assembly elections.[53] The two leaders seemed to agree on a power-sharing agreement, with Musharraf president and Bhutto prime minister. However, the details never were finalized. Musharraf was gambling that by allowing Bhutto to return home and participate in free elections, that he would give his regime a greater semblance of a democracy. The exiled Bhutto would rely on this deal to risk returning to Pakistan. However, both leaders saw themselves as the sole savior of Pakistan, and so neither one really wanted to share power with the other.[54]

On October 5, 2007, Musharraf carried out part of the Bhutto-Musharraf "deal" by issuing a National Reconciliation Ordinance (NRO). The NRO granted amnesty to politicians who had been accused of corruption and terrorism, and this allowed Bhutto to return to Pakistan without having to face the corruption charges that were pending against her.[55] In return, Bhutto's PPP Party would carry out Bhutto's promise not to have PPP legislators boycott the next day's National Assembly vote in the presidential election.

On October 6, the great majority of National Assembly legislators cast their votes for Musharraf for president—the first step for his winning the presidency. The Constitution required that to become president, one needed to win a majority vote of the 1,170-member electoral college, made up of the members of the National Assembly and the four provincial assemblies.[56]

On October 18, 2007, Benazir Bhutto arrived in Pakistan, ending her long exile. This was a risky move since while Musharraf had been discussing her return, the details of the Musharraf-Bhutto "deal" had not been agreed upon. Also, Bhutto had returned many weeks before the date set by Musharraf for her earliest acceptable return. Musharraf also had warned her that Islamist jihadists were planning to kill her, and he told her that he could not guarantee her safety.[57]

Bhutto soon discovered how great a risk she had taken in returning to Pakistan. When Bhutto's plane arrived in Karachi she began a slow, dangerous ride in a small convoy through Karachi's streets—which were lined by two million adoring supporters. Hundreds of unarmed young male volunteers surrounded her truck holding hands to form a human shield to protect her. Her heavily armored truck became increasingly vulnerable as the convoy proceeded, since the street lights were being purposely shut off as her convoy approached, and after eight hours the convoy's cell phone jammers (carried to prevent bomb detonations) had stopped working.[58] At 12:06 a.m., right after she had gone into the truck to rest her feet, two large bombs exploded near her convoy, killing 179 persons and wounding over 600—the worst terrorist attack in Pakistan's history.[59] Bhutto miraculously escaped uninjured, and was whisked away in a jeep to her home. The government and police didn't investigate who was behind the attack and prevented others from doing so.[60] While Bhutto's mistrust of Musharraf grew due to this attack, she decided to continue campaigning for seats in the upcoming National Assembly elections so she could become the next prime minister.

Musharraf's "Second Coup"

On November 3, 2007, President Musharraf declared a six-week state of emergency—his "second coup." He suspended the Constitution and postponed the national and provincial assembly elections—which would eventually be held on February 18, 2008. Musharraf also took blunt measures to gain control of the Supreme Court, which still was deliberating on whether Musharraf's second term was legal. He dismissed Chief Justice Chaudhry for a second time. He also dismissed those Supreme Court and High Court justices who had refused to take a new oath of allegiance to him, and he replaced them with loyal judges. Musharraf also jailed all the leaders of the Lawyers' Movement and raided their headquarters.[61] He also carried out the harshest suppression of the media in Pakistan's history.[62]

Musharraf's "second coup" had several repercussions. First, it turned the increasingly important middle class against him. In addition, Benazir Bhutto pulled out of any power-sharing deal she might have had with him, since she couldn't join with a dictator who was crushing democratic institutions. She publicly denounced his state of emergency and she called for an end to his military government. In addition, former cricket star Imran Khan joined the campaign to unseat Musharraf. Imran had led the PTI party as a virtual one-man party for 15 years. He now reemerged as a firebrand orator and attacked Musharraf's regime for supporting the status quo and for being an "American stooge."[63] Also, Musharraf lost the support of the army's leaders, who feared that the army's reputation was being damaged by Musharraf's ruthless suppression of his opponents.

President Musharraf had become so concerned with Bhutto's surging popularity that on November 13, he arrested Bhutto and 18,000 of her supporters.[64] When lawyers and their supporters protested outside courthouses, police viciously clubbed them. These arrests led to widespread revulsion against Musharraf.

Musharraf soon faced new opposition from other quarters. A complaint was filed with the Supreme Court challenging Musharraf's right to serve a second presidential term. The Supreme Court held that he could serve—after the ISI had blackmailed three of the justices with incriminating sex tapes.[65]

Then on November 25, 2007, former Prime Minister Nawaz Sharif returned to Pakistan after a seven-year exile. Sharif had tried to return to Pakistan two months earlier, but Musharraf had responded by illegally deporting him. This time, Musharraf wasn't able to deport him, and Sharif's return further increased the number of powerful politicians who challenged Musharraf's rule.

The First Battle of Swat

Pakistan's army had been focusing its efforts on destroying foreign fighters in FATA's South and North Waziristan. However, it now became concerned that the Islamist Maulana Fazullah and his TNSM had gradually taken control of the Bajaur, the northernmost agency in FATA. Fazullah had been receiving arms from tribal chief Behtullah Mehsud in South Waziristan.[66] The army also was concerned that the TNSM had gradually taken control of most of the Swat District in the NWFP to the east. Fazullah had been nicknamed "Radio Mullah" because he had set up over 22 pirate FM-radio stations which broadcast jihadist messages over street loudspeakers round-the-clock. His evening messages announced which officials, tribal leaders and collaborators would be killed the next morning. The goal of his reign of terror was to eliminate all of Swat's police and government officials.[67]

To destroy Fazullah's TNSM insurgents, the army on October 24, 2007, for the first time sent regular troops into the Swat Valley (the "First Battle of Swat"). During the first phase of the battle, the army deployed over 3,000 troops in Swat to bolster the 15,000 paramilitary and police who were having trouble there controlling Radio Mullah's extremists. When heavy fighting broke out, some of the insurgents crossed into the Shangla District on Swat's southern border. On November 12, the army began pushing the TNSM out of the Shangla District, and started recapturing some strategic Swat hilltops.

The First Battle of Swat ended on December 8, 2007. The six-week battle had been a short-term army victory, with the army having forced the TNSM out of the Swat and Shangla districts. The TNSM fighters withdrew to their base in FATA's Bajaur agency, but they eventually would return. Fazullah would reopen his FM radio stations, spread his radio messages without army interference, and build up his military forces. A year later the army would strike his TNSM forces again in the Second Battle of Swat.

On November 29, 2007, Musharraf had himself sworn in for a second five-year term as President, even though he had not met the constitutional requirement that he be elected by an electoral college. On that same day, Musharraf surrendered his position as army chief which he had held for nine years. He believed that he had all the powers that he needed. He retained his presidential powers as commander-in-chief, and he had acquired new powers during his "second coup." However, Musharraf's authority had been considerably diminished, since now his powers were limited to those given to the president by the Constitution.

Having resigned as Army Chief, Musharraf had to find a replacement. He appointed ex-ISI chief Ashfaq Parvez Kayani to succeed him, and Kayani would remain army chief for six years. Kayani wanted to return the army to its primary mission of defending the country from outside attack. Therefore, he banned all officers from contacting politicians, and he withdrew hundreds of them from government positions.[68] He also had the ISI close its notorious "political wing," which had rigged elections and had blackmailed and bribed politicians. Kayani also personally insured that Islamist extremists were denied promotion to the rank of Brigadier or above.[69] In addition, Kayani stepped up operations against Islamist insurgents and foreign fighters in South Waziristan and Swat. However, Kayani was indecisive and he seemed unwilling to hold any of his officers accountable for their mistakes.[70] He also would refuse to grant repeated American requests to conduct an army offensive against militants in North Waziristan, where many terrorists had fled seeking sanctuary. He claimed that his troops were not ready to conduct a new offensive because they were weary, they weren't motivated, and they lacked public support.[71]

The Formation of the Pakistan Taliban (TTP)

President Musharraf faced a new challenge when dozens of Pakistani insurgent groups formed a united front to coordinate their attacks on his regime. This united front was formed on December 14, 2007, and called itself the Tehreek-e-Taliban Pakistan (TTP)—also referred to as the "Pakistan Taliban." The TTP included half of Pakistan's 40 Taliban factions, and their commanders led a total of over 15,000 fighters. These commanders had been drawn together in response to the government's Red Mosque attack. The TTP factions set aside their rivalries so they could better coordinate their attacks. Its goals were to overthrow Musharraf's pro–American government and replace it with Islamist rule. It also wanted to overthrow Karzai's Afghan government and drive out Karzai's NATO protectors.

The TTP chose South Waziristan's tribal chief Baitullah Mehsud as its leader ("emir"), and he would become the most powerful and ruthless militant in FATA.[72] Emir Baitullah would preside over a 40-member Shura, and the TTP soon would dominate all the other Pakistani insurgent groups. The TTP would transform the defensive war fought by Pakistan's individual Muslim insurgent groups into a loosely coordinated offensive war.

However, the TTP was not a monolithic group. Instead it was a conglomerate of some two dozen Islamist extremist groups, whose commanders ("deputy emirs") acted independently from Baitullah's TTP headquarters at Sararogha in South Waziristan. However, the TTP's headquarters did offer valuable inspiration, guidance and logistical support. The army and ISI would try to weaken the TTP by offering support to disgruntled TTP members and rivals who were forming their own militias.[73] During the next seven years, TTP terrorist attacks would kill over 23,000 civilians and security personal in Pakistan, and these killings would turn most Pakistanis against this ruthless group.[74]

Benazir Bhutto Assassinated

President Musharraf now focused on winning seats in the upcoming National Assembly elections, which would determine who would be the next prime minister. Musharraf had two main challenges to his PML (Q) Party—Sharif's PML (N) Party and Bhutto's PPP Party. Musharraf's rival Sharif was dismissed from the race by Pakistan's Election Commission, which declared that he could not be a candidate due to alleged criminal activities. Musharraf's other major rival, Benazir Bhutto, would meet a worse fate.

On December 27, 2007, Bhutto was at an election campaign rally in a park near Rawalpindi. She had just given a campaign speech. While her speech had gone well, one of her former security guards on the dais had been acting suspiciously during her presentation.[75] After her speech, the police failed to stop crowds from exiting the park as she left, and they swarmed around her Land Cruiser. At that moment, Bhutto popped her head out of her car's roof hatch to wave to the crowds. As she did so, an assassin fired a pistol at close range, and then detonated his explosive vest. Bhutto was thrown back into her vehicle. She was mortally wounded either by bullets or by the roof retraction latch which may have contacted her head as she dropped down through the closing roof.[76] The TTP had probably organized the assassination, but due to an inadequate investigation, the group behind the assassin never would be conclusively determined.[77]

There were several repercussions to Benazir Bhutto's assassination. First, Bhutto's death deprived Pakistan of its only relatively progressive politician with a large national following. During her long exile abroad, she had formed plans to move Pakistan toward democracy.[78] She might have transitioned Pakistan to a sustainable democracy had she survived, won the election, and served a third term. Also, most Pakistanis believed that Musharraf was in some way responsible for Bhutto's death, and so any remaining support for him totally collapsed. Even active and retired generals believed that Musharraf should withdraw from politics and leave the country.[79] While Musharraf's support collapsed, the popularity of Bhutto's PPP party increased. This would help the PPP win the next parliamentary elections. In addition, Musharraf became more arrogant and autocratic than ever now that his rival Bhutto was gone. He was in total denial that he had been primarily responsible for her death by failing to provide her with adequate security.

Benazir Bhutto's widower, Asif Zardari, quickly returned to Pakistan after his wife's assassination. He presented to the PPP leaders Benazir's handwritten will which named him interim leader of the PPP in case anything happened to her.[80] However, Zardari, recognizing his own unpopularity, agreed to serve as interim PPP chairman for only three years. At that time his son Bilawal Zardari would graduate from Oxford University and would take over the PPP's leadership.

On January 9, 2008, Islamist suicide bombers attacked policemen on duty outside the Lahore High Court—killing 19 policemen and five civilians. This was one of the first major terrorist attacks on targets in Punjab Province, and showed how Musharraf had failed in his plan to contain terrorism in FATA and the NWFP. The terrorists were assisted by he "Punjabi Taliban," who provided intelligence and logistical support. Further terrorist attacks would continue in Punjab Province, moving north and eventually reaching the country's capital itself. The attackers seemed to be trying to force Musharraf from the presidency by demonstrating that he could not protect the public. This rash of suicide attacks in Pakistan's settled areas forced frightened Pakistanis to hide in their homes, and led investors to place their money in foreign countries. The attacks became more frequent because the attackers knew that even if they were brought to trial, few would ever be convicted.[81]

Meanwhile, Pakistani and American forces kept attacking the Islamist extremists. On January 24, 2008, Pakistan's army launched an offensive against the TTP's base in South Waziristan ("Operation Earthquake"). The 10,000 army troops captured the town of Spinkai Raghzai and shut down a suicide training facility and suicide vest factory there. However, the army antagonized the tribesmen in the area by destroying most of the towns, displacing 200,000 residents and forbidding them from returning home for four months.

Then on February 1, an American Reaper drone missile killed Abu Laith al-Libi in North Waziristan—al-Qaeda's third most senior leader. This was the first success inside Pakistan of the new Reaper drone—the Predator drone's replacement. Reapers could fire the more deadly Hellfire missiles and also could drop 500-pound bombs. The drone attacks also would be more successful because the CIA now had permission to fire missiles without prior Pakistani consent. Now the American could call in strikes much more quickly, and wouldn't have to worry that a rogue ISI officer might warn an intended target.[82]

The PPP Returns to Power

On February 18, 2008, Pakistan held elections for the national and provincial assemblies. While Musharraf and his PML(Q) supporters had hoped that the ISI would rig the elections in their favor, Army Chief Kayani made sure that this did not happen. The PPP won 121 seats, Nawaz Sharif's PML(N) Party won 90 seats, and Musharraf's PML(Q) won 54 seats. The PPP won the most Assembly seats partly because it was the only party that still had support in all four provinces. There was immense joy and relief throughout the country over these successful, free and democratic elections. The PPP returned to power for the first time in 12 years. PPP head Zardari succeeded in putting together a PPP-led five-party "Grand Coalition" which included Sharif's PML(N).

In the provincial elections, the ANP won the NWFP elections, and formed a coalition government with the PPP. In voting for the mainstream ANP, NWFP voters repudiated the MMA Islamist coalition which had governed for five years. During those years, the MMA had focused on imposing strict sharia customs throughout the province while ignoring the terror threat. However, while the MMA Islamists no longer were in power, the MMA carried out a campaign of intimidation, threats and assassinations against the government. This campaign made it very difficult for the ANP government to perform its duties, and many government officials and police officers would leave their posts in fear for their lives.

18

Civilian Rule Under Gillani and Zardari

During the four years and four months covered in this chapter, (February 2008–June 2012), Prime Minister Gillani and Bhutto's widower Zardari would dominate Pakistan's civilian government. The army would launch operations against the TTP in the NWFP and FATA's South Waziristan (but not in North Waziristan). America's new president, Barack Obama, would step up drone attacks against the militants who were using FATA as a safe base for attacking NATO troops in Afghanistan. However, U.S.-Pak relations would deteriorate—especially after the Americans conducted a raid inside Pakistan and killed Osama bin Laden. The chapter ends with Sharif being elected prime minister for a third non-consecutive term.

Prime Minister Gillani Assumes Office

On March 24, 2008, soon after the National Assembly elections, the PPP-PML(N) coalition selected PPP loyalist Yousef Raza Gillani as prime minister. Gillani would serve in that post for four years and three months. Gillani disappointed many supporters by breaking his campaign promise to immediately reinstate Chaudhry as Supreme Court chief justice—the justice who had been dismissed a second time during Musharraf's "second coup." The PPP's refusal to restore Chaudhry would provoke a revival of the "Lawyers' Movement," with the lawyers now targeting the PPP's government.

Pakistan faced many problems when Gillani took over the government. First, the government was divided, with Musharraf still president and determined to reassert control. Gillani and Zardari would consume valuable time trying to find a way to remove him. Also, the TTP and other militant groups were growing larger and deadlier. The TTP had seized more territory in FATA and in the NWFP's Swat Valley. Sunni attacks on Shia mosques were rising, with the government and police unable or unwilling to stop them.[1] The city of Karachi was a center of violence, as criminals, sectarian groups, and Taliban factions killed each other along with innocent civilians. In this city, some 1,200 of its 18 million residents were being killed each year. The city's ethnic groups lived in fortified ghettos that barred the entry of outsiders.[2] In addition to the country's violence, Pakistan's economy was in terrible shape. Most of the government's revenue was going to the military and to repaying the huge national debt, and so there was little money left to pay for public services. Most Pakistanis suffered from high unemployment, rising food prices, and shortages of food, drinking water and electricity. Power outages were forcing factories to severely reduce production or close altogether.

The Army Takes on the TTP Terrorists

The TTP continued attacking military targets. Terrorists had been targeting trucks and buses which had been transporting soldiers and police. Now they escalated their attacks by targeting military and ISI facilities.[3] On March 4, 2008, two suicide bombers on motorcycles detonated explosives at the Navy War College in Lahore, killing eight persons.

The army still was reluctant to take on the Islamist extremist forces, and it continued to support the government's peace agreements with the terrorists. On May 21, 2008, the PPP-ANP provincial coalition government in the NWFP signed a generous peace agreement with Maulana Fazlullah's TNSM—a TTP member. The government gave the TTP very generous concessions in return for the TNSM's agreeing not to attack army and government personnel and facilities. As usual, the insurgents quickly violated the agreement.

Pakistan continued to intervene in Afghanistan by supporting the deadly Haqqani network. On July 7, 2008, a suicide bomber from the Haqqani network detonated explosives in his car close to the Indian Embassy in Kabul, killing 58 persons. The ISI had helped the Haqqani plan this attack, and had provided it with vital intelligence.[4] The United States was angry at Pakistan for its close ties and support of the network, which was killing NATO troops in Afghanistan.

On July 12, 2008, American Admiral Mike Mullen visited Pakistan and demanded that Kayani undertake a major offensive against the Haqqani network and other terrorists in North Waziristan. Kayani refused on grounds that he was still building up the army and waiting until the local population in Waziristan was more supportive.[5] The Americans responded by expanding CIA drone targets to include the Haqqanis. The Americans also decided to start making drone "signature strikes"—strikes against gatherings which had not been clearly identified, but which were exhibiting signs of threatening behavior.[6]

The expanded American drone strikes against al-Qaeda targets would become so successful that some al-Qaeda leaders began leaving Pakistan's tribal areas for sanctuary in Somalia and Yemen. The CIA followed up their success with a three-month Reaper drone campaign against al-Qaeda in the Waziristans. The campaign began on July 28, 2008, with an attack in South Waziristan which killed Abu Khabab al-Masri—al-Qaeda's chemical and biological weapons expert. During the next three months, CIA Reaper drones carried out over 150 missile strikes in the Waziristans. Afghan public criticism of the drones increased as the drones began flying lower and more often.

Pakistan's army finally launched a major offensive against TNSM forces in FATA's northernmost Bajaur Tribal agency ("Operation Lionheart"). The TNSM (a TTP member) had gained control of the Bajaur Agency, and from its base there had secured control of the NWFP's Swat District. The army had driven the TNSM out of Swat back to its base in the Bajaur Agency, and now the army decided to destroy this TNSM stronghold itself.

The operation began on August 6, 2008, when some 8,000 army and Frontier Corps troops moved into the Bajaur agency seeking to destroy the 2,500 TNSM fighters there. The army had difficulty clearing the TNSM from Bajaur since the TNSM defenders were well-trained, well-armed, and fought from well-prepared defensive positions connected by trenches and tunnels. However, the army overcame the enemy by flattening villages with artillery and air strikes.[7] During the next six months, the army succeeded in clearing the TNSM fighters from Bajaur, although it also displaced over 500,000 civilians from their homes. The campaign was the first of a series of army operations designed to prevent the Waziristan insurgency from spreading into the NWFP. The campaign would be the longest and most consistent campaign that the army had conducted against the Taliban in many years.

The army retained a residual force in the Bajaur agency which prevented the TNSM from returning after its main force had withdrawn. Taliban violence in the agency would decline significantly.

Zardari Becomes President

On August 18, 2008, Pervez Musharraf resigned as president. General Kayani, Prime Minister Gillani and Nawaz Sharif had pressured him to resign immediately because parliament was preparing to impeach him. Musharraf was in a weak position, since he had given up his powerful position as army chief. He submitted to this pressure because he had lost the support of the army's generals, who had grown tired of his arrogance and unwillingness to share decision-making.[8] He also had lost the people's support by suppressing his political opponents and by attacking the Supreme Court. They also were angry that he had failed to protect them from violent Islamists. Musharraf left the country and wouldn't return for four years.

Musharraf left a mixed legacy. He had damaged Pakistan in several ways. First, he had failed to develop democratic institutions which might have offered the diverse provinces a fair share of political and economic power. Also, he had allowed the ISI to expand its efforts to control politicians, elections and the media. In addition, he had failed to subdue Sunni jihadist groups which had been attacking Shias and non–Muslims.

However, Musharraf had improved Pakistan in several ways. First, Pakistan's economy had expanded during his rule and more Pakistanis had prospered and entered the middle class. Also, Musharraf was the first Pakistani ruler who had recognized that Pakistan needed to make peace with India. He had persuaded several senior generals that making peace was in the army's best interests.

Under the Constitution, a new president was to be selected by an electoral college of the national and provincial assemblies. This college chose 53-year-old PPP leader Asif Zardari by a large margin. Zardari was sworn in as president on September 6, 2008.

Zardari had a number of strengths. First, he enjoyed residual sympathy, since his wife Benazir Bhutto recently had been murdered and he had spent many years in jail on unproven charges. Also, Zardari invoked the legendary Bhutto family name, and many believed his claim that Pakistan's democracy could survive only if he were elected. In addition, Zardari turned out to be a skillful politician, and his leadership enabled the PPP to stay united and form a coalition government.[9]

However, Zardari also had some weaknesses. First, he made no attempt to make his government more representative and he had no desire to work with his opponents.[10] Also, Zardari didn't recruit or listen to competent advisers. He tended to make decisions after consulting just a few loyal and submissive aides.[11] In addition, he had no plan for combatting Islamist extremism, and instead he claimed that the growing violence was normal.[12] Also, his reputation for corruption and the pending corruption charges against him would overshadow his presidency. He was immune from prosecution for corruption as long as he remained president, and so he would become fixated on staying in office. Finally, he would isolate himself in his palace due to his constant fear of assassination—especially by the assassins who had murdered his wife and were still at large. His isolation added to his unpopularity, reduced his ability to gauge public sentiment, and made him unwilling to make major decisions without military approval.

Terrorist Attacks on High-Profile Targets

Terrorists stepped up their attacks after Zardari became president. With al-Qaeda support, the TTP sought to spread its attacks into the settled regions of the NWFP. The first attack occurred on September 20, 2008, when an al-Qaeda terrorist rammed a dump truck loaded with explosives into a barrier outside the Marriott Hotel in Islamabad's high security zone. The blast killed 53 persons, wounded 266, and reduced the hotel to a shell. This was the first major terrorist attack inside Pakistan's capitol.

There were several repercussions to the Marriott Hotel attack. First, it exposed the ISI's folly in having supported Pakistan's Islamist extremist groups, since these groups were turning on their ISI handlers. The chickens "had come home to roost." Also, the Marriott attack shocked Zardari, who now realized that tougher measures had to be taken against Pakistan's terrorists. He soon would authorize unrestricted American drone strikes inside Pakistan. In addition, the attack on the hotel where foreigners often stayed dissuaded foreign businessmen and investors from visiting Pakistan. Pakistan's fragile economy would suffer accordingly. Also, the killing and wounding of so many innocent civilians turned more Pakistanis against all Islamist extremists.

Pakistan's Islamist terrorists now carried out several major attacks in November 2008. The first attack came on November 11 when TTP suicide bombers struck outside a sports stadium in Peshawar—the capital of the NWFP. While the terrorists failed in their goal of killing a government minister, the bomb killed five others. This was part of a TTP campaign to intimidate provincial leaders in the NWFP and FATA into leaving the region.

On November 26, ten LeT terrorists struck eleven sites in Mumbai—India's financial capital. The terrorists had arrived in small boats and for two days rampaged through Mumbai. They targeted two famous hotels, a major train station and a Jewish center. They killed 185 persons. During the attack, the terrorists received cell phone orders from a command center in Karachi, Pakistan.[13] Their goal had been to divert the Pakistan Army's attention from its anti-terrorist campaign in FATA. Pakistan's government vigorously denied that the attackers had any connection with Pakistan, but it soon was discovered that the ISI had helped plan the attack and had trained the LeT how to carry it out.[14] The ISI had supported the attack to prove to its radical Islamist clients that it hadn't gone soft on Western targets.[15] The Mumbai attack forever ended the Bush administration's sympathy for Pakistan, which had revealed itself to be a deeply untrustworthy and unpredictable ally.

President Obama's New Approach to Pakistan

On January 20, 2009, Barack Obama became president of the United States, after having campaigned to end the wars in Iraq and Afghanistan. To conclude the war in Afghanistan, he pledged to conduct an aggressive campaign against al-Qaeda in both Pakistan and Afghanistan, including using more drone attacks—if necessary without Pakistan's consent. Obama favored drone attacks over ground offenses since they avoided American casualties, reduced civilian deaths, and ended the problem of bringing captured terrorists to trial.[16] Obama quickly instructed his CIA chief Leon Panetta to intensify its search for Osama bin Laden, and Panetta's team would focus on tracking him through his couriers.[17] President Obama also secretly instructed the CIA to recruit Pakistanis and hire American contractors without ISI knowledge to collect intelligence on terrorist groups inside Pakistan.[18] The CIA didn't notify the ISI of this new recruiting drive.

President Obama's approach to Pakistan's government also would be different from his predecessors. First, Obama's team would adopt a more understanding, non-confrontational approach toward Pakistan's leaders. He would accept Pakistan's status as a nuclear power. Also, Richard Holbrooke, Obama's special representative for Pakistan and Afghanistan, would work tirelessly to improve Pak-American relations. He would improve cooperation in non-military matters such as education, health care, and agriculture. In addition, Obama would develop a new Af-Pak strategy to pressure Pakistan to stop providing terrorist groups with sanctuary and other support.

At the same time, the United States would step up its drone attacks in Pakistan, and during 2009, it would launch 53 drone strikes—more than during President Bush's entire two terms in office. Most of the drones hit targets in FATA, partly because drone strikes inside the NWFP and Baluchistan Province had been forbidden by Pakistan's government.[19] Pakistan still supported the Afghan Taliban and so it forbade drone attacks against the pro–Taliban

Haqqani network based in FATA. During the year, the civilian death toll rose to 3,021, with 7,300 more wounded.[20] Many of the deaths were caused by 87 suicide attacks carried out by Islamist extremists.

While the United States increased its drone attacks on Islamist extremists in Pakistan, the army and the NWFP provincial government sought to appease these same extremists. On February 21, 2009, the provincial government reached the Swat Peace Accord with TNSM leader Maulana Fazlullah. The TNSM promised to abandon its campaign of violence in return for the provincial government's allowing sharia to become law in Swat. However, the TNSM had no intention of complying with the new peace accord, and they used the lull in the fighting to increase their control over Swat.

The TTP attacks in Pakistan continued with a daring attack in Lahore. On March 3, 2009, a dozen TTP terrorists attacked a convoy, killing ten policemen. The convoy included a bus carrying the Sri Lankan cricket team to a stadium, but the players escaped harm only because their bus sped away from the scene. The country was stunned at the audacity of the attackers and at the massive lapse in security.

President Zardari not only faced threats of growing Islamist terrorism, but he also faced protest demonstrations by Pakistan's lawyers. Zardari had delayed reinstating Chaudhry as Supreme Court chief justice for fear that Chaudhry might end his presidential immunity from prosecution on corruption charges.[21] On March 12, 2009, the lawyers responded by starting a "Long March" from Lahore to Islamabad, demanding Chaudhry's reinstatement. Thousands of lawyers and political activists joined the march. A showdown developed when Zardari banned the march and blocked the highway that the marchers planned to use into the capital.

This "Second Lawyers' Movement" soon ended when Army Chief Kayani notified Zardari that the army would not stop the marchers.[22] Having lost his ability to stop the march, Zardari reinstated Chaudhry on March 16. Chaudhry's reinstatement was a landmark in several ways. First, it marked the transition of the Supreme Court from a meek supporter of the army to a respected independent institution. Also, it marked the start of a period in which the army and its political allies would be challenged by judges, lawyers, and the newly independent media.[23]

During the three years that Chaudhry would remain in office, the strong-willed Chief Justice would lead the Supreme Court to unprecedented heights of judicial activism. Chaudhry quickly removed all the judges that Musharraf had appointed when the dictator had packed the courts during his "second coup." Chaudhry even began intervening in cases that hadn't yet reached the Supreme Court which he believed needed immediate Supreme Court resolution.[24]

President Obama's New Approach to Afghanistan

Karzai's relations with the Americans deteriorated further yet after Barack Obama was inaugurated President in January 2009. Obama was determined not to "coddle" Karzai like Bush had done, and he immediately ended the videoconferences. However, Obama was willing to commit more assets to fight the Afghan insurgents, and he quickly ordered a troop surge. However, when these additional troops caused more civilian casualties, Karzai lashed out at the United States—even though the Taliban and Afghan Army were responsible for more civilian deaths than the Americans.

On August 20, 2009, Afghanistan held its second presidential elections. Karzai was declared the winner even after millions of votes in his favor had been thrown out as fraudulent.[25]

During Karzai's second term, Karzai's anger at the Americans turned to hatred. He criticized everything the Americans did, and he believed far-fetched conspiracy theories—such as that the Americans didn't really want to defeat the Taliban, but just wanted to keep troops in Afghanistan so it could use the country as a regional base.[26]

In November 2009, President Obama announced that there would be a second troops surge into Afghanistan, but that all American troops would start withdrawing in July 2011.[27] The plan was to increase the size and training of the Afghan Army to the point where it could protect Karzai's government after the Americans departed. In November 2010, NATO announced that it would withdraw all its troops from Afghanistan within four years.

There were several repercussions to the announcements of the troop surge and the two troop withdrawals. First, Pakistan's leaders were worried that the American troop surge would push many Afghan Taliban fighters into Pakistan, thereby threatening the gains that Pakistan had made in South Waziristan and the Swat Valley.[28] Also, Afghan President Karzai would redouble his efforts to make peace with the Taliban. He feared that unless he brought the Taliban into his government, the Taliban would overthrow him once NATO troops left.

Pakistan Army Offensives in Swat and South Waziristan

The TTP and its member the TNSM continued their terrorist campaign in the NWFP against Pakistan's police and paramilitary forces. On April 28, 2009, 450 TNSM fighters took control of the NWFP's Buner District—just south of the Swat District. The TTP was anxious to expand into the NWFP, since this would give it a base for attacks into northern Pakistan's major cities, including the capital Islamabad. Also, the NWFP had better communications facilities that it could utilize, and drones were prohibited from striking there.[29] Two weeks later, the TNSM seized three police stations in the region and kidnapped 70 policemen and paramilitary troops. Then the militants, in an act of supreme defiance, decapitated four army commandos who had been inserted into the area on a reconnaissance mission.

There were several repercussions to these attacks in the Buner district. First, public opinion turned dramatically away from the TTP, since the seizure of Buner clearly violated the sharia-for-peace deal. The public now began calling for the army to attack the TTP and the TNSM. Also, while army leaders had tolerated TTP control in faraway FATA, they were unwilling to accept TTP moves into the Buner District—just 65 miles from the capital Islamabad.

Army Chief Kayani soon launched an offensive to retake the Buner and Swat districts in the NWFP. In its largest operation ever against the TTP, on May 16, 2009, the army deployed 15,000 or more regular soldiers against TNSM fighters in Swat and Buner (the "Second Battle of Swat"). There were several reasons why the army would succeed in this second Swat campaign. First, the army's 15,000 troops gave them a substantial numerical advantage over the 2,500 TNSM insurgents. Also, the troops were supported by heavy artillery, attack planes and troop-carrying helicopters.[30] In addition, the troops were highly motivated and sought revenge for the TNSM's decapitation of their commandos.[31] Also, Swat residents had turned against the TNSM, which had brought to Swat assassinations and suicide bombings. In addition, the army had forced the evacuation of most of the population, so it could hit the TNSM with artillery without having to worry about hitting civilians.

The army drove the TNSM out of Swat in just two months, claiming that it had killed 1,200 militants. While TNSM commander Maulana Fazullah and most of his fighters escaped, they would not come back for several years, because the army left troops behind to prevent their return.

There were several repercussions to the army's Second Battle of Swat. First, the army's success led to calm returning to Swat, and the Swatis became confident that the army and security forces would prevent the TNSM militants from returning.[32] Also, this was the first major army success against insurgents in FATA and the NWFP, partly because the army had followed classic counterinsurgency tactics. The success of these tactics led the army and Frontier Corps (FC) to increase the number of troops receiving counterinsurgency training and equipment.[33] In addition, the army's success bolstered its prestige and morale. Finally, the army's successful campaign led to a marked shift in public sentiment in favor of more military action against Islamist insurgents and less support for negotiating peace deals with them.

The TTP soon retaliated against the army for its Swat offensives by conducting a terrorist attack in the NWFP capital of Peshawar. On June 9, 2009, TTP terrorists stormed Peshawar's luxury Pearl Continental Hotel. They also detonated a huge truck bomb outside the hotel, starting a fire which destroyed most of the hotel. Seventeen persons were killed in the attack. The increasing TTP violence was making it impossible for the new ANP-PPP coalition's NWFP provincial government to carry out its basic functions without army assistance.

Baitullah Mehsud's TTP had been terrorizing Pakistan for two years, killing 1,200 or more victims. For two years, Pakistan's leaders had been pleading with the Americans to add Baitullah Mehsud and other TTP leaders to their list of drone targets—instead of focusing just on al-Qaeda leaders. The United States finally complied with their wishes and on August 5, 2009, an American drone missile killed Baitullah at his TTP base in South Waziristan, catching him at night on a house rooftop. This was the first major TTP leader killed by a drone attack. Pakistan's leaders and the people cheered the death of this ruthless terrorist who had been Pakistan's "Public Enemy No. 1." Baitullah's death was an enormous triumph for the Pak-American anti-terror alliance. However, the Pakistanis wouldn't be celebrating Baitullah's death for long, since on August 22 the TTP replaced him with the equally ruthless Hakimullah Mehsud. Hakimullah would remain the TTP's leader for over four years, and under his leadership TTP's suicide attacks would become even deadlier.

In October 2009, TTP's new leader Hakimullah Mehsud launched a series of deadly attacks in FATA and the NWFP, seemingly to avenge the killing of his predecessor. During the TTP's first attack on October 9, 2009, terrorists detonated a massive suicide car bomb in a crowded market in Peshawar, killing 53 persons and injuring over 100. The next day, ten TTP fighters, disguised as soldiers and driving an army jeep, attacked Pakistan Army Headquarters in Rawalpindi and took hostages. This bold al-Qaeda-planned attack killed two high-ranking officers and seven other soldiers.[34] The TTP's ability to penetrate the country's most sensitive national defense area helped turn the army even further against the TTP. TTP terrorists followed up with a series of bold, well-planned attacks on police and government facilities throughout the country.

In response to these TTP attacks, Pakistan's army launched another offensive against the TTP in FATA's South Waziristan ("Operation Path to Salvation"). The operation began on October 17, 2009, when the army sent 28,000 or more troops into South Waziristan, with a goal of removing the 10,000 TTP fighters and 1,500 foreign fighters who controlled the region.[35]

The army had several advantages in this offensive. First, the army had a relatively small population to deal with in South Waziristan—500,000 compared to two million in Swat. Also, the army had three times as many troops as the TTP, used helicopter gunships, and had live video drone surveillance feed of the battlefield. Also, the army had timed its offensive to begin right after the Taliban had been discredited by its major attacks against innocent civilians in the Continental Hotel and the Peshawar marketplace.

The army's "Path to Salvation" operation would last over five months, during which it retook all of South Waziristan. The army would claim that it had killed over 600 militants during the operation while losing 360 of its own soldiers. The surviving TTP fighters withdrew northwards to FATA's North Waziristan agency, where the Haqqani network provided them with sanctuary.

While Pakistan's army was carrying out its offensives against insurgents in FATA, American President Barack Obama on October 15, 2009, signed into law the Kerry-Berman-Lugar (KBL) bill. The law authorized giving Pakistan $7.5 billion in non-military economic aid over a five-year period—considerably more non-military aid than the United States had ever given to Pakistan. This massive aid was designed to show Pakistan that America had a long-term commitment to help Pakistan's economic development. While Zardari's government initially welcomed the KBL package, the army soon began criticizing what it described as the "humiliating" and "insulting" conditions written into the bill on how the funds were to be spent. These conditions included making the aid conditional on Pakistan's proving that progress was being made on strengthening civilian control of the government.[36]

American Drone Strikes Peak

Despite the Pakistan Army's successful operations against them in Swat and South Waziristan, the TTP united front managed to conduct two major attacks on army and government facilities in December 2009. On December 4, four LeT terrorists stormed a crowded mosque in the high-security army zone at Rawalpindi—with sympathizers in the army providing them with intelligence. The attack killed 36 worshipers, including a general, four brigadiers and seventeen children. Then on December 28, TTP terrorists detonated a remote-controlled bomb, killing 44 in a Shiite religious procession in Karachi. An outraged Shiite mob retaliated by plundering and burning thousands of Sunni shops, and conducting a general strike which brought Karachi to a standstill.

Al-Qaeda struck the Americans hard on December 30, 2009, when the CIA allowed Humam al-Balawi to enter its remote Chapman base in Khost Province in eastern Afghanistan. The CIA was anxious to debrief Balawi, who

18. Civilian Rule Under Gillani and Zardari

they believed had been turned into a cooperating double agent. However, as Balawi stepped from his car, he detonated a suicide vest with over 30 pounds of explosives and shrapnel, killing seven CIA officers.[37] The furious CIA responded with a wave of deadly drone strikes against Taliban targets in Northern Waziristan—primarily against Haqqani Network bases.

The year 2010 would mark the height of the American drone campaign in Pakistan, with the number of strikes doubling to 118. The drone campaign focused on attacking the TTP in North Waziristan which was killing NATO troops in Afghanistan. To avoid being targeted by drones, the Taliban in FATA stopped using cell phones, stopped meeting in large groups, and stopped sleeping in buildings at night.[38] They also executed tribesmen whom they suspected of having helped the Americans target them for drone attacks. Finally, they started to quickly remove bodies of Taliban victims of drone attacks to conceal the high Taliban casualties.[39] The number of terrorist suicide attacks began dropping.

The American drone strikes were largely killing terrorists who had been purposely killing innocent civilians. Relatively few civilians were being killed during these drone attacks.[40] However, Pakistan's media chose to portray the drones as intentionally targeting civilians, and this reporting stoked anti-American sentiment.[41]

The American drone strike campaign began targeting the deadly Haqqani network, which was based in North Waziristan. On February 18, 2010, American drone missiles struck a Haqqani target in North Waziristan, killing three Haqqani members. Pakistan's leaders were angry at this attack, since Pakistan had been supporting the Haqqanis because while they were attacking NATO troops in Afghanistan, they were not hitting targets inside Pakistan.[42]

Pak-American relations were severely strained on May 1, 2010, when Faisal Shehzad, a Pakistani-born American citizen, attempted to detonate a bomb in an SUV in New York City's Times Square. Shehzad had recently spent five months in Pakistan at TTP and JeM training camps, and the bomb plot had been planned in FATA.[43] While his primitive bomb failed to explode, it could have killed many people had it detonated. Shehzad was arrested two days later while his plane was taxiing for takeoff bound for Dubai.

There were several repercussions to the Times Square bombing attempt. First, the bombing attempt led the Americans to pressure Pakistani officials to take further action against the Islamist militants in FATA and the NWFP. Also, the incident convinced the CIA to step up its hiring of hundreds of Americans on contract to work inside Pakistan to secure the intelligence needed to prevent future attacks on American soil. In addition, it reconfirmed America's view that Pakistan had become a base for international Islamist terrorism.

The TTP had become a much more dangerous challenge to Pakistan and the United States since its founding three years before. By now it had adopted al-Qaeda's vision of global jihad and it was willing to train Western militants to carry out attacks in foreign countries.[44] Also, it had transformed itself from a loose umbrella for diverse militant groups in FATA to a much more sophisticated organization with links across the country and abroad. What was even more troubling for Pakistan was that the army and ISI had lost control of the TTP members which it had been supporting. This became clear when a TTP commander kidnaped two well-known retired ISI officers and murdered them as alleged "spies," despite ISI pleas for clemency.[45]

While the army continued to face the challenge of containing deadly TTP attacks, it also faced a legal challenge to its use of extraordinary measures it had been using to combat terrorists and insurgents. On May 4, 2010, Supreme Court Chief Justice Chaudhry set up a commission to investigate claims that the ISI had been detaining Baloch nationalists and terrorist suspects and placing them in undisclosed prisons—sometimes torturing and killing them. This was the first serious attempt by the judiciary to hold the ISI and military accountable for their violations of human rights. The ISI responded to this challenge by delays, denials and claims of immunity.[46]

The United States continued its drone campaign inside Pakistan against al-Qaeda. On May 21, 2010, American drone missiles killed Sheikh Saeed al-Masri while he was visiting a compound in North Waziristan. Saeed was al-Qaeda's financial chief and his death was one of the most severe blows ever suffered by al-Qaeda.

President Zardari Makes Concessions

President Zardari became desperate when on December 16, 2009, the Supreme Court struck down the National Reconciliation Ordinance (NRO) which had given government officials and bureaucrats amnesty from criminal prosecution while in office. The Court's ruling threw Zardari's government into chaos, since corruption charges had been filed against many of his officials.[47] His government limped along from crisis to crisis, as pressure mounted for Zardari to step down. While Zardari refused to resign, he began allowing his powers to be reduced in order to improve his chances of remaining in office. He hoped that such concessions would appease his critics and preserve his own presidential immunity from prosecution.[48]

President Zardari made his first concession on April 19, 2010, when he signed into law the Eighteenth Amendment to the Constitution. The amendment provided that the presidency would become a ceremonial office, while Pakistan would return to a full parliamentary democracy with a strong prime minister. The amendment also gave the provinces more autonomy. Finally, in a move to the Pashtun majority in the NWFP, the NWFP was renamed "Khyber Pakhtunkhwa Province" (KKP). Prime Minister Gillani continued in his office with enhanced powers.

President Zardari made another concession on July 22, 2010. He gave General Kayani a three-year extension to his term as army chief—partly as insurance for Zardari's own personal safety and partly for the survival of his government.[49] The extension satisfied most army leaders, since it insured Pakistan's stability and guaranteed the army's continued dominance in the country. The extension also satisfied Pakistan's politicians, since although they opposed Zardari's presidency, they would rather retain him in order to prevent the army from taking over the government.[50]

Soon after Kayani's term had been extended, Kayani and Zardari faced new trouble. On July 25, WikiLeaks began releasing a collection of 92,000 American diplomatic cables and reports covering Pakistan and Afghanistan during the prior seven years. The cables infuriated both Zardari and Kayani, since they exposed America's strong criticism of the two leaders. The reports also revealed the true extent of the Pakistan Army's secret collaboration with the CIA in their drone attacks. They also revealed Pakistan's continued support of the Afghan Taliban and the Haqqani network.[51]

General Kayani was furious. In an angry briefing to selected Pakistani journalists he claimed that the United States wanted to perpetuate chaos in Pakistan and that its real aim was to de-nuclearize the country.[52] The Americans soon learned of Kayani's angry remarks.

However, despite the growing hostility between the two countries, their leaders would continue to work together. While Pakistan's army hoped the United States would leave Afghanistan, they also wanted them to stay for fear of losing over $2 billion in American military aid they were receiving.[53] The Americans wanted to stay in Afghanistan until they were sure that it would not be used again as a base for future attacks on the American mainland.

President Zardari soon came under new criticism due to his government's handling of a catastrophic flood. On July 29, 2010, record monsoon rains began to fall in the northern mountains. The Indus River began overflowing its banks, and as the river flowed southwards, it flooded thousands of miles of farmland all the way down to Sindh Province. The flooding was so extensive because Pakistan didn't have sufficient dams and dikes—especially in impoverished areas.[54] Pakistan appealed for assistance from international sources, but the response was disappointing. Foreign donors told the government that it needed to start collecting more taxes from its own people so it could do more for itself—instead of always expecting foreign bailouts.[55]

There were several repercussions to the flooding. First, President Zardari was widely criticized for his lack of concern for the victims, which was highlighted by his refusal to cut short his vacation at his French chateau at the height of the crisis. He also showed poor leadership in the relief effort. Also, the army demonstrated its superior ability in handling this crisis, and thereby burnished its self-image as being the nation's savior. In addition, the LeT and other Islamist groups rushed to rescue flood victims and provide them with immediate food and shelter. This quick response greatly improved their popularity. While the United States made the largest contribution to the $1.7 billion international flood relief effort, most Pakistanis still disliked the Americans.

Afghanistan Tries to Make Peace with the Taliban

Afghan President Karzai had wanted to make peace with the Afghan Taliban ever since he had taken office. Karzai was an ethnic Pashtun (as were the Taliban), and the Taliban were all natives of Afghanistan. Karzai initially wanted to offer the Taliban generous reconciliation terms, including amnesty to anyone willing to give up arms and agree to respect the Afghan Constitution.[56] However, any amnesty offers were soon withdrawn because at that time and for several more years, the Americans opposed making peace with the Taliban, hoping to destroy them on the battlefield.[57] But gradually the Americans decided to support peace negotiations. They had come to realize that a military victory was impossible, especially once the United States and NATO starting withdrawing their troops from Afghanistan.

However, even after the Americans started backing peace negotiations, Karzai still faced many obstacles in securing a peace agreement with the Taliban. First, Pakistan's leaders insisted that they be part of any negotiations between Karzai and the Afghan Taliban. They wanted to be sure that any agreement resulted in a friendly, pro–Pakistan Afghan government. Their position seemed to be that if they couldn't get a peace agreement that met Pakistan's interests, there would be no agreement. The ISI even warned Taliban leaders living in Pakistan not to meet with Karzai without Pakistani officials present, and they arrested and even killed those trying to meet Karzai directly.[58] Also, the Afghan Taliban had fought NATO troops to a stalemate, and so Taliban hard-liners were more inclined to wait until the NATO troops withdrew and then overthrow Karzai's government. In addition, the emboldened Taliban initially insisted on very tough peace terms.

Despite these obstacles, Afghan President Hamid Karzai still worked toward a Karzai-Taliban peace agreement. On September 5, 2010, President Karzai created the Afghan High Peace Council (HPC) to negotiate a peace agreement between his government and the Afghan Taliban.[59] However, since the Taliban insisted that all foreign troops withdraw from Afghanistan

18. Civilian Rule Under Gillani and Zardari

before it would negotiate with Karzai's government, the first step toward a permanent peace had to be securing an American-Taliban agreement with an American commitment to withdraw all its troops.

The possibility of an American-Taliban peace agreement advanced on November 28, 2010, when Americans had their first meeting with a legitimate Taliban representative.[60] The Taliban leaders had become more flexible than before and seemed agreeable to joining an Afghan coalition government representing all ethnic groups.[61] However, it would take over ten more years before an American-Taliban peace agreement would be signed.

Pak-American Relations Continue to Deteriorate

Pak-American relations would continue to deteriorate due to their different interests. The Americans focused on capturing or killing al-Qaeda fighters, and to a lesser degree seizing Afghan Taliban leaders. However, Pakistan's ISI mainly focused on collecting information on President Zardari and monitoring anti–Indian militant groups.[62] Tensions between the two countries had become so strained that even relatively minor incidents led to major confrontations. For example, on September 30, 2010, two NATO helicopters fired missiles at a Pakistani military post, killing two soldiers and wounding four. The pilots claimed that they were reacting to fire coming from the post. Pakistan responded by closing the Af-Pak Torkham border crossing for eleven days. Pakistan's leaders seemed to have closed the crossing to gain leverage by demonstrating how indispensable Pakistan was in resupplying NATO troops in Afghanistan.

There were several repercussions to the closing of the Torkham border crossing. First, the closure forced the Americans to set up new supply routes to Afghanistan which by-passed Pakistan. Within a year, half of the supplies for NATO forces in Afghanistan would travel through a new northern route which by-passed Pakistan altogether.[63] Also, while the Torkham crossing was closed, over 100 NATO supply trucks stranded between the port of Karachi and the Torkham crossing were destroyed.

On November 19, 2010, a new development further strained Pak-American relations. Relatives of Americans who had been killed during the Mumbai massacre in India filed a lawsuit against ISI chief Ahmed Pasha for having facilitated the Mumbai attack. Pasha was furious. Soon afterwards, a FATA tribesman whose relative had been killed in a CIA drone attack claimed he would sue the CIA station chief in Islamabad, whom he identified as Jonathan Banks. Disclosing the identity of the CIA station chief led to death threats against Banks, forcing him to leave the country. The CIA suspected that the ISI chief had been behind the disclosure.[64]

Pakistan's relations with the United States further deteriorated after Richard Holbrooke died of a heart attack on December 13, 2010. Holbrooke had been President Obama's Special Representative for Pakistan and Afghanistan, and he had worked tirelessly to promote Pak-American good will and cooperation. Holbrooke's death crippled America's campaign to improve relations between the two countries.

Pakistan's religious intolerance was on full display on January 4, 2011, when a police bodyguard assassinated Punjab's Governor Salman Taseer, the moderate leader of Pakistan's most populous province. The bodyguard shot the governor 27 times with his automatic rifle. Taseer had been known for his courageous backing of the rights of women and religious minorities, and his opposition to Pakistan's harsh blasphemy law. The killer immediately turned himself in and confessed to the murder. He was convicted and sentenced to death. The sentencing judge fled the country out of fear for his life. What was most troubling was that mainstream Sunni religious leaders didn't condemn the murder and many Sunnis applauded the assassin as a hero.[65] The Supreme Court upheld his conviction but upheld the Blasphemy law's constitutionality. While the murderer was executed, the country's leaders were too frightened the attend his funeral—which was attended by over 100,000 mourners.

Taseer's assassination was a sign of growing Sunni Muslim intolerance toward religious minorities. The government's weak response to the governor's assassination and its refusal to try to reform the Blasphemy Law emboldened Sunni extremists to demand that Pakistan be converted into a "pure" Islamic state. These extremists would kill hundreds of Shias, Christians, Hindus, and Ahmadis. Many members of these minority groups fled the country.[66]

The Davis Incident and the Killing of Osama Bin Laden

Pakistan's leaders were becoming very concerned with growing CIA activities inside Pakistan. The leaders felt they were losing control of their own country since the ISI couldn't monitor all the CIA intelligence operatives who were roaming around their country.[67] The Pakistanis were especially upset that the CIA had hired hundreds of private contractors to gather intelligence on Islamist extremists inside their country. These contractors behaved arrogantly as they drove their SUVs down city streets and threatened and sideswiped Pakistani drivers who bothered them.[68]

This issue came to a head on January 27, 2011, when Raymond Davis, an American collecting intelligence for the CIA, stopped at a red light in Lahore. Two young Pakistanis who had been following him on a motorcycle pulled up next to him. When one of them flashed a pistol, Davis fired his own pistol

18. Civilian Rule Under Gillani and Zardari 235

five times through his windshield, killing one of the men. As the second man fled on foot, Davis pursued him on foot for ten yards and shot him dead.[69] Davis called for assistance, and the vehicle sent to "rescue" him struck and killed a Pakistani pedestrian while racing down the wrong side of a street trying to reach him.

While Davis claimed that his two victims were common thieves trying to rob him, it is more likely that they were working for Pakistani intelligence.[70] The incident stirred up great anger inside Pakistan. A Lahore court freed Davis after the CIA paid $2.3 million in "blood money" to the victims' families.[71] Davis left Pakistan on March 16.

The Davis incident impacted Pak-American relations in several ways. First, Pakistan's army ordered 350 CIA officers and contractors to leave the country. It also severely restricted the issuance of visas to American officials who were seeking to enter or stay in the country.[72] Also, during the six weeks while the Americans and Pakistanis were resolving the Davis crisis, the Americans had temporarily suspended their drone strikes.

Pakistan's leaders grew increasingly angry at independent American operations in their country, including American drone attacks. The drone attack issue came to a head when on March 17, 2011, a drone fired four missiles into a gathering of tribal leaders in North Waziristan, killing 38 persons. While the Americans claimed that the heavily armed group had been acting like militants, local villagers claimed that most of the group had been peaceful civilians. The deaths added to the feeling of Pakistan's leaders that they had no control over American operations inside their country. FATA civilians also didn't like the American drones constantly buzzing overhead, and vowed revenge whenever an innocent family member was killed when in proximity to the targeted militants.

Al-Qaeda leader Osama bin Laden had been hiding in a compound in Abbottabad, Pakistan for over five years.[73] During those years, he had commanded al-Qaeda members throughout the world.[74] The Americans had concluded that bin Laden probably was living in the Abbottabad compound, since they had tracked his personal courier there. Bin Laden's location also may have been corroborated by an informer seeking to collect America's $25 million reward being offered for bin Laden's capture. The Americans decided not to notify Pakistan's leaders that it would be conducting the raid for fear that bin Laden might be tipped off.

The Americans conducted a night raid on the Abbottabad compound on May 1, 2011 ("Operation Neptune Spear"). Two helicopters dropped off 23 Navy SEALs at the compound—100 miles inside Pakistan and 40 miles from its capital. The SEALs broke into the buildings and overcame light resistance. When two SEALs reached the third floor of the building which housed bin Laden's family, a SEAL wearing night-vision goggles shot bin Laden dead.[75]

The SEALs shot him without hesitation because he had always claimed he would never be taken alive, and they feared he was about to detonate an explosive vest.[76] The SEALs then boarded helicopters carrying bags of computers, computer drives and flash drives—along with bin Laden's body for more positive identification and burial at sea.[77]

There were several repercussions to the raid and the killing of Osama bin Laden. First, Pakistan's media criticized Pakistan's army for having failed to prevent the SEALs from penetrating deep inside their country. The media also ridiculed the army for having told the public for years that bin Laden was dead or hiding in Afghanistan—whereas in fact he had been living inside Pakistan all along. Many Pakistanis believed conspiracy rumors that suggested that ISI leaders had cooperated with the Americans in locating and killing bin Laden.[78] Also, after a short period of subdued reaction, the army strongly criticized the American raid—perhaps to place the blame elsewhere.[79] Army Chief Kayani never punished anybody for allowing Bin Laden to live six years inside Pakistan.[80] Pakistan's leaders were angry that the Americans had conducted a raid deep inside Pakistan without even giving them advance notice. However, the Americans were angry at Pakistan's leaders because they had allowed bin Laden to reside in Pakistan—probably with their knowledge and assistance.[81] Also, CIA teams would begin sifting through over a million documents recovered from hard drives and thumb drives that had been seized during the raid. The few documents that the CIA did release seemed to have been picked to support its view that al-Qaeda had been destroyed.[82] In addition, bin Laden's death was a huge setback for al-Qaeda. Bin Laden had been coordinating terrorist attacks right up to his death. His ability to survive a global manhunt had helped al-Qaeda retain an aura of invincibility. This was crucial for al-Qaeda at a time when al-Qaeda had been losing popularity and significance. Bin Laden's successor Zawahiri, never would command the respect and loyalty that bin Laden had, and he lacked bin Laden's fund-raising abilities.[83] However, al-Qaeda would still remain a threat as it broke into franchises and affiliates around the world.

Pak-American relations deteriorated further over the "Memogate" incident. On May 10, 2011, American Admiral Mullen received an unsigned memo warning of a possible military coup in Pakistan in retaliation for the Abbottabad raid. It asked for American help in averting the coup. Pakistan's generals learned of the memo, and even though it may have been a fake, they were furious, since it implied that the Americans might be willing to interfere in key Pakistani affairs.[84] The generals suspected that Zardari had asked Hussain Haqqani to write and send the memo. Haqqani, Pakistan's ambassador to the United States, denied any involvement in the memo. He resigned under pressure on November 22, 2011. The memogate scandal created even more mistrust between the civilian government and the military.

Pak-American Relations Deteriorate Even Further

The bin Laden raid was soon followed by a series of TTP terrorist attacks to avenge Bin Laden's death. On May 13, 2011, a TTP suicide attack at a Frontier Corps training camp in the NWFP killed 80 cadets and wounded 140 more. Then on May 22, 2011, a 15-man TTP team conducted a well-organized night raid on the Mehran Naval Base outside Karachi—Pakistan's largest military installation. During the ten-hour attack, the terrorists breached the perimeter fence, destroyed two aircraft, and killed thirteen sailors.[85] This was the most serious in a series of attacks on major military facilities—attacks which had been assisted by sympathetic servicemen inside the bases.

The American raid on Abbottabad and the TTP attack on the naval base embarrassed Pakistan's army, navy and ISI. The ISI reacted by denouncing and intimidating journalists who had been exposing ISI links to al-Qaeda and other terrorist groups. The ISI would even kill journalists who criticized it, and Afghanistan became the most dangerous country in the world to be a reporter.[86] One widely publicized attack on a journalist murder occurred on May 29, 2011, in Islamabad, when ISI agents abducted Syed Saleem Shahzad of the *Asia Times* Online. Shahzad had been writing articles linking al-Qaeda with the ISI and navy personnel.[87] The ISI even tried to shut down the independent Geo TV television station for running stories on the ISI's attacks on journalists.[88]

The United States now conducted a series of drone strikes which would further decimate al-Qaeda's leadership. While the strikes didn't kill al-Qaeda's new chief al-Zawahiri, they would kill four of Zawahiri's seconds-in-command—one after the other. On August 22, 2011, a drone strike in North Waziristan killed Atiyah Abd al-Rahman (a/k/a Mahmud)— al-Qaeda's second-in-command. This was a serious blow to al-Qaeda, since al-Zawahiri had come to depend heavily on Rahman's experience and connections to help manage al-Qaeda.

The Americans were pleased with the success of their drone strikes and with the Pakistan Army's ground offenses. However, for several reasons, the anti-terrorism fight inside Pakistan was not going well. First, the TTP had become self-sufficient using revenues from the opium trade and from kidnappings for ransom. The kidnapers moved their victims awaiting release to Haqqini camps which were close to Pakistan Army units.[89] Also, the TTP maintained control over FATA by assassinating tribal leaders suspected of trying to set up anti–Taliban militias. They also killed hundreds of tribesmen suspected of cooperating with the Americans. In addition, the Americans and Pakistanis couldn't agree on which militant groups should be attacked or supported. This was especially true over their different treatment of the 4,000 fighters in the deadly Haqqani network based in North Waziristan.

The Americans wanted to destroy the network, since it was killing NATO troops in Afghanistan. The Americans even launched drone attacks against the network without bothering to secure Pakistani clearance.[90] However, at the same time, Pakistan's leaders continued to support the Haqqani network. In addition, army officers were tiring of fighting an interminable war (which they considered "America's war") while suffering heavy casualties.[91] They particularly resented American criticisms that they weren't doing enough against the insurgents, since actually Pakistani troops had been suffering higher casualties in Pakistan than NATO troops had been suffering in Afghanistan.[92] Finally, NATO troops were suffering heavy casualties from roadside bombs and land mines which were made from fertilizer made in Pakistan. However, Pakistan refused American requests to shut down Pakistani fertilizer companies that were shipping truckloads of fertilizer to Islamic militants in Afghanistan for use in making these deadly IEDs.[93]

America's military leaders also were losing patience with Pakistan's leaders for supporting the deadly Haqqani network, which was based in North Waziristan. The network's fighters continued to cross into Afghanistan and attack NATO troops there. On September 10, 2011, the network detonated a massive truck bomb outside a NATO combat outpost in Wardak Province, killing five Afghans and wounding 77 American soldiers. Three days later, six Haqqanis occupied a high-rise building under construction in Kabul and used it to strike the nearby American Embassy with mortars and rockets.[94]

These attacks led to a searing public rebuke of the ISI from an unexpected source—the long-standing Pakistani army supporter Admiral Mike Mullen. On September 22, 2011, Mullen, the retiring chairman of the Joint Chiefs of Staff, testified before the Senate Armed Service Committee. He accused the ISI of having supported the Haqqani network in its two attacks just days before. He described the Haqqani network as "a veritable arm" of Pakistan's ISI. On October 13, the Americans took direct action against the Haqqani network by firing a drone missile which killed Jalil Haqqani, a top network official. The network retaliated on October 29 by ramming an-explosive laden vehicle into a military bus in Kabul. The explosion killed five NATO soldiers and eight American contractors.[95] The Americans suspected that Pakistan's ISI had supported these attacks.[96]

Pak-American relations frayed further on November 25, 2011, when NATO aircraft mistakenly strayed over the ill-marked Af-Pak border and struck troops at two Pakistani posts, killing 24 Pakistani soldiers (the "Salala Incident"). The Americans claimed that the Pakistanis had fired at them first and that the attack had been caused by mistakes on both sides. However, Pakistan's leaders insisted that the attack had been intentional. While American officials offered private "condolences" for the incident, this didn't satisfy

Pakistan's army leaders, who insisted on a formal public apology. The Americans refused to make such an apology.

Pakistan retaliated for the Salala Incident three days later by shutting down the Torkham and Chaman border crossings through which American supplies were being sent to NATO troops in Afghanistan. Pakistan had shut down the Torkham border crossing a year before for 11 days, but this time the border posts would stay closed for seven months. However, during this closure, NATO sent most of its supplies destined for Afghanistan through new northern routes which avoided Pakistan altogether. NATO had developed these alternative routes for such an occasion for such an emergency. Although using the northern routes was slower and cost $100 million more a month, it demonstrated to Pakistan that it was not as indispensable to NATO as it had believed. These two border crossings would reopen seven months later after the Americans had made an official but guarded apology for the incident.

For decades, there had been no neutral process to insure fair elections after a government left office. A step to resolve this was taken on February 14, 2012, when the Twentieth Amendment to the Constitution was approved. The amendment provided a procedure for creating a neutral interim government to rule until the next elections were held, and provided for an independent election commission to oversee those elections.

Supreme Court Activism and an Election

On June 19, 2012, the Supreme Court removed Prime Minister Gillani from his office, after he had served 4 years and two months. The Court ruled that Gillani was in contempt of court for having refused to comply with its order to reopen the corruption case against President Zardari involving Swiss bank accounts. The Court held that Gillani's contempt disqualified him from holding office. Gillani's removal was Chief Justice Chaudhry's boldest act yet of judicial activism, and a number of lawyers criticized this unusually broad use of the Court's contempt powers. Two days later, the PPP hastily selected Raja Pervez Ashraf as caretaker prime minister in order to resolve the crisis. Ashraf would serve until elections would be held nine months later.

It had been over a year since bin Laden's death, and Pak-American relations had gradually improved. The United States government had softened its public criticisms of Pakistan—although it still issued strong private warnings. The Americans still found Pakistan's support of the Haqqani network intolerable. On September 7, 2012, the United States even designated the Haqqani network as a terrorist organization, although Pakistan continued to support it.

The TTP continued its violent campaign against Pakistani girls' schools. On October 9, 2012, a Taliban terrorist shot 15-year-old activist Malala Yousafzai through the eye as she rode a school bus from her school in the NWFP's Swat District. Malala was shot because she had been campaigning for the right of girls to attend school. Malala was rushed to a British hospital where the bullet was removed and she made a miraculous three-month recovery. Malala's remarkable recovery from the hideous crime and her continued campaign for girls' education gained her international attention. She would receive the Nobel Peace Prize for her championship of children's rights to attend school.

President Obama was concerned that the CIA's drone strikes were killing so many innocent civilians along with the targeted terrorists. Therefore, when he appointed John Brennan as the new CIA director on March 8, 2013, he asked Brennan to reassess America's drone program. Brennan would recommend fewer drone attacks, and under Brennan the number of drone strikes began to fall—along with the number of civilian casualties. There had been 48 drone strikes in 2012, and they would drop to 21 strikes in 2014.[97]

Former military dictator Musharraf returned home to Pakistan on March 23, 2013. He returned after a four-year exile, hoping to make a comeback in the upcoming parliamentary elections. However, Musharraf was disappointed when only a small crowd greeted him on his arrival, when the government limited his right to run as a candidate, and when the government prosecuted him for treason. The army intervened on his behalf by warning Sharif not to humiliate their former chief. Sharif's continued harassment of Musharraf damaged Sharif-army relations.

Mullah Mohammad Omar had been the leader of the Afghan Taliban movement since its founding 19 years before. On April 23, 2013, he died of tuberculosis in a Karachi hospital. However, his lieutenant Mullah Akhtar Mansour would conceal his death for two years—even from other Taliban leaders. During these two years, Mullah Mansour acted as the Taliban's de facto leader, claiming that he was acting on Omar's behalf.[98]

Pakistan now held its national and provincial parliamentary elections on May 11, 2013. There was a relatively high 55 percent voter turnout in the National Assembly election, despite a Taliban campaign of voter intimidation. Nawaz Sharif's PML(N) Party won 189 of the 342 seats in the National Assembly, giving it an outright majority of seats. Zardari's PPP won 36 seats, while Imran Khan's PTI won 28 seats. Sharif's PML(N) prevailed because it had run a solid campaign, it had a strong party machine, and it had promoted Sharif's proven abilities and past achievements. Sharif also had campaigned on the promise of holding peace talks with the TTP.

There were several noteworthy features of this election. First, it was the first election held in compliance with the Constitution's 20th Amendment,

18. Civilian Rule Under Gillani and Zardari

which had set up fair election procedures. Also, the large turnout in the face of Taliban violence, and the victory of Sharif's mainstream party, revealed that most Pakistanis craved a stable efficient government. Also, political parties had discovered a better way to blunt the terrorist violence which had been interfering with election campaigns. They avoided rallies and instead reached voters using media advertisements, door-to-door contacts and Facebook.[99] In addition, the ISI had not intervened in the elections, and the modest rigging that did occur was largely ignored in light of Sharif's overwhelming lead in the voting. Also, former cricket star Imran Khan and his PTI Party made a remarkable political comeback, and for the first time had won many National Assembly seats.

19

Sharif's Third Term

During the four-year period covered in this chapter (June 2013–July 2017), Sharif would serve his third term as prime minister. A year later, the army would conduct its first offensive against terrorists in North Waziristan. Two years after Sharif took office, Imran Khan would begin anti-Sharif protests which would continue for the rest of Sharif's rule. The chapter ends when the Supreme Court removed Sharif as prime minister.

Sharif Begins His Third Term

On June 5, 2013, 63-year-old Nawaz Sharif was sworn in as prime minister for an unprecedented third non-consecutive term. Sharif anticipated serving as prime minister for many years, since his PML(N) Party had won a majority of National Assembly seats by a wide margin in a relatively fair election. This wide support made it unlikely that the army would risk removing his civilian government before his term had expired.

Two months later, Hussan Mamnoon was elected president by a majority vote of the electoral college of the national and provincial assemblies. His predecessor Zardari had not sought reelection, which in itself was an important milestone in Pakistan's democratic development.

Pakistan faced many problems when Sharif took office. First, Pakistan's population had been growing at an alarming rate, making it difficult for the government to provide basic services to the people. Also, Pakistan's economy was weak, primarily because government revenues were stunted by tax evasion, and the revenues couldn't cover military expenditures and servicing of the national debt. The country was experiencing high unemployment, crippling inflation, and electric power shortages. Half the people lacked access to any electricity, while the rest suffered from frequent blackouts.[1] In addition, Pakistan was running out of water for human consumption and crop irrigation.[2]

Terrorist Attacks in Pakistan and Afghanistan

Both Pakistan's Prime Minister Sharif and Afghan President Karzai sought to end the Islamist terrorist attacks on their respective governments. Sharif was willing to make peace with the TTP but he handled the negotiating poorly and allowed the TTP to take the initiative in the talks.[3] Also, he insisted that the TTP disarm as a condition for making peace—a condition that the TTP clearly would never accept. So the peace talks went nowhere and Sharif would order the army to attack TTP strongholds.

The army's first target was Karachi, where TTP terrorists had secured control of one-fourth of the city's outskirts. The TTP's extensive criminal activities in Karachi were generating funds for its TTP operations throughout the country. On September 7, 2013, the army began an operation in Karachi against the TTP terrorists and common criminals. The TTP fought back, and four months later assassinated Chaudary Aslam by detonating explosives in a parked taxi as he drove by. He had led the Karachi police department's anti-extremist cell. However, soldiers and police gradually restored order by detaining tens of thousands of suspects.[4]

While the army was trying to suppress the TTP in Karachi, the TTP began a series of attacks on army targets. On September 15, 2013, a TTP roadside bomb killed General Khan Niazi while he was on an inspection trip. The general was the army's commander in the Swat Valley, and his death shocked army leaders.

At the same time, the Americans continued their drone attacks against TTP insurgents. On November 1, 2013, a drone missile killed the TTP's ruthless leader Hakimullah Mehsud in North Waziristan. The TTP had killed thousands of Pakistani civilians and security personnel. Nevertheless Sharif and Imran Khan condemned the attack, claiming that it had impeded peace negotiations with the Taliban. The TTP chose Mullah Fazlullah as its new leader.

Prime Minister Sharif's Army Chief General Kayani had avoided attacking the TTP terrorists in North Waziristan. This was about to change. On November 29, 2013, following General Kayani's retirement as army chief, the prime minister appointed General Raheel Sharif as Pakistan's army chief. Raheel Sharif was a counterinsurgency expert, and he would become a popular hero for his tough suppression of terrorists—especially in North Waziristan and Karachi.

Supreme Court Chief Justice Chaudhry retired on December 12, 2013, after a stormy eight years in office. During his tenure, the courageous Chaudhry had converted the Supreme Court from a submissive court to a bold one which dared to challenge civilian and military leaders when they abused their powers. Even after Chaudhry's retirement, the Supreme Court would continue preventing prime ministers from exceeding their legal powers, and even removing those whom it deemed had violated the Constitution.

The United States had been cutting back its drone program in Pakistan, and the number of drone attacks fell from 122 strikes in 2010 to just 26 in 2013. The numbers had been falling mainly because so many terrorists on the CIA target list had been killed. The number of drone strikes would decline further because on February 5, 2014, the United States announced that it would narrow its CIA drone target list in Pakistan to 20 known terrorists. The Americans would add no new names to the list after a listed terrorist was killed.

During this period the Baluchistan rebellion revived. On February 9, 2014, Baloch terrorists blew up three of the four gas pipelines of the Sui Northern Gas Pipelines Ltd. in Baluchistan. The attackers detonated all the bombs by remote control within 30 minutes of each other. This attack was one of 84 Baluchistan gas line attacks during the year. The Baloch nationalists were relying more on violence because Pakistan's government refused to negotiate over sharing the revenues from the Sui gas fields.

To suppress the Baluchistan insurgents, the army and ISI had been seizing Baloch militants and jailing them without trial at undisclosed locations. Some brave Pakistani journalists were reporting these illegal detentions. The army and ISI didn't tolerate these criticisms and may have been responsible for some of the violent deaths of these journalists. For example, on April 19, 2014, gunmen on motorcycles shot the popular news anchor Hamid Mir while he was riding in a car. Mir was hit three times in the lower body—probably as a warning to deter him from continuing to report on the "missing persons" campaign.[5] Hamid survived and openly accused the ISI of orchestrating the attack. During the year, a record fourteen Pakistani journalists were murdered.

Pakistan's Army Finally Attacks Terrorists in North Waziristan

On June 8, 2014, ten TTP and IMU terrorists made a bold attack on Karachi's airport—some dressed as security personnel. The attackers killed 19 airport personnel and destroyed two warehouses containing weapons destined for NATO forces in Afghanistan.

There were several repercussions to this terrorist attack. First, Prime

Minister Sharif temporarily abandoned his attempts to negotiate a peace deal with the TTP. Also, Sharif would allow Army Chief Raheel Sharif to launch an offensive against terrorists in North Waziristan. In addition, parliament passed the Protection of Pakistan Act, which allowed police to conduct warrantless searches, arrests and weapons seizures.[6]

Pakistan's army had never conducted offensive operations in North Waziristan, and this inaction had allowed the TTP, al-Qaeda, and Haqqani network to freely build strong bases there. However, the army's leaders had come to realize that these terrorist groups had become a threat to the country and must be destroyed. Therefore, on June 26, 2014, the army sent 25,000 or more troops to North Waziristan to attack some 3,500 militants based there ("Operation Zarb-e-Azb"). The army methodically advanced against the militants and flattened two Haqqani strongholds—the towns of Miranshah and Mir Ali. The army killed many foreign fighters and pushed most of them out of the region. Then on April 3, 2016, the army began a 10-month clearing phase. The army declared the operation over on February 22, 2017.

During the 2.5-year campaign, Pakistan's army had killed 2,600 militants, while suffering over 600 deaths of its own. It had pushed most insurgents out of the last areas that they had occupied in Pakistan. The operation had shown the Pakistani people that the army had the power and commitment to destroy the terrorists who had been killing so many innocent Pakistanis. Terrorism inside Pakistan would significantly diminish.

Imran Khan now began a campaign to remove Prime Minister Sharif. Imran had founded the PTI political party years before, but it had relied mainly on Imran's popularity as a former cricket star. His PTI party had languished for 18 years without attracting grassroots support. Now Imran Khan revived the party with a popular campaign criticizing Sharif's regime for its corruption and its backing American drone strikes. On August 14, 2014, Imran's PTI kicked off its campaign with a 185-mile "Freedom March" from Lahore to Islamabad, with marchers demanding Sharif's resignation. The army didn't stop the marchers from entering the center of the capital, where the protesters set up a tent city and refused to leave. The army didn't disperse the demonstrators, while the ISI gave them moral support and probably some funds.[7] While many of the 50,000 protesters left after a few weeks, some 7,500 held out for another four months. Then Imran Khan abandoned the tent city and began a nationwide anti–Sharif campaign.

Afghanistan After Karzai

On April 5, 2014, Afghanistan held a presidential election. Hamid Karzai did not run, since he had just completed two five-year terms—the most consecutive terms allowed by the Constitution. Abdullah Abdullah won 45 percent of the votes, and Ashraf Ghani won 31 percent. Since neither candidate won 50 percent of the vote, a runoff election was required between the two candidates with the most votes—unless the two could reach a settlement. Abdullah and Ghani did reach a power-sharing agreement in which Ghani became President, while Abdullah Abdullah would serve as his "chief executive."[8]

On September 29, 2014, Ashraf Ghani was sworn in as President. He quickly signed a Bilateral Security Agreement (BSA) with the United States—the same BSA that the American-bashing Karzai had refused to sign. The BSA allowed some American troops to remain in Afghanistan, with the provision that no soldier could be tried in Afghan courts for crimes committed on Afghan soil. This was the standard immunity provision required by the Americans in return for agreeing to keep its troops on foreign soil to protect the host country's government. Pursuant to the BSA, the United States would keep some 10,000 troops in Afghanistan as a reserve force.[9]

During his first term, President Ghani hoped that his government could reach a peace deal with the Afghan Taliban. However, the Taliban had demanded that before it would start negotiations, the Americans must agree to withdraw its troops from Afghanistan. Therefore, the first step to a permanent peace deal was for the Taliban to reach a peace deal with the United States.

On September 28, 2019, Afghan presidential elections were held. Five months later, the Election Commission declared that Ghani had won the election with 50.64 percent of the votes cast—thus not requiring a runoff. However, his main rival, Abdullah Abdullah, who had won 39.52 percent of the vote, alleged fraud and refused to concede defeat. The two wouldn't resolve the standoff for many months, during which time they set up two parallel governments.

The first step towards a permanent peace was completed on February 29, 2020, when the Americans and the Taliban signed a peace agreement in Qatar. Under the agreement, the United States pledged to reduce its troop presence from 13,000 to 8,600 in four months, and withdraw its remaining soldiers in 14 months. The Taliban committed to renounce al-Qaeda and prevent any terrorist group from ever using Afghan soil to threaten the United States or its allies. While this American-Taliban peace agreement was a major accomplishment, it could fall apart if either party violated its terms.

The second step to a permanent peace in Afghanistan would be for the Taliban to reach a peace deal with the Afghan government. However, Taliban-Afghan government peace talks could not begin until it first was determined who would represent the Afghan government in the talks—

Ghani or his rival Abdullah Abdullah. This obstacle was overcome on May 17, 2020, when the two rivals signed a power-sharing agreement. Ghani would remain president, but Abdullah Abdullah would appoint half the cabinet members and lead the government in the peace negotiations with the Taliban. Those peace negotiations actually began on September 13, 2020, in Doha, Qatar.

New Terrorist Groups Join in the Mayhem

Al-Qaeda had revived despite Osama bin Laden's death, and under its new leader Zawahiri it had decentralized and organized affiliates. On September 3, 2014, Zawahiri announced al-Qaeda's new affiliate—"Al-Qaeda of the Indian Subcontinent" (AQIS).[10] AQIS's goal was to overthrow the governments of Pakistan, India, Bangladesh and Myanmar, and form a unified Islamic state in the region.

AQIS quickly made its presence known. On September 6, ten of its fighters tried to hijack a Pakistan Navy frigate—hoping to use its cruise missiles against American naval ships. Four terrorists in military uniforms boarded the ship after displaying military ID cards. However, the plot was foiled when an alert sailor on watch duty prevented the six other hijackers in marine uniforms in their dinghy from boarding the ship and joining the four on board.[11] It was later learned that the ship had been carrying a nuclear warhead.

Most of Pakistan's terrorists had belonged to the TTP umbrella group. However, a disgruntled JuA group had broken from the TTP and began its own series of vicious terrorist attacks. The JuA's first attack took place on November 2, 2014, after a routine daily military parade ceremony near a border crossing near Lahore. A JuA suicide bomber detonated a powerful bomb in a nearby restaurant parking lot which killed over 60 persons.

The next terrorist attack was a TTP massacre at an army school for children of military servicemen. On December 16, 2014, seven terrorists entered the army Public School in Peshawar by scaling a back wall using a ladder. They attacked some 400 students who had gathered in an auditorium, and then sought out students in classrooms. The terrorists killed 145 students—mostly very young children.[12]

There were several repercussions to the army school massacre. First, the killing of so many innocent children strengthened the army's resolve to destroy terrorist groups. Also, Pakistan's civilians were shaken and outraged at the massacre. As never before, the great majority of Pakistanis opposed the TTP, and they put tremendous pressure on the army and government to stop the TTP's terrorist attacks.[13] In addition, the government reacted by setting up special military courts to handle captured TTP fighters.[14] Finally, Sharif lifted a five-year moratorium on carrying out death sentences, and some 60 terrorists on death row soon were executed.

The TTP suddenly had a new terrorist rival when on January 26, 2015, the Islamic State (IS) declared that its caliphate now had expanded to include a new IS "province"—the Islamic State of Khorasan (ISK). IS already had decreed that it controlled IS "provinces" in Iraq, Syria, and other countries. The new ISK province was to include parts of Pakistan and Afghanistan. The ISK began recruiting TTP members who had become disturbed with the TTP leadership's new desire to secure peace.

While the Islamic State (IS) competed with its rival Al-Qaeda (AQ) for dominance of world terrorism, al-Qaeda seemed better-positioned to prevail. AQ's patience, long-term planning and decentralized organization made it a very formidable and elusive enemy. In contrast, the impatient IS's premature attempts to seize territory for its caliphate exposed its forces to attacks by powerful national armies. Also, its ruthless treatment of those within its occupied territory would make it very unpopular.[15]

Pakistan's troubled economy received a boost when its Communist ally China offered to assist Pakistan in improving its infrastructure. The Chinese offer was made during a two-day visit by China's President Xi Jinping, which began on April 20, 2015. During the visit, China and Pakistan signed an agreement for a massive Sino-Pakistan Economic Corridor development program (CPEC). The two countries agreed to develop a 2,000-mile network of roads and railways between Kashgar (in southern China) and Pakistan's southern port of Gwadar. The massive project would be financed by $62 billion in Chinese loans and investments, and Chinese workers were required to be used on some projects. There would be no outright grants. China committed to this massive project because it considered the CPEC to be the only trade and energy corridor that could enable China to overtake India's interests in the region. It also could guarantee China with a source of raw materials to produce electrical power.[16] The CPEC also sought to develop Pakistan's Gwadar port, which would give Pakistan a second port in addition to its crowded main port at Karachi. China also committed to greatly increase Pakistan's weak electrical capacity by building new power plants. The CPEC project would be beset with many obstacles, including Baloch terrorists who would kill Chinese road construction workers. In addition, Pakistan would have difficulty raising the money needed to repay the loans.

Pakistan's leaders had been supporting the Afghan Taliban ever since Mullah Omar had founded it over 15 years before. The secretive and mysterious Mullah Omar had done a good job holding together the diverse factions in the group. However, in a startling development, the media reported on July 29, 2015, that Mullah Omar had died of tuberculosis two years before.

The delayed announcement of Omar's death exacerbated the bitter dispute between the Zakir and Mansour factions of the Afghan Taliban. While the Afghan Taliban finally agreed to make Mullah Mansour its new leader, the Zakir faction never would forgive the Mansour faction for having concealed Mullah Omar's death from it for two years.

While the Afghan Taliban was facing a leadership change, the TTP and the breakaway JuA terrorist groups continued killing innocent civilians. On January 20, 2016, four TTP terrorists stormed the campus of Bacha Khan University in Charsadda, 80 miles west of Islamabad. The attackers killed 21 or more victims before being themselves killed by security forces.

The TTP attack on the university campus was soon followed by an attack by the vicious JuA terrorist group. On March 27, JuA terrorists detonated explosives in a Lahore park, killing at least 72 civilians and injuring 300 more. The terrorists had been targeting Christian women and children who were celebrating Easter Sunday, but most of the victims turned out to be Muslims.

Four Apartments in London

On April 3, 2016, news broke that there had been a leak from the Panama law firm Mossack Fonseca (the "Panama papers" story). The Fonseca firm had secretly created thousands of off-shore accounts for their clients in order to help them avoid paying taxes in their country of residence. Eventually 13.4 million legal documents would be released to the public, including those showing that three of Prime Minister Sharif's children were owners of four luxury apartments in London. This disclosure would prompt anti-Sharif politician Imran Khan to ask the Supreme Court to investigate whether Sharif himself didn't really own those apartments and had purchased them with funds obtained illegally. This matter was critical, since the Constitution provided that lawmakers who were "dishonest" were not qualified to hold office.

While the Panama papers were being examined, violence in Baluchistan Province broke out again. On May 21, 2016, an American drone over Pakistan fired a missile killing Mullah Mansour—the Afghan Taliban's second leader (emir). The Americans hoped that his successor would be more amendable to making peace.[17] Then on August 9, 2016, terrorists mortally wounded the president of the Baluchistan Bar Association. Many of the victim's colleagues converged on the hospital where he had been taken for emergency treatment. A suicide bomber stepped into their midst, detonated his explosives and killed over 65 in the crowd—mainly Baloch lawyers. The JuA claimed responsibility for the attack which had killed an entire generation of Baloch lawyers.

The Islamic State (IS) now joined the terrorist attacks in Baluchistan. By now, the IS had lost much of its territory and was trying desperately to bolster its image of continued strength. On November 24, 2016, an IS suicide bomber detonated explosives inside a packed Sufi shrine in Baluchistan, killing 52 worshipers. The IS considered Sufi Muslims to be heretics. Three months later another IS suicide bomber killed 80 worshipers at another Sufi shrine in southern Pakistan.[18]

On January 20, 2017, Donald J. Trump became president of the United States. Trump would gradually develop plans for dealing with Pakistan and Afghanistan. First, he would pledge to expand America's military presence in Afghanistan. Also, he would exert more pressure on Pakistan's leaders to end safe havens for terrorists based in Pakistan. In addition, Trump returned to the CIA authority to conduct drone attacks in order to restore secrecy to these attacks.

Pakistanis now shifted their attention to the Supreme Court's investigation of Prime Minister Sharif for corruption. At first it appeared that Sharif would survive the scandal. On April 20, 2017, the Supreme Court voted 3–2 against removing Prime Minister Sharif from office on corruption charges. However, the Court ordered the National Accountability Bureau (NAB) to conduct an investigation into whether Sharif had dishonestly secured the funds that were used to purchase four London apartments which were now in the names of his three children. Sharif was arguing that the apartments had been given to his children in settlement of an old family business deal with a Qatari prince. However, the NAB investigation team concluded that Sharif had bought the apartments with funds acquired dishonestly.

On July 28, 2017, the Supreme Court removed Prime Minister Sharif from office on grounds that he had not been "honest," which was a constitutional requirement for holding office.[19] The Court also ordered that civil corruption charges be brought against Sharif, his two sons and his daughter Maryam—his preferred political heir.

The Supreme Court's removal of Sharif set back democracy by creating the precedent that the Supreme Court could dismiss a prime minister in mid-term if it believed that he had been "dishonest." This was the second time the Supreme Court had removed a prime minister—the first time being the Court's dismissal of Gillani for contempt of court five years before.

Epilogue

On July 25, 2018, Imran Khan was elected to succeed Sharif as prime minister. For years, Imran had criticized prime ministers Bhutto and Sharif while they were in office. During his election campaign, he had criticized their support for the United States and the IMF. He had promised to make Pakistan a socialist "welfare state" during his five-year term by creating ten million jobs, building five million low-cost homes, and revamping the health care and education systems. However, once in office, he soon ran into a number of obstacles that would make it impossible for him to achieve his "welfare state" pledge.

Imran Khan's first immediate problem was how to fix Pakistan's economy and prevent the government from defaulting on its huge foreign loans. His predecessors had greatly increased Pakistan's foreign debt by excessive spending and by signing an agreement to join in a massive development project—the "Sino-Pakistan Economic Corridor" (CPEC). The CPEC provided that China would loan $62 billion to Pakistan for use in building roads, power plants, and a port at Gwadar. Many of these projects were in various stages of completion.

During Imran's first year in office, he had tried to raise the funds needed to increase the Treasury's reserves so that it had the money needed to repay its Chinese and other creditors. Unable to borrow enough from non-western sources, Imran was forced to seek help from the International Monetary Fund (IMF). On May 13, 2019, it was reported that Pakistan had secured a $6 billion loan from the IMF. However, as a condition for receiving the loan, the IMF required Pakistan to raise its tax rates, improve tax collections, and raise gasoline and electricity prices. These conditions would prevent Imran from fulfilling his campaign promise of making Pakistan a welfare state.

A second problem involved the Pak-Indian dispute over control of Kashmir. On February 14, 2019, a Pakistani-based JeM fighter killed 44

Indian paramilitary troops in a suicide attack on a convoy. In retaliation, on February 27, Indian planes attacked the site of a former or current JeM terrorist training camp 25 miles inside Pakistani territory—the first Indian military attack on a target inside Pakistan in many years.

Then on August 5, 2019, India's Prime Minister Narendra Modi placed Indian-controlled IJK territory under direct Indian control. He also had parliament revoke IJK's special status given to Muslims living inside Indian-controlled IJK territory in Kashmir. This special status had given local Muslim leaders in IJK some political authority, and had prohibited non–Muslims from investing in or owning property there. Modi claimed that giving IJK's Kashmiris special status had encouraged militancy and separatist sentiment. Modi sent 10,000 more troops to IJK's capital Srinagar to discourage mass protests to the decision. Indian soldiers detained 2,300 or more local political leaders and young men, and closed government offices, schools, and mosques. They pressured residents to stay off the streets. India also imposed a communications blackout which prevented the use of phones, television, and the Internet. Kashmir's IJK's Muslims were furious at their loss of special status, and they were very concerned that Indians might flood into IJK, buy real estate, and convert IJK into a Hindu-dominated region.

While India slowly restored some communications, the IJK still had no Internet access. However, on January 10, 2020, India's Supreme Court ruled that the indefinite suspension of Internet services in Kashmir violated India's constitutional guarantee of freedom of speech.

Pakistan's Long-Standing Problems

In addition to the above immediate problems, Imran Khan faced problems that had been distressing Pakistan's leaders for decades. First, the country has been dominated by powerful army generals, feudal landowners, and industrialists. These elites had a common interest in protecting their power and wealth.[1] They have prevented Pakistan from developing a mature political system in which political parties are used to reconcile the differences between its ethnic and religious groups. Another long-standing problem has been Pakistan's high illiteracy and its lack of a vigorous public school system. The public schools that do exist don't encourage students to think for themselves—an ability needed to critically analyze current events, political campaign promises, and conspiracy theories.[2] In addition, the country's unity has been disrupted by religious intolerance and discrimination. Also, armed Islamist jihadist groups have been killing thousands of innocent civilians, and even threatening to topple the government itself. In addition, Pakistan's government has failed to meet its financial obligations, since its revenues have been lost through massive tax evasion and smuggling of consumer goods into the country.[3] For decades the government's revenues have been unable to meet current expenditures, and Pakistan has had to rely on IMF loans to cover the deficits. However, government leaders keep ignoring IMF demands to become more self-sufficient through improving tax collections and cutting government spending. Finally, Pakistan's army leaders keep promoting the idea that Pakistan is in imminent danger of being invaded by its neighbor—long after India has ceased to be a credible threat.[4] Pakistan's army leaders justify its need for this large army and for improving its nuclear arsenal on the questionable grounds of the Indian threat. These large military expenditures continue to be a huge drain on the country's resources. Also, Pakistan's unwillingness to develop economic ties with India has retarded the development of both countries.

Some Hopeful Signs

There are some encouraging signs that Pakistan might one day become more united, stable, and peaceful. First, the country has operated under its Constitution for the last 47 years, and even during periods of military rule, army leaders have largely adhered to its provisions. Also, Pakistan's civilian leaders seem to recognize the value of adhering to the rule of law when there is a change in governments. Army leaders haven't ruled the country for 12 years, and they seem willing to let the Supreme Court take over the job of removing prime ministers who don't follow the law. During these 12 years, civilian governments have peacefully succeeded each other through reasonably fair elections, with the losing parties abiding by the election results. In addition, some of Pakistan's civilian and military leaders have come to realize that Pakistan should use diplomacy instead of force in dealing with India. The majority of Pakistani citizens favor talks between Pakistan and India.[5] In addition, the stranglehold of the wealthy feudal rural landowners over the government has shown signs of loosening, as mid-size independent farmers have grown more prosperous and stronger politically.[6] Finally, Pakistanis have become more critical of religious terrorist groups.[7]

Appendix
List of Pakistan Army Chiefs[1]

General's Name	Date of Post	Time at Post
Sir Frank Messervy	August 15, 1947	6 months
Sir Douglas Gracey	February 11, 1948	2 years, 11 months
Ayub Khan	January 16, 1951	7 years, 9 months
Muhammad Musa	October 27, 1958	7 years, 8 months
Yahya Khan	June 18, 1966	4 years, 6 months
Tikka Khan	March 3, 1972	4 years
Zia ul-Haq	March 1, 1976	12 years, 5 months
Mirza Aslam Beg	August 17, 1988	3 years
Asif Nawaz	August 16, 1991	1 year, 5 months
Abdul Waheed	January 11, 1993	3 years
Jahangir Karamat	January 12, 1996	2 years, 9 months
Pervez Musharraf	October 6, 1998	9 years, 1 month
Ashfaq Kayani	November 29, 2007	6 years
Raheel Sharif	November 29, 2013	3 years
Qamar Javed Bajwa	November 29, 2016	

1. From August 1947, the official title of the head of Pakistan's army was the "Army Commander-in-Chief." Ever since March 1972, the title has been the "Chief of Army Staff" (COAS). For simplicity, this book refers to all heads of the army as the "Army Chief."

Chapter Notes

Introduction to Pakistan

1. Abbas, Hassan, *Pakistan's Drift Into Extremism*, p. 193; Constable, Pamela, *Playing with Fire*, p. 174.
2. Afzal, Mahida, *Pakistan Under Siege*, p. 164.
3. Afzal, Madiha, *Pakistan Under Siege*, pp. 129–131.
4. Afzal, Madiha, *Pakistan Under Siege*, pp. 79, 81–83.
5. Afzal, Madiha, *Pakistan Under Siege*, pp. 131, 138.
6. Jaffrelot, Christophe, *The Pakistan Paradox*, pp. 341–344, 371.
7. Constable, Pamela, *Playing with Fire*, pp. 110–112; Munoz, Heraldo, *Getting Away with Murder*, p. 173.
8. Munoz, Heraldo, *Getting Away with Murder*, pp. 172, 179–180; Jaffrelot, Christophe, ed., *Pakistan at the Crossroads*, pp. 51, 67.
9. Cloughley, Brian, *A History of the Pakistan Army*, pp. 336–337; Akhund, Iqbal, *Trial and Error* pp. 298–299; Ahmad, Musutaq, Government and Politics in Pakistan, p. 159.
10. Ahmad, Mushtaq, *Government and Politics in Pakistan*, p. 292.
11. Lamb, Christina, *Waiting for Allah*, pp. 170, 192–194.
12. Ahmad, Mushtaq, *Nawaz Sharif*, p. 177.
13. Ziring, *Pakistan in the Twentieth Century*, p. 450.
14. Ahmad, Mushtaq, *Nawaz Sharif*, p. 14.
15. Ahmad, Mushtaq, *Nawaz Sharif*, pp. 27, 40.
16. Cloughley, Brian, *A History of the Pakistan Army*, p. 41.
17. Ahmad, Mushtaq, *Government and Politics in Pakistan*, pp. 93–95, 170; Ahmad, Mushtaq, *Nawaz Sharif*, pp. 17, 84.
18. Ahmad, Mushtaq, *Government and Politics in Pakistan*, pp. 246, 251.
19. Ahmad, Mushtaq, *Nawaz Sharif*, p. 15.
20. Ahmad, Mushtaq, *Nawaz Sharif*, pp. 32–33, p. 220.
21. Ahmad, Musutaq, *Government and Politics in Pakistan*, pp. 238, 246.
22. Ahmad, Mushtaq, *Nawaz Sharif*, p. 142.
23. Ahmad, Musutaq, *Government and Politics in Pakistan*, p. 159.
24. Ahmad, Mushtaq, *Nawaz Sharif*, pp. 12–13.
25. Lamb, Christina, *Waiting for Allah*, pp. 61–65, 68.
26. Lamb, Christina, *Waiting for Allah*, p. 68.
27. Ahmad, Mushtaq, *Nawaz Sharif*, p. 66.
28. Jalal, Ayesha, *The Struggle for Pakistan*, pp. 380–381; Ahmad, Musutaq, *Government and Politics in Pakistan*, p. 159.
29. Jaffrelot, Christophe, ed., *Pakistan at the Crossroads*, p. 106; and Jaffrelot, Christophe, *The Pakistan Paradox*, p. 385.
30. Jaffrelot, Christophe, *The Pakistan Paradox*, pp. 407–408; Ahmad, Musutaq, *Government and Politics in Pakistan*, p. 194; Constable, Pamela, *Playing with Fire*, p. 236..
31. Constable, Pamela, *Playing with Fire*, pp. 229–230.

Chapter 1

1. Ziring, Lawrence, *Pakistan in the Twentieth Century*, p. 22.
2. Ziring, Lawrence, *Pakistan in the Twentieth Century*, p. 28.
3. Collins, Larry, *Freedom at Midnight*, p. 172.
4. Collins, Larry, *Freedom at Midnight*, p. 193; Tunzelmann, Alex von, *Indian Summer*, p. 199.
5. Cloughley, Brian, *A History of the Pakistan Army*, p. 7.
6. Tunzelmann, Alex von, *Indian Summer*, pp. 199–201.
7. Abbas, Hassan, *Pakistan's Drift Into Extremism*, p.16.
8. Collins, Larry, *Freedom at Midnight*, p. 235.

Chapter 2

1. Ahmad, Musutaq, *Government and Politics in Pakistan*, pp. 95, 103, 111.
2. Ahmad, Mushtaq, *Nawaz Sharif*, p. 83.
3. Ahmad, Mushtaq, *Nawaz Sharif*, p. 83.
4. Cloughley, Brian, *A History of the Pakistan Army*, p. 7.
5. Collins, Larry, *Freedom at Midnight*, pp. 333–334.
6. Collins, Larry, *Freedom at Midnight*, pp. 330–334.
7. Tunzelmann, Alex von, *Indian Summer*, p. 239.
8. Tunzelmann, Alex von, *Indian Summer*, p. 228.
9. Von Tunzelmann, Alex, *Indian Summer*, p. 239.
10. Ispahani, Farahnaz, *Purifying the Land of the Pure*, p. 76; Jones, Owen, *Pakistan: Eye of the Storm*, p. xxiii.
11. Burke, S.M., *Pakistan's Foreign Policy*, p. 4; Jones, Owen B., *Pakistan: Eye of the Storm*, p. xxiii.
12. Collins, *Freedom at Midnight*, pp. 128–129; Afzal, *Pakistan History and Politics*, p. 16; Cohen, *The Idea of Pakistan*, p. 42.
13. Afzal, *Pakistan History and Politics*, p. 18; Collins, *Freedom at Midnight*, p. 340; Cloughley, *A History of the Pakistan Army*, p. 21.
14. Ziring, *Pakistan in the Twentieth Century*, p. 442; Talbot, *Pakistan: A Modern History*, pp. 369–370.
15. Jaffrelot, *The Pakistan Paradox*, p. 202.
16. Bose, Samantra, Kashmir, *Roots of Conflict*, pp. 32–33; Burke, *Pakistan's Foreign Policy*, p. 24; Von Tunzelmann, *Indian Summer*, p. 247.
17. Bose, *Kashmir, Roots of Conflict*, p. 35; Collins, *Freedom at Midnight*, pp. 403–404; Von Tunzelmann, *Indian Summer*, p. 248.
18. Bose, Samantra, Kashmir, *Roots of Conflict*, p. 37; Burke, *Pakistan's Foreign Policy*, p. 24; Afzal, *Pakistan History & Politics*, p. 27.
19. Von Tunzelmann, *Indian Summer*, p. 249; Jones, *Pakistan: Eye of the Storm*, pp. 65–66.
20. Bose, *Kashmir, Roots of Conflict*, p. 34; Von Tunzelmann, *Indian Summer*, pp. 251–252.
21. Bose, *The Challenge in Kashmir*, p. 88.
22. Burke, *Pakistan's Foreign Policy*, pp. 19–23; Von Tunzelmann, *Indian Summer*, p. 246.
23. Akhund, *Trial and Error*, p. 286.
24. Akhund, *Trial and Error*, pp. 286–287.

Chapter 3

1. Ahmad, Musutaq, *Government and Politics in Pakistan*, p. 25; Ziring, Lawrence, *Pakistan in the Twentieth Century*, pp. 100–102.
2. Ziring, *Pakistan in the Twentieth Century*, p. 102.
3. Bose, Sumantra, *The Challenge in Kashmir*, pp. 67–68.
4. Jaffrelot, Christophe, *The Pakistan Paradox*, pp. 202–203; Ziring, Lawrence, *Pakistan in the Twentieth Century*, pp. 104–105.
5. Haqqani, Hussain, *Pakistan Between Mosque and Military*, p. 18.
6. Ziring, *Pakistan in the Twentieth Century*, p. 203.
7. Ziring, Lawrence, *Pakistan in the Twentieth Century*, p. 113; Afzal, M. Rafique, *Pakistan History & Politics*, p. 72; Cloughley, Brian, *A History of the Pakistan Army*, p. 26; Nawaz, Shuja, *Crossed Swords*, pp. 83–84; Abbas, Hassan, *Pakistan's Drift Into Extremism*, p. 33.
8. Afzal, M. Rafique, *Pakistan History & Politics*, p. 82.
9. Munoz, Heraldo, *Getting Away with Murder*, pp. 38–39; Ziring, Lawrence, *Paki-*

Chapter 4

1. Talbot, *Pakistan: A Modern History*, pp. 141–142.
2. Ahmad, *Government and Politics in Pakistan*, p. 46.
3. Ziring, *Pakistan in the Twentieth Century*, p. 122.
4. Ziring, *Pakistan in the Twentieth Century*, pp. 125–126.
5. Ziring, *Pakistan in the Twentieth Century*, p. 130.
6. Ziring, *Pakistan in the Twentieth Century*, pp. 142–143.
7. Ispahani, *Purifying in the Land of the Pure*, pp. 53–54.
8. Ziring, *Pakistan in the Twentieth Century*, p. 150.
9. Bose, *The Challenge in Kashmir*, p. 184; Bose, *Transforming India*, pp. 252–253; Burke, *Pakistan's Foreign Policy*, p. 42; Afzal, *Pakistan History and Politics*, p. 301.
10. Bose, *Kashmir, Roots of Conflict*, pp. 67–68.
11. Bose, *The Challenge in Kashmir*, pp. 32, 184–185.
12. Jaffrelot, *The Pakistan Paradox*, p. 639.
13. Jaffrelot, *The Pakistan Paradox*, pp. 640–641; Haqqani, *Between Mosque and Military*, p. 323.
14. Haqqani, *Magnificent Delusions*, p. 78.
15. Ziring, *Pakistan in the Twentieth Century*, pp. 156–160.
16. Ziring, *Pakistan in the Twentieth Century*, pp. 164–165.
17. Ziring, *Pakistan in the Twentieth Century*, p. 170.
18. Ziring, *Pakistan in the Twentieth Century*, p. 173.
19. Cloughley, Brian, *A History of the Pakistan Army*, pp. 36, 40.
20. Ziring, *Pakistan in the Twentieth Century*, p. 176.
21. Afzal, M. Rafique, *Pakistan History & Politics*, p. 207.
22. Ahmad, Musutaq, *Government and Politics in Pakistan*, p. 179.
23. Afzal, M. Rafique, *Pakistan History & Politics*, pp. 144–145, 216; Ziring, Lawrence, *Pakistan in the Twentieth Century*, p. 179.
24. Ziring, *Pakistan in the Twentieth Century*, p. 178.
stan in the Twentieth Century, p. 115; Nawaz, Shuja, *Crossed Swords*, p. 86.
25. Ziring, *Pakistan in the Twentieth Century*, p. 187.
26. Ahmad, Musutaq, *Government and Politics in Pakistan*, p. 53.
27. Ahmad, Musutaq, *Government and Politics in Pakistan*, p. 34.
28. Ziring, *Pakistan in the Twentieth Century*, p. 184.
29. Ahmad, Musutaq, *Government and Politics in Pakistan*, pp. 54–55.
30. Ahmad, Musutaq, *Government and Politics in Pakistan*, pp. 56–57; Ziring, Lawrence, *Pakistan in the Twentieth Century*, p. 189.
31. Ziring, *Pakistan in the Twentieth Century*, p. 202.
32. Ahmad, Musutaq, *Government and Politics in Pakistan*, pp. 165–166; Ziring, Lawrence, *Pakistan in the Twentieth Century*, pp. 198–199.
33. Haqqani, Husain, *Magnificent Delusions*, pp. 83–84.
34. Ahmad, Mustaq, *Government and Politics in Pakistan*, pp. 70–71; Ziring, *Pakistan in the Twentieth Century*, pp. 217–218.
35. Ziring, *Pakistan in the Twentieth Century*, pp. 215–216.
36. Ziring, Lawrence, *Pakistan at the Crosscurrent of History*, p. 79; Weaver, Mary A., *Pakistan in the Shadow of Jihad and Afghanistan*, p. 100.
37. Ziring, *Pakistan in the Twentieth Century*, p. 219.
38. Ziring, *Pakistan in the Twentieth Century*, p. 222.
39. Ziring, *Pakistan in the Twentieth Century*, p. 224.
40. Jaffrelot, Christophe, *The Pakistan Paradox*, pp. 303–304.
41. Ahmad, Musutaq, *Government and Politics in Pakistan*, pp. 177–178.

Chapter 5

1. Nawaz, Shuja, *Crossed Swords*, pp. 173–174, 255.
2. Ahmad, Mushtaq, *Government and Politics*, p. 233.
3. Ahmad, Mushtaq, *Government and Politics*, p. 232.
4. Ispahani, Farahnaz, *Purifying the Land of the Pure*, pp. 68–70.
5. Ziring, Lawrence, *Pakistan at the Crosscurrent of History*, p. 298; Jones, Owen, *Pakistan: Eye of the Storm*, p. 276.

6. Jones, Owen B., *Pakistan: Eye of the Storm*, pp. 277–278.
7. Ziring, Lawrence, *Pakistan in the Twentieth Century*, p. 230.
8. Ahmad, Musutaq, *Government and Politics in Pakistan*, p. 228.
9. Ahmad, Musutaq, *Government and Politics in Pakistan*, p. 299; Ziring, *Pakistan in the Twentieth Century*, pp. 237–238.
10. Ziring, *Pakistan in the Twentieth Century*, pp. 238–239.
11. Ahmad, Musutaq, *Government and Politics in Pakistan*, pp. 283; Ziring, *Pakistan in the Twentieth Century*, p. 235.
12. Ahmad, Musutaq, *Government and Politics in Pakistan*, pp. 200–203.
13. Ziring, Lawrence, *Pakistan in the Twentieth Century*, p. 241.
14. Ahmad, Musutaq, *Government and Politics in Pakistan*, p. 187.
15. Ahmad, Musutaq, *Government and Politics in Pakistan*, p. 187.
16. Ahmad, Musutaq, *Government and Politics in Pakistan*, pp. 228–229.
17. Jaffrelot, Christophe, *A History of Pakistan and Its Origins*, p. 70.
18. Jaffrelot, Christophe, *The Pakistan Paradox*, p. 306.
19. Ziring, *Pakistan in the Twentieth Century*, pp. 249, 254–257.
20. Ziring, *Pakistan in the Twentieth Century*, pp. 257, 259–260.
21. Ahmad, Musutaq, *Government and Politics in Pakistan*, pp. 190–191; Jalal, Ayesha, *The Struggle for Pakistan*, pp. 105–106; 115.
22. Kux, Dennis, *The United States and Pakistan*, p. 113.
23. Burke, S.M., *Pakistan's Foreign Policy*, p. 267.
24. Burki, Shahid and Baxter, *Pakistan Under Bhutto*, p. 155; Jaffrelot, Christophe, *A History of Pakistan and Its Origins*, pp. 167–169.
25. Burki, Shahid and Baxter, *Pakistan Under Bhutto*, p. 155.
26. Kux, Dennis, *The United States and Pakistan*, pp. 122–123.
27. Ziring, *Pakistan in the Twentieth Century*, p. 265.
28. Ahmad, Musutaq, *Government and Politics in Pakistan*, pp. 214–216.
29. Ziring, *Pakistan in the Twentieth Century*, p. 273.
30. Ziring, *Pakistan in the Twentieth Century*, pp., 270, 272.
31. Kux, Dennis, *The United States and Pakistan*, p. 133.
32. Kux, Dennis, *The United States and Pakistan*, p. 131.
33. Ziring, *Pakistan in the Twentieth Century*, p. 277.
34. Kux, Dennis, *The United States and Pakistan*, p. 132.
35. Ziring, *Pakistan in the Twentieth Century*, p. 276.
36. Ziring, *Pakistan in the Twentieth Century*, pp. 276–277.
37. Ziring, *Pakistan in the Twentieth Century*, p. 295.
38. Ziring, *Pakistan in the Twentieth Century*, p. 282.
39. Ahmad, Musutaq, *Government and Politics in Pakistan*, p. 302.
40. Ziring, *Pakistan in the Twentieth Century*, pp. 284–285, 291.
41. Ahmad, Musutaq, *Government and Politics in Pakistan*, pp. 286–295.
42. Ziring, *Pakistan in the Twentieth Century*, p. 289.
43. Ziring, *Pakistan in the Twentieth Century*, p. 288.
44. Ziring, *Pakistan in the Twentieth Century*, p. 293.
45. Ziring, *Pakistan in the Twentieth Century*, p. 303.
46. Ziring, *Pakistan in the Twentieth Century*, p. 306.
47. Burki, Shahid and Baxter, *Pakistan Under the Military*, p. 15.
48. Ahmad, Musutaq, *Government and Politics in Pakistan*, pp. 305–310.
49. Jaffrelot, Christophe, *The Pakistan Paradox*, pp. 220–221.
50. Bergen, Peter, ed., *Talibanistan*, p. 311; Jones, Owen B., *Pakistan: Eye of the Storm*, p. 158.
51. Bhutto, Benazir, *Daughter of Destiny*, p. 51.
52. Kux, *The United States and Pakistan*, p. 178.
53. Ziring, *Pakistan in the Twentieth Century*, p. 318.

Chapter 6

1. Nawaz, Shuja, *Crossed Swords*, p. 312.
2. Ahmad, *Government and Politics in Pakistan*, p. 323.
3. Ziring, *Pakistan in the Twentieth Century*, pp. 320–321.

4. Ziring, *Pakistan in the Twentieth Century*, p. 326.
5. Ahmad, Musutaq, *Government and Politics in Pakistan*, pp. 319-320; Afzal, *Pakistan History & Politics*, p. 363.
6. Cloughley, Brian, *A History of the Pakistan Army*, p. 140.
7. Haqqani, *Pakistan Between Mosque and Military*, pp. 62, 66; Jalal, *The Struggle for Pakistan*, p. 141.
8. Ziring, *Pakistan in the Twentieth Century*, pp. 344-345.
9. Jones, *Pakistan: Eye of the Storm*, p. 160.
10. Jalal, *The Struggle for Pakistan*, p. 171.
11. Cloughley, Brian, *A History of the Pakistan Army*, p. 147.
12. Ziring, *Pakistan in the Twentieth Century*, pp. 346, 352-353, 356.
13. Afzal, *Pakistan History & Politics*, pp. 417-418.
14. Haqqani, *Pakistan Between Mosque and Military*, p. 75; Jalal, *The Struggle for Pakistan*, pp. 135-136.
15. Ziring, *Pakistan in the Twentieth Century*, p. 357.
16. Haqqani, Husain, *Pakistan Between Mosque and Military*, pp. 73-75.
17. Jalal, Ayesha, *The Struggle for Pakistan*, p. 175; Haqqani, Husain, *The Struggle for Pakistan*, p. 74; Ispahani, *Purifying the Land of the Pure*, p. 89.
18. Guha, Ramachandra, *India After Gandhi*, New York, 2007, p. 458.
19. Guha, Ramachandra, *India After Gandhi*, New York, 2007, p. 458; Nawaz, *Crossed Swords*, p. 285.
20. Cloughley, Brian, *A History of the Pakistan Army*, p. 168.
21. Nawaz, Shuja, *Crossed Swords*, p. 315.
22. Cloughley, Brian, *History of the Pakistan Army*, p. 166.

Chapter 7

1. Raza, *Bhutto and Pakistan*, pp. 134-135; Nawaz, *Crossed Swords*, pp. 321-322; Haqqani, *Pakistan Between Mosque and Military*, p. 90.
2. Wolpert, *Zulfi Bhutto of Pakistan*, p. 263; Raza, *Bhutto and Pakistan*, pp. 301, 381.
3. Ziring, *Pakistan in the Twentieth Century*, pp. 379, 396.
4. Kiessling, *Faith, Unity, Discipline*, pp. 45-46.

5. Ziring, *Pakistan in the Twentieth Century*, p. 383.
6. Jalal, *The Struggle for Pakistan*, p. 202.
7. Jalal, *The Struggle for Pakistan*, p. 382.
8. Ziring, *Pakistan in the Twentieth Century*, p. 409.
9. Cohen, Stephen, *the Idea of Pakistan*, pp. 139-140.
10. Ziring, *Pakistan in the Twentieth Century*, p. 384.
11. Haqqani, *Magnificent Delusions*, pp. 175-176, 184.
12. Ahmad, Mushtaq, *Nawaz Sharif*, p. 85.
13. Burki, *Pakistan Under Bhutto*, pp. 120, 132-136; Jaffrelot, *The Pakistan Paradox*, p. 229.
14. Cohen, *The Idea of Pakistan*, p. 82; Jalal, *The Struggle for Pakistan*, pp. 182-183.
15. Ahmad, Mushtaq, *Nawaz Sharif*, p. 122.
16. Cohen, *The Idea of Pakistan*, p. 146.
17. Frantz, Douglas, *The Nuclear Jihadist*, pp. 18-20.
18. Burki, *Pakistan Under Bhutto*, p. 122.
19. Raza, *Bhutto and Pakistan*, p. 280; Quddus, *Nawaz Sharif*, p. 86.
20. Ahmad, Mushtaq, *Nawaz Sharif*, p. 10.
21. Cloughley, *A History of the Pakistan Army*, pp. 218-219; Nawaz, *Crossed Swords*, p. 325.
22. Abbas, *Pakistan's Drift Into Extremism*, p. 72.
23. Haqqani, *Pakistan Between Mosque and Military*, pp. 100.
24. Ziring, *Pakistan in the Twentieth Century*, pp. 388-390.
25. Haqqani, *Pakistan Between Mosque and Military*, p. 110; Ziring, *Pakistan in the Twentieth Century*, pp. 381, 398.
26. Ziring, *Pakistan in the Twentieth Century*, pp. 381-383, 398.
27. Lamb, *Waiting for Allah*, p. 12.
28. Ziring, *Pakistan in the Twentieth Century*, p. 391.
29. Haqqani, *Magnificent Delusions*, p. 196; Raza, *Bhutto and Pakistan*, p. 269.
30. Abbas, Hassan, *Pakistan's Drift Into Extremism*, pp. 73-77; Nawaz, Shuja, *Crossed Swords*, pp. 335-337.
31. Abbas, Hassan, *Pakistan's Drift Into Extremism*, p. 75.
32. Jaffrelot, *The Pakistan Paradox*, p. 385.
33. Ahmad, Mushtaq, *Nawaz Sharif*, p. 86.

34. Ahmad, Mushtaq, *Nawaz Sharif*, pp. 149–150.
35. Ziring, *Pakistan in the Twentieth Century*, p. 398.
36. Wolpert, *Zulfi Bhutto of Pakistan*, p. 240; Raza, *Bhutto and Pakistan*, p. 300; Ziring, *Pakistan in the Twentieth Century*, pp. 398–399.
37. Burki, *Pakistan Under Bhutto*, pp. 145–146.
38. Ziring, *Pakistan in the Twentieth Century*, p. 400.
39. Afzal, *Pakistan Under Siege*, p. 61.
40. Ispahani, *Purifying the Land of the Pure*, p. 98; Bhutto, *Daughter of Destiny*, pp. 90–91.
41. Burki, *Pakistan Under Bhutto*, pp. 145–146.
42. Burki, *Pakistan Under Bhutto*, pp. 153–154, 163.
43. Wolpert, Stanley, *Zulfi Bhutto of Pakistan*, pp. 244–246; Talbot, Ian, *Pakistan: A Modern History*, p. 257.
44. Levy, Adrian, *Deception*, p. 27; Frantz, *The Nuclear Jihadist*, pp. 31–38.
45. Levy, *Deception*, p. 27.
46. Frantz, *The Nuclear Jihadist*, p. 48.
47. Nawaz, *Crossed Swords*, pp. 551–555.
48. Levy, *Deception*, p. 45; Frantz, *the Nuclear Jihadist*, p. 75.
49. Bose, Sumantra, *The Challenge of Kashmir*, p. 44; Bose, *Transforming India*, p. 273.
50. Abbas, Hassa, *Pakistan's Drift Into Extremism*, pp. 76–77.
51. Jaffrelot, *the Pakistan Paradox*, p. 233
52. Ziring, *Pakistan in the Twentieth Century*, p. 413.
53. Wolpert, *Zulfi Bhutto of Pakistan*, pp. 279–280; Raza, *Bhutto and Pakistan*, pp. 331, 364; Jalal, *The Struggle for Pakistan*, p. 210.
54. Haqqani, Hussain, *Pakistan Between Mosque and Military*, p. 120.
55. Ziring, *Pakistan in the Twentieth Century*, p. 412.
56. Haqqani, Husain, *Pakistan Between Mosque and Military*, p. 119; Ziring, *Pakistan in the Twentieth Century*, p. 414..
57. Haqqani, Husain, *Pakistan Between Mosque and Military*, pp. 119–121.
58. Ziring, *Pakistan in the Twentieth Century*, p. 417.
59. Haqqani, Husain, *Pakistan Between Mosque and Military*, p. 121.
60. Haqqani, *Pakistan Between Mosque and Military*, pp. 125–126.
61. Ziring, *Pakistan in the Twentieth Century*, p. 417.
62. Ziring, *Pakistan in the Twentieth Century*, p. 421.
63. Ziring, *Pakistan in the Twentieth Century*, pp. 420, 422, 426, 456.
64. Wolpert, *Zulfi Bhutto of Pakistan*, p. 263; Raza, *Bhutto and Pakistan*, p. 162.

Chapter 8

1. Ziring, *Pakistan in the Twentieth Century*, p. 453–454.
2. Ziring, *Pakistan in the Twentieth Century*, pp. 458–459.
3. Haqqani, *Pakistan Between Mosque and Military*, pp. 127–129, 131.
4. Ahmad, Mushtaq, *Nawaz Sharif*, pp. 5–6.
5. Jalal, *The Struggle for Pakistan*, p. 276; Nawaz, *Crossed Swords*, pp. 387, 445–446, 576.
6. Burki, *Pakistan Under the Military*, p. 116; Ziring, *Pakistan in the Twentieth Century*, pp. 443–444.
7. Jalal, *The Struggle for Pakistan*, pp. 264–265.
8. Jaffrelot, *The Pakistan Paradox*, p. 416.
9. Ziring, *Pakistan in the Twentieth Century*, pp. 424, 431.
10. Wolpert, *Zulfi Bhutto of Pakistan*, p. 305; Ziring, *Pakistan in the Twentieth Century*, pp. 424–426.
11. Wolpert, *Zulfi Bhutto of Pakistan*, pp. 322–323; Jaffrelot, *The Pakistan Paradox*, p. 384.
12. Kiessling, *Faith, Unity, Discipline*, p. 41.
13. Bhutto, Benazir, *Daughter of Destiny*, pp. 128–131.
14. Jaffrelot, *The Pakistan Paradox*, pp. 328–329.
15. Kiessling, *Faith, Unity, Discipline*, pp. 128–129.
16. Burki, *Pakistan Under the Military*, pp. 124–125; Ziring, *Pakistan in the Twentieth Century*, p. 465.
17. Haqqani, *Pakistan Between Mosque and Military*, pp. 145–147; Hussain, *The Scorpion's Tail*, p. 53; Lamb, *Waiting for Allah*, pp. 44, 85.
18. Jalal, *The Struggle for Pakistan*, pp. 283–284.
19. Ispahani, *Purifying the Land of the Pure*, pp. 130–131; Afzal, *Pakistan Under Siege*, pp. 75–76.

20. Cohen, *The Idea of Pakistan*, pp. 108-109.
21. Lamb, *Waiting for Allah*, pp. 186-187; Cohen, *The Idea of Pakistan*, p. 86.
22. Jaffrelot, Christophe, *The Pakistan Paradox*, p. 486.
23. Jaffrelot, *The Pakistan Paradox*, p. 494.
24. Frantz, Douglas, *The Nuclear Jihadist*, p. 103.
25. Kux, *The United States and Pakistan*, pp. 242-243; Jalal, *The Struggle for Pakistan*, p. 228.
26. Jalal, *The Struggle for Pakistan*, p. 229; Kux, *The United States and Pakistan*, pp. 242-245; Haqqani, *Pakistan Between Mosque and Military*, p. 182.
27. Jalal, Ayesha, *The Struggle for Pakistan*, p. 229.

Chapter 9

1. Jalal, *The Struggle for Pakistan*, p. 230; Akhund, Iqbal, *Trial and Error*, p. 151.
2. Coll, Steve, *Ghost Wars*, p. 62; Haqqani, *Pakistan Between Mosque and Military*, pp. 180, 185-186; Crile, *Charlie Wilson's War*, p. 103; Bradshere, Henry S, *Afghan Communism and Soviet Intervention*, Oxford 1999, p. 215.
3. Kux, *The United States and Pakistan*, p. 263; Gul, Imtiaz, *The Unholy Nexus*, p. 116; Levy, *Deception*, p. 130.
4. Kiessling, *Faith, Unity, Discipline*, pp. 53-54.
5. Markey, Daniel, *No Exit from Pakistan*, p. 94.
6. Haqqani, *Magnificent Delusions*, p. 245.
7. Ispahani, *Purifying the Land of the Pure*, p. 148.
8. Ziring, *Pakistan in the Twentieth Century*, pp. 469-470.
9. Ziring, *Pakistan in the Twentieth Century*, pp. 466-467; Bhutto, *Daughter of Destiny*, pp. 314-315; Jaffrelot, *The Pakistan Paradox*, pp. 474-475.
10. Coll, *Ghost Wars*, pp. 66-67.
11. Frantz, *The Nuclear Jihadist*, p. 110.
12. Bhutto, *Daughter of Destiny*, pp. 187-189, 200-201; Weaver, Mary, *Pakistan in the Shadow of Jihad and Afghanistan*, p. 185-186.
13. Ziring, *Pakistan in the Twentieth Century*, pp. 462-464.

14. Ispahani, *Purifying the Land of the Pure*, p. 144.
15. Jaffrelot, *The Pakistan Paradox*, pp. 496-497.
16. Ziring, *Pakistan in the Twentieth Century*, pp. 470-474.
17. Levy, *Deception*, pp. 124-126.
18. Nawaz, *Crossed Swords*, pp. 490-491.
19. Frantz, *The Nuclear Jihadist*, p. 133.
20. Franz, Douglas, *The Nuclear Jihadist*, p. 135.
21. Levy, *Deception*, pp. 102-103.
22. Kiessling, *Faith, Unity, Discipline*, p. 101.
23. Jaffrelot, ed., *Pakistan at the Crossroads*, pp. 77-78.
24. Nawaz, *Crossed Swords*, p. 380; Talbot, *Pakistan: A Modern History*, p. 261.

Chapter 10

1. Ziring, *Pakistan in the Twentieth Century*, p. 173.
2. Rashid, *Taliban*, p. 130; Coll, *Ghost Wars*, p. 144.
3. Ispahani, *Purifying the Land of the Pure*, p. 142.
4. Perkovich, *India's Nuclear Bomb*, p. 278.
5. Perkovich, *India's Nuclear Bomb*, p. 280.
6. Crile, *Charlie Wilson's War*, pp. 420-421.
7. Kux, *The United States and Pakistan*, p. 290; Lamb, *Waiting for Allah*, pp. 42, 223-234; Jalal, *The Struggle for Pakistan*, p. 256; Levy, *Deception*, pp. 131-132.
8. Abbas, *Pakistan's Drift Into Extremism*, pp. 122-123.
9. Akhund, *Trial and Error*, pp. 14-15; Nawaz, *Crossed Swords*, pp. 385, 392-393; Kux, *The United States and Pakistan*, pp. 290-291.
10. Nawaz, *Crossed Swords*, pp. 384-385.
11. Akhund, *Trial and Error*, p. 25.
12. Lamb, *Waiting for Allah*, p. 89; Kiessling, *Faith, Unity, Discipline*, pp. 71-72.
13. Kux, *The United States and Pakistan*, p. 292; Nawaz, *Crossed Swords*, pp. 397, 400-403; Kiessling, *Faith, Unity, Discipline*, pp. 64-65.
14. Akhund, *Trial and Error*, pp. 25-26.
15. Akhund, *Trial and Error*, p. 26; Nawaz, *Crossed Swords*, pp. 400-403.
16. Ziring, *Pakistan at the Crosscurrent of History*, p. 280; Nawaz, *Crossed Swords*,

p. 396; Weaver, *Pakistan in the Shadow of Jihad*, pp. 50–52; Lamb, *Waiting for Allah*, pp. 92–93; Kiessling, *Faith, Unity, Discipline*, pp. 64–65.
  17. Nawaz, *Crossed Swords*, pp. 403–404; Lamb, *Waiting for Allah*, pp. 38, 91.
  18. Nawaz, *Crossed Swords*, p. 400.
  19. Talbot, *Pakistan: A Modern History*, p. 46; Burki, *Pakistan Under the Military*, pp. 87.
  20. Kiessling, *Faith, Unity, Discipline*, p. 55.

Chapter 11

  1. Ziring, *Pakistan in the Twentieth Century*, p. 507.
  2. Frantz, *The Nuclear Jihadist*, p. 163.
  3. Weaver, *Pakistan in the Shadow of Jihad and Afghanistan*, p. 191; Haqqani, *Magnificent Delusions*, p. 277; Haqqani, *Pakistan Between Mosque and Military*, pp. 202, 207; Levy, *Deception*, p. 185; Jaffrelot, *The Pakistan Paradox*, p. 241.
  4. Ziring, *Pakistan in the Twentieth Century*, p. 510; Akhund, Iqbal, *Trial and Error*, pp. 39–40, 305.
  5. Akhund, Iqbal, *Trial and Error*, pp. 43–45.
  6. Akhund, *Trial and Error*, p. 318.
  7. Frantz, *The Nuclear Jihadist*, pp. 181–182.
  8. Akhund, *Trial and Error*, pp. 70–71.
  9. Ziring, *Pakistan in the Twentieth Century*, pp. 510–511, 520.
  10. Ziring, *Pakistan in the Twentieth Century*, pp. 512–513.
  11. Akhund, *Trial and Error*, pp. 53, 68.
  12. Akhund, *Trial and Error*, p. 297.
  13. Lamb, *Waiting for Allah*, pp. 178–179, 181, 282–283.
  14. Ziring, *Pakistan in the Twentieth Century*, pp. 555–556, 563–564; Munoz, Heraldo, *Getting Away with Murder*, pp. 64–65.
  15. Ziring, *Pakistan in the Twentieth Century*, pp. 515, 517.
  16. Akhund, *Trial and Error*, p. 307; Burki, *Pakistan Under the Military*, p. 191; Levy, *Deception*, pp. 188–189; Lamb, *Waiting for Allah*, pp. 40, 109, 286.
  17. Peters, Greetchen, *Seeds of Terror*, p. 60; Lamb, *Waiting for Allah*, pp. 195–197.
  18. Lamb, *Waiting for Allah*, pp. 170, 172–174, 192–197.
  19. Kiessling, *Faith, Unity, Discipline*, pp. 87–88.
  20. Lamb, *Waiting for Allah*, pp. 270–272.
  21. Haqqani, *Pakistan Between Mosque and Military*, p. 209; Levy, *Deception*, pp. 191–192; Akmund, *Trial and Error*, p. 60.
  22. Jones, Owen, *Pakistan: Eye of the Storm*, p. 231–235.
  23. Jones, *Pakistan: Eye of the Storm*, pp. 231–233.
  24. Abbas, *Pakistan's Drift Into Extremism*, pp. 12–13.
  25. Ziring, *Pakistan in the Twentieth Century*, p. 536.
  26. Kux, *The United States and Pakistan*, p. 323; Nawaz, *Crossed Swords*, p. 371; Rashid, Ahmed, *Taliban*, p. 122; Rashid, *Descent Into Chaos*, p. 332; Griffin, Michael, *Reaping the Whirlwind*, p. 122.
  27. Peters, Greetchen, *Seeds of Terror*, p. 60; Lamb, *Waiting for Allah*, pp. 195–197.
  28. Bradsher, Henry S., *Afghan Communism and Soviet Intervention*, Oxford, 1999, pp. 347–348.
  29. Akhund, Iqbal, *Trial and Error*, p. 172.
  30. Akhund, *Trial and Error*, p. 177.
  31. Akhund, Iqbal, *Trial and Error*, p. 176.
  32. Levy, *Deception*, pp. 193–194, 199–200; Nawaz, *Crossed Swords*, p. 424; Ziring, *Pakistan in the Twentieth Century*, p. 517; Hussain, Zahid, *Frontline Pakistan*, p. 24.
  33. Akhund, *Trial and Error*, p. 20; Munoz, *Getting Away with Murder*, pp. 60–61; Jaffrelot, *The Pakistan Paradox*, pp. 400–401; Bhutto, *Reconciliation*, p. 326.
  34. Akhund, Iqbal, *Trial and Error*, pp. 280–281; Ziring, *Pakistan in the Twentieth Century*, pp. 518–519.
  35. Frantz, *The Nuclear Jihadist*, pp. 170–171; Levy, *Deception*, pp. 200–201; Haqqani, *Magnificent Delusions*, p. 279; Haqqani, *Pakistan Between Mosque and Military*, p. 216.
  36. Bose, *The Challenge in Kashmir*, p. 45; Bose, *Transforming India*, p. 275.
  37. Bose, *The Challenge in Kashmir*, p. 173.
  38. Bose, *The Challenge in Kashmir*, p. 173.
  39. Jones, *Pakistan: Eye of the Storm*, p. 215.
  40. Perkovich, George, *India's Nuclear Bomb*, p. 310.
  41. Bose, *Kashmir, Roots of Conflict, Paths to Peace*, pp. 113–114, 128.

42. Bose, *Kashmir, Roots of Conflict*, pp. 113–114.
43. Haqqani, *Pakistan Between Mosque and Military*, pp. 289–290; Bose, *Kashmir, Roots of Conflict*, pp. 106–107, 129.
44. Lamb, *Waiting for Allah*, pp. 161, 289.
45. Lamb, *Waiting for Allah*, p. 136.
46. Ziring, Pakistan in the Twentieth Century, p. 523.
47. Frantz, *The Nuclear Jihadist*, p. 185; Burki, *Pakistan Under the Military*, p. 130; Hussain, Zahid, *Frontline Pakistan*, p. 24; Lamb, *Waiting for Allah*, p. 290.
48. Akhund, Iqbal, *Trial and Error*, pp. 305, 307.
49. Kiessling, *Faith, Unity, Discipline*, p. 117.

Chapter 12

1. Kiessling, *Faith, Unity, Discipline*, pp. 118–121; Abbas, *Pakistan's Drift Into Extremism*, p. 142; Levy, *Deception*, p. 217; Nawaz, *Crossed Swords*, pp. 435–436; Haqqani, *Pakistan Between Mosque and Military*, p. 219.
2. Ispahani, *Purifying the Land of the Pure*, p. 170.
3. Ahmad, Mushtaq, *Nawaz Sharif*, pp. 4–5.
4. Ahmad, Mushtaq, *Nawaz Sharif*, p. 146.
5. Jaffrelot, *The Pakistan Paradox*, p. 492, 614.
6. Ziring, *Pakistan in the Twentieth Century*, p. 534.
7. Ahmad, Mushtaq, *Nawaz Sharif*, pp. 162–166.
8. Ahmad, Mushtaq, *Nawaz Sharif*, p. 122.
9. Ahmad, Mushtaq, *Nawaz Sharif*, pp. 153–155.
10. Ahmad, Mushtaq, *Nawaz Sharif*, pp. 143–145; Ziring, *Pakistan in the Twentieth Century*, p. 551.
11. Nawaz, *Crossed Swords*, pp. 467–468; Gul, *The Unholy Nexus*, pp. 16–17; Haqqani, *Pakistan Between Mosque and Military*, p. 292; Hussain, *Frontline Pakistan*, p. 27.
12. Abbas, *Pakistan's Drift Into Extremism*, p. 147; Kiessling, *Faith, Unity, Discipline*, pp. 102–103; Talbot, *India and Pakistan*, p. 262.
13. Ziring, *Pakistan in the Twentieth Century*, p. 540.
14. Kux, Dennis, *The United States and Pakistan*, p. 322; Hussain, Zahid, *Frontline Pakistan*, p. 27.
15. Ziring, *Pakistan in the Twentieth Century*, p. 541; Talbot, *Pakistan: A Modern History*, p. 325.
16. Ziring, *Pakistan in the Twentieth Century*, pp. 542–543.
17. Ziring, *Pakistan in the Twentieth Century*, p. 543.
18. Ziring, *Pakistan in the Twentieth Century*, p. 545; Cohen, *The Idea of Pakistan*, p. 252.
19. Frantz, *The Nuclear Jihadist*, pp. 254–255.
20. Frantz, *The Nuclear Jihadist*, pp. 180–181, 254.
21. Frantz, *The Nuclear Jihadist*, pp. 202–203.
22. Franz, Douglas, *The Nuclear Jihadist*, pp. 207–208.
23. Frantz, *The Nuclear Jihadist*, pp. 207–209.
24. Frantz, *The Nuclear Jihadist*, pp. 223–227.

Chapter 13

1. Ziring, *Pakistan in the Twentieth Century*, p. 558.
2. Ziring, *Pakistan in the Twentieth Century*, pp. 556–567.
3. Bhutto, *Reconciliation*, pp. 334, 493–495.
4. Ispahani, *Purifying the Land of the Pure*, p. 180.
5. Kiessling, *Faith, Unity, Discipline*, pp. 118–122.
6. Ziring, *Pakistan in the Twentieth Century*, pp. 565–566.
7. Matinuddin, Kamal, *The Taliban Phenomenon*, pp. 25–26.
8. Coll, Steve, *Directorate S*, p. 167.
9. Kiessling, *Faith, Unity, Discipline*, pp. 147–148.
10. Gul, Imtiaz, *The Al Qaeda Connection*, pp. 217–218.
11. Kiessling, Hein, *Faith, Unity, Discipline*, p. 149; Rashid, Ahmed, *Taliban*, pp. 28–29.
12. Nojumi, Neamatollah, *The Rise of the Taliban in Afghanistan*, p. 134.
13. Rashid, Ahmed, *Taliban*, p. 29.
14. Kux, *The United States and Pakistan*, p. 329; Levy, *Deception*, p. 253.
15. Bose, *Kashmir, Roots of Conflict*, pp. 133–134.

16. Levy, Adrian, *Deception*, p. 253-254.
17. Rashid, Ahmed, *Taliban*, p. 25.
18. Ispahani, *Purifying the Land of the Pure*, p. 197.
19. Peters, Gretchen, *Seeds of Terror*, p. 79.
20. Jaffrelot, *The Pakistan Paradox*, p. 506.
21. Gul, Imtiaz, *The Al Qaeda Connection*, pp. 219-222.
22. Soufan, Ali, *Anatomy of Terror*, pp. 65-67.
23. Jaffrelot, *The Pakistan Paradox*, pp. 505-506.
24. Soufan, Ali, *Anatomy of Terror*, p. 69.
25. Bergen, ed., *Talibanistan*, pp. 142-143.
26. Ziring, *Pakistan in the Twentieth Century*, p. 569.
27. Ziring, Pakistan in the Twentieth Century, p. 570
28. Munoz, *Getting Away with Murder*, p. 67; Ziring, *Pakistan in the Twentieth Century*, pp. 563, 571, 585; Kux, *The United States and Pakistan*, p. 337.
29. Akhund, *Trial and Error*, pp. xv-xvi; Munoz, *Getting Away with Murder*, p. 66; Ziring, *Pakistan in the Twentieth Century*, p. 575; Kux, *The United States and Pakistan*, p. 338.
30. Ziring, *Pakistan in the Twentieth Century*, pp. 575-577.
31. Kiessling, *Faith, Unity, Discipline*, pp. 130-131.

Chapter 14

1. Nawaz, Shuja, *Crossed Swords*, p. 490.
2. Haqqani, *Pakistan Between Mosque and Military*, p. 319.
3. Rashid, *Pakistan on the Brink*, pp. 59, 61.
4. Gul, *The Al Qaeda Connection*, p. 227.
5. Soufan, Ali, *Anatomy of Terror*, pp. 76-77.
6. Abbas, *Pakistan's Drift Into Extremism*, p. 180; Rahid, *Descent Into Chaos*, p. 45; Coll, *Ghost Wars*, pp. 438-439; Hussain, *Frontline Pakistan*, p. 4; Musharraf, *In the Line of Fire*, p. 84.
7. Haqqani, *Pakistan Between Mosque and Military*, p. 251; Riedel, Bruce, *The Search for Al Qaeda*, Washington, 2008 p. 72.
8. Haqqani, Husain, *Pakistan Between Mosque and Military*, p. 251.
9. Haqqani, Husain, *Pakistan Between Mosque and Military*, p. 250.
10. Nawaz, Shuja, *Crossed Swords*, p. 517.
11. Haqqani, Husain, *Pakistan Between Mosque and Military*, p. 253.
12. Musharraf, Pervez, *In the Line of Fire*, pp. 102-106.

Chapter 15

1. Abbas, *Pakistan's Drift Into Extremism*, pp. 235-236.
2. Jaffrelot, *The Pakistan Paradox*, p. 339.
3. Levy, *Deception*, p. 396.
4. Talbot, *Pakistan: A Modern History*, pp. 386-387; Jalal, *The Struggle for Pakistan*, p. 312; Ziring, *Pakistan at the Crosscurrent of History*, p. 266.
5. Jaffrelot, *A History of Pakistan and Its Origins*, p. 265.
6. Jalal, *The Struggle for Pakistan*, p. 313; Abbas, *Pakistan's Drift Into Extremism*, p. 184.
7. Weaver, *Pakistan in the Shadow of Jihad and Afghanistan*, p. 23; Jones, *Pakistan: Eye of the Storm*, pp. 286-290.
8. Rashid, *Descent Into Chaos*, p. 51.
9. Bose, *Kashmir, Roots of Conflict*, p. 161; Bose, *Transforming India*, p. 281.
10. Jalal, Ayesha, *The Struggle for Pakistan*, p. 317.
11. Riedel, Bruce, *The Search for Al Qaeda*, pp. 119-121.
12. Jaffrelot, *A History of Pakistan and Its Origins*, pp. 266-267.
13. Jaffrelot, *A History of Pakistan and Its Origins*, pp. 266-267.
14. Jaffrelot, *The Pakistan Paradox*, p. 346.
15. Talbot, *Pakistan: A Modern History*, pp. 382-385.
16. Gul, *The Al Qaeda Connection*, pp. 221-223.
17. Levy, *Deception*, pp. 304-305; Rashid, *Descent Into Chaos*, p. 59.
18. Frantz, *The Nuclear Jihadist*, pp. 253-255.
19. Frantz, *The Nuclear Jihadist*, pp. 253-257.
20. Levy, *Deception*, pp. 308-309.
21. Gul, *The Unholy Nexus*, p. 84; Talbot, *Pakistan: A Modern History*, p. 390; Jones, *Pakistan: Eye of the Storm*, p. 24.
22. Jaffrelot, *The Pakistan Paradox*, p. 529.

Chapter 16

23. Gall, Carlotta, *The Wrong Enemy*, pp. 52–53.

1. Kiessling, Hein, *Faith, Unity, Discipline*, p. 183.
2. Soufan, Ali, *Anatomy of Terror*, p. 90; Scott-Clark, *The Exile*, p. 47.
3. Soufan, Ali, *Anatomy of Terror*, pp. 86–89; Ziring, *Pakistan at the Crosscurrent of History*, p. 354.
4. Afzal, *Pakistan Under Siege*, p. 12.
5. Jones, Seth, *In the Graveyard of Empires*, pp. 88–89; Nawaz, *Crossed Swords*, pp. 541–542; Musharraf, *In the Line of Fire*, pp. 204–206.
6. Rashid, *Descent Into Chaos*, pp. 29–30; Hussain, *Frontline Pakistan*, p. 41; Levy, *Deception*, p. 313; Musharraf, *In the Line of Fire*, pp. 202–203.
7. Scott-Clark, *The Exile*, p. 33; Kiessling, *Faith, Unity, Discipline*, p. 179.
8. Gopal, Anana, *No Good Men Among the Living*, New York 2014, p. 62.
9. Hussain, *Frontline Pakistan*, p. 43.
10. Levy, *Deception*, pp. 87–88.
11. Kiessling, *Faith, Unity, Discipline*, pp. 180–181.
12. Hussain, *Frontline Pakistan*, p. 46; Kiessling, *Faith, Unity, Discipline*, p. 185.
13. Rashid, *Descent Into Chaos*, pp. 80–81.
14. Scott-Clark, *The Exile*, pp. 35–36.
15. Blehm, Eric, *The Only Thing Worth Dying For*, pp. 63, 76, 104–111; Gopal, Anand, *No Good Men Among the Living*, pp. 35–43.
16. Blehm, Eric, *The Only Thing Worth Dying For*, pp. 131–137.
17. Rashid, *Descent Into Chaos*, pp. 91–92; Jalal, *The Struggle for Pakistan*, pp. 326–327.
18. Rashid, Ahmed, *Descent Into Chaos*, p. 93.
19. Rashid, Ahmed, *Descent Into Chaos*, p. 96.
20. Gall, Carlotta, *The Wrong Enemy*, p. 34.
21. Fury, Dalton, *Kill Bin Laden*, New York, 2008, p. 239.
22. Fury, *Kill Bin Laden*, pp. 220–226.
23. Fury, Dalton, *Kill Bin Laden*, pp. 260, 262.
24. Soufan, *Anatomy of Terror*, pp. 277–279; Scott-Clark, *The Exile*, pp. 146–147, 301, 470.
25. Scott-Clark, *The Exile*, p. 132.
26. Gall, Carlotta, *The Wrong Enemy*, pp. 74–75.
27. Gopal, Anand, *No Good Men Among the Living*, pp. 189–190, 197.
28. 28. Gopal, *No Good Men Among the Living*, pp. 194, 196–197.
29. Gopal, Anand, *No Good Men Among the Living*, p. 195.
30. Gul, *The Most Dangerous Place*, p. 12; Bergen, *Talibanistan*, p. 133; Jaffrelot, *The Pakistan Paradox*, pp. 560.
31. Nawaz, *Crossed Swords*, p. 544.
32. Rashid, *Descent Into Chaos*, pp. 221–222.
33. Rashid, *Descent Into Chaos*, pp. 248–249.
34. Coll, Steve, *Directorate S*, pp. 151–152.
35. Coll, Steve, *Directorate S*, p. 150.
36. Munoz, Heraldo, *Getting Away with Murder*, p. 109.
37. Rashid, Ahmed, *Descent Into Chaos*, pp. 221–222.
38. Munoz, Heraldo, *Getting Away with Murder*, p. 111.
39. Khalilzad, Zalmay, *The Envoy*, pp.133–134.
40. Partlow, Joshua, *A Kingdom of Their Own*, p. 386.
41. Jaffrelot, *The Pakistan Paradox*, p. 534.
42. Hussain, *The Scorpion's Tail*, pp. 36–38; Jones, Seth, *In the Graveyard of Empires*, pp. 104–105; Gall, *The Wrong Enemy*, pp. 177–178.
43. Isby, *Afghanistan*, p. 249.
44. Hussain, *Frontline Pakistan*, pp. 59–60.
45. Hussain, Zahid, *Frontline Pakistan*, p. 59; Constable, Pamela, *Playing with Fire*, p. 87.
46. Isby, *Afghanistan*, p. 251.
47. Soufan, Ali, *Anatomy of Terror*, p. 104.
48. Cohen, *The Idea of Pakistan*, p. 208.
49. Hussain, *Frontline Pakistan*, pp. 127–128; Rahid, *Descent Into Chaos*, p. 155.
50. Scott-Clark, *The Exile*, pp. 116–117, 146.
51. Hussain, *Frontline Pakistan*, p. 99; Ziring, *Pakistan at the Crosscurrent of History*, p. 337.
52. Rashid, Ahmed, *Descent Into Chaos*, p. 149.
53. Coll, Steve, *Directorate S*, pp. 173–174.

54. Coll, *Directorate S*, pp. 170-171.
55. Weaver, *Pakistan in the Shadow of Jihad and Afghanistan*, p. 215; Rashid, *Descent Into Chaos*, p. 215; Markey, *No Exit from Pakistan*, p. 116.
56. Munoz, Heraldo, *Getting Away with Murder*, p. 109.
57. Jaffrelot, *The Pakistan Paradox*, p. 350.
58. Jalal, Ayesha, *The Struggle for Pakistan*, p. 331.
59. Hussain, Zahid, *Frontline Pakistan*, p. 175; Rashid, Ahmed, *Descent Into Chaos*, p. 156.
60. Bergen, Peter, *Talibanistan*. p. 266.
61. Bergen, Peter, *Talibanistan*, pp. 266-267; Jaffrelot, *The Pakistan Paradox*, p. 568.

Chapter 17

1. Rahid, *Descent Into Chaos*, p. XLI.
2. Chua, Amy, "Group Identity Is All," *Foreign Affairs*, July/August 2018, pp. 28-29.
3. Gopal, Anand, *No Good Men Among the Living*, pp. 194-197.
4. Peters, *Seeds of Terror*, pp. 139-140; Rashid, *Pakistan on the Brink*, pp. 50-51.
5. Scott-Clark, *The Exile*, p. 246.
6. Bergen, *Talibanistan*, pp. 344-345.
7. Jones, Seth, *in the Graveyard of Empires*, p. 115.
8. Jones, Seth, *In the Graveyard of Empires*, pp. 118-124.
9. Gall, *The Wrong Enemy*, p. 74.
10. Jaffrelot, *The Pakistan Paradox*, pp. 536-539.
11. Frantz, *The Nuclear Jihadist*, pp. 271-272.
12. Frantz, *The Nuclear Jihadist*, p. 243.
13. Frantz, *The Nuclear Jihadist*, p. 294.
14. Frantz, *The Nuclear Jihadist*, pp. 303-304.
15. Frantz, *The Nuclear Jihadist*, p. 310.
16. Frantz, *The Nuclear Jihadist*, pp. 312-313.
17. Frantz, *The Nuclear Jihadist*, p. 321.
18. Frantz, *The Nuclear Jihadist*, pp. 337-339, 342.
19. Levy, *Deception*, pp. 388-389; Rashid, *Pakistan on the Brink*, p. 63; Nawaz, *Crossed Swords*, pp. 554-555.
20. Frantz, *The Nuclear Jihadist*, pp. 341-346.
21. Musharraf, Pervez, *In the Line of Fire*, p. 246.
22. Musharraf, Pervez, *In the Line of Fire*, pp. 246-257.
23. Rashid, *Descent Into Chaos*, p. 270; Hussain, *The Scorpion's Tail*, p. 65; Gall, *The Wrong Enemy*, pp. 84-85.
24. Scott-Clark, *The Exile*, pp. 218-219, 222-223; Coll, *Directorate S*, pp. 208-209.
25. Coll, *Directorate S*, p. 210.
26. Gul, *The Al Qaeda Connection*, pp. 27, 122-123.
27. Cloughley, *A History of the Pakistan Army*, p. 348.
28. Rashid, *Descent Into Chaos*, p. 275.
29. Jaffrelot, *The Pakistan Paradox*, pp. 592-593.
30. Jones, Seth, *In the Graveyard of Empires*, p. 262; Scott-Clark, *The Exile*, p. 225.
31. Bergen, *Talibanistan*, p. 167.
32. Coll, Steve, *Directorate S*, p. 285.
33. Gul, *The Al Qaeda Connection*, p. 234.
34. Rashid, Ahmed, *Pakistan on the Brink*, p. 165.
35. Rashid, *Pakistan on the Brink*, pp. 164-165.
36. Rashid, Ahmed, *Descent Into Chaos*, p. 291.
37. Gul, *The Most Dangerous Place*, pp. 171, 174, 185.
38. Markey, *No Exit from Pakistan*, p. 44.
39. Scott-Clark, *The Exile*, pp. 223-224.
40. Rashid, *Descent Into Chaos*, p. 275.
41. Coll, *Directorate S*, pp. 261-265; Gul, *The Al Qaeda Connection*, pp. 135-139, 145-148.
42. Coll, *Directorate S*, p. 226.
43. Isby, *Afghanistan*, p. 269.
44. Rashid, *Descent Into Chaos*, pp. 277-278, 384; Hussain, *The Scorpion's Tail*, pp. 86-87; Jalal, *The Struggle for Pakistan*, pp. 339-340; Gul, *The Al Qaeda Connection*, pp. 64, 67.
45. Rashid, *Descent Into Chaos*, pp. 290-291; Nawaz, *Crossed Swords*, pp. 557-558.
46. Rashid, *Descent Into Chaos*, pp. 290-291; Nawaz, *Crossed Swords*, pp. 557-558.
47. Rashid, *Descent Into Chaos*, pp. 381-382; Jalal, *The Struggle for Pakistan*, p. 141; Constable, *Playing with Fire*, p. 160.
48. Hussain, *The Scorpion's Tail*, p. 111; Gall, *The Wrong Enemy*, p. 167; Constable, *Playing with Fire*, pp. 107-108.
49. Coll, *Directorate S*, p. 346.
50. Gul, Imtiaz, *The Al Qaeda Connection*, pp. 58-59; Bergen, *Talibanistan*, p. 188.
51. Afzal, *Pakistan Under Siege*, p. 46; Jaf-

frelot, *The Pakistan Paradox*, p. 577; Markey, *No Exit from Pakistan*, pp. 131, 139–140.
52. Constable, *Playing with Fire*, pp. 27–28.
53. Musharraf, Pervez, *In the Line of Fire*, pp. 122–123.
54. Coll, *Directorate S*, p. 283.
55. Hussain, *The Scorpion's Tail*, p. 129; Gall, *The Wrong Enemy*, p. 174; Rashid, *Descent Into Chaos*, pp. 376–377.
56. Scott-Clark, *The Exile*, p. 2; Rashid, *Descent Into Chaos*, p. 387; Hussain, *The Scorpion's Tail*, p. 129.
57. Jalal, *The Struggle for Pakistan*, p. 345; Bhutto, *Reconciliation*, pp. 6–9, 219; Gall, *The Wrong Enemy*, pp. 174–175.
58. Bhutto, *Reconciliation*, p. 354.
59. Rashid, *Descent Into Chaos*, p. 375; Hussain, *The Scorpion's Tail*, pp. 136–137; Constable, *Playing with Fire*, p. 165; Bhutto, *Reconciliation*, pp. 220–221.
60. Bhutto, Benazir, *Reconciliation*, pp. 14–15, 222, 360; Hussain, Zahid, *The Scorpion's Tail*, p. 138.
61. Constable, *Playing with Fire*, p. 222.
62. Jaffrelot, *The Pakistan Paradox*, p. 421.
63. Jaffrelot, *Pakistan at the Crossroads*, p. 75.
64. Bhutto, *Reconciliation*, p. 360.
65. Kiessling, Hein, *Faith, Unity, Discipline*, p. 200.
66. Isby, *Afghanistan*, p. 256.
67. Hussain, *The Scorpion's Tail*, pp. 92–102; Rashid, *Descent Into Chaos*, p. 385; Gul, *The Most Dangerous Place*, pp. 243–244; Constable, *Playing with Fire*, pp. 183–186.
68. Constable, Pamela, *Playing with Fire*, p. 118.
69. Kiessling, *Faith, Unity, Discipline*, p. 227.
70. Rashid, *Pakistan on the Brink*, p. 147.
71. Jaffrelot, *The Pakistan Paradox*, pp. 593–595, 603; Constable, *Playing with Fire*, p. 119.
72. Hussain, *The Scorpion's Tail*, pp. 135–136; Gul, *The Most Dangerous Place*, pp. 38–41; Constable, *Playing with Fire*, p. 191; Gul, *The Al Qaeda Connection*, p. 51.
73. Isby, *Afghanistan*, p. 264; Gul, *The Al Qaeda Connection*, pp. 55–63.
74. Afzal, *Pakistan Under Siege*, pp. 8–9.
75. Munoz, *Getting Away with Murder*, pp. 33–34.
76. Rashid, *Descent Into Chaos*, pp. 374–375; Hussain, *The Scorpion's Tail*, pp. 140–141; Gall, *The Wrong Enemy*, p. 179; Gul, *The Most Dangerous Place*, p. 226.
77. Constable, *Playing with Fire*, pp. 224–225.
78. Bhutto, *Reconciliation*, pp. 404–444, 461–475.
79. Kiessling, *Faith, Unity, Discipline*, p. 204.
80. Jalal, Ayesha, *The Struggle for Pakistan*, p. 350; Hussain, Zahid, *The Scorpion's Tail*, p. 143.
81. Constable, *Playing with Fire*, pp. 226–227.
82. Scott-Clark, *The Exile*, p. 311.

Chapter 18

1. Ispahani, *Purifying the Land of the Pure*, pp. 222–224.
2. Rashid, *Pakistan on the Brink*, p. 167.
3. Jaffrelot, *The Pakistan Paradox*, p. 611.
4. Coll, *Directorate S*, pp. 308–309; Kiessling, *Faith, Unity, Discipline*, p. 211; Munoz, *Getting Away with Murder*, p. 179; Bergen, *Talibanistan*, p. 148.
5. Coll, *Directorate S*, p. 325.
6. Coll, *Directorate S*, pp. 310–311.
7. Rashid, *Pakistan on the Brink*, p. 65; Gul, *The Most Dangerous Place*, pp. 83–85.
8. Nawaz, *Crossed Swords*, pp. 557–559; Hussain, *The Scorpion's Tail*, p. 144; Rashid, *Descent Into Chaos*, pp. 290–291.
9. Jaffrelot, *Pakistan at the Crossroads*, p. 70.
10. Rashid, *Pakistan on the Brink*, p. 137.
11. Constable, Pamela, *Playing with Fire*, pp. 268–269.
12. Rashid, *Pakistan on the Brink*, pp. 138–140.
13. Coll, *Directorate S*, pp. 342–343.
14. Coll, *Directorate S*, pp. 343–345; Haqqani, *Magnificent Delusions*, pp. 329–332; Rashid, *Pakistan on the Brink*, pp. 57–58; Jaffrelot, *The Pakistan Paradox*, pp. 590–591.
15. Coll, *Directorate S*, p. 346; Jalal, *The Struggle for Pakistan*, p. 355; Rashid, *Pakistan on the Brink*, p. 58; Kiessling, *Faith, Unity, Discipline*, pp. 215–216.
16. Markey, *No Exit from Pakistan*, pp. 24, 157.
17. Scott-Clark, *The Exile*, p. 319.
18. Rashid, *Pakistan on the Brink*, p. 171.
19. Isby, *Afghanistan*, p. 269.
20. Rashid, *Pakistan on the Brink*, pp.

139-140; Gul, *The Most Dangerous Place*, p. xiii.
21. Constable, Pamela, *Playing with Fire*, p. 231.
22. Constable, Pamela, *Playing with Fire*, p. 232.
23. Jaffrelot, *The Pakistan Paradox*, p. 435; De Mesquita, *The Dictator's Handbook*, New York, 2011, p. 188.
24. Constable, *Playing with Fire*, p. 233.
25. Partlow, *A Kingdom of Their Own*, p. 41.
26. Partlow, *A Kingdom of Their Own*, p. 10; Khalilzad, *The Envoy*, p. 223.
27. Woodward, Bob, *Obama's Wars*, New York, 2010, p, 387.
28. Hussain, *The Scorpion's Tail*, pp. 11, 185.
29. Rashid, *Pakistan on the Brink*, p. 142.
30. Rashid, *Pakistan on the Brink*, pp. 143-144; Kiessling, *Faith, Unity, Discipline*, p. 206; Constable, *Playing with Fire*, p. 120.
31. Rashid, *Pakistan on the Brink*, pp. 143-144.
32. Bergen, *Talibanistan*, p. 307.
33. Rashid, *Pakistan on the Brink*, p. 143.
34. Hussain, *The Scorpion's Tail*, pp. 167-168; Rashid, *Pakistan on the Brink*, p. 62; Gall, *The Wrong Enemy*, pp. 171-172.
35. Hussain, Zahid, *The Scorpion's Tail*, pp. 174-178.
36. Haqqani, *Magnificent Delusions*, pp. 334-335; Hussain, *The Scorpion's Tail*, pp. 181-183.
37. Scott-Clark, *The Exile*, pp. 326-329,336-337.
38. Bergen, *Talibanistan*, pp. 238, 242.
39. Bergen, Peter, *Talibanistan*, pp. 234, 242.
40. Bergen, *Talibanistan*, p. 232.
41. Bergen, Peter, *Talibanistan*, p. 246.
42. Kiessling, *Faith, Unity, Discipline*, p. 222; Rashid, *Pakistan on the Brink*, pp. 133-134.
43. Coll, Steve, *Directorate S*. pp. 450-451.
44. Rashid, *Pakistan on the Brink*, pp. 154-155.
45. Bergen, *Talibanistan*, pp. 182-183; Rashid, *Pakistan on the Brink*, p. 154.
46. Jaffrelot, *Pakistan at the Crossroads*, pp. 48, 96-97.
47. Constable, *Playing with Fire*, pp. 235, 270-271.
48. Constable, *Playing with Fire*, p. 271.
49. Rashid, *Pakistan on the Brink*, pp. 152-153.
50. Constable, Pamela, *Playing with Fire*, pp. 271-272.
51. Rashid, *Pakistan on the Brink*, p. 157; Constable, *Playing with Fire*, p. 246.
52. Rashid, *Pakistan on the Brink*, pp. 157-158.
53. Rashid, *Pakistan on the Brink*, p. 161.
54. Constable, *Playing with Fire*, pp. 42-43.
55. Rashid, *Pakistan on the Brink*, p. 154.
56. Jaffrelot, Christophe, *Pakistan at the Crossroads*, p. 202.
57. 57. Gopal, *No Good Men Among the Living*, pp. 192-193.
58. Jaffrelot, *Pakistan at the Crossroads*, p. 202; Hussain, Zahid, *The Scorpion's Tail*, pp. 202-204; Rashid, *Pakistan on the Brink*, pp. 130-132.
59. Rashid, *Pakistan on the Brink*, p. 130.
60. Coll, *Directorate S*, pp. 505-508.
61. Rashid, *Pakistan on the Brink*, pp. 117-119.
62. Coll, *Directorate S*, p. 514.
63. Rashid, *Pakistan on the Brink*, pp. 53-54.
64. Coll, *Directorate S*, p. 515; Scott-Clark, *The Exile*, p. 380.
65. Ispahani, *Purifying the Land of the Pure*, pp. 228-229; Rashid, *Pakistan on the Brink*, p. 162; Jalal, *The Struggle for Pakistan*, p. 362.
66. Rashid, *Pakistan on the Brink*, pp. 162-164.
67. Rashid, *Pakistan on the Brink*, p. 171; Gall, *The Wrong Enemy*, pp. 258-259.
68. Coll, *Directorate S*, pp. 515-516.
69. Coll, *Directorate S*, pp. 518-519.
70. Kiessling, *Faith, Unity, Discipline*, p. 221.
71. Coll, *Directorate S*, pp. 527-529.
72. Rashid, *Pakistan on the Brink*, p. 172.
73. Scott-Clark, *The Exile*, pp. 319-321, 360-367; Rashid, *Pakistan on the Brink*, pp. 5-6; Gall, *The Wrong Enemy*, pp. 242-245.
74. Rashid, *Pakistan on the Brink*, pp. 5-6; Gall, *The Wrong Enemy*, pp. 242-245.
75. O'Neill, Robert, *The Operator*, New York, 2017, pp. 309-310.
76. O'Neill, Robert, *The Operator*, New York, 2017, pp. 309-310.
77. Kiessling, *Faith, Unity, Discipline*, pp. 224-225.
78. Scott-Clark, *The Exile*, p. 430; Jaffrelot, *Pakistan at the Crossroads*, p. 248.
79. Haqqani, *Magnificent Delusions*, pp. 345-346; Rashid, *Pakistan on the Brink*, pp.

8–9; Jaffrelot, *Pakistan at the Crossroads*, pp. 247–248; Gall, *The Wrong Enemy*, p. 256.
80. Rashid, *Pakistan on the Brink*, pp. 147–148, 177.
81. Coll, *Directorate S*, pp. 551–553; Gall, *The Wrong Enemy*, pp. 247–253.
82. Scott-Clark, *The Exile*, pp. 451–452, 491–492.
83. Bergen, *Talibanistan*, pp. 391, 399–401.
84. Scott-Clark, *The Exile*, p. 439; Jaffrelot, Christophe, *The Pakistan Paradox*, pp. 266–267.
85. Rashid, *Pakistan on the Brink*, p.178.
86. Jaffrelot, *Pakistan at the Crossroads*, pp. 252–253.
87. Rashid, *Pakistan on the Brink*, pp. 178–180; Scott-Clark, *The Exile*, pp. 435–436.
88. Jaffrelot, *Pakistan at the Crossroads*, p. 45.
89. Rashid, *Pakistan on the Brink*, p. 151.
90. Rashid, *Pakistan on the Brink*, p 148.
91. Rashid, *Pakistan on the Brink*, pp. 149–150.
92. Rashid, *Pakistan on the Brink*, pp. 148–149, 174–175; Coll, *Directorate S*, pp. 439–440.
93. Rashid, *Pakistan on the Brink*, pp. 150–151.
94. Rashid, *Pakistan on the Brink*, p. 180.
95. Rashid, *Pakistan on the Brink*, p. 180.
96. Coll, *Directorate S*, pp. 575–576; Rashid, *Pakistan on the Brink*, pp. 180–181.
97. Jaffrelot, *Pakistan at the Crossroads*, p. 246.
98. Coll, *Directorate S*, pp. 637–638, 676.
99. Jaffrelot, *Pakistan at the Crossroads*, pp. 849–853.

Chapter 19

1. Munoz, *Getting Away with Murder*, p. 225; Markey, *No Exit from Pakistan*, pp. 35–36.
2. Markey, *No Exit from Pakistan*, pp. 36–37.
3. Afzal, *Pakistan Under Siege*, p. 31.
4. Jaffrelot, *The Pakistan Paradox*, p. 179.
5. Kiesslling, Hein, *Faith, Unity, Discipline*, p. 243.
6. Jaffrelot, *The Pakistan Paradox*, p. 283.
7. Jaffrelot, *The Pakistan Paradox*, pp. 286–289; Kiessling, *Faith, Unity, Discipline*, pp. 233, 240, 244.
8. Coll, *Directorate S*, pp. 649–653.
9. Coll, *Directorate S*, pp. 668–669.
10. Soufan, *Anatomy of Terror*, p. 285.
11. Coll, *Directorate S*, pp. 657–659.
12. Jaffrelot, *The Pakistan Paradox*, p. 643
13. Afzal, *Pakistan Under Siege*, pp. 8–10, 30.
14. Jaffrelot, *The Pakistan Paradox*, p. 644.
15. Soufan, *Anatomy of Terror*, pp. 287–288.
16. Jaffrelot, *Pakistan at the Crossroads*, pp. 293–294.
17. Coll, *Directorate S*, pp. 676–677.
18. Afzal, *Pakistan Under Siege*, p. 140.
19. Afzal, *Pakistan Under Siege*, p. 153.

Epilogue

1. Ahmad, Mushtaq, *Nawaz Sharif*, pp. 122, 188, 188.
2. Afzal, *Pakistan Under Siege*, pp. 82–83.
3. Ahmad, *Government and Politics in Pakistan*, p. 292; Lamb, *Waiting for Allah*, pp. 170, 192–194.
4. Rashid, *Pakistan on the Brink*, pp. 59, 61.
5. Afzal, *Pakistan Under Siege*, p. 20.
6. Burki, *Pakistan Under the Military*, p. 155.
7. Afzal, *Pakistan Under Siege*, pp. 8–9, 20.

Bibliography

Abbas, Hassan, *Pakistan's Drift Into Extremism*, London: M.E. Sharpe, 2005.
Afzal, M. Rafique, *Pakistan History & Politics, 1947-1971*, Oxford, 2001.
Afzal, Madiha, *Pakistan Under Siege*, Haryana, India: Penguin, 2018.
Ahmad, Mushtaq, *Government and Politics in Pakistan*, Karachi: Royal Book Company, 2009.
_____ *Nawaz Sharif, Politics of Business*, Karachi: Royal Book Company, 2001.
Akhund, Iqbal, *Trial and Error: The Advent and Eclipse of Benazir Bhutto*, Oxford: Oxford University Press, 2000.
Bergen, Peter, ed., *Talibanistan*, New York, NY: Oxford University Press, 2013.
Bhutto, Benazir, *Daughter of Destiny*, New York ,1989.
_____. *Reconciliation*, New York, 2008.
Burke, S.M., *Pakistan's Foreign Policy*, Oxford, 1973.
Burki, Shahid, and Baxter, Craig, *Pakistan Under Bhutto, 1971-1977*, New York: St. Martin's Press, 1980.
_____. *Pakistan Under the Military*, Oxford, 1991.
Cloughley, Brian, *A History of the Pakistan Army*, 3rd ed., Karachi: Oxford University Press, 1999.
Cohen, Stephen P., *The Idea of Pakistan*, Washington, 2004.
Coll, Steve, *Directorate S: The CIA and America's Secret Wars in Afghanistan and Pakistan*, New York: Penguin, 2018.
_____. *Ghost Wars*, New York: Penguin, 2004.
Collins, Larry, and Lapierre, Dominique, *Freedom at Midnight*, NewYork, 1975.
Constable, Pamela, *Playing with Fire: Pakistan at War with Itself*, New York, 2011.
Crile, George, *Charlie Wilson's War*, New York, 2003.
Frantz, Douglas and Collins, Catherine, *The Nuclear Jihadist*, NewYork: Hachette Book Group, 2007.
Gall, Carlotta, *The Wrong Enemy*, Boston, 2014.
Girardet, Edward, *Killing the Cranes*, Vermont, 2001.
Gopal, Anand, *No Good Men Among the Living*, New York: Holt & Company, 1980.
Griffin, Michael, *Reaping the Whirlwind: Afghanistan, Al Qa'ida and the Holy War*, London, 2003.
Gul, Imtiaz,. *The Al Qaeda Connection*, Oxford, 2009.
_____. *The Most Dangerous Place. Pakistan's Lawless Frontier*, London: Penguin Books, 2010.
_____. *The Unholy Nexus: Pak-Afghan Relations Under the Taliban*, Lahore, 2002.
Haqqani, Husain, *Magnificent Delusions*, New York, 2013.

_____. *Pakistan Between Mosque and Military*, Washington, D.C.: Carnegie, 2005.
Hussain, Zahid, *Frontline Pakistan: The Struggle with Militant Islam*, New York, 2009.
_____. *The Scorpion's Tail: The Relentless Rise of Islamic Militants in Pakistan—and How It Threatens America*, New York, 2010.
Isby, David, *Afghanistan*, New York: Pegasus Books, 2010.
Ispahani, Farahnaz, *Purifying the Land of the Pure*, Noida, India: HarperCollins, 2015.
Jaffrelot, Christophe, *A History of Pakistan and Its Origins*, London: Anthem Press, 2004.
_____. *The Pakistan Paradox*, New York: Oxford University Press, 2015.
_____, editor. *Pakistan at the Crossroads*, New York, 2016.
Jalal, Ayesha, *The Struggle for Pakistan*, London, 2014.
Jones, Owen B., *Pakistan: Eye of the Storm*, New Haven, CT: Yale University Press, 2002.
Jones, Seth, *In the Graveyard of Empires*, New York, 2009.
Khalilzad, Zalmay, *The Envoy*, New York: St. Martin's Press, 2016.
Kiessling, Hein G., *Faith, Unity, Discipline: The Inter-Service-Intelligence (ISI) of Pakistan*, Noida: HarperCollins, 2016.
Kux, Dennis, *The United States and Pakistan*, Washington, D.C.: Woodrow Wilson Center Press, 2001.
Lamb, Christina, *Waiting for Allah*, London, 1991.
Lapping, Brian, *End of Empire*, New York, 1985.
Levy, Adrian and Scott-Clark, *Deception*, New York, 2007.
Markey, Daniel S., *No Exit from Pakistan*, Cambridge, 2013.
Matinuddin, Kamal, *The Taliban Phenomenon*, Oxford, 1999.
Munoz, Heraldo, *Getting Away with Murder*, New York, 2014.
Musharraf, Pervez, *In the Line of Fire*, New York, 2006.
Nawaz, Shuja, *Crossed Swords. Pakistan, Its Army, and the Wars Within*, New York: Oxford University Press, 2008.
Partlow, Joshua, *A Kingdom of Their Own*, New York: Alfred Knoff, 2016.
Peters, Gretchen, *Seeds of Terror: How Heroin Is Bankrolling the Taliban and Al Qaeda*, New York, 2009.
Rashid, Ahmed, *Descent Into Chaos: The U.S. and the Disaster in Pakistan, Afghanistan, and Central Asia*, London: Penguin, 2008.
_____. *Pakistan on the Brink*, London: Allen Lane, 2012.
_____. *Taliban*, New Haven: Yale University Press, 2000.
Raza, Rafi, *Bhutto and Pakistan, 1967–1977*, Oxford, 1977.
Soufan, Ali, *Anatomy of Terror*, New York: W.W. Norton, 2017.
Talbot, Ian, *India and Pakistan*, London, 2000.
_____. *Pakistan: A Modern History*, New York: St. Martin's, 1998.
Tunzelmann, Alex von, *Indian Summer*, New York, 2007.
Weaver, Mary A., *Pakistan in the Shadow of Jihad and Afghanistan*, New York: Farrar, Straus & Giroux, 2002.
Wolpert, Stanley, *Zulfi Bhutto of Pakistan*, New York: Oxford University Press, 1993.
Ziring, Lawrence, *Pakistan at the Crosscurrent of History*, Oxford: Oneworld Publication, 2003.
_____. *Pakistan in the Twentieth Century*, Karachi: Oxford University Press, 1997.

Index

Abdullah, Farooq ("Lion Cub"") 100, 141, 158
Abdullah, Sheik ("Lion of Kashmir") 28, 61, 99; death 100
Afghan High Peace Council (HPC) 232–233
Afghan-Soviet War: 116–117; additional funding 123–124; American support 117–118, 123; arms distribution 126; Geneva Accords 128–129; Soviet withdrawal 138; Stingers 128; Zia support 117
Afghanistan: 111; AIG 139; Constitution 187; Northern Alliance offensive 181–183; troop surges and withdrawals 225
Agartala Conspiracy 71
Agra Summit 177
Ahmadis 41, 97
Ahmed, Gen. Mahmood 170, 180, 181
AJK *see* Provisional Government of Azad (Free) Kashmir
Al-Jufikar organization (AZO) 119
Al-Qaeda: 200, 248; Al-Qaeda of the Indian Subcontinent AQIS) 247; embassy attacks (1998) 166, 177; escaped to Pakistan 183–184; New York attack (2001) 179; Osama bin Laden killed 235–236
Ali, Chaudhri Mohammad 46, 49
Alliance for the Restoration of Democracy (ARD) 175
amendments to 1973 Constitution: (1st) 96; (2nd) 97; (8th) 126; (13th) 163; (14th) 163–164; (17th) 199–200; (18th) 230–231; (20th) 239
Anti-Terror Law 164
Army: civilian duties 41; attacks on insurgents 192, 200, 216, 220, 226–228, 243
Aslam, Chaudary 243
Attock Conspiracy 93–94
Awami League (AL) 40, 50, 63

Awami National Party (ANP) 123, 217
Azhar, Maulana Massood 173
Aziz, Shaukat 202

Badaber air base 57–59, 70
Baghdad Pact 45
Bajaur Agency 213, 220
Baluchistan: insurgencies 30, 92–93, 202–203, 244; joins Pakistan 30
Baluchistan Bar Association 249
Baluchistan Liberation Army (BLA) 203
Bandung Conference 45
Bangladesh 80, 96
Basic Democracy system 57–58
Bhutto, Benazir: 111, 119, 122, 134–135; assassinated 215; exiled to Dubai 166–167; family feud 160; first dismissal 144; first term (1988) 34; foreign policy 136–137, 140–141, 155; husband Zardari 128, 160; legacy 144; returned home 211; second dismissal 161; second term (1993) 152–154
Bhutto, Murtaza 112, 119, 135; killed 160–161
Bhutto, Nusrat 135, 160
Bhutto, Zulfikar: 54, 70, 82, 86–87; 110–111; executed 111; foreign minister 62, 68–69; foreign policy 88; FSF created 92–93; legacy 104–105; martial law ended 90–91; moving right 96–97; nationalizations 88–89, 95; nuclear bomb 89–91; POW release 95–96; prime minister 86; reforms 90–101; removed 104
Bilateral Security Agreement (BSA) 246
Bin Laden, Osama 140; arrived Abbottabad 205; arrived Afghanistan 159; killed 235–236
Blasphemy Law 234
Bogra, Mohammed Ali 42, 44; death 62
Bonn Agreement 182

275

border crossing closures: Chaman & Torkham (2011) 239; Torkham (2010) 233
Brass Tacks 127
Buddha statues 176
Bugti, Nawab A. 203
Buner District 225–226
Bush, George H. 140–141
Bush, George W. 190, 196

Cabinet of Talents 45
Carter, Jimmy 117–118
Central Intelligence Agency (CIA): 182; Chapman base 228–229; contractors 229, 233–234
Chaudhry, Justice Iftikhar: dismissed 209, 212; reinstated 224, 230; retired 244
Chief Martial Law Administrator (CMLA) 74
Chinese-Indian border dispute 61–62
Chinese-Pakistan relations 35–36, 62, 101, 248
Chundrigar, Ibrahim 51
civil wars: Afghanistan (1992) 150; Pakistan (1971) 80–81
Cleanor Lahore Campaign 41
Clinton, Bill 166, 168; doormat visit 174
coalition support funds (CSF) 181
Colony Textile Mill 110
Combined Opposition Party (COP): of Fatima Jinnah 64–69; of Nawaz Sharif 140
Constituent Assembly: First CAP 24, 44–45; Second CAP 46–47
constitutions: abolished 52; first (1956) 47–48; second (1962) 60–61; third (1973) 94–94; *see also* amendments
Convention Muslim League (ConML) 64
currency devaluations 35, 91, 152
cyclone 77

Davis, Raymond 234–235
Decade of Development 69–70
Direct Action Day 20
Dostum, Abdul Rashid 182
drone strikes 202, 205–207, 216–217, 220, 223, 227, 229–230, 237, 240, 243–244, 249

earthquake 206
East wing grievances 26, 30, 36, 40, 44, 63
economy: 26; agriculture 59–60
education 14
Eisenhower, Dwight 50, 58
Eisenhower Doctrine 50
elections, Afghan presidential: (2004) 187; (2009) 225; (2014) 245–246
elections, Pakistan: 18; legislative (1962) 61; legislative (1970) 77; legislative (1977) 101–102; legislative (1985) 124; legislative (1988) 133; legislative (1990) 146; legislative (1993) 152; legislative (1997) 162; legislative (2002) 193; legislative (2008) 217; legislative (2013) 240; presidential (1965) 64–65; presidential (2008) 221
Elective Bodies Disqualification Order (EBDO) 57
embassy attacks: American in Africa 166; American in Islamabad 114–115

Fazullah, Maulana 213, 243
Federal Security Force (FSF) 92
Federal Shariat Court 118
Five-Year Plans: first (1956) 48; second (1960) 59; third (1965) 66
floods 231

Gandhi, Indira 69
Gandhi, Rajiv 127, 137
Gates, Robert 142
Geneva Accords 128–129
Ghani, Ashaf 245–246
Gillani, Yousef Raza 218; removed 239
government: finances 25; general 15–17
Government of India Act of 1935 21, 24, 41
Gracey, Gen. Douglas 29, 37
Great Migration 25
Green Revolution 59–60
Gul, Hamid: 133, 139–140; removed 140
Gwadar 203, 248

Haqqani, Hussain 236
Haqqani network 219, 237–239
Harkatul-ul-Mujahidden (HUM): 142, 167–168; hijacking 173
Hassan, Gen. Gul 88; resigned 90
Hassan, Mumbashir 89, 97
Hekmatyar, Gulbuddin 129, 150
hijacked airliners 119, 173; World Trade Center (2001) 179
Holbrooke, Richard 223; died 234
Hotel Marriot 222
Hotel Pearl Continental 227
Hudood Ordinances 113
Hussein, Saddam: invaded Kuwait 143
Hyderabad massacre 133

independence from Britain 19–21
India: American arms 61–62; hot nuclear tests 98, 165
India Jammu Kashmir (IJK): 28, 33, 66, 99–100, 157–158; fidayeen campaign 173; Intifada 141; special status ended 252
India-Pakistan relations: 37, 59, 66, 123, 151, 167, 177, 200, 203; Brass Tacks 127; Kargil infiltration 167–168; nuclear alert 142

Indian Independence Act 21
Indus Waters' Treaty 59
Inter-Service Intelligence (ISI): 15, 29–30, 156–157, 177, 207, 223; abuses 230, 237; assisted Taliban 196
Iran: Shah overthrown 113
Iraq: seized Kuwait 143–144; U.S. invasion 195
Ishaq *see* Khan, Ishaq
Islamabad: bombing 222; built 63
Islamabad Declaration 200
Islami Jamhoori Ittihad (IJI) 133, 146
Islamic State (IS) 248–250
Islamic Summit Conference 96
Islamization Program 112–113

Jagmohan 141
Jaish-e-Mohammad (JeM): 251–252; formed 173–174
Jalalabad, siege of 139–140
Jamaat-ul-Ahrar (JuA) 247, 249
Jamali, Zafarullah 194; resigned 201–202
Jamiat-e-Ulema-e-Pakistan (JUP) 31
Jamiat-i-Islami (JI) 31, 114
Jammu & Kashmir Liberation Front (JKLF) 141–142
Jinnah, Fatima 29, 64
Jinnah, Mohammed 19–22, 24; cancer 29; died 31; foreign policy 26; legacy 31; promoted Urdu language 30
Johnson, Lyndon 63
journalists 206, 237, 244
judicial system 18, 118
Junejo, Muhammad Khan 125–126, 128–129

Kahuta nuclear facility 99
Kalat, Khan of 30, 51
Kallu, Gen. Shamsur R. 104
Karachi 120, 143, 150, 157, 207, 211, 219, 243–245
Karamat, Gen. Jahangira: 160; resigned 167
Kargil 167–168
Karzai, Hamid: 182, 245; first term (2004) 187; peace negotiations Taliban 232; relations Obama 225; second term (2009) 225
Kashmir *see* Indian Jammu Kashmir (IJK); Provisional Government of Azad (Free) Kashmir (AJK)
Kasuri, Ahmad Raza 98
Kayani, Gen. Ashfaq: 204; Army Chief 214; retired 243; term extended 231
Kennedy, J.F. 60
Kerry-Berman-Lugar Act 228
Khalilzad, Zalmay 187
Khan, A.Q.: 98–99, 152–153, 196–198; cold test (1983) 121; hot tests (1998) 165; interviews 121
Khan, Ayub: 37, 45, 54–55; 64–65, 70; coup 52; legacy 72–73; lifted martial law 61; new capital 63; reforms 56–58; resigned 72
Khan, Imran: 212, 240–241, 245; prime minister 251
Khan, Ishaq Ghulam 133, 135, 144, 151; resigned 152
Khan, Liaquat 24, 32–33; assassinated 37–38; prime minister 32
Khan, Gen. Tikka 80, 82; Army Chief 90; retired 100
Khan, Wali 97–98
Khan, Gen. Yahya 69, 75, 78; resigned 86; took control 74
Khomeini, Ayatollah 113–114
Korean War 36, 42

Lahore 51
Lahore Conference 96
Lahore Declaration 167
languages 30
Lashkar-e-Jhangvi (LeJ) 177
Lashkar-e-Taiba (LeT) 173, 222–223, 228
Lawyers' Movement: first 209, 212; second 224
Legal Framework Order (LFO) 192
Leghari, Farooq 154, 160–161; resigned 164
Line of Control: 34; formal cease-fire 204
Local Bodies Electoral System 112
Lost Decade of Democracy 137

Madrassas 14, 117, 177
Mahmood, Masood 92; killed 177
Majlis-i-Shoora 120
Mamnoon, Hussan 242
Mansour, Mullah Akhtar 240
Martyrs' Day 40–41
Mehran Naval Base 237
Mehrangate 156
Mehsud, Baitullah 202; heads TTP 215; killed 227
Mehsud, Hakimullah: heads TTP 227; killed 243
Memogate 236
military 14–15
military coups: Ayub Khan (1958) 52; Musharraf (1999) 169; Zia (1977) 104
Mir, Hamid 244
Mirza, Iskandar 44, 46, 48, 52
Modi, Narendra 252
Mohajir Qaumi Mahaz (MQM) 143, 150; formed 123
mohajirs 31
Mohammed, Bakshi Ghulam 43

Mohammed, Khalid Sheikh (KSM): captured 195
Mohammed, Nek 200; killed 202
Mountbatten, Lord Louis 20–22, 28
Movement to Restore Democracy (MRD) 119, 122
Muhammad, Ghulam 40–41; 44, 46
Mujib *see* Rahman Mujibur
Musharraf, Pervez 170–171, 175, 177; assassination attempts 190–191, 199; foreign policy 172; legacy 221; presidency 177, 194, 221; Red Mosque 209–210; removed Sharif 169; resigned as Army chief 214; resigned presidency 204; returned from exile 240; returned to Pakistan 240; "second coup" 212; two-track policy 186
Mutahhida Majlis-i-Amal (MMA) 193, 199, 217

Najibullah, Mohammed 139, 149
Najimuddin, Khwaja 32, 39–41
Nasir, Gen. Javed 149, 151
National Accountability Bureau (NAB) 172
National Awami Party (NAP) 50
National Conference (NC) Party 28
National Reconciliation Ordinance (NRO): 211; struck down 230
Nawaz, Gen. Asif 148; death 150
Nehru, Jawaharlal: 20–21, 61–62; died 64
Nixon, Richard 76, 81
"no-confidence" vote 140
Noon, Feroz 51
Northern Alliance 181–183
Northwest Frontier Province (NWFP) 93, 217
nuclear development: 89–90, 98–99; cold test (1983) 121; hot tests (1998) 165
nuclear proliferation 152–153, 197–198

Obama, Barack 223
Ojhiri camp: 126; explosions 128
Omar, Mullah Mohammed: 166, 180; death reported 248–249; died 240; formed Taliban 156
one unit 47, 75
Operation al Mizan 192
Operation Earthquake 216
Operation Enduring Freedom 181–183
Operation Gibralter 67
Operation Kaloosha 200
Operation Lionheart 220
Operation Neptune Spear 235
Operation Path to Salvation 227
Operation Searchlight 80
Operation Zarb-e-Azb 245

Pakistan Democratic Movement (PDM) 71

Pakistan Election Commission 215
Pakistan Muslim League Q (PML(Q)) 192–193
Pakistan Movement for Justice Party (PTI) 212, 240–241, 245
Pakistan Muslim League (PML) 27, 33, 42
Pakistan Muslim League N (PML(N)) 146
Pakistan National Alliance (PNA) 102–103
Pakistan Peoples Party (PPP) 70, 97
Panama Papers 249
Pasha, Ahmed 233
Pearl, Daniel 189
Peshawar 222, 227
Peshawar Accord 149–150
Peshawar Seven Islamic Alliance 125
Pressler Amendment 122
princely states 22
Protection of Pakistan Act 245
provinces 13
Provisional Constitution Order (PCO) 120
Provisional Government of Azad (Free) Kashmir (AJK) 27, 33–34; earthquake 206
Pucca Qila fort 143
Punjab Province 41; terrorism 216; Gov. Taseer killed 234

Qazi, Javed A. 149
Qureshi, Moeen 152

Rabbani, Burhanuddin 150
Radcliffe Boundary Award 21, 25
Rahim, J.A. 70, 96–97
Rahman, Mujibur ("Mujib") 40, 63, 89; Six-Point Plan 69
Rann of Kutch 65–66
Rawalpindi 228
Rawalpindi Conspiracy 37
Reagan, Ronald 119, 121–122
Red Mosque 209–210
referendums: (1960) 58; (1984) 124; (2002) 191
religions 14
Republican Party 51; formed 47
Roundtable conferences 72
Rushdie, Salman 137

Sadiq, G.M. 43
Salala incident 238–239
Sararogha 204, 215
Satanic verses 137
Sayeed, Mufti Mohammad 174
Shakai Agreement 200–201
Shangla District 213
Sharif, Nawaz: 134, 144–148, 152, 161, 169, 174, 213, 250; foreign policy 164; presi-

dent: 1st term (1990) 146; 2nd term (1997) 163; 3rd term (2013) 242
Sharif, Gen. Raheel 243
Sharia Act 148
Shastri, Lal B. 64; died 69
Siachen Glacier 123
Sindh Province 31, 91–92, 123, 133, 150; language bill 91–92
Singh, Maharaja Hari 28
Singh, Manmohan 203
Sino-Pakistan Economic Corridor Development Program (CPEC) 248, 251
Sipah-e-Mohammed Pakistan (SMP) 120, 177
Sipah-e-Sahaba-i-Pakistan (SSP) 120, 155–156, 177
Six-Point Plan 69
Solarz amendment 122
Stinger missiles 128
Suez Canal 49–50
Sufis 250
Suhawardy, Husain S. 49, 50; died 89
Sui gas fields 203
Sunni-Shiite violence 41, 120, 177, 190, 207, 219
Supreme Court 54, 111, 151–152,161, 174–175, 192, 212–213, 230, 244; removes Gillani 239; removes Sharif
Swat battles: first 213; second 226
Swat District 213
Swat Peace Accord 224

Taliban, Punjabi 216
Taliban, Afghan: attacked NATO 197; Buddha statutes destroyed 176; formed 156; Mullah Omar's death 240; overthrown 181–183; revived 196; seized Kabul 159; seized Kandahar 157; suicide attacks 206; support from Pakistan 159, 207
Taliban, Pakistani see Tehrik-e-Taliban (TTP)
Taliban peace deals: Sararogha Agreement 204; Shakai Agreement 201; Swat Peace Accord 224; Waziristan Accord 208
Tarrar, Mohammed R. 164, 177
Taseer, Gov. Salman 234
Tashkent Declaration 68
Tehrik-e-Taliban (TTP): formed 214–215, 227; funding 237, 243; more deadly and independent 230; peace talks 243, 246
Tehriki e Nifaz c Shariat-e-Muhammad (TNSM) 213, 219–220, 224–226

Times Square bombing attempt 229
Trilateral policy 63, 65
"True Democracy" system 175
Truman, Harry 35
Trump, Donald 250
TTP see Tehrik-e-Taliban

IJK see India Jammu Kashmir (IJK)
Ul-Haq, Gen. Ehsan 181
United Front 42
United States, Indian relations 50; civilian nuclear program 205
United States, Pakistan 30, 51–52, 57, 70–71, 114–115; 174, 180–181; arms 43–44, 119
United States, Soviet relations: 58–59; USSR broke up 148–149
United States, Taliban relations: peace deal signed 246; talks 232–233

Vajpayee, Atal Behari 177, 200

Waheed, Gen. Abdul 150
wars, Indo-Pakistan: first (1947) 28–29; second (1965) 67; third (1971) 81–82; fourth (1999) 168
wars, Kashmir: first (1947) 29, 33; second (1965) 67; third (1999) 168
Washington Agreement 168
Waziristan Accord 208
Wikileaks 231
Wilson, Charlie 123–124
World Muslim Congress 35
World Trade Center attacks: center destroyed (2001) 179; garage bomb (1993) 150–151

Yellow Cab Scheme 149
Yousafzai, Malala 240
Yousef, Ramzi: 150–151; captured 157

Zadari, Asif: 128, 155 216, 221; concessions 230–231; minister 160; president 221
Zakat alms tax 118–119
Zawahiri, Ayman 236
Zia, Gen. Ul-Haq 107; Army Chief 100–101; coup 104, 106; executed Bhutto 111; Islamization 112–113; killed in plane crash 129–130; legacy 130–131; martial law ended 127; presidencies 111, 125; referendum 124
Zubeida, Abu 190

www.ingramcontent.com/pod-product-compliance
Lightning Source LLC
Chambersburg PA
CBHW032033300426
44117CB00009B/1046